W9-BNW-859

The Handbook of
ORGANIZATION DEVELOPMENT
in Schools and Colleges
Fourth Edition

Richard A. Schmuck
Philip J. Runkel
University of Oregon

WAVELAND
PRESS, INC.
Prospect Heights, Illinois

LIBRARY

For information about this book, contact:
Waveland Press, Inc.
P.O. Box 400
Prospect Heights, Illinois 60070
(847) 634-0081
www.waveland.com

Copyright © 1994, 1985 by Richard A. Schmuck and Philip J. Runkel

ISBN 0-88133-798-6

All rights reserved. No part of this book may be reproduced, stored in a retrieval system, or transmitted in any form or by any means without permission in writing from the publisher.

Printed in the United States of America

12   11   10   9   8   7   6   5

Contents

Chapter 10   Institutionalizing OD in Colleges and Schools   **407**

Preface

We have written this *Handbook* for educators at every level of the educational enterprise from kindergarten to graduate school. It is suitable both as a text for college classes and as a resource kit for administrators, consultants, counselors, instructors, and psychologists. It can be used for courses on counseling and guidance, curriculum and instruction, educational administration, school psychology, the community college, higher education, organizational psychology, public policy, the social psychology of education, and special education. It can also be used by consultants in county offices, intermediate education agencies, regional laboratories, and state departments having responsibility for facilitating planned change. We intend for this book to be used as a guide for institutional reform and restructuring, site-based management, staff development, strategic planning, teambuilding, and "total quality" programs.

Most important, we have written this book for educators everywhere who want to bring about constructive organizational change in their work settings. We have in mind administrators (e.g. deans, department heads, or principals), and instructors (e.g. college professors, elementary teachers, or high school teachers) who hope for better organizational and classroom climates. We also have in mind school superintendents and college provosts who strive for more effective faculty teamwork, and in-house specialists who have been designated to operate as organizational facilitators with their colleagues. Indeed, this *Handbook* addresses any educator who wants to lift morale and raise achievement levels of students through more humane, consistent, and effective management and instruction. The two of us do not think of educational organization and academic curriculum as separate spheres; for us good organization offers the soil from which good teaching can grow.

This, our fourth *Handbook*, differs from the first three in four ways:

1. We include here information about organization development (OD) in higher education, a domain of interest and activity in OD that has been increasing since 1985. In particular, Schmuck has spent more than half his consulting time during the last decade facilitating change in colleges and universities. Runkel has been helping a cadre of graduate students deliver OD services in the University of Oregon for the past six years. We introduce information about OD in higher education into every chapter to achieve a balance in our treatment of OD between our long-term interest in kindergarten through high school and our newer interest in colleges and universities.

2. We include here equal amounts of information about OD facilitated by external consultants and about OD carried out by administrators and instructors inside the educational organization. In previous editions our sole focus was on the tasks of the external consultant in starting, implementing, and ending an OD contract. In this book we change that focus because most schools and colleges do not seek assistance from outsiders for their OD efforts and because professors of education increasingly seek to introduce OD concepts and techniques to their graduate students. Thus, we introduce information about how key educators in line and staff positions within schools and colleges can carry out OD.

3. We include here a new chapter (chapter 2) on the alternative uses or versions of educational OD. For example, along with a discussion of various uses of OD in strengthening organizational aspects of schools and colleges, we discuss the use of OD concepts and techniques for improving one-to-one relationships, classroom interactions, interpersonal relations on boards, and the functioning of externally based citizens' groups. We also point out how a variety of role-takers in schools and colleges can implement OD.

4. We exclude from this book separate chapters on "Diagnosis and Readiness" and on "Evaluation." In their place we integrate information about those topics particularly into the new chapter on macrodesigning (chapter 3) and throughout the revised chapters 4–9. We believe that the changes will make it easier for the reader to see how diagnosis, readiness, and evaluation fit into the flow of an OD design.

Since the third edition, the use of OD in schools, much like its use in higher education, has grown by leaps and bounds. OD has become commonplace in work on site-based management, staff development, strategic planning, and teambuilding in non-graded elementary schools and middle schools. What is done in such change efforts might not be called OD, but much of it nonetheless entails activities central to OD. From studying such change efforts, we have learned more about the OD techniques that work and that don't work. This fourth *Handbook* takes account of what we learned by adding a few new techniques that work and by removing a few old techniques that no longer work. We note that the lion's share of the OD techniques that appeared in the third edition continue to be useful and effective.

Although this new book is the sole responsibility of Schmuck and Runkel, portions of it still remain the contributions of our coauthors of the first two editions. We are grateful to Jane H. Arends, Richard I. Arends, C. Brooklyn Derr, Ronald T. Martell, and Steven L. Saturen for their contributions. In addition, we appreciate Eleanor Perry's constructive criticism about parts of this edition, and Claire Runkel's conscientious and skilled assistance with indexing and editing. We dedicate this book to the more than 200 students who have worked closely with us on OD projects at the University of Oregon from the summer of 1967 to the present.

Richard A. Schmuck
Philip J. Runkel

Chapter One

What OD Is and How It Works

Schools and colleges are social organizations. Without human collaboration and commitment, they are only wood, concrete, and paper. Typically, educational improvement requires less change in the paper and more change in the patterns of human action. Deliberate efforts at educational improvement usually affect not only the administrators and faculty as individuals, but also relationships among them and their collective relationships with students. For example, changes in curriculum or instruction are almost always accompanied by changes within schools and colleges in such relationships as authority, communication, status, and even friendship. Consciously capitalizing on such social phenomena to bring about and stabilize a desired state of affairs is a major concern of organization development (OD).

Examples of OD

Every two weeks for the past three months, Mike has been driving from a nearby college of education to the central office of a school district, where he consults with the superintendent's cabinet. Before each visit, he talks with the convener of the upcoming meeting, both to coach the convener in ways to run the meeting and to find out what has happened in the cabinet since his last visit.

Once the meeting begins, Mike observes the way the cabinet members work their agenda. He observes the norms and attitudes through the way the members phrase questions and comments and in their nonverbal behavior. From time to time, he comments on the distribution of the participation, the clarity of the decisions, the commitment to the decisions, or the ways in which the group is collecting information to solve its problems. Occasionally he offers a summary of his observations to support his comments or to encourage cabinet members to talk with one another about how the group is working. Mike is using the OD technique of *process observation and feedback*.

At the college, Mike heads the Department of Teacher Education. When he became the head two years ago, he took the departmental faculty of 11 on a weekend retreat in the countryside so that they could set goals and make group agreements about how they would operate. At that retreat, Mike introduced the ideas of a process observer and of debriefing as a part of departmental meetings. Mike's colleagues decided to rotate the role of process observer so that everyone would perform the role once every 11 meetings. They agreed that the process observer would lead the group in a discussion about the strengths and weaknesses of its group processes at the end of every meeting. Mike's colleagues, too, are using the OD technique of *process observation and feedback*.

Paula chairs the English department and Don is a counselor at a small community college. Both received training in organizational consultation from a nonprofit organization while on their sabbatical leaves last year, and both became aware of their frustration with the small role most students played in improving the organizational climate of the college. Working together, they persuaded the executive dean to allocate money so that other faculty members could join them in planning a new student-involvement strategy. They then addressed a faculty meeting to explain what they wanted to accomplish and to recruit volunteers for a task force. During the following month, Paula and Don convened a three-day retreat at which task-force members composed a formal proposal to create a representative group made up of one administrator, three instructors, and three students, all to be elected by their constituencies. The function of this group would be to find more ways for students and faculty to help one another improve their lives as members of the college. The faculty adopted the proposal, and the executive dean agreed to try out the new organizational structure if Paula and Don would train the group in collaborative problem solving and joint decision making. After elections to the group were held, Paula and Don carried out a four-hour training session with the new group that included practice in the skills of communication, problem solving, and consensual decision making. Paula and Don were using the OD techniques of *training*.

Jane, the local high school principal, heard about Paula and Don's capabilities in OD, and asked them to help her administrative cabinet (i.e., Jane, an assistant principal, a counselor, and nine department heads) learn the skills of communication, problem solving, and consensual decision making. Paula and Don agreed to carry out a four-hour session, similar to the one they carried out at their college, with Jane's cabinet. They called it "teambuilding."

Later, Jane worked together with Paula and Don on similar teambuilding meetings at the college, in the school district, and at a church. From those experiences, Jane became confident enough to carry out teambuilding meetings on her own. Now, Jane starts each academic year in August by training the administrative cabinet in the skills of communication, problem solving, and consensual decision making. She is using the OD techniques of *training* in her job as high school principal.

Pat (an elementary school principal), Lee (a junior high counselor), and Lynn (a senior high biology teacher) are members of a cadre of organizational specialists in their school district. As an ad hoc consulting team, the three of them are collaborating with an elementary school faculty—the principal, teachers, counselor, reading specialist, three aides, and a secretary—who agreed last year to try out team teaching. Pat, Lee, and Lynn volunteered to help those faculty members move out from their self-contained classrooms into new role relationships as team leaders and team members.

As OD specialists, Pat, Lee, and Lynn attend all team meetings at the school and frequently serve as facilitators when conflicts surface. A lot of conflict has erupted this year as faculty members try to articulate their goals and negotiate the sharing of materials, space, and resources. Plenty of time in staff meetings is left open to permit team leaders and members to discuss how instruction should be supervised in the school. The specialists help organize these role-clarifying discussions so that the faculty can uncover disagreements and arrange to work collaboratively on important instructional problems. Pat, Lee, and Lynn are making use of the OD techniques of *constructive confrontation*.

When Alice, the executive dean of a community college, learned about angry strife between the department head of Fine Arts and a veteran faculty member in that department, she decided to intervene. She started by interviewing each antagonist individually about the conflict. While trying to persuade each to work with her to reduce the strife, she also taught them the communication skills of paraphrasing and behavior description. Then, she asked both to employ those communication skills in a meeting with her to discuss their differences. During the meeting she asked each party to discuss actions of the other that they would like increased in frequency, decreased, or maintained. Next, she urged them to reach agreements about behavioral changes that they both would make in their attempt to salvage their working relationship. She also offered a few behavioral changes that she, herself, would try in working with the two of them. After the meeting, Alice typed a memorandum of agreement for each of the three of them to sign. Alice was making use of the OD techniques of *constructive confrontation*.

Vera, head of art education, and Dick, an associate professor in psychology, are also members of a cadre of OD specialists in their small state college. They have been asked by their cadre coordinator, the dean of students, to help a planning team in the college with an effort to improve the climate of the entire college. As a first step, the team prepares a climate questionnaire to collect data from everyone in the college. Vera and Dick's role is to offer the planning team examples of climate questionnaires, to help the team prepare its own questionnaire, to facilitate collecting and analyzing the data, and to collaborate with the planning team in feeding back those data to the faculty. After the data are discussed by the faculty, Vera and Dick will help the faculty form problem-solving groups to create plans for climate improvement. Vera and Dick are using the OD technique of *survey-data-feedback*.

Randy, a high school English teacher, routinely seeks feedback from students after instructing them for four or five weeks. He hands each student a 3"x 5" index card with a plus sign in a corner of one side and minus sign in a corner of the other side. He tells them that the plus sign stands for things he has been doing that are helping them learn English, and that the minus sign stands for things he should try to change to help them learn English better. He asks them to write a short list of things on both sides of the card. He also tells them not to put their names on the card.

After Randy analyzes the contents of the cards, he reports the results to the class. In particular, he tells them that he appreciates their telling him about favorable aspects of his teaching. More important for Randy, he tells the students about aspects of his teaching that they would like to see changed and how he intends to attempt change. Randy is using the OD technique of *survey-data-feedback*.

OD Defined

Certain features of those eight projects are characteristic of organization development in schools. All eight projects were *systematically planned* by the prime movers in collaboration with school and college participants. All showed *sustained effort* over time and encompassed arrangements for continued effort. All focused on altering the dynamics of the *social system* in which the individuals were embedded. All showed *self-study*—conscious examination of present social conditions, actions, and procedures. All instituted *planned change*. All brought about new group or organizational *structures*. All dealt with formal and informal *procedures*, *processes*, and *norms*. All had the intent of improving group or organizational *functioning*. Finally, all had a direct or indirect focus on *educational issues*.

The italicized words are features of a definition of organization development summarized by Fullan, Miles, and Taylor (1980, p. 135) from dozens of definitions in the literature:

> Organizational development (OD) in school districts (or colleges) is a coherent, systematically planned, sustained effort at system self-study and improvement, focusing explicitly on change in formal and informal procedures, processes, norms, or structures, and using behavioral science concepts. The goals of OD include improving both the quality of life of individuals as well as organizational functioning and performance with a direct or indirect focus on educational issues.

Although the eight examples are similar in the several ways listed above, they also demonstrate the variety of possible approaches to OD in education. For example, by sitting with the cabinet during its meetings and offering his perceptions of the cabinet's group dynamics, Mike was using the technique of process observation and feedback. Mike also applied the same technique in his own department at the college where he worked. Paula and Don, in contrast, designed and executed a four-hour training session at their college in which they took on the high-profile role of trainers. Jane, who had worked with them, applied those same training techniques to her own administrative cabinet in the high school. Pat, Lee, and Lynn dealt primarily with uncovering conflict, constructive confrontation, and role negotiation, while Vera, Dick, and Randy employed the classical OD technique of collecting survey data from staff or students and feeding it back to them for subsequent problem solving and improvement.

The undertakings in our eight examples might seem of a kind that arises ordinarily in educational settings. They might not seem to deserve a special label such as organization development. But one more feature of the definition makes the important difference: the use of concepts from behavioral science. Many educators assume that some people are skillful at working in groups like administrative cabinets, and some are not, and that's it. Mike and Jane, however, believe that skill in group work can be learned. They know that people can learn to talk about their group processes and that they can be encouraged to practice new skills. Furthermore, Mike and Jane know that they can help by modeling skilled participation, by training people in particular skills, and by stopping the work occasionally to enable cabinet members to talk explicitly about what they see themselves doing. In carrying out the responsibilities of their roles as process observer and trainer, they use the concepts of communication skills and the techniques of process observation and training.

Paula and Don believe that work is more likely to get done if the people who will do it have a voice in planning it. Some administrators, if they agreed with Paula and Don in wanting students to participate more in the college, would simply appoint a faculty group to recruit students to participate. Paula and Don, knowing that the success of such a venture requires active participation by faculty, asked for volunteers from the faculty to form a working core and then allowed three days for those faculty members to agree about and commit themselves to action. That group, knowing that students are best recruited by students, insisted that some members of the task force be students elected by students. Finally, Paula and Don, like Mike and Jane, know that skill in problem solving and joint decision making is needed if the task force is to be effective. They therefore trained the new group.

Pat, Lee, Lynn, and Alice are alert to the conflicts that inevitably arise in teaching teams and academic departments. When people find themselves in conflict with others, they often begin to fear they will lose something they want. They find that demands are made upon them that they do not want to satisfy, and they begin to worry. Naturally, they wish the fears, demands, and worry would go away. Pat, Lee, Lynn, and Alice, however, believe that conflict is inevitable when people are deeply committed to their work, and they know that it can be an occasion for creativity. They know that fears, blunt language, demands, and worries are side-effects of resolving an array of differing goals, values, and ways of working, and they know that skills in working with interpersonal strife are usually poorly developed. Thus, they choose to conduct confrontation sessions, in which the conflicts can be dealt with in a disciplined way.

Vera and Dick believe that data collected from everyone on a staff permit the sort of self-analysis in a college that can lead to productive change. They also believe that faculty members won't come to believe in the validity of the data unless they have some say in the sorts of data that are collected. The two have therefore adopted a strategy in which a planning team participates collaboratively with them in developing and executing survey-data-feedback. Vera and Dick believe that problem clarity and ownership are prerequisites to problem solving and college improvement.

Randy believes that data feedback should be a two-way street. When he receives feedback from students, he makes certain that he gives his data analysis back to the students. He believes that students will work hard to improve themselves if he shows them that he, the teacher, is willing to improve himself.

Mike, Paula, Don, Jane, Pat, Lee, Lynn, Alice, Vera, Dick, and Randy all believe that the well-meaning professionals, service personnel, and students who make up schools and colleges often work in ineffective and poorly coordinated groups. They understand, too, that educators typically do not make deliberate efforts to examine their communication patterns, their customary ways of working together in meetings, or the ways in which they are linked together to get their work done. To legitimize the examination of these important phenomena, OD practitioners bring to their colleagues both a conceptualization of organizational life and a strategy for change.

An underlying assumption of OD is that educational organizations consist of behavioral and programmatic regularities that do not depend for their existence primarily on particular personalities. Further, OD practitioners theorize that many efforts at educational reform have failed or passed by without effect precisely because of the limited attention given to the organizational context in which the reforms were attempted. The conclusion follows that major innovation in curriculum or instructional techniques requires alterations in the educational organization's behavioral and programmatic regularities—in short, educational innovations require changes in the "culture" of the school or college.

The tenacity of organizational culture lies in the power of its norms; that is, how well they are adhered to and how resistant they are to change. Norms are shared expectations, usually implicit, that guide the thoughts and behaviors of group members. Note that this definition of norm emphasizes interpersonal sharing; norms occur in groups and are not merely intrapsychic. When a norm is present, most people know that their view of things is shared by others, and that the others expect them to have the same viewpoint and to behave accordingly.

The following additional assumptions guide our thinking and action in relation to educational improvement and the work of most OD practitioners, whether they are external consultants or administrators and instructors working within the school or college.

1. *Groups differ from a sum of individuals.* A group has a character that is more than the pooling of its members' personalities. The ability of a group to do work stems not merely from the individuals' abilities and attitudes, but also from the ways in which the individuals coordinate, dovetail, and complement the uses of those abilities and attitudes. Working together socially requires skills that cannot be contained within a single individual. Those interpersonal skills come into play when two or more individuals are acting in concert. An educational organization's potentiality is greater than the sum, but its performance can be less than the sum.

2. *Change occurs through work groups.* Because a work group is more than an assembly of individuals, an organization can change its way of working more surely by directing the effort to intact work groups rather than to individuals.

3. *Members' goals and motives have relevance for action.* Since coordination depends on knowing what actions people are likely to take, knowledge of others' goals and motives aids coordination. Knowing the goals and motive satisfactions of its members can be as useful to a school staff as knowing members' knowledge, skills, or other capabilities.

4. *Members' feelings have relevance to action.* Humans become emotionally aroused when they encounter frustration or gratification, and those feelings affect their actions. Since coordination depends on being able to predict what actions people are likely to take, knowledge of others' feelings can aid coordination. Knowing members' feelings can be as useful to a faculty as knowing members' knowledge, skills, or other resources.

5. *Untapped resources have relevance.* Individuals and groups usually possess abilities, information, and skills beyond those typically expected of them. If tapped, these resources can be used to facilitate improved organizational functioning. The wherewithal for problem solving, for example, frequently already resides within the members of the faculty.

6. *Change is made from within.* Although an initial prod toward changing an educational organization often comes from outside, people within often possess much of the knowledge and skill needed to create and implement new programs, especially when the change involves reorganizing group structure or altering ways in which staff members work together. The long-range purpose of OD is to transmit necessary knowledge and skills to the group members themselves. A faculty that has internalized OD knowledge and skills and that has members who can facilitate the faculty's joint work can be regarded as *self-renewing* and as possessing *adaptability.*

The History of OD

Organization development has been used in industrial and governmental organizations since the mid-1950s. Its use continues to spread. As good a marker as any for the beginning of OD is the workshop directed by Kurt Lewin at the Connecticut State Inter-Racial Commission, at New Britain, Connecticut, in June 1946. The workshop was conducted as an experiment in change and as training for workers in intergroup relations. The following summer, the National Training Laboratories were established at Gould Academy in Bethel, Maine. For a detailed and delightful description of how Lewin's initiatives influenced the history of OD during the 40s and 50s, see Weisbord (1987, pp. 88–105).

In the early part of this century, the dominant theory of organizational design was that of "scientific management," which too many people interpreted as meaning that the work of humans, after analysis by time-and-motion studies, should be made as machinelike as possible. That view was weakened, however, after a series of studies was conducted from 1924 to 1932 at the Hawthorne plant of the Western Electric Company. Several social scientists writing between 1933 and 1947 interpreted those experiments as showing that workers would respond favorably, with higher production, to interested and sympathetic attention from supervisors and managers. Though the validity of that interpretation has been challenged, there is no doubt that the Hawthorne experiments drew intense interest from social scientists nor that the experiments prompted further research and theorizing that became a part of the "human relations movement"—one important strand in the history of OD.

The human relations movement fit nicely with the results of the training and experimentation conducted at Bethel by the National Training Laboratories. The followers of Lewin discovered at Bethel that members of groups could examine explicitly the social processes that made their groups effective. In group after group, it was also discovered that members cared a good deal about their relationships with one another. Especially when the group was given no explicit task to carry out and when it was free from a close time limit, members spontaneously made known their feelings toward one another. That discovery led to "sensitivity training" in "T-groups," a way of purposely training people to become more aware of the emotions that typically develop in people working in groups.

The early development of OD was in part a reaction against "scientific management," and it was therefore natural for some of the early consultants to pay attention almost exclusively to the "human" side of the work, giving short shrift to the technical side. For some years, OD had the reputation of ignoring the work that had to be done, focusing instead on participants' emotions and going round in interminable circles to reach consensual decisions. One heard the derogatory phrase "touchy-feely" and stories of hours spent in seeking consensus on picayune matters.

Organization development, as we conceive it, is not sensitivity training, and its designs typically do not include T-groups. OD honors people's feelings *when they are relevant to their work*. Feelings *are* aroused when people find strong satisfactions or experience deep frustrations in doing their jobs and working with others. Those feelings become one—only one—of the interpersonal conditions affecting the course of action people choose.

Seeking consensual decisions is important when the success of a task depends on coordinated action by all. People are more likely to carry out the actions called for by a decision when they understand the implications of the decision and when they have committed themselves publicly to shouldering their parts of the task. That principle has been shown to hold not only in educational organizations, but in industry, government, human services, and the military. It is one of the reasons that OD facilitators advise that decision making occur low in the hierarchy, at the level of those who will do the work called for by the decision.

But that principle does *not* imply that all decisions should be made consensually or, in schools and colleges, only by instructors. Sometimes instructors are willing to carry out a decision no matter which way it goes. In a large college, for example, instructors know that putting together the schedule is a very complex matter, with many criteria to be balanced against one another. They know that the schedule is best made by only a few people—that trying to get the details ironed out in a large group would require more time and energy than the benefits would justify.

Nowadays, people practicing OD still respect the importance of members' feelings and consensual decision making, but only as they relate to solving educational problems. Instructors' feelings are brought into OD meetings when they are relevant to getting the work done effectively, and consensual decision making is used only when it will facilitate mutual helpfulness and group effectiveness. Contemporary OD gives balanced attention to all sides of work, adopting the view of educational organizations as *sociotechnical* systems.

Though organization development in schools and colleges has been strongly influenced by the earlier developments in industry, numerous modifications of industrial methods have been made to suit the special characteristics of the educational setting. In particular, three social-psychological conditions set schools and colleges off from most industrial organizations: (1) the nature of educators' goals, (2) the amount and types of hierarchy and specialization of work in educational organizations, and (3) their unique vulnerability to short- and long-term pressures.

1. *Educators' goals.* In contrast to people in business, the goals of educators are special in at least four ways. First, educators exert a great deal of effort toward ends that are seldom concretely defined. For example, while tests measure some features of student achievement, considerable debate goes on continually among educators about how to measure intellectual outcomes. And such diverse outcomes as mental health, creativity, and citizenship are abstract and difficult to measure. Second, the benefits sought from public education are immensely diverse, and their number is steadily increasing. Indeed, each new critic of public education and each new alternative program provides evidence that another list of pedagogical and social pursuits is being articulated. Instructors do not typically have time or energy to understand the new ends as fast as they are promulgated. Third, even the agreed-upon citizenship goals of educators take considerable time— usually a decade or more—to become actualized in the behavior of large numbers of students when they reach adulthood. Educators must face the frustration of coping with this time span with a new cohort of students each year; this perennial frustration is further complicated by the absence of indicators and a sophisticated technology for assessing progress at interim points. Fourth, educators strive to make human beings humane; they don't grow vegetables, manufacture auto-mobiles, or construct cellular telephones. In the daily work of schools and colleges, educators and students are in relation-

ships of circular causation. As one exerts influence on the other, so too does the other exert influence on the initiator, creating circles of reciprocal influence that continue in every educational activity throughout every day. Thus, educators cannot measure progress or achievement simply by assessing student outcomes. They often feel compelled to judge effectiveness with assessments of difficult-to-measure indicators of social well being, such as teacher-student rapport, classroom climate, organizational health, and the community's quality of life.

2. *Hierarchy and specialization of work.* Some large organizations have many hierarchical layers of management. The federal civil service has 18 grades. The U.S. military has a couple dozen ranks. Schools and colleges, even very large ones, typically have three or four levels of hierarchy. Very large school districts and universities have perhaps five or six levels, rarely more. A great many levels of hierarchy make it difficult for OD to make changes at one level that will remain stable for long, because people at that level are so strongly influenced by their bosses. That is one reason that OD consultants strongly prefer for a project of any size to include the top officers of an organization as active participants.

   Aside from relationships of power among levels, the varieties of work also demand special attention in OD work. When jobs of people differ, special time and procedures must be used to help them understand one another's work better. A person in one job will often find it difficult to take the point of view of a person in a different job. Furthermore, people often suspect persons in other jobs to be competing with them for resources even when it seems obvious to an outsider that the two kinds of work depend inseparably on each other.

   Specialization of labor laterally poses difficulties for OD that are similar to those posed vertically. Even when there are no complications from differences in level in the hierarchy, persons are often reluctant to take time to talk with others in other kinds of jobs, because they think the difference in jobs gives them nothing important in common to talk about. Sometimes, too, people feel their own work to be more important in some way, or more correct, or more beautiful, and feel a disdain for people in other kinds of work. Both those attitudes show up in colleges and universities among professors in different departments, and to some extent in high schools also.

3. *Social pressures.* Compared with many industrial organizations, schools and colleges are typically less vulnerable to competition but more vulnerable to short-term community pressures. Although public schools and colleges typically are not required to compete against one another to sustain themselves, the effects of many of their day-to-day procedures are readily visible to citizens. Still, though educational institutions stand largely in a noncompetitive relationship, educators often respond laggingly or defensively to shifts in their cultural, social, and intellectual environments, and tend to respond to crises brought on by students and the population at large as short-term difficulties, not as indications of long-term trends that require serious adaptations. When students, parents, local merchants, or legislators become stakeholders in the work of a school or college, the work of OD can become very difficult because the numbers of people who must communicate, the number of points of view that can come into conflict, and the difficulty of finding times and places for the stakeholders to meet face to face.

These special features of educational organizations—features that in many ways run counter to the early theory and technology of organization development—have been at least partly responsible for the slowness with which organization development has caught on in schools and colleges. It was not until the 1960s, therefore, that the first systematic effort to carry out and conduct research on organization development in school districts was launched by Mathew Miles (1963). His three-year project on organization development in schools, headquartered at Teachers College, Columbia University, was carried out in collaboration with one school district near New York City and another near Pittsburgh. Later, in that same decade, Dale Lake, a student of Miles, carried out the first OD intervention in a community college in New York state. Since those historic projects, organization development in schools and colleges has grown slowly but steadily. It has now established sufficient credibility and legitimacy to make it an important part of the educator's repertoire.

Reasons to Do OD

Various people can have various purposes in the pursuit of which they believe OD can help them. The most far-reaching kind of aid we think OD can give, however, is in enabling educational organizations to achieve a sustained capacity for solving their own problems. The people in schools and colleges having that capacity will monitor their environment and take action to control inputs from that environment. Members of the problem-solving school or college find, maintain, and use their resources, ideas, and energy. The personnel are conscious of the skills they need and take steps to improve them when necessary. They periodically review their goals and alter them to suit the organization's capacities and circumstances. The activities of OD, which take a school or college along the road to a sustained capacity for solving its own problems, are to clarify communication, establish clear goals, uncover and resolve conflicts and problems in groups, make clear decisions that capture commitment, and self-consciously assess the directions the work is taking.

Above all, OD practitioners value the collaborative effort among themselves, educators, and students, in striving to create new, more democratic social structures and more humanized interpersonal relationships. Other values are (1) expanding all the participants' consciousness about how others think and feel, (2) continually finding more choices for new action, (3) authenticity in interpersonal relations, (4) a collaborative, democratic conception of freedom and control, (5) participation and interpersonal respect, and (6) establishing commitment to new directions the organization might take.

Why do we insist that educational organizations should be able to sustain a heightened capacity for solving their own problems? After all, some might say, schools and colleges do solve problems, if only in the sense of muddling through. We do not object to muddling through if staff members have, with some consensus, deliberately chosen that method for dealing with a particular problem. Staff members, however, often let themselves in for much wasted effort, frustration, and conflict when they expect to progress from A to B to C but in fact are only muddling. The methods of OD can save much effort from being wasted, solve some sorts of educational problems more surely than is typical now, and generate feelings among the staff of competence, solidarity, and pride.

Practitioners of organization development aim at improving the interpersonal and group procedures used by administrators, instructors, and students to reach their educational objectives. They focus primarily on the *how* of interpersonal and group interactions rather than on the *what* of their content. The success of an organization development intervention as an improvement strategy is measured by the effectiveness with which the recipients—whether they be educators, students, or concerned citizens—work together in reaching their respective objectives. The success of an OD endeavor is determined by how effective the recipients are in defining their problems and goals (which may, for example, have to do with the content of a program of remedial writing); how resourceful they are in devising ways to reach their goals (which may include conferring with a content consultant in reading methods); and how stable, adaptive, and effective the group's products are over time (as indicated, for example, by measuring the long-term effectiveness of a writing program).

Strategies Other Than OD

Three fundamental strategies employed today for educational improvement will clarify OD further: (1) expert assistance, (2) content instruction, and (3) process facilitation.

Expert Assistance

The strategy of *expert assistance* employs proficient specialists to fulfill an educational need usually, though not always, considered temporary by the faculty. An adjunct instructor may be hired to teach a course, or a management firm might be hired to help administrators decide on optimal allocations of money for classroom space or athletic facilities. Sometimes business firms are hired to take over instruction when they guarantee to improve students' mastery of certain subjects. Expert assistance can help schools and colleges fill a temporary gap, but it does not typically improve the skills of other educators in the same organization. Nor does this strategy give the educators a personal understanding of the nature of the expert assistance. As a result it is difficult for the educators to pick up any of the specialist's skills and become more self-sufficient. Indeed, most adjuncts who do short-term work on limited problems have a vested interest in keeping their skills to themselves. OD practitioners, in contrast, try to make their interventions long enough and their methods participative enough to enable educators to acquire some OD skills and lessen their dependence on outside specialists.

Content Instruction

The strategy of *content instruction* employs specialists to teach educators about the content of their jobs to improve their performance as individuals. The specialist sets out to raise participants' cognitive understanding of new procedures and their commitment to the change. The most typical way the content specialist works is through an in-service workshop in a subject such as writing, mathematics, social studies, or the arts. In other examples, a psychologist might teach instructors about human development, a mathematician could help instructors develop new instructional strategies, a mental health consultant could help staff members cope with students having emotional problems, and a management consultant might offer administrators instruction in management skills. Although the potential for organizational change is present, content specialists do not focus directly on social system improvement. Rather, they try to bring about changes in cognitions, attitudes, and skills within individuals, and therefore do not directly facilitate organizational changes. OD practitioners spend only a little time with individuals apart from the working group and almost no time with individuals collected for academic instruction. OD practitioners do take some time to heighten participants' cognitive understanding of the new collaborative procedures, but only enough time at one sitting to enable participants to move with more awareness into the next state of practice.

Process Facilitation

The strategy of *process facilitation* employs specialists to improve the *procedures* used to reach educational objectives. Process specialists deal with such phenomena as patterns of communication, leadership attempts, underlying tensions, and decision-making procedures. Process specialists do not deal directly with the subject matter—the immediate content—of the interactions. In that respect, they work like OD practitioners. Indeed, OD makes use of many of the techniques of process facilitation. We list process facilitation here as a strategy separate from OD, however, because it can be used—as indeed it often is—with one small group in an organization without touching the organization as a whole. Though OD usually includes process facilitation with small parts of the organization, it goes beyond that. OD practitioners do not expect their efforts to have long-term effects until they reach throughout an organization—to the entire school or college.

OD Theory for Educational Organizations

Like any organization, schools and colleges contain individuals. In one sense, individuals constitute the most fundamental subsystems of the educational enterprise, but we shall spend little time in this book on the individual participant per se. For, while educational organizations seem by and large to be attuned to the challenges of individual development, they are notoriously weak in their capabilities to nurture their own social subsystems for organizational development. College staffs, in particular, are weak in their abilities to cooperate, and often even the college's smallest groups, its departments, teams, and committees, experience difficulties. By and large, colleges and schools should give higher priority to their own organizational development.

Subsystems

By *subsystems* we mean an intact work group—several individuals organized to carry out one or more tasks. Subsystems have tasks to perform, require interdependence among the members, and exhibit a structure through which patterned social interaction occurs. A curriculum committee, the administrative cabinet, the classroom containing students and instructor, and the custodial staff are all subsystems. An individual usually belongs to more than one subsystem. The name of a subsystem is often a good clue to its primary function.

Schools and colleges are composed of subsystems that perform various functions from designing curricula to ordering textbooks, and each subsystem includes people, supplies, space, and information. Some subsystems are easy to draw on an organization chart, some are not. People belong to a subsystem if its function depends on them, regardless of where they lie on an organization chart. That is true of equipment, too, no matter what room it is in. The boundaries of subsystems are both formal and informal. To be sure where the boundaries lie, where they are unyielding and where they are permeable, the OD practitioner must often do a good deal of analysis and observation.

Some subsystems have vague, easily penetrable boundaries. The subsystem in a high school or college that serves the function of socializing new instructors, for example, might not have a designated space in which to carry out its task, a budget, or a stable roster of members. Other subsystems have more definite boundaries, which make them easier to locate. For example, the counseling staff is different from the math department, and that is obvious to everyone. In some cases, legal arrangements entailing contracts and credentials prevent outsiders from penetrating the boundaries of an educational subsystem.

Some OD practitioners find the classification by Katz and Kahn (1978) to be helpful. Their scheme categorized the organization's functions as *production, support, maintenance, adaptation,* and *management*. The production subsystem carries on the fundamental work of the organization—in schools and colleges, that is teaching students the curriculum. The support subsystem provides the material needed by the production subsystem to operate—library, classroom aides, curriculum specialists, texts, and supplies. The maintenance subsystem coordinates and motivates action close to production (instruction)—committees, informal helpfulness among faculty members, and norms about "the way we do things around here." The adaptation subsystem anticipates changes in the environment and alters internal procedures accordingly—the superintendent's or provost's dealings with their respective boards, curriculum committees anticipating the demands of employers or technological changes in the society, budgeting decisions to anticipate tax revenues, and so on. The management subsystem coordinates the school or the college as a whole—making decisions to convert policy into procedure, specifying job descriptions, and allocating funds.

However one prefers to classify subsystems, the key concept for the OD practitioner is that of the *intact group*. Whenever one wishes to improve some function in an educational organization, the change agent almost always encounters interdependence among several people whose work carries out that function. The work proceeds partly because the members of that group can predict adequately some of one another's actions, and because they demand certain outcomes from one another. Those predictions and demands hold the work in place. If the manner of work is to be changed, there must be changes in the predictions and demands among the individuals who work together, and the *intact group thus becomes the best strategic target of change.*

Conflict Among Subsystems. Most OD practitioners assume that conflict is inevitable in organizations, and some say that organizations cannot be creative unless they allow participation that exposes conflicts. Kouzes and Mico (1979) write persuasively that schools (or colleges) have conflicts built into their structure. They say that three kinds of subsystems are inevitably in conflict— those in the domains of *policy, management*, and *service*. For school districts, the policy domain is primarily occupied by the school board. In the main, the administrators make up the management domain, and the teachers and counselors the service domain. For many colleges, the policy domain is occupied by an elected or an appointed board. The president, provost, and deans make up the management domain, and the instructors and counselors the service domain.

Often, people working in the policy domain feel as though they are representatives of others. They measure their success by whether they make just, impartial, and fair decisions. Their work entails negotiating, bargaining, and voting. Those in the management domain view the organization more as structure and bureaucracy. They measure their success in terms of cost efficiency and organizational effectiveness. Their work is linear and rational. Those in the service domain typically operate by autonomy, collegiality, and self-regulation. They measure their success by the quality of instruction or counseling and by whether they act according to professional standards. Their attention goes to process more than product, and their work is client-specific and oriented to problem solving.

Management's insistence on conformity to rules conflicts with the service domain's focus on the needs of students. The policy domain's norm of airing disagreements in public conflicts with the management's norm of keeping problems private until decisions are made. The norm of fair and equitable treatment among the policy makers conflicts with the demand for cost efficiency and political reciprocity in the management domain, and that in turn conflicts with the maintenance of professional standards in the service domain.

Representation among the policy makers, bureaucracy in the management, and collegiality for those performing service require different kinds of interpersonal norms, and conflicts arise when a participant in one domain expects to be treated by norms that seem inappropriate to persons in another domain. The linear style of work in the management domain, the individualized treatment of complex human problems in the service domain, and the negotiation and bargaining in the policy domain call for different interpersonal norms and values. It would be fruitless for participants in all three domains to try to adhere to the same work norms and professional standards.

Meyer and Rowan (1977) argued that the board and the administrators (policy and management domains) have the job of looking outward toward the public, while teachers (service domain) have the job of looking inward toward students. Board and administrators must deal with the public through a large—and simplified—picture of the organization. Instructors and counselors must deal with students through detailed and technical procedures. That difference, too, is a source of conflict.

One important way to reduce the likelihood of conflict is to arrange work so that people from different domains do not often interact with one another. Division of labor is the typical strategy— among individuals, committees, departments, and so on, with specific resources allocated to each. To the extent that interdependence among persons or groups of diverse domains can be minimized, the occasions for conflict can be minimized. Weick (1976) and others call that reduced interdependence *loose coupling.* High schools and colleges are notoriously loosely coupled.

Features of Educational Organizations

One or more features of schools or colleges distinguish them from industrial firms, the military, and churches. These features generate both opportunities and restrictions not found in other organizations. We have already mentioned the built-in conflicts among the policy, management, and service domains, and the organization's loose coupling. Below are some other features that OD practitioners have found noteworthy.

Nonvoluntary. Although faculty members take their jobs voluntarily, the membership of students, at least for public schools and many community colleges, is coerced. Hirschman (1970, p. 4) points out that members can express their dissatisfaction with an organization in two ways: they can leave it or they can voice their complaints. Faculty members can quit and find employment elsewhere, even though it is sometimes difficult. Up to a specified age, students are constrained from leaving, and even when they become old enough to leave, the lack of employment opportunities can work to keep them in school. Thus, students often express their complaints by word or action while staying in school. Some of those words and actions (vandalism or drinking, for example) become a main source of problems for the school.

Funding. The funding of public schools and colleges is loosely coupled to its performance. If a manufacturing firm turns out a poor product, it loses customer revenues. Schools can experience a drop in funding, too, if taxpayers become dissatisfied, but the action is delayed, and it is often difficult to trace the connection between the dissatisfaction and events in a particular school or college.

Near-monopoly. Competition among schools and community colleges, even where it is felt, has in the past had little effect on joining or leaving by teachers or students. Recently in many parts of the nation, however, a greater proportion of parents have been sending their children to private schools, or their graduating high school seniors out of state to college.

The Membership of Students. Students are members of the educational organization in some ways, and in other ways they are clients. As members of the same educational organization, students and professionals communicate in groups to carry out teaching and learning. Students are like clients, on the other hand, in that they receive services from the professional faculty. They are also like clients in that they have little voice in the operation of the school, no career line within the college (they cannot be promoted to teacher), an officially limited tenure, and almost no possibility of being paid for their work, except of course, for graduate students who become research assistants.

Permeability. Schools are highly permeable to the environment. Customers of an industrial firm have very limited ways of making known their dissatisfactions. Taxpayers and others with special interests, however, can do many things: vote against levies, vote for different board members, voice complaints at board meetings, initiate meetings of interest groups and demand that administrators attend, visit the school or college and complain to administrators, complain to instructors, and teach their children to make various kinds of demands on the instructors and counselors.

Multiple and Unclear Goals. Typically, factions in schools and colleges have differing visions of educational goals, sometimes radical differences, and it is difficult for one group to describe its goals clearly to another. Whatever other goal a commercial firm may have, the "bottom line" is making a profit. Perhaps the bottom line for schools is maintaining order, though most educators are not satisfied with that. But it is difficult to be specific, when framing educational goals, about the kinds of behavior the education should produce, the preferred domains of behavior, acceptable evidence, and the point in the student's career when a judgment of success should be made.

Information, Not Goods. Almost the whole business of schools and colleges is to deal with information and the skills to use it. Schools and colleges do not manufacture goods or provide services connected with goods such as washing laundry, repairing typewriters, or transporting groceries. The stuff educational organizations deal with is information, by which we mean more than the formal curriculum. When instructors transmit skill in writing, painting, or basketball, they do the transmitting by communicating information and values. Some business firms or churches come close to educational organizations in having information and values as their sole stuff but schools and colleges are the purest case.

Formal and Informal Structures

The formal structure of an educational organization, the result of tradition and rational planning, often limits its capacity to deal with unpredictable contingencies. Even when administrators try to provide jobs, communication channels, committees, ombudsmen, personnel directors, or some other scheme for adapting to the uniqueness of different individuals, unusual problems still arise that cannot be contained within the formal routines. When unusual demands stir urgent demands, when the formal arrangements become too cumbersome, people find help quickly by opening their own communication channels to informally offered helping roles. No doubt, too, people sometimes feel safer with the informal than with the formal arrangements. In sum, the "informal structure" arises because the organizational members have abilities, needs, and feelings that cannot be encompassed by the formal structure.

Although it is true that the informal subsystems sometimes subvert the operations of the formal subsystems, we should not look upon the informal side of the school or college as clandestine or always subversive. Since rational planning and formal structure are inevitably inadequate, the informal structure is a necessary part of the complete organization. OD practitioners work with both the formal and the informal subsystems with equal openness.

Norms, Roles, Structures, and Procedures

A *norm* exists when, within a collection of people, certain ranges of behavior are approved, others are disapproved, and still others are neither approved nor disapproved. If, in a high school class in writing, most students express acceptance of a student who writes an essay of 10 pages but make resentful remarks both to a student who "tries to get away" with five pages and also to one who "tries to show us up" with 20 pages, then a class norm exists regarding essay length. For a norm to have effect, people must express approval or disapproval about certain ranges of behavior. If the norm is to be clear, it must be *shared*—that is, most people must agree on the ranges of behavior to be approved and disapproved. Where people give mixed approval and disapproval, the norm is weak because it is confusing.

Norms hold together the organization's patterns of behavior. Some norms are official rules and regulations. Such formal norms have effect when a large proportion of the members of the school give approval to those who conform and disapproval to those who do not. The rules are ineffective or "on paper only" when they are contravened without disapproval.

Roles are norms about how a person in a particular organizational position should perform—or, more exactly, how two or more persons should interact on the job. Colleges have norms, for example, about how faculty members should behave toward students and how students should behave toward faculty members; there can be no instructor's role without students and no student's role without instructors.

Structures are norms about roles assigned to several interrelated jobs: about performance in those jobs, responsibilities among jobs, and so on. Structures have vertical dimensions which have to do with authority and hierarchy and horizontal dimensions which have to do with the division of labor or specialization of work.

Procedures are the actions taken through the structure for accomplishing a specific task—for example, a procedure for becoming enrolled in a course or for requisitioning paper. Procedures can be formal or informal, and they are held in place by norms. Norms, roles, structures, and procedures combine to make up the culture of the educational organization.

When innovations are undertaken in schools or colleges, norms must be changed, because they hold the current structures and procedures in place. Since norms exist among role takers, not within individuals, the OD practitioner should expect to work mostly with the intact group to change them. The OD practitioner strives to help educational staffs become explicit about the norms they wish to have in their organization. When norms are decided upon explicitly, we call them *group agreements*.

OD Strategy in Educational Organizations

To change norms, roles, structures, and procedures so that a school or college can become self-renewing, the OD practitioner keeps three goals in mind: (1) organizational adaptability, (2) individual motive satisfaction, and (3) effective work groups.

Organizational Adaptability

In our view the ultimate reason for developing an organization is to bring it to a sustained capacity to solve its own problems. We call that quality *organizational adaptability*. By *adaptability* we mean that the organization constructively manages change, that it does not merely adjust or acquiesce to externally imposed change. By *adaptable*, we mean what Gardner (1963) meant by *self-*

renewing, what Buckley (1967) called *morphogenetic*, what Williamson (1974) called *inquiring*, what Hedberg, Nystrom, and Starbuck (1976) called *self-designing*, and what Weisbord (1987) called the *learning organization*. We see organizational adaptability in educational organizations as composed of four metaskills: the ability to (1) diagnose the functioning of subsystems within, (2) gather information and other resources from within and outside, (3) mobilize synergistic action among the faculty, and (4) monitor the other three metaskills. A school or college with high levels of those skills can deal productively with changing demands and circumstances.

Diagnosis. Diagnosis is the systematic inspection by school participants of their own current functioning. In diagnosis, participants ask whether what the educational organization is actually doing matches the way the members talk about what they are doing, and whether what they are doing is what they want to be doing. Diagnosis does not merely mean a yearly review, though that is usually a good idea. Rather, formal and informal diagnosis should be done as often as necessary to prevent stressful responses to crises.

By *systematic diagnosis*, we refer to two things. First, we mean collecting data in a manner that will give answers in which one can have reasonable confidence. If information is sought about what frustrations staff members are feeling, for example, it will not do to ask only the principal or the dean, or simply to ask for statements at a faculty meeting. Methods are needed that will survey all important segments of the staff and that will enable the respondents to feel safe in answering.

Second, we mean using a checklist, written or mental, to make sure that important aspects of organizational functioning are covered. The make-up of the particular list used is less important than the fact that a list exists that does in fact itemize all the important features of organizational life. (See the list below in "Effective Work Groups" for an example.)

Searching for Information and Other Resources. Searches are initiated whenever currently available information or any other resource is inadequate to plan an effective solution to a problem. A group skillful in dealing with problems will assess the degree to which later action depends on resolving an uncertainty. ("Do we need to know what might happen at that juncture?") If the possible answers to an uncertainty will have little effect on further action, the skillful group ceases discussion of the uncertainty. If clarifying the uncertainty can make a difference, the skillful group decides when the uncertainty must be resolved, how to get information to resolve it, and who will take the necessary steps. Those are the components of searching out information and sources.

Obviously, skill in gathering information and other resources is important in solving problems. A solution to a problem can founder if it turns out that staff members have less than they need of information, status, affection, services, materials, or money.

Mobilizing Synergistic Action. Even if an educational organization were to exhibit well-developed norms, structures, and procedures for systematic diagnosis and for getting information and resources from inside and outside, it would still not show an exemplary capacity for solving problems. Even when all concerned had agreed on an accurate diagnosis of the present situation, when they had consensually chosen a clear and specific target, and when participants had declared their commitment to realistic and well-understood steps of action, a crucial step would still remain. Some faculty members would actually have to take the first, risky, irretrievable action in the new mode.

We emphasize the necessity for *synergistic* group action in organizational change, because new norms and role relationships are more than the sum of all individual actions. Administrators, and others too, often try to bring about change by instructing every individual what to do and then saying, in effect, "On next Monday morning, do things the new way, not the old way." As everyone but a few top administrators seems to know, that method often thrusts people into high risks. Participants may lack the confidence that they can do the new thing correctly—in a manner that will please the others involved in the change, or at least not draw their wrath. It is often safer for them to go on doing things in the old way.

If change is to proceed, faculty members must be in frequent communication up, down, and laterally to keep up with the latest developments. Collaboration must replace isolation and hierarchical direction so that all concerned can be aware of new action when it occurs, see for themselves who committed it, and give it their own support. Cooperation in processing problems and making decisions will yield new patterns of coordinated action that directives to separate individuals could not possibly have brought into being.

Monitoring the First Three Metaskills. The monitoring ability is the crowning skill necessary to sustaining a capacity for solving organizational problems. The skill consists of the ability to observe one's own group and to ask, "Are we as skillful as we need to be in diagnosing our functioning, getting appropriate information and resources, and mobilizing our action? Are we able to move ourselves in the direction we want to go?" Answering those questions gives the faculty an awareness of its shared capacity to deal productively with problems and change.

Individual Motive Satisfaction

In choosing ways to improve educational organizations, we must not disregard the satisfaction of human motives. Most of us would agree that a strong, resilient school or college that is able to meet internal and external challenges with competence will be populated by faculty and students who are satisfied with their academic lives together.

Though many people work at jobs they find dissatisfying, many others look to their jobs for greater personal satisfaction than they find elsewhere. And it is not generally true that people dissatisfied at work make up for it at home or elsewhere. Indeed, when work is dull and passive, people usually do *not* choose leisure pursuits that answer needs for variety and vigorous activity, but turn instead to activities that are as undernourishing as their work. To ignore the satisfaction of human needs in the school or college is inevitably to bring about two undesirable results: students and faculty will in one way or another increasingly remove themselves from serious work, and they will drag through each additional unrewarding day with growing discouragement.

Individuals act, when they can, to maximize their chances of taking initiative and being successful (the *achievement motive*), of enjoying friendship (the *affiliation motive*), and of exercising influence over their own fate (the *power motive*). They make choices: between behavior producing more achievement and that producing less; between behavior that is helpful and affectionate and that which is obstructive and expresses hostility; and between behavior that yields mastery of the environment and that which requires acquiescence to the will of others. OD practitioners believe that people are more likely to remain motivated, to keep more paths open to further satisfaction, and to become more productive if their motives for achievement, affiliation, and power can be expressed and satisfied in their work.

Effective Work Groups

Because the functions of educational organizations are carried out through coordinated effort within work groups, understanding what makes them effective is crucial to understanding what makes schools and colleges adaptable. Indeed, improving work group effectiveness, coupled with efforts to improve interpersonal skill and satisfy human motives, constitutes the core of organization development. The following list describes seven highly interdependent capabilities of an effective work group. When one capability is increased, it is easier to increase others.

1. *Clarifying communication.* Because skill in communication opens channels within the work group and between it and other work groups or segments of the environment, clarity of communication is essential to effectiveness.

2. *Improving group procedures in meetings.* The face-to-face meetings in which most organizational activity occurs need not be frustrating or unproductive. Procedures to facilitate task productivity and group maintenance can make meetings more satisfying.

3. *Establishing goals.* Because people's educational goals are diffuse and ambiguous, sharpening goal definitions can lead to exploring the differentiation and integration of effort needed to achieve them. Recognizing the pluralism of goals within a work group, school, and community can be a vital step toward an acceptance of differences and a greater commitment to common goals.

4. *Uncovering and working with conflict.* Just as clarifying communication and goals will lead to increased awareness of areas of conflict, so confronting conflict can help to clarify the norms that will aid the organization in accomplishing its tasks. Norms for collaboration can replace norms for avoiding conflict.

5. *Solving problems.* Adaptability implies continual active engagement in problem-solving cycles for pinpointing, analyzing, and acting on environmental contingencies. Work groups that harness human resources to extract creative solutions are more successful than are those that merely extrapolate past practice.

6. *Making decisions.* Effective work groups, like adaptable organizations, must be capable of moving decisions into action; that can be done effectively only when people clearly understand a decision and are committed to it. Although it is not necessary for some members to have less influence and others to have more, it is usually helpful for those with more knowledge and competence on a topic to have more influence on decisions about that topic.

7. *Assessing changes.* Change for its own sake does not necessarily lead to adaptability. Schools and colleges must develop criteria for measuring and evaluating progress toward meeting short-range and long-range goals.

OD Technology in Educational Organizations

OD practitioners try to increase the clarity with which participants choose what they want to do, the steps through which they will do it, and the signs by which they can decide whether they have succeeded. OD practitioners help school participants to visualize those organizational procedures that will help and those that will hinder, to bring into open discussion opinions or feelings that can affect the job at hand, and to find ways the participants themselves can put to use conflicts that are ordinarily suppressed. Above all, OD practitioners *teach* participants how to work with their colleagues in solving organizational problems together.

Types of OD Designs

We distinguish four designs for organization development— (1) training, (2) survey-data-feedback, (3) constructive confrontation, and (4) process observation and feedback. The four call for different behavior from the OD practitioner.

Training. The type of OD design carried out most often with schools (not colleges) is training. As trainer, the OD practitioner determines the learning outcomes for a particular period of time and organizes and directs the activities. Thus, training entails highly planned teaching and experience-based learning in structured formats that often feature lecturettes and assigned readings. In our examples of OD in action presented at the beginning of this chapter, Paula, Don, and Jane were engaged in training designs. Paula and Don trained both within their own college and as disinterested outsiders with Jane's administrative cabinet. Jane acted as an outside trainer initially, but, with experience, became a trainer to her own cabinet.

Certain *skills, exercises,* and *procedures* are regarded as the building blocks of organizational training. A *skill* may be one of communication, such as paraphrasing what a speaker has said to allow the speaker to verify your understanding of the message. Other examples of communicative skills are the ability to guide a group through a quick oral survey of opinion and to write interview queries that successfully elicit diagnostic information about the organization.

An *exercise*, or simulation, is a structured, gamelike activity used to enable participants to become consciously aware of their own interpersonal behavior and that of others. Participants usually find it easy to see parallels between their experience in the exercise and their previous workday experience in the organization. Exercises have two important advantages: they can be designed to produce specifiable learning, and they typically have content very different from that of an educational organization's ordinary day-to-day work. By enabling participants to learn the advantages of one form of behavior over another, an exercise helps them plan to establish more productive behavior.

Unlike exercises, whose content is determined by the trainer, *procedures* are content-free and are used for the purpose of making work toward a specific goal chosen by the group more effective. Under most conditions, experiencing an exercise takes a group away from its primary tasks. Procedures, on the other hand, are introduced to accomplish a task the work group is already facing. As steps or routines by which a group can move forward in its actual business, procedures are less gamelike and also less obtrusive to the group's normal functioning. Procedures such as taking surveys and doing systematic problem solving are useful in colleges, schools, departments, and cabinets, and sometimes to faculty members who have tried them with their students to improve the teaching and learning environment in their classes.

Survey-Data-Feedback. In *survey-data-feedback*, information is collected systematically usually through questionnaires, interviews, and observations and then reported back to appropriate work groups as a basis for diagnosis, problem solving, and planning. Three aspects of survey-data-feedback are central to its success. First, the OD practitioner must be adept at collecting data and at putting the data into a feedback form that will be understandable and energizing to the participants. Second, the practitioner must strive to show essential significance in mundane data to capture participants' interests. Third, the practitioner must find ways of incorporating data feedback into the natural ebb and flow of larger OD designs. Vera, Dick, and Randy were using survey-data-feedback designs in our earlier examples. Vera and Dick applied their design to the challenge of climate improvement in their state college. Randy applied survey-data-feedback to his high school English class.

Constructive Confrontation. The social relationships between two or more work groups can often be clarified by a *constructive confrontation*. This strategy also sharpens and clarifies problems that are causing conflicts between the groups. The OD practitioners bring together the conflicting groups and help them to communicate explicitly the perceptions that each has of the others; to spell out the ways each views the others as helpful or unhelpful; to increase the openness, or at least the clarity, of communication; to propose procedures for problem solving that can facilitate collaborative inquiry into mutual problems; and to find common concerns, if any, among the parties. Ultimately, the OD practitioner aims to get the parties to make some new agreements. Pat, Lee, and Lynn were using elements of a constructive-confrontation design in their consultation with the elementary school that was converting to team teaching. Alice applied a similar OD design in her role as executive dean at a community college.

Process Observation and Feedback. In carrying out *process observation and feedback*, the purpose of which is to help group members become more aware of how they are working together, the OD practitioner sits with the work group during its work sessions, observes the ongoing group processes, and offers occasional comments and questions to turn the participants' attention to their way of working and its effects on getting the job done. The goal of this type of OD intervention is to involve participants in talking about their working relationships and in making group agreements to modify their ways of working together in the future. Mike was engaged as an outsider in that sort of design with the superintendent's cabinet. Later, Mike also used process observation and feedback when he became department head in the Department of Teacher Education of his college.

The Stages of OD

Although one or another type of OD design can be used to help solve small problems over short periods (to improve meetings, for example), a project in organization development that reaches throughout an educational organization and aspires to bring to maturity its organizational adaptability is inevitably complex. Such a project typically goes through six stages.

Start-up and a Memorandum of Understanding. An educational organization acknowledges a problem when some influential person or group within it conceives a state of interpersonal and group affairs significantly more satisfactory than the current one. In our view, productive change is unlikely to occur unless a significant part of the faculty acknowledges a discrepancy between an ideal and actual state of affairs before an OD design is started. That is, a sizable portion of the faculty, and especially its more powerful members, should accept the problems as their problems and become reasonably committed to solving them instead of merely acquiescing to a project that originates on the initiative of a single administrator. OD practitioners should make it a rule to start a formal OD project only with intact work groups that are to some extent calling out for help.

What happens during the first phase foreshadows later phases. If the project is to have support, a practitioner must get at least oral commitment to the enterprise from all members of the work groups that will participate in it. To that end, it is critical for the practitioner to establish rapport, credibility, and legitimacy at the outset, and to arrive at clear statements about motives, competencies, and shared expectations. OD practitioners should be explicit about their role, their goals, the project's budget, and the time and effort they are willing to devote to the project. They will also have to make explicit whether they will endeavor to implement the OD project from within, without outside assistance, or if they will seek to hire an external OD consultant.

Although outside consultants may initially be contacted by a single administrator who is particularly interested in OD, interactions are best begun between the outsider and all administrators with authority, because those administrators hold crucial gatekeeping power and can control subsequent contacts with other members of the system, and it is therefore helpful if they become allies early rather than enemies. In school districts, colleges, and universities, powerful parties with authority typically include the board members, the superintendent or president and his or her cabinet, the principals and provosts or deans, and faculties' organizations. In individual schools or colleges, the powerful parties with authority may be particular instructors, department heads, counselors, deans, and, increasingly, formal students' groups.

Although gaining the approval and collaboration of key authorities is essential, that alone will not necessarily win commitment or acquiescence from others in the educational organization. OD practitioners, whether they are inside change agents or external consultants, must keep in mind that they are working not just with individuals but with a social system and with numerous work groups, and they will want to test the willingness of authorities to carry to others introductory discussions of the potential OD project.

During the first phases of start-up, it is vital that the OD practitioner communicate, if possible, with an entire work group, and not allow the less powerful participants to believe that they are less important to the OD project than administrators or others in authority. If the project is organization-wide, the practitioner will want to get acceptance from the significant work groups within the whole organization. If it is limited to a single division or department, it will be necessary before proceeding to win support not only from the powerful persons on that faculty but from as many other relevant staff members as possible. Practitioners can often win staff acceptance for OD by working in close collaboration with a carefully chosen steering committee composed of administrators and faculty members representing both formal groups and informal factions of the organization.

Although discussions of organizational processes, intervention techniques, OD designs, and schedules are important, a sound relationship between the OD practitioners and the staff members is not forged by agreement about tasks alone. The dynamics of start-up can arouse intense feelings ranging from suspicion to trust, dissatisfaction to well-being, caution to a willingness to invest, and reserve to complete openness. Directly acknowledging those feelings is a prime requisite for starting up well.

One way to signal that a new project is indeed under way is for the OD practitioners and a steering committee to prepare jointly a memorandum of understanding. It describes in summary the OD project's goals, steps, and approximate schedule of key events. It is available for editing by anyone and eventually agreed upon by everyone. The memorandum of understanding serves as a preamble for the OD project.

Diagnosing Current Functioning. OD practitioners must have detailed information on which to base their macrodesigns. Furthermore, they must communicate to staff members the importance of having particular data on the organization both for designing a tailored OD intervention and for enhancing the staff's problem solving. In fact, collecting relevant data on goal clarity, conflicts between work groups, processes at meetings, methods for solving problems, and procedures used for reaching decisions often demonstrates the foci of OD far better than the memorandum of agreement.

Diagnosis, however, often stirs fears, even when faculty members manifest great interest in becoming engaged in OD. Nowadays, for example, educational personnel who have experienced diagnosis and intervention frequently in the past may regard them as old hat. It is also true that although the innovative *zeitgeist* has reigned supreme in many colleges and school districts, promises of change have often failed to materialize. If resistance, change attempts, and a subsequent failure of change have been part of an organization's history, the OD practitioner must nevertheless insist that diagnosis of the current situation is still critical, since no rational change design can be developed without an accurate picture of the here and now.

Diagnosis should occur with even the most sophisticated faculty. Indeed, pessimistic comments by faculty members are important data in themselves. OD practitioners need to take special care with cautious or cynical faculty members to assess the amount of worry about OD in general and about the diagnosis in particular. OD practitioners should strive to discover the kinds of workshop events that occurred within the organization before, the kinds of organizational problems that were targeted, and the reasons, from the faculty members' point of view, previous problem-solving efforts were aborted. Attacks on problems that occur later in the OD project, such as ineffective meeting procedures, can take into account the frustration of previous problem-solving efforts.

During the diagnostic period, the OD practitioner should use multiple methods, of which self-report questionnaires, interview guides, and planned observations are the most typical. In addition to those formal methods, conversations with organizational members also bring important information, and so do organizational memos and letters.

Collecting formal data can strengthen organizational members' view of the validity and legitimacy of the OD project. Ideally, OD practitioners will let their first impressions, however they are obtained, guide the selection of formal questionnaires, interviews, and observations. The results of these data-gathering efforts will be augmented in turn by insights gained from further data informally collected.

Another useful procedure to employ for collecting diagnostic data grows out of the tradition of action research. Here the OD practitioners collaborate with a project steering committee in the construction of a diagnostic procedure tailored to the organization. Together the practitioners and the committee collect and analyze the diagnostic data.

Designing the OD Project. OD designs can usually be divided into macroaspects and microaspects. *Macroaspects* include the design's overall structure and outline, sequence of parts, and the general forms through which activities flow. *Microaspects* include the specific activities carried out during a limited period such as a week, a day, or even an hour of intervention. Tailoring macroaspects and microaspects of the design to specific objectives and participants is a major challenge for the OD practitioner, who must be able to distinguish between what is most effective in a particular time and place and what the practitioner personally is most comfortable doing.

Different diagnoses usually call for different emphases in macrodesigns—that is, different sequences of training, survey-data-feedback, constructive confrontation, and process observation and feedback. For example, although OD practitioners should deal early with actual organizational problems among sophisticated faculties, with unsophisticated staffs they might choose to offer more simulated skill-training in the beginning phases of OD. A lack of goal clarity, as another example, might lead the practitioner to begin with an agenda-building activity that would enable participants to deal with very short-term goals as a prelude to dealing with those of longer term.

When designing, the practitioner always does some detailed, rational planning in advance. We have found it useful during initial meetings, for example, to attempt to describe the total OD effort or to post the agenda and plans at the beginning of an event to invite clarification from participants. Still, even the best-laid plans must allow a certain amount of free time to accommodate the unanticipated. This slack allows an unexpected event to turn a highly task-oriented, unexciting OD session into one in which participants can arrive at their own insights, invent creative solutions to their problems, and find the confidence and zeal to go on.

An effective OD effort must meet the challenges of improving interpersonal and work group skills, changing work group norms, and improving organizational structure. These goals are often dealt with in the following sequence.

First, the OD practitioner focuses on interpersonal and work group skills, typically trying to increase openness and ease of interpersonal communication by training participants to paraphrase, describe behavior, describe their own feelings, and confirm their impressions of others' feelings. In addition, the OD practitioner tries to build skills in conceiving problems and in responding, until participants are able to exhibit constructive openness and confidence that communication with colleagues can be worthwhile.

Second, the OD practitioner focuses on norms. Even while improving interpersonal and work group skills, practitioners can raise participants' awareness of the functioning of norms. They can point out the discrepancies between what is being approved and what everyone wants to approve. By giving members a chance to applaud one another for moving plans into action, for example, OD practitioners can evoke pressures to "put up or shut up" that create new norms in support of responsiveness. In addition, they can show how deviations from norms help to pinpoint problems and resources in the organization. Helping people in a school or college to see that deviation from norms is a resource rather than a threat can move the group a long way toward organizational adaptability.

As a lever for changing work group norms, the OD practitioner can attempt to ameliorate actual problems by asking participants to describe some of the frustrations they encounter in their jobs and then to practice a sequence of cooperative problem solving to reduce them. Cooperative problem solving not only reduces frustrations but also yields the satisfaction of knowing that one's contribution toward reaching a solution is valued by others. When staff members behave in new ways (according to new norms), they enable one another to see the new norm taking hold. They see that others are not only *saying* they are willing, but that they are *acting* willingly.

Third, the OD practitioner turns to the organization as a whole—the school or college. Now, using the same techniques, strategies, and skills as before but in larger scope, participants arrive at the time for building new functions, roles, procedures, policies, or subsystems and making them formal and institutionalized, with budgetary support, so that these new structures become part of the basic fabric of the organization.

Assessing Designs and Monitoring Progress. As we see it, OD designs cannot be expected to fit well if they are made in Peoria and shipped to Little Rock, or vice versa. They should be tailored to fit the local diagnostic data. Two parts of tailoring are to assess the feasibility of a design before it is carried out and to assess progress after each event in the design is carried out.

OD practitioners assess a design before putting it into motion by scrutinizing it and trying to anticipate what could go wrong before it does go wrong. They ask how the macrodesign relates to the diagnosis and how it furthers the overall goals of the project. They might also invite steering committee members to examine and criticize the plan for possible weaknesses. Moreover, OD practitioners assess progress by watching alertly both during each microaspect of the design and during the first few hours afterward for signs of unwanted side-effects. If the episode turns out to have fallen short of what was hoped or to have gone well beyond, the OD practitioner redesigns the next episodes accordingly.

Terminating the OD Project. Inevitably, participants in an OD project develop some amount of dependency on their facilitators, and that is particularly true when the OD practitioners are outside consultants. The latter must prepare participants for the consultants' eventual withdrawal by giving repeated advance notice of their date of leaving and then sticking firmly to schedule. The macrodesign should move toward increasingly greater client control over the course of the OD effort, and the outside consultants should give participants ample practice in taking over the functions of organization adaptability before they leave.

Similarly, when the OD practitioners are staff members who belong to the organization, they too, should gradually adopt a lower-profile role in leading the OD project as the project moves along. The problem of dependency on OD practitioners can become serious, particularly when the OD design has been featured primarily by training in skills and exercises. OD practitioners inside the organization will want to create macrodesigns in which intervention procedures are more and more executed by the organizational participants themselves as the OD moves toward conclusion.

Institutionalizing OD. If an innovation like OD is to continue in a school or college for some years, it must be made a more or less routine part of the organization's operation. That is, if educational managers do not want a new way of doing things to fade quickly away, they must try to institutionalize it. OD itself can be institutionalized by establishing procedures, roles, and structures to maintain the metaskills necessary for organizational adaptability. For an educational organization, perhaps the most powerful support for OD, as well as the most economical one, is the *cadre of organizational specialists*, which we describe in chapter 10.

Chapter Two

Applications of OD

OD projects in schools and colleges differ in their system levels, process goals, educational contents, and the organizational positions of the facilitators.

The system levels include one-to-one relationships, small work groups, relationships between small work groups, whole organizations, and relationships between whole organizations and their external stakeholders.

The process goals entail either building on strengths or overcoming weaknesses. They lie in clarifying communications, improving meetings, solving problems, making decisions, and working with conflicts.

The educational contents pertain to curriculum change, group and organizational restructuring, and staff development. Curriculum change entails innovation in any subject taught to students. Group and organizational restructuring focuses on establishing new role relationships, as must occur when desegregating, forming new schools, mainstreaming, managing at the site, and team building. Staff development entails introducing knowledge, skills, and values to individual educators.

The organizational positions of the facilitators can be either inside or outside the system that is targeted for OD. If they are inside the targeted system, they are members of it. For example, a principal might undertake to facilitate OD in his or her own school, or the faculty might ask the principal to do so. Typically, inside facilitators are administrators, but other skillful people such as counselors or department heads can be called on. If facilitators are outside the targeted system, they can be either inside or outside the larger organization. For example, a facilitator for school A might be found in school B of the same district. Or a facilitator for department A of a college might be found in department B. But facilitators can also come from farther afield. Consultants can come from universities, private firms, across town, or from across the nation.

System Levels

OD projects can be implemented at different levels of educational systems, ranging from very small, one-to-one relationships to far-ranging relationships between the educational organization and its community.

One to One

The typical focus for OD in one-to-one relationships is on how well the parties understand and agree on the roles they will take in their formal relationships. For example, a student and teacher agree on what constitutes an acceptable essay, a counselor and student agree on how they will act to maintain confidentiality, a principal and teacher agree on how clinical supervision will unfold, an associate dean and department head agree on responsibility for organizing and spending money in the budget, and a president and provost agree on criteria for faculty promotion and tenure.

Frequently, role clarification in one-to-one relationships focuses on procedures; on how the parties will be expected to act in carrying out their roles. Thus, OD also focuses on making agreements about interpersonal procedures. For example, a student and teacher agree that if the student turns in an essay to the teacher on Wednesday, that the teacher will return the essay with critical comments by Friday; a counselor and student agree that the student will start each meeting by talking about events between meetings that bolstered or undermined the student's self esteem; a principal and teacher agree that they will hold a conference before and after the principal observes the teacher teaching; an associate dean and department head agree to keep each other informed about expenditures and other changes in the budget by electronic mail; and a president and provost agree that although the provost will make final decisions about faculty promotions and tenure, the president must be informed of the reasons for the provost's decision in writing no more than two weeks after the decision.

One-to-one partnerships also can be encouraged and nurtured during a larger OD project. For example, during an organizational-training event for a middle-school faculty, two teachers agree to help each other implement cooperative learning in their classrooms. Or during a strategic-planning event in a college of education, two faculty members decide to carry out a research project together. Or during a survey-data-feedback event in a senior high school, the principal and a counselor decide to work together to improve the efficiency of faculty meetings. Support groups, even as small as two people can help participants in them feel integral to the organization and satisfied with their work.

Small Work Group

OD has been applied most frequently with the small work group. Indeed, OD practitioners' concern for small group effectiveness dates back to Lewin's pioneering initiatives in New England 50 years ago. Still today, OD practitioners spend the lion's share of their time on what they call group development or teambuilding.

Small work groups are featured by high task interdependence and regular face-to-face meetings. To be effective, the members of small work groups must communicate clearly with one another, under-stand the group's primary purposes, run efficient meetings, solve problems together, make decisions that are acceptable to everyone, and work with interpersonal conflicts constructively.

In most of their efforts at planned change, OD practitioners in schools and colleges target six types of small work groups: classroom groups, teams, committees, departments, boards, and cadres. An application of OD to the classroom, for example, could use questionnaire data from students to increase the teacher's understanding about how the students are reacting to teaching methods or class procedures. Or the students could be trained in how to run effective meetings before the teacher asks them to become engaged in cooperative learning. Or weekly class meetings could be scheduled for the teacher and students to discuss their thoughts and feelings about how the teaching and learning is going. Or an elected committee of students could meet weekly with the teacher to plan for improvements in class functioning. Or a class could discuss the differences between group norms and group agreements in an effort at self-governance.

Teams and Committees. Compared with most classroom groups, teams are smaller and characterized by a higher degree of required interdependence. Two or three teachers who teach in a team, for example, must plan, execute, and debrief their teaching together. Four or five students who work in a project team depend on one another to contribute ways to complete the project. A few administrators who strive to manage a school or a college as an administrative team must have trust and confidence in one another. Thus, OD with teams very often focuses upon clarifying or negotiating roles, giving and receiving information from others about the effects of one's actions, building trust and cohesiveness, and the like. For us, teambuilding in OD means helping team members to take initiative to sharpen role clarity, heighten constructive openness, and increase their trust in one another.

Another title for a small work group is the committee. Like some teams, it is established by administrators to perform specific tasks. Administrators officially delegate to committees either an advisory capacity of reporting or the sole responsibility of acting. Committees can vary in size from a very few people to perhaps a quarter of a school staff. Sometimes they require less interdependence and cohesiveness than do teams. Nevertheless, the primary challenges of OD faced by committees are to reach agreements about goals, roles, norms, and group procedures. Examples of typical committee tasks in education are curriculum change, evaluation of students and instructors, improvement of staff climate, parent or citizen participation in an educational program, and textbook selection.

Departments and Boards. Departments are official units of schools or colleges that focus on academic disciplines or fields of knowledge. They are responsible for carrying out teaching and research and for monitoring the professional activities of their members. Departments are integral parts of the formal social structures of educational organizations, serving to connect administrators with teachers and teachers with students. Applications of OD to departments often focus on such activities as running meetings, resolving conflicts, solving problems, and making decisions.

Boards set policy for a school or college, select and hire the chief administrator to manage the educational organization, and monitor the professional actions of that head. Policies are plans or general blueprints of action intended to affect the norms, structures, and procedures of the educational organization. The head administrator typically is the superintendent of schools or the president of a college. Boards hold the heads accountable for implementing the policies set by the boards. Applications of OD to boards focus on teambuilding, communicating with constituents, meeting skills, problem solving, and decision making.

Cadres. Cadres are groups of specially trained personnel from which the larger organization of the school district or university can receive continual assistance in organization development. They typically are made up of a cross section of the membership of the whole organization and could include teachers, administrators, counselors, psychologists, students, and classified personnel. Their members know how to implement aspects of OD and act as OD planners, facilitators, trainers, and consultants. In striving to establish a cohesive and effective group of their own, cadre members apply techniques of teambuilding to themselves.

Relationships Between Work Groups

OD projects also focus on improving relationships between small work groups. Here, OD consultants facilitate communication between the client groups by helping members of the groups understand their different norms and roles in the organization, their respective functions vis-à-vis each other, and the procedures they will use to perform instructional or organizational tasks effectively. Examples are:

1. In an elementary school, a 5th grade class and a 2nd grade class taking part in a cross-age tutoring program.
2. In a middle school, 6th, 7th, and 8th grade teacher teams working on how to dovetail their science curricula.
3. In a senior high school, the principal's administrative council and an elected group of faculty members deliberating on how to implement site-based management.
4. In a community college, the academic vice-president's management team and officers of the faculty union developing agreements about the role of affirmative action in hiring and promoting personnel.
5. In a four-year college, the English and psychology departments developing plans for interdisciplinary, interdepartmental courses.
6. In a university, department heads of selected disciplines in the arts and sciences and members of the teacher education

department developing programs for the preparation of teachers of secondary schools.

7. In a school district, a cadre of OD specialists and the superintendent's staff clarifying their respective roles in a district-wide staff development program.

Whole Organizations

Educational OD originally focused primarily on whole organizations, which we define as a body of persons organized by at least three hierarchical levels of authority for some end or work. During the 60s and 70s, the initial decades of educational OD, action researchers such as Christopher Keys, Dale Lake, Matthew Miles, and the two of us applied OD to public schools or districts, parochial schools, and community colleges. Although the applications of OD have become more varied today, we still think of OD for whole schools or colleges as classical OD. Examples are:

1. In an elementary school, the entire certificated faculty receiving organizational training in meetings' skills.
2. In a junior high school, the whole staff, including the classified personnel, taking part in workshops on interpersonal communication, personal goal setting, group problem solving, and consensus decision making.
3. In a senior high school, the certificated staff receiving feedback from a questionnaire it had completed, pinpointing its goals for school improvement, applying a problem-solving procedure to reach the goals, and agreeing on specific actions to try in striving to reach the goals.
4. In a community college, the academic vice-president's management team cooperating with a group of OD facilitators in a retreat intended to build trust and community with the entire teaching faculty.
5. In a school district, its own cadre of OD specialists collaborating with a group of OD consultants to carry out a two-year macrodesign in site-based management.

Relationships Between Whole Organizations and Their Stakeholders

OD projects have as their most far-ranging focus the relationships between whole organizations and their external stakeholders. Examples include: a parents' group in an elementary school confronting the teachers about weaknesses in the school's program, a district engaging its board and community in "strategic planning," and a college initiating "partnerships" with corporations. Lately, educational OD has been affected by a philosophy of administration labeled *Total Quality Management* (TQM). In particular, TQM stresses the importance of the customer's perceptions and attitudes about the targeted organization. In education, we can think of "customers" ranging from students and parents to employers, state departments of education, legislators, and various pressure groups. Up to now, educational OD projects following the TQM thinking have usually involved parent or citizen groups and partnerships with corporations. The sheer multiplicity of people who are stakeholders in the educational establishment offers a considerable challenge to OD practitioners.

Process Goals

In chapter 1 we wrote that effective work groups spend time clarifying communication, improving meetings, establishing goals, working with conflicts, solving problems, making decisions, and assessing changes. Those seven capabilities also are the primary process goals of educational OD.

Early OD projects typically were carried out in schools and colleges that already had reasonably effective group processes in the staffs. Action researchers such as Keys, Lake, Miles, and the two of us sought, by and large, to test OD designs in educational organizations where staff members wanted to make their work environments better. The researchers picked educational organizations to work with that could start OD from a position of strength. In our own early research and development during the late 60s and early 70s, we looked for schools and districts that we believed would benefit from OD. We did not search out the highly troubled or turbulent schools. After the OD was under way, however, we often found meetings that were inefficient, goals that were unclear to the members, problems that were ignored, decisions that were not implemented, and conflicts that were covered up.

Over the years we have found that weaknesses in the group processes of educational work groups are typical, not unusual. In working within schools and colleges as facilitators, consultants, and trainers, we have often uncovered breakdowns in communication between two people, within small groups, between small groups, and from the bottom to the top of the organization. We have observed numerous staff meetings with no agenda or agreed-upon procedures for solving problems or making decisions. We have consulted with many community colleges in which the roles of individuals and work groups have been unclear to most staff members. We have worked with school districts in which interpersonal and intergroup conflicts have festered for many years. Indeed, we conclude that virtually all schools and colleges need assistance in working on their group processes. We do not conclude, however, that everyone in education should become engaged in an OD project.

We view an educational system's ability to improve its own group processes to depend on the amount of tension its participants feel about how well they are working together. OD works best in educational systems that have participants with moderate degrees of tension about improving their interpersonal processes. Our thinking follows the classical Yerkes-Dobson law in the psychology of learning which states that concept learning is optimal when the learner's anxiety is in a middle range. Too much anxiety blocks the concentration required to learn new concepts, while too little anxiety does not supply the impetus for concentration and concept learning. With one exception, OD procedures should be applied only when most participants in a targeted system feel moderate degrees of tension about the effectiveness of their group processes. The exception is the confrontation design, discussed in chapter 8, and applied when a serious conflict between individuals or groups has become public, at least to the extent that the conflicting parties, however high their feelings of tension may be, can both agree with the OD consultant that conflict is present and that both parties know it is present.

Examples of OD interventions aimed at building on the strengths of a school's or college's group processes are:

1. In an elementary school, the faculty establishing group agreements about how to make decisions consensually.

2. In a middle school, an interdisciplinary team of teachers systematically collecting questionnaire data from students about the students' attitudes toward the school's curriculum and climate.

3. In a senior high school, the administrative team, composed of the principal, a counselor, and seven department heads, taking time during their meetings to discuss the strengths and weaknesses of their meetings' procedures and how to improve them in future meetings.

4. In a community college, the administrators spending two days yearly away from campus to discuss the helpful and unhelpful aspects of the college's norms, structures, and procedures and to plan for how to change them.

5. In a four-year college, the members of the sociology department engaging a consultant to interview students about the students' perceptions of the quality of communications on the faculty.

Along with confrontation designs that have been used in schools and colleges to deal constructively with serious intergroup or interpersonal strife, examples of other OD interventions aimed at overcoming process weaknesses are:

1. In a large elementary school of 44 professionals with serious communication breakdowns, the administration initiating a "matrix organization" to enhance communication up and down and across grade levels. The matrix organization has face-to-face work groups linked vertically and horizontally; team leaders link grade-level teams to the administration, while representatives from every grade level link their teams to one another through participation in school-wide committees.

2. In a middle school fraught with conflict between the elementary and secondary teachers who make up the faculty, the administration attending to improving meetings' procedures as a first step in working toward better communication in the school. Writing agendas, convening discussions, taking surveys, and recording decisions are safe foci for launching OD.

3. In a senior high school where several teachers avoid talking to one another altogether, and where most others are reluctant to voice their opinions at meetings, an ad hoc leadership team of administrators and teachers hiring outside consultants to implement a survey data feedback design in order to create new staff norms, structures, and procedures.

4. In a large community college with morale problems, the president and provost creating an advisory group of faculty and students to design and carry out "community-building" activities in the college.

5. In a four-year college with declining cohesiveness on the faculty, the deans and department heads holding a series of monthly meetings to carry out problem solving about the quality of relationships on the faculty.

Educational Contents

Altering the content of school and college programs is a frequent target of planned change in education. As an appropriate aide for facilitating change of educational contents, OD concepts and procedures can be applied specifically to curriculum change, group and organizational restructuring, and staff development.

Curriculum Change

A curriculum is the aggregate of courses of study presented to students in a school or college. Although courses of study have traditionally been created by individual teachers, textbook publishers, or specially formed committees of experts, more and more, teams of instructors inside the schools or colleges are assuming the challenge of collaboratively preparing courses that are appropriate for particular types of students. For example, a team of middle-school teachers, with the learning styles of early adolescent students in mind, might prepare some integrated course topics incorporating two or more traditional subject areas, or a team of community college instructors, with the attitudes of middle-aged adults in mind, might prepare courses in world literature and social science that incorporate the unique life experiences of their students. Whatever the specific focus of the curriculum change, the demands for faculty cooperation to complete the task give rise to the application of OD concepts and procedures. Other examples are:

1. In an elementary school in which 50 percent of students are having difficulty with reading, a team of k–3rd grade teachers integrating a whole-language curriculum into all their subjects.
2. In a middle school with 30 percent of students having arrived recently from El Salvador, a team of teachers preparing a bilingual curriculum.
3. In a senior high school, a committee of English, science, and social studies teachers developing interdisciplinary units to enhance writing across the curriculum.
4. In a community college, members of the business department collaboratively conferring with representatives of the business community to revise the college's business curriculum.
5. In a four-year college, professors of curriculum, educational administration, and educational psychology working together to create a certification program for prospective middle-school teachers.

Group and Organizational Restructuring

Restructuring refers to changes in the patterns of relationships and interaction between the members of a social system. It includes changes in interpersonal relationships, such as those that must occur among students when a teacher implements cooperative learning in the classroom. It also includes changes in *intergroup relationships*, such as those that must occur among blacks and whites when a district or college strives to transform itself into a racially integrated institution. OD concepts and procedures are appropriately applied to facilitate restructuring, particularly when, as in the examples above, educators wish to transform social patterns of status hierarchy and unfamiliarity into status equality and friendship. Examples are:

1. In an elementary school, a school psychologist and teachers representing each grade engaging in problem-solving meetings to establish more effective ways of integrating students with learning and physical disabilities into the daily learning activities of the regular classrooms.

2. To establish a new middle school in which half the staff are elementary teachers and half are secondary teachers, a team from the district's cadre of OD specialists training the new faculty in communication and meetings' skills, group problem-solving techniques, and collaborative decision-making procedures.

3. In a senior high school, a counselor and two teachers doing problem solving with 12 student leaders from the student government to reduce instances of racism and to increase friendly interactions between blacks and whites during the school's extracurricular activities.

4. In a community college, a committee of administrators, counselors, and instructors using questionnaire and interview data collected from the Native-American students to propose changes in the college's advising procedures and curriculum.

5. In a four-year college, a committee of female and male faculty and students using interview data from their peers on sexual harassment to design and carry out workshops for faculty and students on reducing unwanted sexual advances on the campus.

Staff Development

Until about a decade ago, staff development was synonymous with in-service workshops for individual teachers. The workshop presenters typically aimed to upgrade each participant's knowledge about curriculum and student psychology or his or her skills of teaching and counseling. Individual teachers chose the workshops they wished to attend, and they went to them as free agents in search of professional development rather than as representatives of their school or college. In many states, in-service workshops for k–12 public school teachers took place on a Friday in October and before or after school during the rest of the year. When government funds were more plentiful, k–12 teachers were paid to attend special in-service workshops in August before the start of the school year. In contrast to the widespread acceptance of in-service training for k–12 teachers, colleges and universities have been much less likely to sponsor professional development courses for their faculty members.

During the last decade, perhaps because of the influence of organization development, more and more in-service workshops were carried out with teachers who worked together in the same school. Those interventions were variously labeled site-based in-service, school-based professional development, school development, and even organization development. Especially in school districts with more than 2,000 students, a district-office administrator, charged with the job of staff developer, would assess each staff's needs for improvement and then arrange for appropriate instructors to present tailored workshops to satisfy some of those needs. Although some district-office-based staff developers thought they were doing organization development, most presenters focused on changing individuals' knowledge and skills. Instead of organization development, they were doing individual development for colleagues working in the same organization.

Today, under the leadership of the National Council on Staff Development, staff developers and school administrators are attempting to integrate the professional development of educators with organization development for schools and districts. Examples are:

1. In an elementary school, a committee of six teachers charged with the responsibility of proposing a new science curriculum to its colleagues receiving training in meetings' skills before it commences work on the new curriculum. While working on the curriculum, members of the committee rotate the roles of convener, recorder, and process observer; during each meeting the members spend a few minutes discussing how to improve their teamwork.

2. In a middle school engaged in trying out more cooperative learning projects, the staff receiving consultation in organization development from members of a local cadre spends time discussing how to apply the OD procedures it is experiencing in the classroom. Staff members refer to their projects as "OD in the classroom."

3. In a senior high school, an assistant principal, a counselor, and a social studies teacher, who together teach a course called Organizational Psychology to students elected to the student

government, preparing students to act as participant observers on the quality of teaching in the school and paving the way for students to give feedback about good teaching to the teachers.

Organizational Positions of OD Facilitators

OD has been designed and implemented traditionally by specialists who are not members of the targeted system. They usually have had advanced education in group dynamics and organizational psychology. Frequently, they have held master's or doctoral degrees in business, education, or the social sciences. In chapter 1, we wrote about Mike, a professor of teacher education, as a prototypical example of an external OD consultant. Mike used the OD technique of process observation and feedback in consulting with the superintendent's cabinet in a school district near his university. It is important to note that much of the jargon used by OD consultants brings to mind images of approaching the targeted system from the outside. OD consultants use such expressions: making entry, confrontation, intervention, and data feedback, to describe their work.

In our various experiments with OD in schools and colleges over the past three decades, we have concluded that OD procedures have a better chance of being sustained if they can be successfully implemented by members of the targeted system. Thus, as we described in chapter 1, Mike, who is head of his college department, can also use the OD technique of process observation and feedback with his colleagues in the department, and Paula and Don trained a task force of their community college colleagues in the skills of communication, problem solving, and consensual decision making. Often, inside facilitators are administrators like Mike, but other skillful people who have the trust of their colleagues also can be called upon to act as OD interveners. Thus, Paula and Don, who did not have administrative authority over the task force, could still be effective OD trainers.

We have raised questions in the past, however, about how effective an insider can be in turning interpersonal strife into constructive problem solving. In chapter 1, we described how Pat, Lee, and Lynn, as members of a district-wide cadre of organizational specialists helped the staff of an elementary school uncover disagreements and arrange to work collaboratively on important instructional problems. The cadre consultants made use of the OD technique of constructive confrontation. We also pointed out that while the cadre was inside the district, neither Pat, Lee, nor Lynn were members of the elementary school in which they were consulting. Not being members gave them the objectivity and distance to see the conflicts in perspective. Moreover, the staff members viewed them as supportive and helpful and saw their interventions as constructive.

We went on, however, to describe how Alice, the executive dean of a community college, could successfully mediate strife between faculty members in the Fine Arts department. Alice was able to apply the OD techniques of constructive confrontation effectively, in part because of the administrative clout she holds in her job, and in part because she herself was not involved in the interpersonal strife. The case of Alice's application of a confrontation design demonstrates that an insider can deal effectively with conflict between parts of his or her own organization.

Survey-data-feedback can also be carried out successfully by inside consultants. In chapter 1 we described how Vera and Dick, members of a cadre of OD specialists in their small college, collected data from everyone in the college about its emotional climate, collaborated with a planning team in feeding back the data to the faculty, and helped form problem-solving groups to create plans for climate improvement.

Even within the smaller, more intense environment of the high school classroom, Randy demonstrated how a teacher can successfully use survey-data-feedback to bring about constructive change.

Today, we believe that OD procedures can be initiated successfully by either insiders or outsiders or a combination of the two. Perhaps the key to the success of OD lies less with the organizational position of the OD facilitators and more with the way the insider or outsider facilitators are introduced and integrated into the OD design. In the next chapter, we discuss the most important intellectual capability of OD facilitators, the capability of macrodesigning.

Chapter Three

Macrodesigning

The overall sequence of a comprehensive OD project is: startup, contract building, diagnosis, macrodesigning, implementing and monitoring microdesigns, evaluating outcomes, and institutionalizing the target system's capability for continuous problem solving. When OD facilitators are members of the target system, as when they are department heads, principals, deans, or presidents, they start an OD effort by articulating a philosophy of democratic management and describing how they personally wish to act as a democratic head. When OD facilitators come in from the outside as consultants or trainers, they typically make an initial presentation about the theory and practice of OD to the administrators who have responsibility for the target system. In either instance, a planning or steering committee for the OD project is usually formed to guide the OD process. When the target is a whole organization, the planning committee is made up of an administrator, a representative group of teachers or instructors, and perhaps representatives of classified staff, citizens, and students. The planning committee collaborates with the head or the OD consultants to engage all members of the system in the OD macrodesign.

Next, the OD planning committee collects diagnostic data about the target system's social functioning and, after analyzing them, feeds back selected high points to system members. At this point, the task of macrodesigning becomes prominent. Whatever macrodesign is used, it eventually serves as a catalyst for active problem solving among staff members of the target system. After several cycles of problem solving, the OD facilitators encourage staff members to agree on ways of institutionalizing problem solving so that the whole OD cycle can repeat itself in the target system after the planning committee is dissolved.

A *macrodesign* comprises the overall structure and outline, sequence of parts, and general forms through which activities flow. Examples include improving group skills, changing norms through problem solving, and changing the target system's structure for continuous problem solving. Other examples are the steps of a survey-data-feedback procedure, explained later in this chapter, and the constructive confrontation design described in detail in chapter 8. The present chapter deals with building effective macrodesigns. *Microaspects* refers to the specific activities played out during any limited period of consultation. Some useful microdesigns for training in skills, exercises, and procedures, along with instruments for survey-data-feedback and for process observation and feedback, are offered in chapters 4 through 8; chapter 9 presents guidelines for microdesigning.

There is no more important skill for OD facilitators than designing. This skill requires knowledge of alternative designs, a sensitivity to the unique characteristics of the target system, and a delicate balance between insight into one's own motives and empathy for the system members. Although matching macro-aspects in effective combinations and microaspects with specific objectives and system members is an important skill of the OD facilitator, an even rarer skill is the ability to monitor one's own proclivities. The ability to recognize one's own defenses, for example, and to use this recognition as information about the conduct of the OD process greatly enhances a facilitator's effectiveness.

System Development

For us, a developing system—whether a small group, a one-to-one relationship, or an organization—is one that is engaged continually in problem solving. This does not necessarily mean that a developing system is also a troubled system. Rather, problem solving here refers to an active striving to meet new challenges, seek improvement, and measure progress. When viewed from such a fundamental perspective, *problem solving* can refer to the thoughtful reflections of two interdependent individuals as well as to planned evaluations by staff of organizational achievements.

Elements of Problem Solving

We view as a problem any discrepancy between an actual state of affairs (a situation) and some ideal state to be achieved (the target). Since both the situation (S) and target (T) are in flux, problem solving must be continual. In many circumstances, moreover, as progress is made in moving S closer to T, participants switch their perception of T to an even higher level of aspiration, recycling the problem and again making the process continual. One might argue that problem solving is so fundamental to a system's life and health that when problem solving is stopped, the system stops developing and loses its vitality.

Organizations, their subgroups, and people in one-to-one relationships should be detecting and working on problems continually, not just during times of crisis, failure, extreme tension, or pain. Furthermore, they should be aware that their understanding of the situation and the target will change as they work toward solutions. As system participants reach new clarity about the problem that brought them together, they will become aware of problems they had not apprehended earlier. This process, however natural in system functioning, has stages, and it is a responsibility of the OD facilitator and planning committee to provide a macrodesign that will enable a system to agree on its present stage and to move ahead in a coordinated manner from stage to stage.

But even as we write about stages, we must point out that they are less like steps moving forever upward and more like rolling circles moving forward; they continually recycle. Problem solving is continuous partly because progress is slow and difficult. Problems must be cycled and recycled as the system pursues a better state.

Working toward a target tests how well the original situation has been understood. New information brought to light while a plan for change is being carried out may call for revising either plan or target. As people approach their target and form a clearer picture of what it might be like to live in the more ideal state, they may not find it as desirable as they did originally, or perhaps they will judge reaching it to be too costly. The second thoughts do not necessarily mean that they had planned poorly or chosen the wrong target. Rather, they point to the fact that no plan or target stays good for long, and that even if a group's vision does not change, circumstances will.

For that reason, participants should tackle concrete problems first, pick targets of moderate scope, and avoid the trap of over-planning. The danger of large-scale problem solving is that after people expend an immense amount of effort, they are reluctant either to waste the spent energy or to put still more into recon-ceiving the goal or changing the plan. If they succumb to the temptation to carry out the plan to the last detail even though the facts show that things are going badly, they face the worse danger of losing the norms and skills of openness. Thus, instead of problem solving on the grand scale, we advocate incremental problem solving informed by regular feedback and replanning. Educators should develop their new world in moderate steps, repeatedly surveying both the wider horizon and the immediate path.

Long-Range and Short-Range Objectives

It is important for the OD facilitator and planning committee to keep in mind the larger, long-term objectives of developing a target system's capacity for continuous problem solving while simultaneously recognizing the shorter-term benchmarks of development. Stated most generally, organization development enables the classroom, college, team, or school to solve its own educational problems more effectively (1) through building more effective communication patterns, group meetings, and joint decision making; (2) by using those more effective group skills to modify at will its own roles, norms, and procedures; and (3) by putting together the improved skills and norms in systematic group problem solving.

To be more specific, some examples of long-range objectives include (1) increasing understanding of how staff members with different jobs interrelate and affect one another; (2) developing clear communication networks up and down and laterally; (3) increasing understanding of the different educational goals in different parts of the target system; (4) uncovering interpersonal, group, and organizational conflicts for constructive problem solving; (5) developing new ways of solving problems through creative uses of group dynamics; (6) involving more personnel at all levels in decision making; and (7) establishing procedures for searching out innovative practices, both within and outside the target system.

Short-range objectives would be (1) clarifying communication; (2) establishing clear goals; (3) uncovering and working with specific conflicts; (4) improving group meetings; (5) making clear decisions; and (6) assessing progress toward goals.

Both kinds of objectives are subordinate in range and scope to establishing norms, structures, and procedures in the target system that support the condition described in chapter 1 as organizational adaptability. The four metaskills of adaptability are (1) diagnosing the functioning of relationships in the system, (2) gathering information and other resources from within and from outside the system, (3) mobilizing synergistic action in the system, and (4) monitoring the other three metaskills. Table 3-1 depicts the several kinds of objectives for OD.

Table 3-1. The Goals of OD

Short-range	Long-range	Ultimate Metaskills
Clarifying communiation	Understanding different	Institutionalized norms,
Establishing clear goals	roles	structures, and
Working with specific	Developing clear	procedures for:
conflicts	communication	Diagnosing
Improving group	networks	Gathering information
meetings	Understanding different	Mobilizing synergistic
Making clear decisions	goals in the system	action
Assessing progress	Uncovering larger	Monitoring other
	conflicts for problem	metaskills
	solving	
	Developing new ways to	
	use groups for	
	problem solving	
	Involving more personnel	
	in decision making	
	Establishing procedures	
	for searching out	
	innovative practices	

Before the Consultation Starts

A widely accepted principle of consultation is that you must start where the people are now. If you act as if the participants know something critical that they actually do not know, or as if they have a necessary skill that they do not have, at least some of them will soon feel confused, deceived, or even betrayed, and your work with them will fall apart. (It will also fall apart if you act as if you know everything critical about the local situation when you don't.) Conversely, if you act as if the participants don't know what they need to know when they do, or as if they've not had experience they believe they have had, many of them will be bored or even insulted.

The principle of readiness is an ancient one. It says that people are likely to take a step that is a reasonable distance beyond where they are now, but that they will give up in hopelessness if the step stretches them too far, and they will give up in boredom if they are asked to retrace steps already familiar to them. The principle applies not only to individuals, but also to groups, schools, and colleges.

Readiness to accept the OD process is of course an important variable at all stages of an OD project, but readiness is crucial at the outset, when members of a target system are asking themselves whether they want to undertake a serious project of change and to participate in it themselves. It is very unwise to begin even a short OD project if it calls for resources, skills, commitments, or values that are nonexistent. At the same time, it often falls to the head or the planning committee to raise the readiness for OD in an unready system.

Readiness at Various System Levels

An organization is not ready for OD when its members stay apart from one another as much as they can, when they try to benefit themselves at the expense of others (and believe that others do the same), and when they are unhappy with life in the organization but believe that they themselves have no hope of making it any better. But an organization is not ready for OD, either, when members find some pleasure in working together, when they are often helpful to one another, but when, despite periodic failures of their joint work, they believe that life in their organization is about as good as one can expect life in organizations to be. For an OD project to take hold, members must have some imagination about a better life at work and some daily evidence that they are capable of working together toward jointly-prized goals. To take the example of the affiliation motive, members must have some experience of the satisfactions of being cherished for their own personal qualities, must believe that an organization could exist while offering more frequent occasions for that kind of personal appreciation, and must believe there to be a reasonable chance that coordinated work to move toward that state could succeed. The facilitator should ask, "Is there some hopefulness here? Is there mostly resignation or complacency here?" If there is almost no hope or if there is mostly resignation or complacency, do not propose an OD project. Or find a pocket of people who have some hope and some confidence that they can join in working toward a better life.

As we have pointed out, the educational organization, whether a college or a school, is a social institution composed of many parts. It is a complex organization with diverse one-to-one relationships and small groups connected to each other by formal and informal relationships, roles, norms, and routine interactions that provide stability. The interrelationships of these organizational features—not primarily the personalities or sheer stubbornness of staff members—create stability and resistance to change in educational organizations.

We identify these interrelationships and interactions by observing the behavior of staff members on three system levels: *individual, group*, and *organization*. In determining a system's readiness for OD, behavior can often be interpreted to give information about more than one level. For example, a staff member who volunteers to work on the planning committee for an OD effort might be seen as satisfying a personal need for affiliation (information about an individual), or adhering to group norms about taking one's share of responsibility (information about a group), or fulfilling the organization role of a staff member in that particular position (information about that part of the organization). All of these interpretations could be simultaneously true. An important skill is deciding which level of interpretation offers the most useful viewpoint for understanding the behavior and taking effective action. The OD facilitator should be attuned to all three levels of the social system of the educational organization when diagnosing its readiness for OD.

The Individual Level. It is useful to concentrate on two influences shaping individual members' responses to OD—namely, motivation and perception. As we wrote in chapter 1, under "Individual Motive Satisfaction," people need affiliation—experiencing feelings of friendliness, warmth, and inclusion; achievement—feeling a sense of accomplishment; and influence—exercising some control over their lives and interactions with others. They seek to satisfy these motives in work and play. For educators, the need for affiliation might be met by joining with other educators to work on a committee, that of achievement by producing a creative lesson plan or an innovative plan for scheduling students, and that of influence by shaping the learning of students or by influencing students in positive ways. Of course, an individual always risks the possibility that his or her attempts to satisfy a motive will be frustrated. Thus, one's involvement on a committee might lead to hostilities and the loss of friends, a new course plan might fall on its face, and attempts to influence students might backfire. It becomes clear, then, that any impending change might on the one hand be a welcome opportunity for motive satisfaction and on the other an exasperating ordeal sure to end in motive frustration. OD facilitators must be attuned to the hopes, fears, and concerns of staff members as they look forward to the OD project.

Along with motives, other factors affecting participants' responses to OD will be their perceptions of themselves, their job situation, their understanding of OD, and the OD planning committee. In particular, staff members' views of OD will be significantly colored by their experience with previous similar efforts. Staff members will be highly sensitive to how OD might disrupt their own personal routines on the job. Public school teachers, for example, will be especially concerned with the impact of OD on classroom management, the curriculum, and the time and energy they have to work effectively with the students. College instructors' images of OD will be shaped, too, by their estimates of how it will fit their classroom routines and their relationships with students.

It is important for OD facilitators to remember that they will not necessarily be seen as they are (or want to be seen), but will be perceived in terms of staff members' previous experiences with similar sorts of self-proclaimed democratic heads or external consultants. When staff members find the label or image that fits the OD facilitator, they act accordingly. They think, "Oh, you're the sort of person who . . .; now I know who and what you are." A significant part of the OD facilitator's task is to establish an open and trusting relationship with staff so that the images become more accurate.

The Group Level. Even though staff members in colleges and schools spend most of their time alone in their own offices or classrooms, their membership in departments, teaching teams, and committees influences much of their behavior. In particular, norms, roles, and cohesiveness make groups powerful molders of behavior. Norms, for example, enable us to predict how others will respond to our actions and how they will behave toward us. Norms protect group members from the embarrassing consequences of inappropriate behavior. They provide a measure of safety by defining the range of acceptable behavior. Since norms are created—implicitly or explicitly—to give stability in groups, introducing OD into an educational system requires abandoning some of the old norms and creating new ones.

Just as norms are expectations for how groups members should behave, roles are shared expectations about the behavior of people in particular positions. Staff members behave toward one another according to their images of their roles. Educators typically develop rather stable role images of one another, so it can be difficult, as in an OD project, for one person to take on new behaviors unless others also alter their role conceptions and behaviors.

Group cohesiveness is another important variable in a staff's readiness for OD. When people identify themselves with others as members of a group, they come to have feelings of solidarity and loyalty to one another. They value their membership in the group and want to protect it. Those feelings of cohesiveness can be a powerful force that keeps individuals from changing their behavior in violation of group norms, but cohesiveness can also be an influential source of support for change if the group supports the OD effort. OD facilitators will seek to identify the cohesive groups in a target system, note the role takers in them as well as their norms, and determine their orientation and image in relation to OD.

The Organization Level. The college or school as an organization is, of course, made up of the individuals' motives and perceptions as well as the groups' norms, roles, and cohesiveness, but it is instructive for the OD facilitator to look beyond such microvariables to see characteristics of the college or school as a totality. Among the relevant variables are the organization's goals, structure, "climate," and environment.

Although colleges and schools exist to reach certain goals, agreement on the priority of the goals is frequently low. Educational organizations strive to reach several goals simultaneously—for example, high writing skills, good citizenship and self esteem, enjoyable extracurricular activities, fiscal accountability, research productivity, high staff morale, a winning basketball team, and so on. Moreover, OD facilitators nearly always find themselves working with staff members whose energy and enthusiasm for a proposed change is severely limited by other goals and demands on their time. Even in the face of such complexity, in most colleges and schools during any two- or three-year period certain goals will be advocated over others. It is crucial for the OD facilitators to point out how OD processes could help the target organization move toward at least a few of its highly rated goals.

Structure is the sum of the relationships of various roles to each other in terms of influence, authority, responsibility, function, and so on. Small elementary schools have simple structures; large community colleges are more complex. In contrast to organizations like the military, which have tightly controlled structures, schools and especially colleges are *loosely coupled*—that is, individuals and groups within them have a good deal of autonomy. Superiors such as central office administrators or members of the provost's staff can rarely mandate a change such as OD. At the same time, the necessity to go through channels can be a major barrier to getting OD going. OD facilitators and a system planning committee need to pinpoint the important parts of the organizational structure affected by OD and work with them to make the adjustments needed.

An educational organization's *climate* has to do with staff members' feelings about being part of the organization, the state of interpersonal relationships, the level of motive satisfaction, shared feelings of success or failure, and so on. In a public school the principal plays a key part in setting the climate of a school, but so do the staff, the district norms and policies, the parents, and the like. Similarly, in a college, the faculty and students are key in setting the climate. Climate is the product of an educational organization's norms, and, as the more global phenomenon, is not as easily assessed and altered as its components. The level of readiness for OD is particularly affected by norms about openness in communication (especially in emotional high-pressure situations), collaboration, willingness to spend extra time in meetings, and willingness to experiment with innovations.

An educational organization's *environment* also can play a significant part in the staff's readiness for OD. In public schools, two potent factors can be parents' desires for improvements in the school and legislative changes that have implications for school programming—for example, those having to do with desegregation and mainstreaming. In colleges, parents' willingness to pay the tuition and legislative changes in funding also can significantly enhance the staff's readiness for change. At the same time, change within a school or college often requires some sort of change or accommodation within relevant parts of the environment. For example, involvement in an OD project requires support from the board in some colleges, and changes in grade-reporting systems require new understandings and behaviors from the parents of students in some public schools.

Raising Readiness Levels

It is frequently unwise to pursue an OD project in an unready system. The effort would probably be wasted. Our experience indicates that some minimal degree of readiness is necessary at the outset to ensure future success. Still, raising the readiness of an educational system for OD is often feasible, and should be tried wherever it does not threaten to become too expensive.

The OD facilitators and planning committees who attempt to raise readiness levels in colleges or schools should be guided by the three system levels described above. The arguments in favor of trying OD are best approached by considering the organization level first, the group level next, and the individual level third. This strategy entails working initially with administrators, next with key staff members, and finally with the entire staff.

It is possible to persuade administrators, department heads, and lead teachers to consider OD by facing them with issues in their systems related to goals, structure, climate, and environment. Goal achievement is problematic for many administrators. They wonder how they can get their staffs to move together in focused directions and how they might build the synergy and motivation for concerted, goal-directed action. Answers to such challenges are embedded in OD theory and technology. Through participation and self-diagnosis, staff members can be brought to attend to the organization's goal achievement. Survey-data-feedback in particular allows staff members to recognize how they view the organization's goals, and constructive confrontation can help them resolve differences and conflicts of interest.

Organizational structure is another aspect of school life that can lead administrators to become involved in OD. Administrators usually feel challenged to make the ideal organizational structure function effectively. But how should they go about encouraging staff members to follow through on their assignments and to communicate effectively through the structure? OD can encourage staff members to look with curiosity at their own functioning. In many macrodesigns that use training activities, for example, a simulation or "serious game" is included during which participants can see and discuss difficulties of functioning that characterize their own organization or group, and can do so without yet risking new action in the real work place. OD can also help colleges and schools to build entirely new structures such as team teaching and multi-unit or multi-departmental structures. OD helps staff members to feel that they "own" the new structures—that they want to protect them. Traditional hierarchical decision making too often produces structures on paper that are subverted and undermined in practice.

Organizational climate, a concern of a great many site administrators, offers an obvious invitation to OD. After all, OD asks the staff members themselves to assess their own educational culture, to decide on ways in which the culture is lacking, and to take new actions to improve its quality. In this regard, OD is virtually synonymous with a climate-improvement program. Some administrators and staff members more readily accept a project to improve organizational climate than something called OD. The wise planning committee or facilitator will always think of such semantic distinctions when approaching other administrators or staff members about an OD effort.

One can also look to the environment. For example, perhaps the legislature demands desegregation, mainstreaming, or student advisory boards. The educational organization is pressured to make genuine modifications in structure. How should it go about making such changes? By fiat, by edict, or by participation? Typically, some form of participation is viewed as essential by administrators. OD offers the sort of techniques that can work in building staff commitment.

Another way to raise readiness is to work with administrators and key staff leaders on the challenges of running effective groups. Perhaps the most universal frustration in colleges and schools stems from ineffective meetings, whether staff, departmental, or committee meetings. An OD effort might be started by concentrating on improving meetings and moving to larger issues after that. Actually, no matter how effective subgroup meetings are, the adept OD facilitator can inspire their improvement through process observation and feedback. But if staff members are not ready for a process observer, the OD facilitator might begin by focusing on helping the subgroup's formal leader to act as a more effective convener of meetings. Here the facilitator acts temporarily as a coach, as a one-to-one helper to the subgroup leader, while keeping in mind the potentialities of a larger OD effect.

Large secondary schools and colleges often show low readiness for OD. One tactic is for the facilitator to work with just a part of the staff, perhaps the dean's cabinet or a particular academic department or committee. The focus of such an OD project would be on improving meeting skills, clarifying roles and norms, and building heightened cohesiveness or team spirit. In the short run, the OD facilitator would be carrying out a team-building effort, but in the long run, this effort could lead to an OD project for more and more parts of the educational organization.

We must also be concerned with individual variables when trying to raise readiness for OD in educational organizations. It is obvious that the facilitator needs to keep individual motives and perceptions in mind when trying to persuade administrators to use OD, but the facilitator should take care to keep the various needs and characteristics of individuals in mind when approaching entire staffs in introductory meetings and OD demonstrations. The facilitator's talk should include concrete illustrations of how the OD project might increase affiliation, achievement, and influence among staff members. One might propose, for instance, a retreat that would give staff members a chance to get to know one another better, some consultative coaching that would help the staff finish a highly valued task, or some new communication channels that would convey more influence to the administration.

Although pointing out the motive satisfactions that OD can bring is important for raising readiness, the indispensable task is clarifying staff members' understandings of what OD is, what it is not, and how it works. It is important to explain that OD is not, on the one hand, direct help on curriculum, or, on the other hand, sensitivity training. The OD process aims to help staff members have open and constructive discussions that could lead to beneficial changes for the educational organization.

The OD Contract

Productive change is unlikely to occur unless staff members acknowledge a discrepancy between an ideal and actual state of affairs (a gap between S and T) even *before* a planning committee launches an OD effort. That is, a sizable portion of the staff (more than 50 percent as a rule of thumb), and especially its more powerful members, should accept the organization's problems as their own and become reasonably committed to solving them instead of merely acquiescing to a project that originates on the initiative of the head of a committee. OD facilitators should make it a rule to enter into contract only with those educational subsystems that are reaching out for help and that exhibit other signs of readiness as described above.

OD facilitators should be aware that what happens during the first phase of OD can foreshadow much of what is to come, and that, if the OD effort is to be built on a solid base of support, it is necessary to gain at least an oral commitment to the enterprise from all key participating groups. To this end, we cannot overstate the critical importance of establishing at the outset relaxed rapport, credibility, and legitimacy, and of arriving at clear statements about motives, competencies, and shared expectations. Facilitators, whether inside or outside the target system, should be explicit about their role, the goals of OD, the project's budget and probable length, and the approximate amount of time everyone will be expected to devote to the project. Also early during start-up, the facilitator should discuss with staff members their own hopes, concerns, and expectations for the change. Those discussions should be two-way, with the facilitator giving informal instruction to staff members about OD and how it works, and with staff members coaching the facilitator in the perspectives of people in their organization. During such discussions, the facilitator should note the extent to which staff members adopt a collaborative attitude and are ready to collaborate with one another in new ways.

Although an external OD consultant might be contacted initially by an individual from any level of the organizational hierarchy, interactions are best begun formally between the outside expert and the legitimate leaders, because those personnel hold crucial gatekeeping power over later contacts with other members of the system, and it is therefore helpful, even critical, for them to become allies rather than enemies. The principal, the legitimate leader in the school, and the dean, the most legitimate leader in the college, must of course spend considerable time with the consultants discussing their respective roles and sharing hopes, concerns, and expectations about a change project. There are, however, other relevant gatekeepers. In school districts, powerful parties typically include the school board, the superintendent and the superintendent's cabinet, and teachers' organizations. In colleges the powerful parties other than the dean might be department heads, counselors, instructors in general, and student groups. Particularly powerful in many schools and colleges are personnel whose work is seen as having unalterable routines to which others must defer; athletic coaches are a good example.

Although gaining the approval and collaboration of key authorities is essential, this alone will not win commitment or even acquiescence from others in the target system. OD facilitators must keep in mind that they are working not just with individuals but with a complex social system, and they will want to test the willingness of authorities to carry introductory discussions of the potential program to others. How the outside consultant is introduced to more subordinate personnel will naturally influence subsequent support and program effectiveness, and outside consultants should not be slow in moving their attention to less powerful groups.

During the first phases of start-up and at every subsequent stage of the OD sequence, it is vital to work with all the clients in mind, and less powerful participants should not be led to believe that they are of less importance to the planning team and facilitators than are administrators or others in authority. If the OD effort is aimed at the whole organization, the planning committee and facilitators will want to gain the support of every significant division or group within the organization. If the OD is limited to a single college or school, it will be necessary before proceeding very far to get approval not only from the powerful persons on the faculty, but from as many other staff members as possible. Toward this end, the facilitator and planning committee should hold one or two meetings with the whole staff in order to find out how many staff members support the project.

OD facilitators should almost never agree to hold a meeting with only "those who can come." Potential participants who are deciding whether to commit themselves to the OD effort will need to know how others involved are judging the prospects. People always want to know which way their colleagues are leaning. That is one reason why facilitators should encourage everyone at the meeting to say something about OD before going very far. Another reason is that since personnel who work together will be consulted within their intact groups at the later stages of the project, it is advantageous to begin early to deal with the groups, thereby setting a precedent as well as facilitating later conceptualization.

Many projects are greatly facilitated by a "memorandum of agreement" signed by the planning committee and key participants. The memo might include a general description of the goals of the OD effort, a paragraph on the role of the facilitator and planning committee, a rough time schedule for the macrodesign, and a statement about decision points—that is, points at which decisions will be made about continuing or stopping the project. A memo of this sort should be no more than a page or two in length. It is important that the signers include a representative committee of faculty members, if not all participants, and that the document be reproduced and given to every staff member involved in the OD project.

Although a memorandum of agreement is important in formalizing the OD project, sound facilitator-staff relationships are not forged by agreement on tasks alone. The facilitator should be mindful that the dynamics of start-up and contract building can arouse intense feelings. Directly acknowledging these feelings at the right time is a prime requisite for valid contract making.

The OD facilitator should realize, too, that any improvement of organizational processes will take time. Research by Wyant (1974), for example, indicated that less than 24 hours of staff training in communication skills and problem solving can actually have detrimental long-run effects. In contrast, staffs that receive more than thirty hours of such training typically show favorable gains.

Portraying OD During Start-Up

As we conduct it, OD is largely experiential. Although facilitators should take a few minutes to describe what the OD process will be like, they should not expect their listeners to get an accurate picture from words alone. The best way of conveying this information is actually to demonstrate OD exercises and procedures via laboratory training activities that communicate the experiential nature of OD to those relatively inexperienced in it.

A few educators still think of OD as highly emotional sensitivity training; others think of lectures and discussion on administrative sciences and group dynamics; still others think of relaxed fun and games having little relevance to the real life of the educational organization. Most educators probably hold no very clear idea about OD, and these unclear expectations often plague the start-up and contract-building phases of an OD effort. By helping a target group to understand OD theory and to experience OD technology, the following sample design for a demonstration workshop should increase the reliability of the decision as to whether OD should continue in earnest.

A complete demonstration calls for two days, but shorter modifications can be designed. Participants are told that the demonstration is being presented to help them determine whether they would like to become engaged in an OD project. They are asked to suspend judgment until the two days are over, since the demonstration events must move along a bit before a clear picture of OD will emerge.

Demonstration goals include (1) developing participants' understanding of the possible benefits of OD to educational systems; (2) presenting an accurate picture of a self-renewing educational organization; (3) helping members of the target system see how they can confront current problems through OD methods; (4) helping them understand the unique functions of OD in contrast to those of management consultation or sensitivity training; (5) acquainting them with the skills to be gained through OD facilitation; and (6) establishing the beginning of a collaborative relationship between participants and the planning committee, communicating that all participants are expected not only to influence the OD project but eventually to own and run it themselves. Demonstrations shorter than two days will have fewer stated goals.

Early in the event, following some warm-up and getting-acquainted activities, participants can be given the handout shown in Figure 3–1. A facilitator guides them through the material, telling them that aspects of the OD strategies will come alive for them during the next day and a half and calling attention to supplemental reading materials available on a display table.

After introducing the handout, the facilitator proceeds to episodes that entail more active client participation. Every subsequent activity should commence with experiential activity and be followed by a debriefing with the help of process observers that focus on both the here-and-now aspects and interpersonal dynamics of the experience. Participants are then asked to comment on the similarities and differences between the OD activity and their actual work experience in their educational organization. Finally, the facilitator shows how the activity is relevant to the real educational organization, presents some research concepts and results related

Figure 3-1. Handout #1 for Start-up Demonstration

What Is OD?

Organization development (OD) is a planned and sustained effort at system self-study and improvement, focusing on change in norms, structures, and procedures, using behavioral science concepts and methods. OD engages system members themselves in the active assessment, diagnosis, and transformation of their own organization.

Organizational development enables the educational system to solve its own educational problems more effectively—by using the consultative strategies of

- training in skills, exercises, and procedures
- data collection, feedback, and action planning
- constructive confrontation and problem solving
- process observation and feedback

1. to improve its capabilities to modify its own roles, norms, and procedures
2. to build more effective communication patterns, group meetings, and joint decision making
3. through systematic group problem-solving processes.

---

to the activity for group members to apply to their own work setting, and suggests more detailed readings on relevant theory and research. This general sequence from experience to comparison to theory can be used profitably with every episode or microaspect of the demonstration.

Many alternative macrosequences can be effective, including the following example, which makes use of materials supplied later in this book (see index): (1) practice in communication skills; (2) feedback on the results of a survey of norms, using, for example, the Team-Expectation Survey; (3) an exercise on group decision making using the Lost at Sea exercise; (4) an exercise on effectiveness between groups using the Planners and Operators exercise; and (5) practice in uncovering conflicts using an imaging procedure. If aspects of the Imaging exercise are used toward the end of the two days, the facilitator must allow time for collaborative problem solving so that conflicts do not remain troublesome at the end of the demonstration. Problem-solving sequences using the S-T-P paradigm, also supplied later, can usefully be introduced as the last object for group study.

Midway through this sequence of activities, at the end of the first day or at the beginning of the second, the facilitator should hand out Figure 3–2 for discussion. The contents of this handout will help to deepen and extend the participants' understanding of where the

Figure 3-2. Handout #2 for Start-up Demonstration

Goals of OD

The goals of OD can be of at least two types: long-range and short-term objectives:

Long-range Objectives

1. To increase understanding of how staff members with different jobs interrelate and affect one another
2. To develop clear communication networks up, down, and laterally
3. To increase understanding of the different educational goals in different parts of the educational system
4. To uncover organizational conflicts for constructive problem solving
5. To develop new ways of solving problems through creative uses of group dynamics
6. To involve more personnel at all levels in decision making
7. To establish procedures for searching out innovative practices, both within and outside the educational system.

Such long-range objectives are reached gradually through small steps. The following is a list of some short-term objectives:

Short-term Objectives

A. Clarifying communication
B. Establishing clear goals
C. Uncovering and working with conflict
D. Improving group meetings
E. Making clear decisions
F. Evaluating progress toward goals

---

facilitators and planning committee hope to go by using the activities. And during the early part of the second afternoon the facilitator should hand out Figure 3–3 for discussion. This handout will help bring alive the steps of OD proposed.

We will discuss more fully the means of introducing OD in chapter 10 when we cover cadres of OD facilitators in educational systems.

The OD Diagnosis

Our research indicates that the most effective organizational diagnoses are carried out collaboratively by the facilitators and an OD planning committee in the educational system. The planning committee serves as a steering committee for the OD project and is composed of a representative body including faculty members, assistant administrators, counselors, and in some cases students. The facilitator, whether an insider or an outsider, serves as a technical assistant to this committee, bringing to it examples of

Figure 3-3. Handout #3 for Start-up Demonstration

Summary of the OD Sequence

1. Administrators or outside facilitators make initial agreements with policy-setting boards to launch an OD project.
2. A planning committee is formed within the target system to guide the OD effort.
3. Agreement is solicited from the professional staff of the target system to join the OD effort.
4. Facilitators and the planning committee diagnose existing organizational processes and climate of the target system.
5. Facilitators and the planning committee feed data back to the staff of the target system.
6. Facilitators, planning committee, and others establish specific goals for the OD effort.
7. Facilitators and the planning committee build a plan for the OD effort and carry it out. It may include one or more of the strategies of training, survey-data-feedback, constructive confrontation, and process observation and feedback.
8. Staff members of the target system engage in active problem solving.
9. Staff members of the target system come to agreement about ways to institutionalize problem solving.
10. Staff gathers data to evaluate the progress of the problem solving. At this point, the planning committee is dissolved and a newly formed staff committee takes the next steps for OD in the system.

---

questionnaires, interview formats, and observation strategies, and helping the steering committee to make wise and practical choices in tailoring its own diagnostic strategy.

The purposes of the OD diagnosis are several. First, OD theory stipulates that making a diagnosis of one's own situation increases feelings of ownership of the data and enhances one's motivation to seek change. This is the central idea behind most "needs assessments" in education. Those who participate in defining their own needs will work harder to seek new ways of satisfying those needs. But in OD a second purpose of diagnosis is as important and central as the first—to uncover data throughout the target system that will permit colleagues to enlighten one another about their diverse and often contrasting views of the social situation. It is easy for people in power to believe that all is going well in an educational system, particularly if most participants collude to keep quiet about their perceptions and feelings. An OD diagnosis helps make public the views and feelings that typically are not brought out into the open. By focusing on a few of the differences among the staff, the steering committee can often mobilize energy and involvement for productive change.

A third purpose of diagnosis is to help build a workable agenda for system-wide problem solving. Most educational organizations, including colleges and schools, have a myriad of organizational problems related to communications, goals, meetings, decision making, and the like. A diagnosis can help to rank the problems, according to both importance and feasibility for change. After a diagnostic exercise in a target system, the staff should feel motivated to work on very specific targets of change. Moreover, the inspiration of the initiators of the effort should have started to spread to others in the system.

A Short Diagnosis of the Organization

A change project in an educational organization can be short or long and involve a few persons or many. The diagnosis should be proportional. It should give sufficient information about the existing situation so that facilitator and participants alike can lay plans for the near future with some confidence. For a project fairly small in scope, you might gather diagnostic data in a concentrated and formal way only once. In a larger project, the first formal data collection might yield more data than in the small project, and special time might be set aside repeatedly for more check-ups (formative evaluation) as the months go by.

In either case, the key is to get information useful in answering the question, "Where are we now and where can we go from here?" In this section, we use a short list of questions to illustrate how an interview can bring out useful information. In a project of small scope, you might use no more than the thirteen questions below when systematically interviewing the participants at the start of the project.

The questions below are adapted from a handout by Dale Lake, Paul Buchanan, and Matthew Miles. The questions are phrased as for an interview guide; that is, the interviewer is to ask the questions orally and write down the answers. In paragraphs following the questions, we comment on the kinds of information the questions might yield.

1. *"Please describe what you do—your area of responsibility."*

Answers to this question would begin to tell us about functions and give us hints about membership in subsystems (see chapter 1). When a respondent said, "Actually, I'm not very clear about some of my responsibilities," we would learn about role clarity. When a respondent went beyond the letter of the question, we might learn about still other matters. We might learn about the press for change: "I don't think I should be the one to do X; I've been talking to the dean about it." We might learn about the support for change: "I'm willing to change my responsibilities, but I don't know whether other people are willing to change theirs to match." We might learn about the stability of the staff: "Anderson and Lidovici are both leaving next year, and I suppose I'll be taking on some of what they've been doing." We might learn about norms supporting collaboration: "I tried for six months to get the other people to do their part and then gave up. When you're put in charge of something, people here seem to think you should do it all yourself." We might learn about skill in collaboration: "I'm chairperson of the X committee, but I wish I weren't. We just seem to argue in circles." We might learn about readiness for taking risks: "The principal says he wants us to make more decisions ourselves, but at the same time, he says he can't promise to go along with what we decide, because the responsibility is really his." We write down everything respondents tell us.

2. *"With whom does your work bring you into contact most often? Whom do you need in doing your work? Are there people in your organization whom you need to see more often?"*

This, too, helps to chart subsystems—the groups with which you must work as facilitator. The last part of the question can suggest possible inadequacies in communication that might be parts of other problems. Again, volunteered comments might give us further information: "We've been having to meet at 6:30 in the morning." "She says she's willing to give us whatever time it may take if we can come up with a plan we all like." "Six of us are working out a new committee structure. I think it's shaping up really well." And so on.

3. *"How would you characterize the amount and type of confidence that your supervisor has in you? That she has in (Person X)?"*

This one, when the answers are tallied, gives us clues about the distribution of trust and therefore the willingness of people to risk new collaborations. If there are clear differences among the answers to the part about confidence in "you," then the head may favor one faction in the staff to the exclusion of others, or the communication of confidence may be so sketchy that the answers arise more from desire and self-deception than from evidence. If there are clear differences among the answers to the part about confidence in "Person X," then the communication net might be distributing reliable evidence only to a part of the staff, or again the communication about confidence may be too sparse to produce agreement. And, again, respondents may volunteer remarks about additional matters.

4. *"How much influence do you think you have over goals and activities in your educational organization? How are the goals set?"*

This question may draw rich information from some people and almost nothing from others. Some people simply do not think in terms of goals; they become either somnolent or impatient during discussions of goals. Those people may answer something like "Oh, I don't know," and mean "and I don't care." Other people like to feel they can count on companions as they move into the future. They use discussions about goals as opportunities to find out who will join them in the direction they want to go. When those people answer that they have little influence over goals and activities, they mean that they feel isolated and lonely. They may be ready for change. They may want greater affiliative satisfaction and yearn for more companionship in their daily work. They may want greater satisfaction of achievement and yearn for collaboration that would enable them to use more of their skills. And regardless of whether respondents think much about goals, the question may draw out their need for power—their yearning for more influence so that they can control more of what they do.

5. *"How would you characterize your head's leadership?"*

This question can draw out information about many aspects of the organization. Some respondents will merely utter an adjective, but most will go on to say more about the head's style and its effects on what they themselves feel they can do. We will learn about aspects of the press for change, the support for change, the stability of the staff, the norms supporting collaborative group work, and the readiness to take risks.

6. *"How are budgets created?"*

This one will tell us where the financial resources lie. It will give us some hint about how money is used for influence (for reward, status, and so on) and about the people who influence the use of money. The question may also uncover some important facts or feelings about centralized and decentralized decision making.

7. *"How do you know when you are being productive? What are the criteria? Who notices? What gives you satisfaction?"*

Be prepared to spend time on this question. Because there are four clearly distinguishable parts to it, almost every respondent will have more than a sentence to offer. The answers are likely to yield a lot of useful information about the norms supporting collaborative work and the skill in it and about the interviewee's readiness to take risks.

8. *"What is currently going very well in your educational organization?"*

When respondents name something, we will get clues about what they believe their organization does well. If most respondents fail to name something, we will get information about morale. Many respondents, too, in that case, will give us hypotheses about the reasons the organization is not doing well. Those hypotheses will be useful in designing the OD project.

9. *"In my (our) brief meeting with your group at _____, certain issues came up that were called _____. Could you tell me more about them?"*

This question assumes the facilitators will have had one or more meetings with some key people during preliminary negotiations, before undertaking this systematic interviewing. The reference is to one of those meetings. The question will draw out a fuller picture and more viewpoints on the participants' conceptions of their current problems. Our design for OD should have some obvious connection with the local problems as the participants see them—not necessarily as the facilitators see them.

10. *"If you were given the head's job for a month or a year what would you change? How would you do that?"*

If many of the answers to this question were no more than "I don't know," we would think ourselves to be in an organization unready for serious change. In most cases, we would expect to learn important things about the press for change, the support for change, the stability of the staff, the norms supporting collaborative group work and the readiness to take risks.

11. *"Is there anything you want to add that I haven't covered?"*

This is always a good question, because respondents often hold back, not because they are reluctant to answer, but because they are waiting for a question that will seem more relevant to the point they are holding in mind.

12. *"What specific things do we need to give attention to at the next meeting?"*

Don't ask this question unless you do in fact intend to bring up most of the matters proposed by respondents. Of course, you can reduce the pressure somewhat by altering the question to "as we move into the project?" Either way, this question, like number 9, will keep us alert to how respondents conceive their problems and to the urgencies they feel.

13. *"Now let's go back over the interview to give you a chance to strike out anything you don't want me to mention in the meeting that's coming up."*

Always be sure to find out what the respondent wants to keep confidential. Often, a respondent will be willing for you to bring up a topic publicly if you don't mention his or her name in connection with it. In addition, this question will often serve the purpose of number 11, because reviewing what the respondent said will give him or her time to think of what could be added and subtracted.

Those 13 questions illustrate five good rules about diagnosis:

1. Get clues to interpersonal dynamics early.
2. Get clues to the satisfaction of social motives early (see chapter 1 for a description of those motives).
3. Take notes of all volunteered information, especially at the beginning of a project, when you don't know yet what you don't know.
4. Elicit the help of the participants in discovering what it is important to know.
5. Maintain confidentiality.

The Selecting of an OD Design

As we discussed in chapter 1, the OD facilitator can follow four themes for macrodesigns in tailoring the right OD design for a particular target system—training, survey-data-feedback, constructive confrontation, and process observation and feedback—each of which calls for special sorts of skill on the part of the facilitator. Training formats are highly structured, requiring that the facilitator adopt a strong leadership role similar to that of an expert scholar or a coach. Training works best when the participants expect to be taught and when the organizational problems of the target system are not terribly pressing. Of course, at some point during the OD process, training will be necessary in most target systems, but as a point of departure it should be used only with professional staffs that are very new to OD and that can set aside a few days to retreat from their work for a serious course of study.

Survey-data-feedback has become the most frequently used OD design, in part because of Bowers's (1973) research, which indicated that it was the most effective kind of OD design in industry, but also because it fits very well into the OD philosophy of sharing power with participants at all stages of the change process. In OD projects where the facilitator works with a steering committee to construct an instrument, collect data, analyze data, feed back the data, and lead faculty committees in problem solving, each of the steps of the data-feedback design involves the participants. Such complete involvement is not typical of training, confrontation, or process observation and feedback.

Furthermore, data-feedback designs can work effectively when the facilitator wants to take a rather low profile, which is not possible in the other three designs. In data feedback, a necessary skill is that of finding or designing a suitable data-collection instrument and advising the steering committee on the construction of the final instrument. (The instrument is usually a questionnaire or an interview guide, but it can also include a guide to direct observation of behavior or to sources of information in existing records.) Persons trained in research and evaluation frequently have the needed expertise.

Once the data-feedback cycle gets going, active participant involvement on the part of a steering committee force is often enough to move toward action planning. We do not mean to imply, however, that it is easy for OD facilitators to play a low-profile role. The effective facilitator learns to exert influence and to back off gracefully at appropriate times; doing so requires a level of personal skill typically acquired through experience as a facilitator.

Several pitfalls are frequently encountered in data-feedback designs. First, participants in the target system might find the first drafts of diagnostic instruments confusing, irrelevant, or even silly. Careful pilot testing can counteract such reactions. Second, data analysis and feedback can be hindered by respondents who don't fill out the instruments as requested. Again pilot testing will help, but steering committees should also try to supplement closed-ended questionnaire items with open-ended items, and even with brief interviews whenever feasible. Third, during discussions of the data, participants can get bogged down in petty arguments about items, formats, and so on. The facilitator and steering committee should take care to keep the discussions focused and to discourage significant deviations from discussions about the target system itself. After all, the data are only "windows on the system"; it is the living target system itself that should be discussed during the staff's OD meetings.

Of the four kinds of designs, constructive confrontation is used least, but this form can be very effective if the circumstances warrant it. It is appropriate when there are obvious disagreements between subsystems in a larger target system and when these disagreements become disruptive. We use the word disagreement because apparent conflicts between groups are often more subjective than objective, and confrontation works best in eliminating hostilities stemming from imagined oppositions and schisms. For confrontation to be effective, however, the facilitator must be perceived as a trusted expert by the participants. Moreover, since it is important that the participants view the facilitator as neutral and disinterested, confrontation designs typically work better when the primary facilitator is not a member of the target system.

Because constructive confrontation calls for dominant behavior by the facilitator, it is often difficult for a colleague to assume the role of facilitator during confrontation. More than in the other three designs, success in constructive confrontation is more sure when it is carried out by an expert outsider, or at least with the help of one. In fact, some of our research indicated that constructive confrontation is most effective when it is carried out by a team composed of both inside and outside facilitators. The outsiders are needed to get the confrontation off the ground, to keep participants on task during the early stages, and to play a significant role in controlling the natural defensiveness that arises during confrontation. Insiders are more important for the latter stages of the confrontation sequence and are crucial for supporting follow-through.

Of course, confrontation designs are risky; they bring into open discussion conflicts that may otherwise have been covered and held down for several years. The catharsis of opening such conflicts can be highly emotional for some participants; it can be so upsetting, in fact, that some people can lose psychological control, however temporarily. Outbursts might be so extreme that the participants reject the whole experience. To control such disruptive outbursts, the facilitator must be strong and forceful in keeping the confronting parties on task.

The last design category, process observation and feedback, is omnipresent in OD. The astute facilitator is always an observer and is always looking for appropriate opportunities to give feedback. However, the most important place for this sort of design is in the second half of most macrodesigns. Process observation and feedback is most useful after problems have been made public and problem solving has proceeded to a point where the target group has agreed on new actions. Process observation and feedback can serve to keep participants honest about their action agreements. The facilitator observes the group's behavior and gives structured feedback on how closely the observed behavior conforms to the spirit of the previously made group agreements. Thus this form of OD design serves as a sort of evaluative monitoring.

Process observation and feedback is often used successfully, however, at the very start of an OD design. Generally, the facilitator sits in on a series of regular meetings and gradually offers constructive feedback to the target group to encourage problem solving. In such circumstances, the group must perceive the facilitator as an astute expert and as one who won't hurt the status positions and rewards of the group members. Although on the surface, process observation seems to call for a low-profile role, the facilitator's inevitable responsibility to offer feedback means that he or she must have a certain degree of charisma to be effective. The need for charisma, however, diminishes as the group accepts as natural and usual the role of process observer. It is the external facilitator's objective, then, to move group participants gradually into being process observers for themselves, giving feedback to one another as an ordinary feature of their meetings. Skillful administrators, too, can gradually remove themselves from the role of process observer by inviting group participants to give feedback to one another as a regular part of a meeting agenda.

We should point out that it is frequently impractical to use process observation and feedback with an entire staff, especially when the college or school is large. OD facilitators prefer to do what they call team building only when subsystems are small enough for face-to-face meeting. It is there that process observation and feedback are especially useful.

The Execution of an OD Design

OD projects consist of a series of organized social events carried out by educators who have continuing, committed interrelationships with one another. Facilitators, too, look forward to continuing interaction with the participants and with one another during most of a macrodesign. If the OD project is of sufficient length and scope, all participants become in effect a temporary society that not only serves as a vehicle for the OD work but can itself exemplify many of the interpersonal procedures and structural forms that facilitators hope to teach.

When designing an OD project, facilitators and steering committees should see to it that this temporary society maintains in good condition the four organizational features that affect interpersonal and subsystem effectiveness: (1) differentiation and integration, (2) norms, (3) role relationships, and (4) satisfaction of motives within the organization. They should also see to it that the macrodesign presents participants with conceptual lessons that can be used to support organized action.

Differentiation and Integration

People in educational organizations perform a variety of differentiated functions, from receiving and transmitting information about the working of the organization to shaping students and materials. For differentiated roles to function effectively, they must also be integrated. OD projects can raise differentiation and integration to the level of conscious awareness in a number of ways. First, selecting as participants people from a variety of jobs and then communicating across this variety invariably reveals to participants the profit inherent in integrating diverse functions. Indeed, that people from heterogeneous but interdependent positions are included in the same OD events at all helps to make salient the concept of integration.

Second, rotating combinations of people through the various subgroups that form during an OD project so that everyone will eventually have interacted at least once with everyone else can have an important multiple effect. In the course of an OD project, people from every level of the educational organization will reveal both competence and incompetence in performing OD tasks, in perceiving organizational functions, and in perceiving how OD tasks relate to everyday life in the organization. By interacting with many people with whom they have either never before communicated or have communicated only superficially, participants have a chance to learn that differentiation of role and function is primarily an organizational reality and not necessarily a matter of personal endowment, that effective interpersonal and group performance is not necessarily more difficult in some positions than in others, and that other people are as worried about interdependence with them as they are about their interdependence with others.

Depending upon the complexity of the macrodesign, rotation can often be achieved by instructing participants to form themselves into groups containing at least one person with whom each individual has not interacted before. When the sequence of OD events is complicated and the facilitator wants the cluster to satisfy goals other than mere spread of interaction, it may be prudent to lay out beforehand a complete schedule describing in detail the groups and their individual members.

Finally, facilitators can design exercises and other activities to ensure both division of labor (differentiation) and active collaboration among different roles (integration). For example, the Fishbowl technique (see chapter 4 under "Communication in the Subsystem") can be used to bring together representatives from different teams to discuss a common problem while they are observed by other members of the team. Or each subgroup can appoint its own convener, recorder, and process observer before a meeting, giving these people time to debrief on how they worked together and with others in their subgroup. In a large event requiring four or five or more facilitators, the use of the facilitators themselves can be designed to exhibit differentiation and integration.

Norms

An educational organization becomes able to change its routines by learning how to replace old norms with new. In outline, this is done by reaching agreement in the relevant groups on what the new norm should be, simulating the new action patterns a few times, and then trying out the new actions a few times on the job. When participants feel rewarded by the new pattern, the new norm has become a reality. In practice, however, establishing new norms causes stress, not only because it means discussing matters that are seldom publicly discussed, but also because older norms may not support the changes being attempted. Clients are less likely to withdraw from an OD design either physically or psychologically if the facilitator guides them through a series of steps that arouse an appropriate amount of anxiety. Specifically, a design can move staff members to new norms if it begins with structured, game-like interpersonal exercises, proceeds to group simulations, and then moves on to real procedures.

At the beginning of one senior high school OD project, for example, staff members told us through interviews that their school had no problems and ran like clockwork. At a series of discussions with all department heads, however, after it was agreed that further discussions could be profitable, members began to discuss the organization for which the facilitator worked and their school as a whole. At a later meeting they mentioned problems they had had in the past and problems they regarded as other people's. In the course of time, the discussion moved closer to people who were present, and from problems present somewhere in the school to participants' current problems. Over the series of meetings, the time perspective moved gradually from the past and a vague future to the present and specified future dates ("Ted and I will see the principal on Friday to tell him what we want to do about this").

As simple as such time focusing is in both concept and action, it could not have occurred at the first meeting because the group's norms did not support it. Uncertain of the extent to which their frustrations were shared and of the degree to which others were willing to invest energy in change, and having as yet no reason to trust the OD facilitator, the group had regarded committed action involving themselves and the principal as inappropriate and too risky at the outset. For these reasons, early discussions had been conceptually vague, general, and interpersonally distant; they were concerned with other people and other times. For the same reasons, early steps in a design encouraging participants to try new norms must allow them, at least initially, to practice at some distance from their ordinary daily entanglements.

Working with functioning units or subsystems, in which group norms tend to be very powerful, we do not typically place two different faculties into close interaction with each other, or members of two separate college office departments into the same training group. Instead we bring together interdependent persons who either have the same supervisors or are bound to one another by some shared function, such as supervising the student registration or selecting new staff members for an academic department. In this way participants are already much closer in their interdependence or common fate than are strangers from different subsystems.

Specifically because they are closer, however, it is important that they be given some protective distance from one another—distance that allows them to protect their views of themselves, that requires no commitments affecting other parts of their lives, and that does not require them to take a stand on matters of local policy or to make specific commitments about what they will do on the job. One way of placing protective distance between colleagues is to begin an OD project during the summer hiatus when the routines and commitments of the new academic year are not yet fully established. Another way is to remove participants from the building or rooms in which they usually work, away from telephones, e-mail, or other continual interruptions. Probably the best technique is to be found in the highly structured games such as those described as exercises in chapters 4 through 8, which, in relation to their daily work on the job, can be seen as "then and there" rather than as here and now. If exercises are to be effective in changing norms, however, they must be introduced early in the OD effort.

For example, exercises offered early with an OD design can help to establish a norm that supports *debriefing*—that is, examining the effectiveness of interactive processes in a group soon after every meeting. Even when done during make-believe activities, debriefing encourages adaptability, because it makes explicit the norm that procedures are alterable. That is, if a survey during debriefing shows agreement that a certain procedure is impeding progress toward a goal, the question of whether to change the procedure arises, and the questioning opens the door to productive self-renewal. Thus exercises that facilitate debriefing, if conducted after every meaningful unit during the first few hours of consultation, can cause debriefing to become an accepted norm among the participants. Further, the facilitator should provide time for debriefing on all written agendas and encourage its use by listing a number of leading questions for group discussion.

The facilitator can also confront norms among participants by modeling behavior that is contrary to their norms—for example, by exhibiting openness, directness, and authenticity about the organization's dynamics to participants who are unwilling to do so themselves. To this end, the macrodesign of data feedback is a useful strategy. The facilitator interviews organization members individually about the variables discussed in chapters 4 through 8, and subsequently feeds group data back to all members of the target system using a style that is direct and open, using living examples, and asking for participants' reactions. Participants are often sufficiently relieved that someone is finally telling them the truth about the organization to begin concerted problem solving on the newly revealed problems.

Roles

Because role taking always occurs in interactions with other role takers, an OD macrodesign should address itself not only to relationships among organization members but also to the relationship between the facilitator and participants (many of whom may expect an "expert" to behave in a more authoritarian manner). At an early stage of execution of the macrodesign, facilitators should therefore distinguish between their own goals and those of the participants in order to distinguish between their respective roles as well.

The role of participants is to state the problems and goals of their educational system; to assign priorities, schedules, and deadlines; and to choose whom they will work with and trust. The facilitator's primary goal is to maximize the participants' ability to deal consciously and purposefully with their own organizational processes. On the question of appropriate group processes, participants will usually defer to facilitators, but on matters of substance, the facilitator will defer to the participants. In addition to drawing attention to role structure during an OD project, the very process of arriving at an understanding of the proper granting of expertness—group process to the facilitators and substance to the participants—will exemplify the introduction of new group-process activities, such as debriefing, that will later prove useful to participants.

Participants can gain wider practice in putting new roles into effect if facilitators treat them equally, without regard to previous deference patterns in the college or school. This is not to say that facilitators should ignore the jobs that people hold or the realities to which they work, but only that they can give practice in flexible role taking if they give special privileges to no one. They should not ask department heads, for example, to act as leaders more often than others or excuse their absences more readily. Treating everyone alike demonstrates that a role relationship established for one purpose in one subgroup of the organization need not apply for other tasks or in other parts of the organization.

Motives

Although individuals differ in the extent to which they attempt to satisfy achievement, power, and affiliation needs in their jobs, participants and facilitators alike bring their own motives with them to an OD project, and facilitators should not allow their own needs to bias them against the needs of others. Indeed, facilitators who work with, not against, the needs of all parties will maximize their influence during the OD effort. Let those with strong achievement motives be initiators and planners; let those who enjoy power be coordinators and conveners; let those enjoy the warmth of affiliative satisfactions who wish to do so.

One way in which all three motives can be expressed is through the exercise of charismatic leadership, a quality that is more cultural than psychological in its dynamics and that can characterize a group as well as an individual leader. When David

Berlew was a consultant to our research team in the early 70s, he set forth three principles underlying the attraction of the charismatic leader (or group), all of which related to the motives of achievement, power, and affiliation:

1. The charismatic leader expresses for other people their own mute longings in a way that makes their longings clear to them.
2. The charismatic leader shows people that the object of their longing is attainable—and not by waiting for someone else to bring it, but by taking matters into their own hands.
3. The charismatic leader inspires people with the conviction that significant action can be taken now, today, not next year or in heaven, and that the action should be taken together.

Insofar as the achiever seeks to reach a goal or outcome, and the achievement of specifiable outcomes is an educational organization's *raison d'etre*, the achievement motive, especially, can energize the planning of innovative programs. Achievement motives are active when problems are real and important, so that requiring participants to choose realistically attainable goals provides the best possible field of action for people with high achievement needs. Indeed, the high achievement motivation of many educators and students is one of the forces acting in the facilitator's favor. When asked to state their goals, most people can reply with some specificity. When they are asked to do so, many groups of educators can seek consensus on some near subgoal. When asked to construct plans for reaching a goal, most groups of educators will put in extra hours in the eager hope of reaching a subgoal.

At the same time, however, program planning and problem solving may not satisfy people whose primary motivations are power or affiliation. These motives are somewhat more difficult to use because many educated Americans believe that it is somehow shameful to exhibit them in public, although inhibiting norms can be considerably weakened by use of appropriate warm-up activities such as those described later in this book.

Even action- or achievement-motivated people may not enjoy large-scale problem solving if their motives have been repeatedly frustrated and their patience for finding gratifying outcomes has grown short. People who have had a great deal of frustrating experience are less likely to do problem solving on real problems than to indulge any of several common attitudes: the scapegoat attitude (blame or punish someone for the problem, and the problem will go away); the savior attitude ("Don't worry, our leader will take care of us"); the prayer-wheel attitude ("If we continue doing what we've always done when threatened, after a while the problem won't look as bad''); or the rabbit attitude (''Freeze, and maybe the problem will go away without noticing us'').

Bridging the gap between the OD effort and independent action is the most far-reaching way of making use of participants' motives. That is, never design an OD activity so that participants go away feeling satisfied and fulfilled, because doing so leaves them no reason to undertake further action. Design each event so that they have committed themselves to action, have formed a clear plan of action and a clear picture of the nature of the action, have expressed mutual expectations, and have perhaps made a first step in the action phase, but have neither completed nor approached completion of the action; doing that leaves them with the motivation to act even in the facilitator's absence.

Learning Themes

When designing a macrosequence, OD facilitators should consider the abstract significance of even the most mundane events in the interests of leaving participants with one or more conceptual lessons that support organized action. While the exercises described in chapters 4 through 8 teach small lessons, it is in the larger lessons taught by the OD event as a whole that facilitators demonstrate their ability at macrodesigning.

The Planners and Operators exercise (see index), for example, teaches among other things that, no matter how carefully people may organize their presentations, one-way instructions are less effective than most people believe them to be. The larger session that includes this exercise, however, may carry the additional lesson that administrators either do or do not care about the effect of unilateral communication on their relations with instructors and that they are or are not willing to take action on the matter. This further lesson is likely to be clear and strong if the exercise is conducted with administrators and the actual instructors they supervise, if it is preceded by a few activities centered on communicative efficacy, and if it is followed by activities and exercises that cause participants to probe their present relationships so that participating administrators get an opportunity to demonstrate their own perceptions and hopes.

Again, an OD activity session that aims at moving into action innovative ideas requiring the collaboration of instructors and administrators might convey the following related lessons. First, while the ordinary routines of the college or school do not facilitate conferring, gathering information from those with veto power, arranging logistics, or planning committed action to begin on a certain date, it is nevertheless possible to design a setting that does facilitate these steps. Second, the behavior of staff members toward one another is almost always more a function of organizational structures and the given situation than of individual interests and personality styles.

A macrodesign that presents participants with cognitive messages they can carry into their educational organization can leave them feeling that their potentialities are different or that their relationships with others are new. We mean, for example, that during the next few days the administrator and a committee of instructors will invent and try out some new modes of bilateral communication, systematically assessing the results of their efforts; that within a few days clusters of instructors will begin doing new things collaboratively; and that the administration will support the new ventures. In short, the lesson we seek always to impart is that new and more worthwhile interdependent actions are not only conceivable and feasible but imminent.

By participating in one particular aspect of a group's plan of actions, facilitators can also help participants move toward their goals. If, for example, educators in a group set a goal of learning how to design meetings they themselves can carry out with students, a particular part of their macrodesign might be a planning session in which outside facilitators sit in as process observers, intervening only when asked or when the meeting process appears unproductive. Participating educators should leave this kind of OD activity feeling closer to their goal than before and more competent to make progress toward it in the future.

The problem-solving sequence described in chapter 6 provides a useful learning theme, one we used in 1970 during the first week of a design to launch the conversion of several public schools from traditional individuated structures to multiunit team-teaching structures. Essentially, the design comprised four stages:

1. During the first five days, skill practice, exercises, and focused training aimed at helping the faculty to articulate its present and ideal conditions, to reach group agreements both for subgroups and for the school as a whole, and to be clearer with one another about their yearnings and frustrations.

2. The staffs were asked next to state formally some problems that were within their power to solve.

3. While working on actual school problems, they were taught the problem-solving sequence. By the time their plans had been detailed and first steps taken in accordance with the plans, the week had ended.

4. During the final day, staff members told one another about the faculty strengths that they believed would help move the school toward its new goals. By adding personal abilities to the list of helping forces, this activity also made some of the staff's diverse resources more accessible.

Successful Macrodesigns

This section offers general guides to good designs.

Eight Techniques for Macrodesigning

Include Key Members. Especially with small subsystems such as teams, departments, committees, cabinets, and college non-academic staffs, designs for OD work best when all group members begin and participate in all phases together; even a few days' difference can raise barriers between those who participate and those who come late. When all members experience the intervention goals, skills, and activities simultaneously, they are better able to remind one another of what happened at the workshops and to transfer what was learned to the educational organization in which they work.

When the organization is large, it is not feasible to include all members in one event. It is difficult, for example, to induce all members of a large secondary school or community college to attend an individual OD event, and it is logistically impossible for all members of a school district or university to attend all training events. The nonparticipant will understand that a great many people cannot be accommodated at one meeting and will not feel threatened when an OD event is held with one fraction of the organization before others.

Thus, when beginning an OD project with a large organization, invite key members—those who are regularly interdependent and who hold formal positions of power—and select them in ways that will be viewed as legitimate and appropriate. If you ask teachers or students to attend a district OD event with the superintendent's cabinet or professors and students to attend a college OD event with the provost's staff, for example, either invite those holding formal positions of leadership, invite a random group, or choose the participants by some other method that will cause them to be viewed as legitimate representatives and not as chosen by some faction. If people do attend an OD event as representatives of a larger body, see to it that they regularly report the content of the proceedings to their constituents.

Clarify OD Goals, Theory, and Technology. The ultimate aim of OD is to develop in the target system a self-renewing culture in which discrepancies between actual and ideal conditions are viewed as target problems and in which creative solutions are sought both inside and outside the organization as problems arise. To bring these goals to life, the macrodesign should include both explicit descriptions (cognitive) and lively experiences (affective). Participants should see that clarifying communication and developing new group norms for working together more effectively are prerequisites to carrying out innovative educational programs, and they should come to view defining and solving problems as a regular repetitive cycle in their work. Handouts can be used to introduce and clarify these concepts: Table 3–1 and Figures 3–1, 3–2, and 3–3, and some of the exhibits in the other chapters as well. Exercises are sufficiently removed from the reality of the target system to allow staff members to participate with little personal risk or anxiety, but they resemble reality enough to spark discussions of the ways the experience in them resembles or differs from what really happens in the system.

Move from Structured Activities to Application. Skill exercises effectively demonstrate in microcosm organizational issues of role relationships, group norms, and human motivation. Indeed, structured exercises enable organization members who attend a training event out of duty rather than by choice to find new interpersonal modes more easily than do freer experiences demanding more personal commitment and initiative. Exercises often stimulate thought about familiar problems and thus encourage problem solving about real issues as a next step. By skillful debriefing, the facilitator can bring participants to the realization that more work is needed to improve oral and written communication, to overcome difficulties in listening, and to gain skill in working together in groups.

Move from Shared Information to Action Planning. Reporting systematically collected information back to appropriate organizational units as a basis for diagnosis, problem solving, and planning is one of the most important intervention modes for OD projects in education. In both survey-data-feedback and constructive confrontation designs, start by sharing important information within and among appropriate subsystems and role takers. Then help group members practice communication skills to assure a flow of clear information across subsystems and persons. Move next to problem solving, and lead participants toward making specific action plans. Continually point out this macrosequence, which can be labeled *action research*, in the hope that participants will adopt it as a regular organizational process.

Rotate Subgroup Memberships. When small subsystems such as an elementary school staff or smaller groups such as the provost's staff become engaged in OD, successful macrodesigns rotate participating members through different groups, especially during the opening days of the OD process. Rotation increases the potential networks of workable relationships on the staff, diminishes the possibility that groups in relative isolation from one another will come to perceive an in-group and out-group (which can occur with surprising speed), and helps to increase members' identification with the whole staff. The latter is necessary to sustain motivation through the project's follow-up phases and to increase group cohesiveness so that members pull together and share resources during problem solving.

When doing OD with large groups such as the faculty of a very large high school or a complex university made up of people with a number of jobs, rotating subgroup memberships is impractical. In this case it is best to begin with homogeneous job groups, introducing occasions for participants to communicate about their performances during the exercises and skill activities. Next, arrange a period when they can discuss larger organizational problems similar to those in the exercises, allowing each group to list its own problems and to tell the others about them. Then, organize problem-solving activities within heterogeneous job groups. Finally, schedule planning of the application of OD techniques to real situations so that homogeneous groups can practice new skills, norms, and actions. Later the OD project should bring heterogeneous groups together again to assess how well the problem solving has been going.

Treat All Ranks Equally. People in educational institutions are generally attributed higher or lower status on the basis of impressions of how much or how well they contribute to valued group goals. Some status differences are both relevant and useful, as when seasoned instructors are accorded high status for knowing their way around the college or when principals are accorded high status for knowing their way around complicated school budget procedures. Other status differences, however, are unnecessary or hampering — as when it is believed that only a department head can convene a meeting or that only the department secretary can take minutes. An effective macrodesign reduces such unnecessary differences in the context of the OD events. That is, the facilitator responds to organization members according to their performance in intervention activities and not according to their job titles.

OD facilitators should explain that every participant is potentially important in carrying out a task and that stereotypes based on job titles can impede effective group functioning. Rotating participants through groups can bring facilitators, administrators, and nonprofessional personnel into closer communication with one another and thus reduce the distance between them. Equal treatment during an OD event will bring them closer psychologically, a prime prerequisite to achieving openness and improved communication for performing the tasks of the educational organization.

To be sure, facilitators sometimes offer special coaching or training to people in certain positions. For example, principals might welcome recommendations for building bilateral communication into their job of supervising teachers. For other examples, we have trained a group of college students to give feedback in ways that aroused less defensiveness from their instructor and have also helped high school students to practice effective meeting procedures before joining teachers and parents on a school's advisory body. Facilitators should not encourage participants to ignore status or other differences that enrich an educational organization's variety pool or resources. Instead, they should together create norms that support retention of differences that are relevant and useful for accomplishing their work together as educators.

Exemplify New Organizational Forms. A successful macrodesign deliberately includes activities that, in their own structure and process, exemplify organization forms potentially useful to participants. Practice in summarizing, group exercises in decision making, procedures such as the Fishbowl or S-T-P Problem Solving—all should be living representations of techniques that can be used in the everyday life of the educational organization. In other words, the facilitators should plan activities that give participants new and improved organizational structures that they can bring to their regular work.

Set Out Continuing Work for the Future. The effective macrodesign should culminate with work specifications that participants will be facing as they leave the OD event. That is, facilitators should design in such a way that the participants feel both some sense of closure about matters learned and interim tasks completed and some unresolved tension concerning important tasks still incomplete. A shared feeling of incompletion, the conviction that continued problem solving will be useful, and a sense of urgency to get on with it are all powerful motivations for self-renewal.

The Design Team of Facilitators

OD projects are typically composed of one facilitator to fifteen or twenty participants. When the target system offers special challenges or when less-experienced facilitators are included in the endeavor, working in pairs can increase the ratio to one facilitator to eight or nine participants, lend emotional support and additional skill to the facilitators, and leave each target system less susceptible to errors during the execution of OD activities.

Especially during brainstorming, the design team of facilitators will gain in total strength if its composition is heterogeneous with regard to information, skills, interests, and personal styles. Because such diversity can also create difficulties in building openness and interdependence, the team of facilitators should spend time developing itself as an effectively functioning adaptive group, and the facilitators should strive to create the kind of team culture that they expect of the target system. Both goals require frank discussion of process as the team of facilitators fashions the OD design.

No matter how large the team of facilitators becomes, it is important that those facilitators who will implement the design participate in some of the planning, although it is unnecessary and often inefficient for all team members to become engaged in all phases of planning. When the design team of facilitators exceeds four members, a division of labor is required. Subteams of two, for instance, can work on diagnosing the target system, defining OD goals, and developing alternative sequences.

Before the rest of the macrodesigning takes place, the whole team of facilitators should react to the diagnosis and goal setting and should brainstorm microdesigns for increasing facilitating forces and reducing restraining forces. Finally, the whole team of facilitators should react to the proposed sequences, select one, and enlist members for refining and implementing each microaspect of the design. After that is done, individual members or two-person subgroups might finish the specific steps of each small part of the total OD design.

Seven Building Steps

The seven steps for building an effective macrodesign are somewhat like the steps employed in problem solving (see chapter 6).

1. The design team of facilitators starts by discussing its general view of organizational self-renewal, using as guides the concepts introduced in chapter 1. Talk about adaptability in relation to how the target system will look at the end of the OD project. Important aspects of this discussion will already have occurred during the entry-and-startup phase, when the memorandum of understanding with the target system was built.

2. Using the instruments and data-collecting procedures described in chapters 4 through 8, collect data on selected organizational attributes of the target system, and seek information about the clarity of communication and education goals (chapter 4), hidden intergroup and inter-role conflicts (chapter 8), and meeting effectiveness (chapter 5). Although these data can be collected by means of questionnaires, interviews and observations are generally more useful for facilitators, allowing them to gather sufficient additional data on the spot to commence characterizing the target system during the interviewing or observing process.

3. For the particular event being designed, list OD goals that are more specific than those discussed during start up. Ideally, observable behavioral evidences for the goals are specified in advance (chapters 4 through 8).

4. List forces present in the target system that will facilitate or restrain the achievement of OD goals. These forces can be categorized as group, interpersonal, or intrapersonal (see chapter 6 for a discussion of Force-Field Analysis).

5. Use brainstorming to generate microdesigns that might increase facilitating forces or reduce restraining forces (see chapter 9 for details about microdesigning).

6. Prepare alternative sequences for the microdesigns.

7. Finally, accept one sequence and assign implementation duties for each microaspect to a specific member of the facilitators. Let the facilitator responsible for each microaspect refine the design of his or her part.

Ten Questions

Designing an OD event requires creativity, knowledge, and flexibility; it is in many ways the most challenging and exciting part of planned change. Judging from our own experience and what we have learned of the work of others, we believe there are 10 questions that should be answered affirmatively before any design is put into action.

1. Will the design allow participants to feel rewarded, challenged, uplifted, and inspired?
2. Does it clearly connect the OD activities to the actual work of the target system?
3. Will it increase communicative clarity, a sense of pulling together, and energy for continuing collaborative work?
4. Does it aid in clarifying problems entailing unclear roles, norms, and decision-making procedures?
5. Does it offer activities through which achievement, affiliation, and power motives can be satisfied?
6. Does it offer a description of some goals of the total educational organization so that members can recognize and adopt superordinate goals?
7. Does it feature a learning theme to leave participants with one or more conceptual lessons?
8. Does it include procedures for monitoring the OD activities events as they are occurring?
9. Does it build structures and schedules that will continue after the formal OD project is over?
10. Does it offer a sense of closure while leaving some tension related to work still to be accomplished?

The Centrality of Problem Solving

Problem solving is fundamental in all OD macrodesigns. It is present in all OD virtually from start to finish and, we always hope, even beyond the end of the formal OD design. Small cycles of problem solving occur during the making of a contract, the system-wide diagnosis, the selection of a macrodesign, and the execution of an OD design.

During contract making, for example, the facilitators offer information about the goals of OD. That gives participants a direction toward targets; it also helps them focus upon the current situation in their own system. And the contract presents guidelines for the ensuing problem solving. Thus, even during contract making we find the rudiments of problem solving: the description of the situation (S), specification of target (T), and proposals for the path (P) to the target.

Collecting diagnostic data also requires several cycles of problem solving. First are the steering committee's discussions on which items and strategies to use in data collection. Often, the best format is one that requires participants to reflect on discrepancies between S and T in the target system. Second is the steering committee's choice of the issues to be given the most attention during the OD. And third are the feedback sessions with all members of the target system that help everyone to see and understand the organizational problems their educational organization faces.

The problem-solving mode of thought comes into play even more significantly during the selection and execution of the macrodesign. Regardless of the macrodesign chosen—training, survey-data-feedback, constructive confrontation, or process observation and feedback—they all help build the structure and motivation for collaborative problem solving among colleagues in the target system.

During training, the organizational problems of the participants are brought into view both indirectly and subtly. During the first few days of training, and particularly toward the end of each minicycle of experiential learning, participants compare and contrast their behavior during the foregoing exercise and their typical behavior at work. These discussions often give rise to problems that, if worked on, can help the staff members strengthen the processes of their organization. The OD facilitator keeps a list of those problems as they arise and later reminds participants about them before proceeding into problem-solving groups.

Compared with training, survey-data-feedback leads straightforwardly to problem solving. The data themselves typically allow participants to see discrepancies between their S and their T's, so that during survey-data-feedback, problems can be listed both by the facilitator and by the participants themselves.

In a different manner, problems also arise from constructive confrontation. Here the facilitator helps subsystems in conflict to see the norms, structures, or procedures that are blocking effective collaboration. Through a step-wise progression from social distance through catharsis to reflection, the confrontation design gradually increases participants' realization that system-wide problems are shared and that if they are to be solved, they must be attacked collaboratively.

Finally, process observation and feedback also facilitates problem identification. The facilitator watches the participants work, noting process problems and giving feedback to raise participants' awareness of the problem. In structure, that procedure is similar to data feedback, except that in process observation and feedback the facilitator replaces the questionnaire as the instrument of problem identification.

Although problem solving goes on continuously from the start, formal problem solving starts, from the participants' point of view, after one of the four macrodesigns has helped the participants to make a list of central educational problems. Our research indicates that it is necessary for participants to go through at least two cycles of formal problem solving for lasting outcomes to occur in the target system.

The initial cycle of formal problem solving should address pressing school issues that, if worked on, can give rather rapid and visible results. Examples could include communication breakdowns between particular subsystems or role takers, confusion over some of the organization's goals, ineffective meetings, and a lack of group agreements about certain role relationships.

A later cycle of formal problem solving should focus on what has to be done to ensure that collaborative problem solving will take place continually in the target system. Here, participants explore the norms, structures, and procedures required to maintain an effective capacity for continual problem solving. We discussed examples of such norms, structures, and procedures in chapter 1.

Figure 3–4 is an abbreviated flow chart summarizing relationships among aspects of a macrodesign.

Examples of Macrodesigns

Although the number of possible macrodesigns is virtually infinite, we have chosen to present here some that have shown promise in our own work and the work of others with which we have been associated. We distinguish among three sorts of designs: classical, complex, and special interest. Classical designs are rather pure examples of survey-data-feedback, training, constructive confrontation, and process observation and feedback. Complex designs are mixtures of those; they are larger in scope and frequently longer in duration than the classical designs. While some differences between classical and complex designs appear obvious, the distinctions are only a matter of degree. Special-interest designs commence with a focus on a specific social or educational problem or challenge—for example, desegregation, consolidation, interdisciplinary curricula, mainstreaming, or student involvement. More and more attempts to use OD in colleges and schools get their impetus from the presence of new societal or educational challenges confronting our educational systems.

Figure 3-4. Main Points of OD Macrodesigns

Making the OD contract (a memorandum of understanding)
↓
The OD diagnosis
    Data collection
    Data feedback
↓
The OD macrodesign
    Data feedback
    Training
    Confrontation
    Process observation and feedback
↓
Pressing organizational problems
are identified
↓
Problem-solving cycle I
(pressing problems)
↓
Problem-solving cycle 2
(problem-solving capacity)

Classical Macrodesigns

Here are illustrations of the four kinds of strategies.

Survey-Data-Feedback: Developing Renewal Processes in Urban High Schools *

Bassin, Gross, and Jordan (1979) developed a practical model based on organization development for strengthening urban high schools. This New York-based project differs from other efforts to apply OD to public schools in several ways. First, it was the largest organization-development effort in inner city schools anywhere in the world; specifically, there were thirty-five participating schools and most of them were very large. Second, it was the largest effort to apply organization development to secondary schools. And third, it was the longest organization development effort in inner city schools, in operation between 1969 and 1985.

Bassin, Gross, and Jordan describe their "renewal model" as involving participatory, systematic planning, and problem solving.

* Adapted from Richard A. Schmuck, "Organization Development in the Schools" in Cecil R. Reynolds and Terry B. Gutkin (eds.), *The Handbook of School Psychology*, 2d ed., (New York: John Wiley, 1990).

The model called for members of the school—including students—to identify, analyze, and develop solutions to school problems. The process required start-up, diagnosis, planning, and implementation, and offered an excellent example of how to apply OD for urban school improvement. The plan worked as follows.

Following exploratory conferences with the principal and other key staff members, the OD facilitator decided whether the school was ready. *Start-up* officially took place when the facilitator met with the principal and other staff to explore the segments of the school that should commence the renewal process.

Next, the principal, a few staff members, and the facilitator designed procedures for selecting an *internal renewal coordinator*. The coordinator initiated, energized, and managed the project (see Porterfield and Porterfield, 1979, for details). The first task of the coordinator was to enlist the aid of a voluntary committee drawn from the school and its surrounding community. The start-up was completed when the OD facilitator, coordinator, principal, and the committee designed the details of the remaining stages of renewal in terms of who would do what and when.

Diagnosis is the data-collection or self-study stage of renewal. The committee decided on issues of concern about which to collect data, carried out an extensive survey of the issues, and thereby diagnosed the school's problems. Several methods of collecting data were used to produce both opinion data and baseline or quantitative data. Most common among the collection methods were survey instruments, group brainstorming, interviews, and observation. The data were used by the renewal committee to establish priorities for planning.

Planning entailed developing ideas and programs to solve priority problems. Bassin, Gross, and Jordan indicated that in their schools planning typically consisted of five steps. First, potential implementers of innovative programs were invited to collaborate with the committee in the planning process. Second, "research and development" was carried out by examining effective practices relevant to the issues in question that were being tried elsewhere. Third, an action plan was created that included a carefully phrased set of objectives, an accountability scheme, and a specific time line listing tasks and people. Fourth, a formative evaluation procedure was established. And fifth, administrative approval was sought to assume that the project was consonant with the goals of the school and to enlist support of the administration during implementation.

Implementation entailed putting the action plans into effect. It often encountered resistance, particularly in the urban school environments where it was being tried. Resistance was often due to political problems in the school, but just as frequently was due to poor management procedures. The facilitator could be helpful in facilitating the prevention or resolution of implementation problems. For example, renewal committees often found fault with the principal for what was perceived as a lack of support. Principals, on the other hand, often tended to view the committee as another pressure group that had to be balanced along side of many others. Those perceptions led to hostilities that obligated the facilitator to act as a third-party negotiator.

Survey-Data-Feedback: Teambuilding for Academic Managers of a Community College

During one academic year, Schmuck worked with the Vice President of Academic Affairs and her 15 department heads to help them establish a more cohesive and better functioning management team. After two introductory meetings in September with the whole group, Schmuck asked for four department heads to form a steering committee for the project. The vice president, Schmuck, and the four heads who volunteered to help, met four times during October and November to write a questionnaire to survey all 16 members of the management team. The questions asked about the participants' perceptions and attitudes about how well the academic managers were acting as a team. A few questions asked about the vice president's effectiveness as the head of the team.

In early December, the steering committee called for a meeting of the whole team to explain the reasons for the questionnaire and to have all 16 members fill it out at the same meeting. All 16 questionnaires were filled out completely without names or departmental affiliations. Before the holiday break the steering committee tallied the responses and prepared charts and tables to summarize the results. A summary write-up of the results was mailed to team members over the holiday.

In January the steering committee convened two meetings with the management team to discuss the results. At another meeting of the whole team in February Schmuck helped the team construct a list of the team's problems. At the same meeting Schmuck spoke briefly about systematic problem solving. Later that month, the department heads divided themselves into five trios; each trio applied the problem solving procedure to one of the problems on the list. Working substantially on its own during March and April, each trio followed a five-step procedure: (1) describing the problem through behavioral description, (2) further defining the problem by diagnostic force-field analysis (see index), (3) brainstorming to find actions likely to reduce restraining forces, (4) designing a concrete plan of action, and (5) trying out the plan behaviorally by means of an activity with the whole management team. During May,

Schmuck and the vice president helped the whole team reach consensus on the new actions it wished to take in trying to become a stronger team. The vice president, for her part, announced changes that she intended to make in how she was carrying out her role. From the middle of May until the end of the academic year, Schmuck convened three meetings in all with the management team to evaluate how well the new actions were working out.

Training: Organizational Training for a School Faculty

The following design, carried out in a junior high school, was fully reported in Schmuck and Runkel (1970); its purposes were to stimulate improved group problem solving among faculty members and generally to help the staff become more responsive to students and parents. The training began with a six-day laboratory in late August with almost the entire building staff present. The 54 participants included all the administrators, all but two of the faculty, plus the head secretary, the head cook, and the head custodian.

The first two days were devoted to group and intergroup exercises and communication skills—e.g., Lost on the Moon, the Five-Square puzzle, and the Planners and Operators exercise (use the index to locate specific exercises) along with paraphrasing and other communication skills described in chapter 4—all of which aimed at increasing awareness of interpersonal and organizational process and at demonstrating the importance of effective communication in accomplishing tasks collaboratively. After each exercise, small groups discussed how the experiences were like or unlike their normal relations in school. All staff members then pooled their experiences and analyzed their relationships as a faculty. Each small group chose its own way of reporting what it had experienced, and the facilitators supported openness in giving and receiving feedback about perceptions of real organizational processes in the school.

During the next four days the faculty pursued a problem-solving sequence, similar to the one described above, working on real issues that were thwarting the school's organizational functioning. On the third day, after a morning of discussion and decision (which also served as practice in decision-making skills), three significant problems emerged and three work groups formed, each to work through a problem-solving sequence directed toward one of the problems. The first six days of training culminated with a discussion in which members described their own strengths and those of their colleagues and reflected on what their school could be like if all faculty resources were used.

Early in the fall, during the regular school year, the facilitators interviewed all faculty members and also observed several committees and subject-area groups to determine what uses were being made of the earlier six-day training. Data gathered then indicated that problems still unresolved were closely related to communicative misunderstanding, an overload of duties in some jobs, and a limited capability for group problem solving.

At the next follow-up OD event with the entire staff, held for one and a half days in December, the facilitators sought to increase the effectiveness of subject-area coordinators as communication links between teachers and administrators, to increase problem-solving skills of the area groups and the principal's advisory committee, to help the faculty explore ways of reducing its duty overload, and to increase effective communication between service personnel and the rest of the staff. OD activities included communication exercises, problem-solving techniques, decision-making procedures, and development of skill in observing and giving feedback to work groups.

On the first day, departmental groups applied problem-solving techniques to their own communication difficulties and received feedback from other observing groups. The problems raised were brought the next day to a meeting of the principal's advisory committee held before the staff. The staff observed the committee in a Fishbowl Arrangement (see index), participated with its members in specially designed ways, and later reflected on how effectively the committee had worked and how accurately its members had reflected them.

The main objectives of the third follow-up event three months later, which also lasted one and a half days, were to evaluate staff progress in solving the problems of use, role clarity, and staff participation and to reanimate any lagging skills. A group discussion was held for each problem, and all teachers were invited to work in the group considering the problem that interested them most. Each work group discussed the favorable and unfavorable outcomes associated with its problem and wrote examples of improvement, instances of no change, and cases of regression. The work groups tried to devise ways to halt backsliding by modifying the school's organizational procedures. Faculty members continued with this activity in work groups during the spring without help from the facilitators.

Training: Improving Meeting Effectiveness in College Departments

The meetings of academic departments in higher education are usually frustrating and unproductive for faculty members. One reason is that the participants themselves usually don't know how to run an effective meeting. A popular training design that is often carried out by an inside facilitator focuses on improving meeting effectiveness.

In one community college in which Schmuck had been carrying out a survey-data-feedback design, for example, he learned that the head of the nursing department was training her departmental colleagues in meetings skills. The steps of her macrodesign followed closely our ideas about meetings in chapter 5.

She started by asking her colleagues to brainstorm features of an effective meeting. Once she had a list of features printed on posters in front of the group, she asked her colleagues to put black check marks by those features that the department was doing well on and red check marks by those features that should be improved.

Setting those data aside she next lectured to the group about how to construct a clear agenda, how to convene a meeting, how to record the high points, how to act as a process observer, and how to debrief the interpersonal processes that take place during a meeting. After discussion on those points, she presented information about the task and maintenance functions of an effective problem-solving group.

She then returned to the list of meeting features and focused on those with the most red marks. She made up 15 index cards, one for each member of the department. On card one she printed the word *convener*, on another she printed *recorder*, and on a third she printed *process observer*. On the other 12 cards she printed one task or maintenance function on each. Then she shuffled the cards and dealt one to each of her colleagues. She told them to run a meeting in which they should try to come up with some group agreements about how to improve upon the weak features of their meetings.

A week later she repeated the cards procedure, this time with the regular agenda as the content for the meeting. Next, she made up three lists, each of which described who in the department would take the roles of convener, recorder, and process observer and the dates on which they would take those roles.

Survey-Data-Feedback: The Charismatic Day

The personal qualities of a charismatic leader, who excites the imaginations of others, encourages them to share in feelings of relevance and power, and imparts a sense of urgency to them, can also become part of the culture of a group. The Charismatic Day, a one-day macrodesign built on this concept, can be carried out with an academic department in a college or with the faculty of a public school late in a year-long OD effort, following a series of training and consultative events such as those described in this chapter.* The intent of the design is to excite the hopes and imaginations of staff members, to help them feel powerful and confident, and to instill in them a pervasive sense of urgency. It encourages organization members to put new ways of working together into immediate action and is also useful in stimulating a staff to upgrade instructional practices in new ways.

First, the facilitator, with the help of steering committee members who have participated in planning the event, quickly lists in the form of goals some changes currently under serious consideration in the college or school, each of which must have the vocal support of at least one small group. Staff members are asked to express their understandings and feelings about these goals in buzz groups and soon afterward to report the discussions to the total staff.

Again in a small group, each person is asked to tell others specifically and realistically what he or she personally wants to do to achieve these broader goals. Then each individual prepares a list headed "what I can contribute toward achieving my preferred action plan." These lists are posted, and staff members try to find others with whom they can profitably work to achieve their personal plans. Clusters of four staff members are encouraged but not required, and time is allowed for the clusters to form.

To induce a sense of urgency, each cluster is asked to produce a plan of action that can be initiated in the next week. After an hour or two of planning, participants are asked to talk about the new things they believe they can do with others in their college or school as a result of this procedure. If nothing they have done in planning has been important, or if they feel discouraged about their action plans, they are asked to talk about their disappointments. The design can end here, or, if group members seem ready, 10 to 15 minutes can be spent at some trust-building procedure.

Constructive Confrontation: Bringing a School Staff and Parents into Effective Interaction**

During one school year, Schmuck teamed with a cadre of organizational specialists within a school district to facilitate conflict resolution at a beleaguered elementary school. The context of this OD project was a national reaction to the presumed dehumanization

---

* For more information about this macrodesign, see Schmuck et al. (1975).

** Adapted from Richard A. Schmuck, "Organization Development in the Schools," in Cecil R. Reynolds and Terry B. Gutkin (eds.), *The Handbook of School Psychology,* 2d ed., (New York: John Wiley, 1990).

in school classrooms and the need for parent involvement at school to turn things around. About 90 parents at an elementary school attended informal neighborhood meetings in the fall to discuss concerns they had with their own school. The outgrowth of these meetings was the formation of a group that called itself the Parents' Advisory Committee.

The committee sent a letter to the school's principal in November that described "wide-spread concerns with school-to-parent communication, curriculum—especially in the arts—and the quality of the staff and its training." The principal passed on the letter to the school's 12 teachers who greeted it with disbelief, resentment, and disappointment. The principal then called on the coordinator of the district's cadre of organizational specialists, asking for "assistance in dealing with the parents' complaints."

Members of the cadre, along with Schmuck, developed a design that had as its overall theme a confrontation between parents and teachers. Within the theme of confrontation were elements of training, data feedback, and process observation and feedback. The macrodesign included six stages:

1. Forming and meeting with a steering committee composed of some teachers and a few parents to explain the macrodesign and get approval to proceed.

2. Providing demonstrations of OD to the staff and to all interested parents so they understand its goals and procedures.

3. Training parents and staff separately in the skills of interpersonal communication and group problem solving and helping each group list top-priority concerns. Collecting data on impressions of intergroup climate and influence.

4. Bringing the two groups together and feeding back data on climate, concerns, and influence. Helping the groups clarify intergroup communication and agree upon top-priority mutual concerns.

5. Forming problem-solving groups of parents and teachers to design proposals to solve important mutual problems. Serving as process facilitators to these groups.

6. Bringing all problem-solving groups together to share their proposals and to make decisions and plans for implementation.

The six stages were carried out as scheduled, beginning with Stage 1 in November and ending with Stage 6 in June. Details about microdesign elements and the intervention's favorable outcomes can be found in Schmuck et al. (1977).

Three kinds of outcomes were documented. The first set had to do with implementation of proposals designed by the parent-staff problem-solving groups. Within a year, there were (1) a new parent organization that included parents in making decisions about curriculum and staffing, (2) new forms of written communication from school to home, (3) improvements to the building and grounds, (4) parties for welcoming new and foreign families to the community and school, (5) many parent volunteers in classrooms and the library, and (6) an artist-in-residence program.

A second set of outcomes had to do with improvements in the climate of interaction between staff and parents and in the climate of interactions among staff members. After the intervention, parents reported that they had better impressions of the school, could now get the information they wanted, and thought their input was welcomed by the staff. When asked about changes they saw in the school, more than two-thirds of the parents singled out the atmosphere as being very different.

The third set of outcomes concerned changes in perceived and attributed influence. Parents perceived an increase in their own influence and did so without attributing less influence to the staff. Staff members, by contrast, did not think they had gained or lost influence but attributed more influence to parents. To both parents and the staff, the PTA in its new structure was the vehicle through which the total amount of influence available to be shared had been increased.

Constructive Confrontation: Reducing Conflict Between the Two Colleagues of a Two-Person Department

Schmuck carried out a similar macrodesign to the one just described in a special situation in a community college. The provost of the college asked Schmuck to help one of her division heads deal with a virulent conflict between two of his faculty members who were the only two teaching a particular curriculum. Schmuck started with Stage 3 described above, but in this application gave special one-to-one tutoring to each of the conflicting individuals separately in the skills of interpersonal communication and group problem solving, while helping each individual list top-priority concerns in his relationship with the other. Schmuck then proceeded through Stages 4 and 5 adapting them to this one-to-one confrontation. Finally, Schmuck asked the pair to meet with their division head to explain to him their agreements.

Process Observation and Feedback: Improving the Meetings of the Staff of a Language Institute in a University

Schmuck used process observation and feedback to help the 14 members of a language department in a large university improve their meetings. After meeting with the department head and subsequently with department members themselves, a joint decision was made to use a Saturday to get the OD project going. Schmuck suggested that the participants meet the Friday evening before the OD day to give him an opportunity to observe the department in action. He recommended that the department run a regular meeting that evening with its own agenda and typical procedures. He would observe the procedures used, offer some immediate feedback, and work up other feedback after that meeting for discussion on the next day. From then on, the department was to do problem solving and to make some new group agreements about its regular meetings.

The work proceeded well as planned. Schmuck observed the department work for 90 minutes. After a break he offered behavioral descriptions of what he saw, along with some of his feelings about the group behaviors. His feedback balanced favorable and unfavorable reflections about the department's group dynamics. While he saw concerted attention to task and participation by all, he also noted that when a few people spoke no one responded to them, that the agenda for the meeting wasn't written down, that no paraphrasing or gatekeeping occurred during the meeting, and that no one checked with others to reinforce decisions that seemed to be made by the team. After a short discussion about the meeting, the session ended.

The next morning Schmuck led off by asking department members for their reflections and feelings about the meeting on the previous evening. This question gave rise to quite a few critical comments about the department's functioning. Schmuck then asked how typical the meeting had been—how it resembled or differed from other meetings. Some participants saw similarities with other meetings in the department's lack of a clear agenda and its failure to clarify who was to do what after decisions were made. Others saw contrasts with other meetings, chiefly insofar as the department was trying to perform well in front of Dr. Schmuck. Typically, they remarked, the department drifted away from its task more than it had the night before.

Next, Schmuck engaged the participants in a discussion to pinpoint key process problems during the group's meetings. The list that developed included (1) a lack of clarity in the agenda; (2) too much dependence on the department head for running the meetings; (3) some sloppy communication; (4) hidden feelings that came out only after the meetings; and (5) unclear decision-making procedures, throwing most of the responsibility for follow-through on the shoulders of the department head.

Then, each person was paired with another, and each pair

selected one of the above-listed problems to work on. Schmuck introduced the *S-T-P* problem-solving process (described in chapter 6). Each pair proceeded through the steps of problem solving while Schmuck moved around the room again acting as a process observer. Finally, the initial cycle of problem solving ended with each pair reporting back its ideas to the whole group.

Schmuck next asked that each individual spend 30 minutes alone listing the actions he or she would like to see the department take to improve its meetings. At the end of that half-hour of reflection, each participant presented his or her list on a large piece of newsprint paper so the others could see it. Schmuck suggested circling any ideas that were on three or more lists. The circled ideas were then discussed by the group and either consensually accepted or tabled for later consideration. No idea was immediately rejected. Schmuck ended the day by asking each participant to state his or her willingness to try out the new ideas, and by scheduling his next visit to the department when he would act as process observer at a regular meeting.

Schmuck visited the department once a month for four months to do process observation and feedback at department meetings. He used as a guide to his observations the lists of ideas that the participants had agreed upon during the Saturday of problem solving. During his third visit, he suggested that the participants themselves start to serve as process observers at future meetings, and suggested choosing a member to pair off with him and observe at the next meeting. Schmuck asked the participants to count off quickly from one to 14, and then arbitrarily chose the number six; the person whose number was six would collaborate with him as an observer of the next meeting. That sort of pairing with Schmuck took place twice, and then all participants felt capable of observing and feeding back information on their own. Schmuck departed from the department five months after the OD Saturday.

The following macrodesigns contain one or another mixture of training, survey-data-feedback, constructive confrontation, and process observation and feedback.

Complex Macrodesigns

Establishing OD Specialists in a School District

As part of a two-year OD project, facilitators from the University of Oregon established an internal cadre of organizational specialists within a school district. Before the specialists were in place, however, the university facilitators carried out organizational training events for several key parts of the district for one year. The goal of the OD events was to increase the communication and problem-solving skills of teams of personnel in a variety of influential positions; an early auxiliary goal was to clarify and define the complex relationships between line and staff personnel. Detailed results of this district-wide effort were presented by Runkel, Wyant, Bell, and Runkel (1980).

Training Personnel with Line Functions

In April the facilitators invited all the key personnel performing line functions in the district to the first training event. They included the superintendent and his cabinet, the elementary and secondary school principals, and selected teachers who were leaders within the local education association. At least one teacher from every school site attended the meeting along with the higher officers in the association. The event lasted for four days, but only the superintendent's cabinet was present all the time.

On the first day, before others had arrived, the superintendent and his cabinet discussed ways in which their communication was breaking down, the lack of clarity in their role definitions, ambiguous norms within the cabinet, and also their strengths as a group.

On the second day, the principals joined the superintendent's specially designed Imaging procedure that brought into the open the organizational problems that each group felt involved the other (see chapter 8 for details). The issues uncovered were earmarked for future problem solving. Now the cabinet and principals divided into three units: cabinet, elementary principals, and secondary principals. Each group met separately to list the other two groups' helpful and unhelpful work-related behaviors toward their own group. At the end of two hours, all agreed-upon behaviors of the other groups were written in large letters on sheets of newsprint. This session ended with a brief period of training to sharpen the communication skills of paraphrasing and behavior description.

Next, one of the three groups sat in a circle surrounded by members of the other two groups. Those in the outer ring read aloud the descriptions they had written of the inner group. A member of the inner circle then paraphrased the descriptions to make sure everyone in the ring had understood. After all items describing the inner group were read, each of the remaining two groups took its turn in the inner circle. Throughout this procedure, inner-circle members were not allowed to defend their group against the allegations made by the others.

Next, the three groups met separately to find evidence supporting the descriptions—that is, to recall examples of their behavior that could have given the other group its impressions. Returning to the Fishbowl Arrangement, each inner group reported evidence it had recalled to verify the others' perceptions. Again, inner-group members were asked simply to describe the evidence without attempting to defend themselves.

On the evening of the second day, teachers joined the principals and cabinet for four hours, and thus, for that period all the district's line personnel with formal authority were together. A modified Imaging procedure was carried out, culminating in a meeting at which the three groups specified the organizational problems that they believed existed in the district. Discussion was lively, penetrating, and constructive; most had never so openly confronted persons in other positions with their perceptions of district problems. The principals returned to their buildings the next day, leaving time for teachers and cabinet to interact. On the fourth day the cabinet met alone to schedule dates for problem solving.

Training Personnel with Staff Functions

Personnel in staff roles in the divisions of Student Personnel Services and Curriculum Development attended a three-day conference in September of the next academic year during which they were joined for a half-day by the principals. This event began with the staffs of Student Personnel and Curriculum meeting separately to discuss the helps and hindrances occurring within each of their groups, with special attention to obvious interpersonal helps and hindrances. Afterward, the two groups plus the principals participated in a period of confrontation. As in April, the confrontation unearthed a number of problems needing work. Finally, each group undertook a systematic process of problem solving, planning to continue these efforts back home.

Demonstrating OD Consultation to Selected School Staffs

From September to March the facilitators worked with five of the school staffs in the district. More than the training events with line and staff personnel, these brief OD events at school sites demonstrated to many of the teachers the benefits of OD procedures in reaching district subsystems. Although as demonstrations they were probably not as successful as that portraying OD during start up, they had the effect of increasing awareness of the meaning and procedures of OD to more people. Perhaps the most significant result of these events was that many of the volunteers to be trained as future OD specialists inside the district came from the buildings in which the OD events took place.

Preparing the OD Specialists

In April, district personnel were informed that a workshop would be held two months later for those who wished to become OD specialists. A mimeographed circular stated that the trainees would become skilled and knowledgeable in group processes and would serve on committees to give feedback or as trainers for special groups within the district. The facilitators solicited applications from all hierarchical levels of the district, and the 23 persons selected represented a wide cross-section of the district, including teachers, counselors, elementary and secondary principals, specialists in curriculum and student personnel, and assistant superintendents who were members of the superintendent's cabinet.

The first (and major) training event was a two-week workshop in June, soon after the active school year was over. The goals of the first half of that workshop were to introduce the trainees to many of the skills, exercises, and procedures that later appeared in the first edition of this handbook; to provide them an opportunity to explore the effect of their behavior on a group; to establish the OD cadre as a cohesive, supportive unit; and to give its members practice in leading training activities.

Trainees spent the first three days experiencing many exercises in small groups, rotating the role of co-trainer for training experience. Each exercise focused on a certain type of group process, such as interpersonal control, sharing of resources, or coordinating efforts to make certain "lessons" easy to comprehend. During the last two days of this week, group members designed exercises that would help strengthen their group as a cadre of OD specialists. They carried out the exercises with their peers, engaged in critical discussion afterward, and reviewed and practiced the skills of paraphrasing, behavior description, describing one's own feelings, and checking one's impressions of the feelings of others.

For the second week, they divided into six subgroups, each convened by an outside facilitator. The entire group determined potential target groups within the district, and each subgroup chose one for its work. Among the targeted groups were several schools that were changing their programs in the coming academic year, the principal and department heads at a senior high school, the principals and counselors serving elementary youngsters, and a community advisory group made up of parents. The remainder of that week was spent establishing goals for the OD projects to be conducted with the target groups, gathering diagnostic data about them, analyzing the data to determine the forces operating within the target groups, and designing OD events. The outside facilitators worked closely with these subgroups, anticipating the follow-up they would give during the academic year.

During the first two-thirds of the next academic year, the outside facilitators continued to work with the new OD specialists, withdrawing in March. Thus, many training events engineered by the specialists were observed and criticized by the outside facilitators to support the development of OD skills within the cadre. Approximately 10 various OD events occurred with their assistance, most of them successful in raising district interest in improving communication, group processes, and organizational problem solving. Other features of this project are described in chapter 10.

Launching Collaborative Colleges and Schools

Colleges and schools are likely to become increasingly characterized by collaborative structures in which teams of teachers work together to individualize instruction for students. Ideally, this format will make fuller use of customized instruction, differentiated staffing, and group decision making. The transition, however, from the self-contained to the collaborative style will not be easy, nor will the abilities and customs in the traditional college or school be sufficient in themselves to make the new organization work. Differentiated staffing and dispersed decision making will require that roles and norms be well understood and that greater attention be paid to coordination among instructors. That in turn will require from staff members improved skills in communication and group problem solving.

The following design aims at helping a previously self-contained college or school move effectively toward a collaborative structure. The OD project calls for a series of events over about nine months. The first, week-long event of approximately 40 hours occurs in August and is followed by several events during the academic year that total another 40 hours.

The first five days in August commence with group exercises, such as Grievances of Black Citizens (chapter 7) and a diagnosis of the organizational structure through the use of Tinkertoys in groups. During the same period, facilitators teach participants communication skills to use during debriefing. To generate organizational concerns, facilitators draw out group agreements in teaching teams by means of intergroup exercises. On the third day, problems are pinpointed and problem solving occurs in heterogeneous groups. Finally, staff strengths are listed on newsprint for all to see. Staff members discuss their group agreements within teams and continue problem solving in the heterogeneous groups after they return to their regular work. The OD project during the academic year should emphasize four major themes in the sequence below, with approximately 10 hours of process facilitation devoted to each theme.

1. *Supporting successful performance of the heterogeneous problem-solving groups.* As a skill, problem solving will not be successful unless it leads to reduced frustrations and new satisfactions on the staff. The plans made during the last few days of the first week of OD should now be reexamined to meet the schedules of the academic day. In general, plans should either be carried through, modified as necessary, or dropped by explicit agreement.

2. *Helping the teaching teams work effectively.* Continued organizational problem solving depends upon norms of interpersonal openness and helpfulness in the teams. During this phase, the teams should be strengthened by continued facilitating and coaching in communication skills, group agreements, meeting skills, and decision making.

3. *Building the leadership team.* The aim of any OD project should be to build new functions, roles, procedures, or policies so that the new structures become part of the basic fabric of the organization. Because the head, departmental leaders, counselor, and resource personnel are crucial to success or failure in the new organization, special process consulting should be extended to them in such functions as the role of the effective group convener, the role of process analysis during a work session, and differences between being the leader and merely performing leadership functions.

4. *Engaging the leadership team in designing an OD learning experience for the rest of the staff.* Facilitators should attempt to establish expectations and skills within the staffs that support continued OD efforts initiated and carried out by fellow staff members. During this phase, outside facilitators might co-plan and co-consult with the leadership team to help the staff solve problems, to help the staff improve group processes in its subgroups (e.g., teaching teams), and to help the entire staff improve organizational processes across subgroups.

Collegial Facilitation

Cameron (1982) described the details of an experiment in collegial consultation in Australian k–12 schools. Eight experienced teachers, three of whom were principals, volunteered to receive training in OD facilitation from experts on the staff of the New South Wales State Department of Education. Those eight, who were to act as OD facilitators in schools other than their own, received seven days of intensive workshop preparation before forming into four pairs, with one facilitating pair to serve each of four schools. The decision to participate in the experiment rested with the staffs of the four schools, with the understanding that once in the project, the school would remain in for two years. For their part, the neophyte facilitators were released from their own schools for one half-day per week to carry out the OD functions and to receive continued training over the two years.

In general, the new facilitators followed a survey-data-feedback design. After they discussed with the staffs the purposes of the OD, they asked staff members to complete a questionnaire about their schools. At several subsequent meetings in each school, results from the questionnaires were given back to the staffs for under-standing and discussion. Then, each staff retreated for a three-day weekend workshop that was intended to teach a structured way of problem solving, to gain a commitment to collaborative problem solving for planned change, and to gain further acceptance of the facilitators as credible process helpers. The facilitators deliberately played low-key roles. While they tried to keep the participants to the task of problem solving, they avoided confrontations and refrained from becoming engaged in the content of the discussions.

After the retreat, temporary task groups of staff members were formed, each to work in earnest on one of the problems selected at the retreat. Examples of problems were role confusions, communicative difficulties, ineffective meetings, need for curricu-lum revision, inadequate counseling services, poor relationships among departments, and the like. The task groups brought suggestions for change back to the whole faculty after doing their own problem solving. In many instances, staffs tried some modifications in work patterns.

The assessment of the change effects revealed some interesting outcomes. While there were some reservations, the majority of responses indicated that, compared with non-OD schools, staffs of the four OD schools felt that there had been an improvement in the problem areas in which change was attempted. The improvements had to do with knowledge, skills, and attitudes for staff members in various aspects of their teaching role, and professional relationships. Also evident were improvements in both the organi-zation of schools and their use of resources. At the same time, the data indicated that the staffs of the OD schools tended to be more critical of their work procedures as staffs than those of non-OD schools. Cameron interpreted that result as an indication that the staffs of the OD schools developed higher standards by which to evaluate their collaborative work than those current in the non-OD schools. Other features of this project are described in chapter 10.

A Design for Renewing Urban Elementary Schools

Scheinfeld (1979) offered a complex macrodesign that showed promise for dealing with the difficult problems of school improvement in inner-city settings. His strategy assumed that the quality of classroom life is multiply determined and that it is advisable to explore improvement strategies that take into account as many factors as possible. The same strategy would be appropriate for college classrooms.

Scheinfeld's design used interventions into three key aspects of school life: the classroom, the organizational climate of the school, and school-community relations. The design employed the roles of classroom advisor, OD facilitator, and school-community organizer working together as a coordinated OD team. Specific features of the design were developed during a three-year action-research project in which Scheinfeld's team worked with two public elementary schools in Chicago.

The most effective tactic, largely developed during Scheinfeld's team's engagement with the second school, used an OD framework for the overall coordination of the OD efforts. An OD facilitator first helped a staff reflect on its problems, needs, and desires. During that activity, diagnostic data were unearthed that the facilitators and the participants could share. Some of the problems raised were high rates of vandalism, poor student discipline, low student achievement, a lack of staff coordination in working with the students, and poor relationships with parents. The OD facilitator was assisted by the OD team's community organizer, who helped members of existing parents' groups to formulate their own concerns and wishes.

The OD facilitator and the community organizer worked closely with the principal to bring the staff and parents into formal meetings to discuss the problems and to formulate a list of challenges. Tightening discipline and raising achievement were included in the list. Once the challenges were chosen, the OD facilitator provided process observation and feedback to the staff to improve communication and group meetings within the school. In addition, the OD facilitator coordinated the use by the parents of the community organizer and the assistance of the classroom adviser.

As the OD project moved along, teachers made more and more

requests for help from the classroom adviser. The classroom adviser typically consulted with individual teachers, helping them set specific goals for their teaching, observing them, and giving them feedback. Later, after several teachers had worked with the classroom adviser, the OD facilitator convened them to talk about what they were doing and to what extent the school's challenges were being met by their new classroom practices.

Later, the school-community organizer invited parents and teachers together to parcel out ideas about how best to dovetail procedures at the school with family support of the student at home. Their efforts led some parents to volunteer as aides at the school and to more dialogue between parents and teachers about the students. There was a noticeable increase in attendance at parent-teacher conferences.

Special-interest Macrodesigns

Here are four designs built to alleviate particular problems: desegregation; faulty group processes in the classroom; interpersonal conflicts; and dissension among parents, students, and teachers.

Desegregation

Milstein (1979) described a project in the Buffalo public schools that used a cadre of internal OD specialists to facilitate court-ordered desegregation in that district. The cadre, called the School Improvement Resource Team (SIRT), was patterned after the project designed by Schmuck and Runkel and described above under the heading "Establishing OD Specialists in a School District." The Buffalo district was obliged to desegregate the elementary schools before desegregating the secondary schools. District administrators believed, however, that it was primarily in the secondary schools that careful preparation of the staff and community was essential, and that is where the SIRT began work.

The rationale was that if desegregation were to succeed in Buffalo, staffs would have to come together to support the change process. Teachers and administrators would have to share their hopes, concerns, and expectations; to anticipate obstacles to good human relations in the school; and to develop a plan together for working with students and the community. The consensus was that it would be disastrous if staff members were in conflict about the desegregation process. The SIRT was created to facilitate staff problem solving.

We can classify the activities of the first year into three relatively sequential phases: team selection and school identification, SIRT development and maintenance, and a first round of OD projects in several schools. In his evaluation, Milstein indicated that after two years of operation, the SIRT was working very well. The SIRT became very cohesive, schools were actively using its consultative services, and the district's administration had become supportive and understanding. During the second year, the services of the SIRT became more diversified; the team worked with a variety of school subsystems including teaching teams, administrative cabinets, grade-level teacher groups, and student groups. SIRT continued to employ a variety of designs, including a considerable amount of training and process observation and feedback and smaller amounts of survey-data-feedback and constructive confrontation.

Improving Group Processes in the Classroom

Although so far we have barely touched on the classroom, successful OD facilitation for a college or school can have favorable direct effects there. As Schmuck and Schmuck (1974) pointed out, macrodesigns that deliberately plan for the transfer of OD and that also include a focus on classroom group processes will have the greatest impact. This section offers two illustrative designs.

The first design, which lasts eighteen months, commences with an OD event in late August, just before the beginning of the academic year. The design for the August laboratory could resemble that described in the subsection above headed "Organizational Training for a School Faculty." Instructors are then asked to volunteer for a program of consultation and training in classroom group processes, and a facilitator skilled in interpersonal relations theory and classroom processes works with them for two hours each week throughout the academic year. During the following summer, an instructor development laboratory is held; perhaps covering communication skills, group techniques, problem solving, and role playing as applied directly to the classroom. Follow-up discussions could occur during the fall semester to help the instructors try out new procedures and to reinforce any insights or new skills developed during the previous year.

The second design, which lasts about six months, is launched with a one-week OD laboratory two weeks before the academic year begins; this is followed by a week of consultation in classroom group processes. Since many colleges and schools now grant some days before opening school for faculty preparation, it may be possible to use these days as part of the second week, which is devoted to facilitating the translation of group processes found useful during the OD phase into classroom innovation. During the fall semester, facilitators can lead supportive discussions, emphasizing the problem-solving process and encouraging instructors to implement their plans in the classroom. For some specific action plans for the classroom, see Schmuck and Schmuck (1992).

Interpersonal Conflict

Schmuck helped a senior high school staff work through some very tense conflicts that had existed for several years. Four years prior to the OD project, the faculty had been divided into two sub-parts. One subgroup stayed in an older building that was a few hundred yards from a new structure in which the other half of the staff worked. Although the newer structure was more desirable because of larger classrooms, better office space, and a brand new library, the older building carried the nostalgia and school spirit of a generation of educational activities. Gradually the two subgroups grew apart psychologically; they also began to develop intergroup stereotypes and feelings of antagonism toward each other. Members of both groups made fun of colleagues in the other group but shared a cohesiveness with the colleagues in their own subgroup. Several times, interpersonal antagonisms between members of the two subgroups came out into the open, and, to the embarrassment of the principal and a number of teachers, students and parents were becoming aware of the intergroup hostility among the teachers. Indeed, the public face of faculty conflict had become so serious that the superintendent and principal, not to mention more than half the staff, thought that some sort of special action was necessary.

Because time and money were limited, Schmuck's macrodesign could span only a few months. He asked first that a representative steering committee be formed of the principal and a counselor from the school and three influential teachers from each of the two subgroups. This group of eight met with Schmuck several times for a total of four hours to share perceptions of the school's conflicts and to react to Schmuck's ideas for design. The major event of the design was a three-hour clearing-the-air meeting of the entire staff on a Friday morning when the students were released from school.

This clearing-the-air event was made up of six parts:

1. Schmuck's introduction, during which his ground rules for the session were explained.
2. Small-group discussions on "perceptions of staff cultures in the two parts of the school."

3. Other small-group discussion on "old behavior that accentuates misunderstanding and conflict between the two parts of the school."

4. Small-group brainstorming on "new behaviors to try to increase understanding between the two parts of the school."

5. Suggestions from the entire staff about possible future behavior.

6. Feedback about this session and expectations about next steps.

As staff members entered the meeting room, they picked up a name tag which indicated, along with their names, the small group to which they were assigned for the entire session. The small groups were made up of four staff members each, two members coming from each of the two parts of the school. The chairs were arranged in clusters of four for the small groups, and the clusters were arranged in a large horseshoe with the opening of the horseshoe reserved for Schmuck, a chalkboard, and two easels of newsprint paper. The chairs were arranged so that at first everyone would be facing Schmuck but later could easily be turned for small-group discussions. There were 44 staff members at the meeting.

Schmuck's introduction covered the following points: "First, a public relations problem exists in this school. No longer are your conflicts simply internal to the staff. Increasingly, students and parents are being affected by your difficulties. There is a need for more understanding on this staff, a need to alter what has become a frustrating climate, and a need for more accurate and more supportive communication. The time to act is now, today. Second, the ground rules for this session are very important. I will expect you to abide by them. Since this is serious business, we must not beat around the bush; we must be open, straight-forward, direct, and succinct. There should be absolutely no kidding or joking. I won't be able to understand the in-jokes here, and they will get in the way of our communication. Today, we should have direct statements about your perceptions and feelings, not how you think others feel. When we don't understand one another, we should ask for clarification or try to paraphrase. I will try to do a lot of paraphrasing. Time is very precious; we must move along."

Next, Schmuck directed small groups to talk about the two staff cultures in the school. What are they like? What are the most favorable and the most unfavorable characteristics of each? The groups were given 20 minutes each. Then each of the 11 groups proceeded with their discussions, and Schmuck circulated personally, asking one member in each group to act as the recorder. Next, he asked the recorders to report to the whole group about their discussions. With the help of several assistants, Schmuck recorded the main points on newsprint in front of everyone.

Similar procedures were employed for the next parts of the design, described as "old behavior that accentuates misunderstanding and conflict between the two parts of the school" and "new behaviors to try to increase understanding between the two parts of the school." Before beginning the second part of the design, Schmuck exhorted the participants to leave the past behind and to think creatively about possibilities for the future.

The fifth part of the design was carried out with all 44 participants acting together in a brainstorming session. Since ideas about "new behaviors to try" were fresh in people's minds, Schmuck asked everyone to reflect on that list and to suggest the most important actions to take first. As the brainstorming proceeded, index cards were passed around to everyone. One side of the card was reserved for ideas for new behavior that didn't get onto the lists, while the other side was for giving feedback about the session.

One week after the clearing-the-air meeting, the steering committee met to debrief and to cluster the action ideas for further work. The decision was made to cluster the action ideas into seven categories and to form seven parallel task forces on the faculty. The seven clusters were (1) developing a more effective total faculty council, (2) establishing an attractive, common faculty room, (3) dispersing staff collaboration in extracurricular student activities, (4) developing an attractive social calendar for the whole faculty, (5) rearranging classroom and office locations to bring different faculty members physically closer, (6) scheduling classroom visits and designing team teaching, and (7) developing a more effective program of community relations.

At a two-hour faculty meeting the following week, the list of task forces was approved unanimously, and virtually all participants agreed to sign up for one of the committees. Steering committee members were designated as the conveners of the task forces, with the principal serving as convener of the conveners. To ensure that all faculty members would have an opportunity to select a committee that interested them, each participant was asked to rank the three committees they most preferred and to jot that information down on their name tags as they left the meeting.

Bringing Students into College Management

The gap between the sporadic, generally ineffective ways in which students currently participate in educational decisions and the well-organized procedures available to this end constitutes a major problem in contemporary higher education. As the following sketchy macrodesign indicates, however, the methods of OD can be adapted to narrow the gap.

First, train each separate body—educators and students—in communication skills, establishing objectives, uncovering and working on conflicts, conducting meetings, solving problems in groups, and collecting data. Second, bring the two together to explore goals, uncover differences, and agree on problems that impede joint decision making and other uses of human resources. Third, allow small heterogeneous problem-solving groups (with students and educators all represented as members) to work collaboratively on problems previously identified. Fourth, build new structural arrangements out of the multiple realities shared during the second and third stages and as part of the solutions to problems worked out during the third stage. The four stages are to be recycled several times and the whole design can last for more than a year.

Chapter Four

Clarifying Communication

For educators to be clear about instructional goals, solve important problems, make effective decisions, and put plans into action, many acts of communication are required. Understanding is particularly important when complex plans are to be developed—plans requiring many people to coordinate their actions. If the educational organization is to remain responsive to demands of all sorts, an open flow of information from and to the various groups must be maintained.

A college or school with organizational adaptability has open and direct channels of communication within the faculty as well as between the faculty and other groups. Members have interpersonal skills that facilitate clear, open, and candid communication. They have norms that support directness, candor, tact, and authenticity. They have procedures for helping those outside the faculty understand "what our institution stands for" and for encouraging members to listen well to what those outside are saying.

Though a college or school with the characteristics we have just mentioned is a happier place to work than one with taboo topics and constrained communication, we are saying more than that. We are saying that an organization without ample and effective communication will carry out only haltingly and feebly the purposes its members hope for it.

Although many different activities, from ringing a fire alarm to reading a computer screen, can function as communication, this chapter will focus mainly on face-to-face verbal and nonverbal interactions between people in subsystems by means of which educational functions are carried out. The first section explains what is meant by unilateral, directive, and transactional communication; the second and third sections describe interpersonal communication; the fourth describes communication processes in subsystems; and the fifth considers communication in the organization as a whole. Instruments that the OD facilitator can use to assess communication are described in the fifth section. The sixth describes some exercises and procedures (microdesigns) we have used to enhance clear communication in educational organizations, and the seventh section summarizes some macrodesigns for raising the level of communicative effectiveness in systems.

Types of Communication

In its simplest form, *unilateral communication* is initiated by a speaker and terminated at a listener; examples in schools include reading the morning bulletins over the loudspeaker or making announcements at faculty meetings. Popular forms of unilateral communication in colleges include memos, newsletters, and e-mail. But much unilateral communication entails a second step as well. In studying the mass media, for example, Katz (1957) found that information from the media reaches certain opinion leaders who in turn relay it, as they understand it, to others in face-to-face interactions. Although this second step entails two-way communication, the event remains unilateral because the person who is the original source of information is unable to clarify any misunderstandings that may have occurred during the transmission of the information. Indeed any error in transmission is likely to be amplified during this second step.

In their study of the transmission of rumors, Allport and Postman (1945) describe three psychological processes that occur in the course of two-, three-, and four-step communications. In the first process, called leveling, the receiver tends to reduce contrasts between parts of a message—by omitting qualifying phrases, for example. In the second, the receiver sharpens certain parts of the information so that a few high points are remembered while most of the rest is forgotten. In the third, the receiver assimilates much of the message into his or her personal frame of reference, coloring memories and interpretations of the message by his or her own thoughts and feelings. For all these reasons, unilateral communication is not an efficient way of transmitting information even when it is supplemented by a second step.

In *directive communication*, which occurs face-to-face, the exchange is complete when the receiver indicates to the sender that the message has been received and understood, as when an instructor gives an assignment and students indicate that they understand the assignment. The distinguishing feature of a directive communication is that the sender influences while the receiver merely complies, as when one student tells another to get out of his way and the second obliges. McGregor (1967) calls this kind of communication coercive because there is no provision for mutual influence and exchange. It is assumed that the source's position is correct. The listener is required only to understand the message; acceptance is implied.

As Figure 4-1 demonstrates, *transactional communication* is a reciprocal process in which each participant initiates messages and attempts to understand the other. Information travels in both directions rather than in one direction only; each message has some impact on the next message, and the roles of source and receiver shift rapidly back and forth as communication takes place. Participants in transactional communication engage in active listening as well. The listener attempts to grasp both the facts and feelings of a message, attempts to increase his or her understanding by discerning the speaker's point of view, and tests this understanding by advising the speaker of personal reactions to the message, thereby helping the speaker know whether the meaning was or was not communicated. Elsewhere in this book we usually refer to this kind of communication as *two-way communication*.

While many misunderstandings can be resolved through transactional communication, carrying out effective transactions

Figure 4-1. Transactional Communication

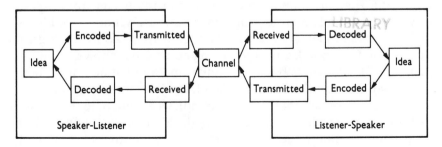

takes a high degree of communicative skill. Participants must be able to state their thoughts and feelings clearly, ask each other for specific information, read the relevance of gestures, and make sure that the message was apprehended correctly. This mutual feedback and spirit of helpfulness between participants is of crucial importance.

Interpersonal Communication

Educators communicate many different kinds of information to one another. They talk about the tasks they perform, the methods they use to get tasks accomplished, and sometimes, though rarely, their relations with one another. The content of face-to-face conversations can also be viewed as belonging to one or another aspect of a problem statement—that is, people talk about how things are (situations), how things ought to be (targets), or how to move from the situation to the target (proposals). As mentioned earlier, this is known as the *S-T-P* model of problem analysis and will be explained in detail in chapter 6.

Features of Effective Interpersonal Communication

Openness, communication during emotion, eliciting personal resources, and trust are features that cut across the three levels of interpersonal skill, subsystem effectiveness, and organizational adaptability described in chapter 1, and are extremely important signs of a readiness to begin organization development. Their presence not only sets a context for interpersonal communication but also oils the way for improving the interpersonal skills and other subsystem processes on which improvements in organizational adaptability depend.

Openness. Luft (1984) depicts openness by means of the following useful illustration known formally as the Johari Awareness Model and informally as the Johari Window (see Figure 4–2). In this model, a behavior, feeling, or motivation is assigned to one of four quadrants on the basis of who knows about it. Quadrant 1 refers to behavior, feelings, and motivation known both to oneself and to others (open); Quadrant 2 refers to that which is known to others but not to oneself (blind); Quadrant 3, to that which is known to oneself but not to others (hidden); and Quadrant 4, to that which is known neither to oneself nor to others (unknown).

Figure 4-2. Johari Awareness Model

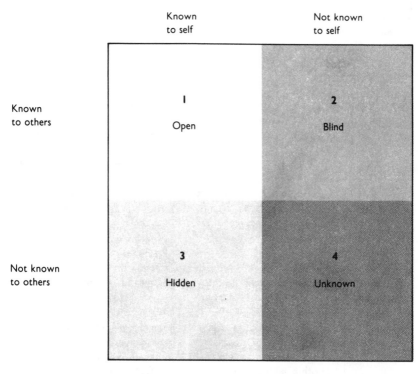

Source: Luft (1984).

Openness is the skill that increases the area of Quadrant 1 in relation to other quadrants.

Openness does not mean telling all, confiding indiscriminately, or giving information that is irrelevant to the work situation. It means giving information that both parties need in order to get work done or describing the feelings that are generated by people working together. By disclosing information that has heretofore been hidden, and by attempting to understand their blind spots, people can increase the total amount of information in the open quadrant.

As Figure 4–3 indicates, people communicate more or less openly depending upon the emotional closeness or distance they feel toward one another. In emotionally distant interactions, people know little about one another and view one another as objects that can either fulfill or frustrate their wishes and expectations. In emotionally close interactions, people recognize their interdependence with others, realizing that other people's behavior simultaneously influences and is influenced by their own behavior.

Figure 4-3. Emotional Closeness and Distance

**Degree of
closeness
depends
upon**
↓   **Close**   **Distant**

The *topic* we are talking about	Concerns our relation, you and me.	Concerns you or me.	Concerns people or things we both know directly.	Concerns people or things known to one of us directly.	Concerns people or things known directly to neither of us.
The *time* perspective	*Now:* Topic is happening now or something that helps us understand what is happening now.			*Then:* Topic is past or future happening, not related to what is happening now. *Or:* No time perspective, as in generalizations, jokes, etc.	
The *importance* of topic	Important to *both* of us.		Important to *one* of us.	Important to *neither* of us.	
How we use our *feelings*	Feelings are seen as natural; openly stating one's own feelings is viewed as helpful to both persons; each accepts the other's feelings.			Feelings are seen as unfortunate and disruptive; openly stating one's own feelings is avoided, so feelings are indirectly reflected in intellectualizations and judgments about the external world, including the other.	
How close the conversation is to *direct experience*	Conversation is composed of specific, tangible reports of observations and examples from direct experience.			Conversation is composed of abstract, vague generalizations without illustrative examples; no evidence is presented. The language is remote from any direct experience.	
How much *coercion* enters the interaction	Personal autonomy is respected; because each knows that the other must lead his own life, make his own decisions, face his own consequences, he offers information but does not try to persuade him to follow a certain course of action.			One or both attempts to convince, persuade, coerce, or manipulate the other to be like him or to do what he thinks should be done.	

Communication During Emotion. It is extremely important to know how to communicate during emotion, whether it is you or another person who is hurt, angry, or embarrassed. When strong feelings rise in a conversation, someone is likely to say, "Let's not get emotional about this." That is the mistake. First, few of us can turn our emotions off at a moment's notice. Over a long period, one can acquire the habit of *repressing* a great deal of emotion, but few of us can, in a fraction of a minute, change ourselves to do so. We can, however, choose certain actions in preference to others *while* feeling anger. For example, we can tell a person what happened to make us angry and tell the person explicitly our emotion: "I've spent an hour hunting for the overhead projector, and now I find that you borrowed it without telling anyone or leaving a note. I'm angry." That action maintains a better basis for future association with that person than silently showing an angry face to that person for the next hour or week, then shouting, "Some people sure don't care about anybody else!" and then punching the person in the face. We call the first kind of action *describing* emotion and the others merely *expressing* emotion.

Second, if you go along with the proposal not to "get emotional," all you can do is to *pretend* not to get emotional. All of us, for one reason or another, watch others closely for signs of emotion. Sooner or later, if only from sudden silences or sudden changes of the topic of conversation, we begin to guess when emotion is rising in the other person (though we may not know the kind of emotion or the cause of it). Agreeing to pretend that participants in a conversation are feeling no emotion merely gives the advantage to those who are more skillful at suppressing signs of their own emotion or more skillful at detecting emotion in others.

Third, if you do hide your emotion, you deprive the other person of information the person could use in being helpful to you. It is useful to your colleagues to know the kinds of ideas or events you want to embrace and the kinds you want to stay away from; emotions give important information about such matters. It is true that others can sometimes use information of that sort to do you harm; that is the reason that open and accurate exchanges of information require some degree of trust. It is also the reason that hiding emotion sends the message that you do not trust the other. That message leads the other person to mistrust you, and that display of mistrust leads you to confirm your distrust of him or her, and so on. But acting constructively and collaboratively while obviously feeling emotion invites reciprocation and trust.

Eliciting Personal Resources. Effective interpersonal communication also requires an awareness of one's need for the resources of others, and an awareness, too, of the virtue of offering one's own strengths, preferences, ideas, and feelings in finding solutions to problems of mutual concern. But some people are far more reticent about some of their personal resources than others, and they frequently require strong encouragement to state their feelings.

Wallen (1972) suggests several reasons that it is difficult to discuss one's feelings. First, many people have an unfavorable attitude toward emotion, often responding to someone else's expression of strong feelings with a variation of "please don't feel that way." Second, while actions and thoughts seem controllable, feelings seem to be uncontrollable. Third, we too often think that others have more control over our feelings than we have ourselves. To believe that others can make one angry, for example, is to acknowledge a surrender of some control over oneself. Feelings, in short, seem to threaten voluntary, planned control over one's own affairs.

Some people think that the teaching of communication skills typically overemphasizes trust and truth and underemphasizes power and conflict, but we like to stress both aspects in OD projects. Helping participants to voice their wants and at the same time helping problem-solving groups collaborate to reach a group consensus are both OD services, and it is true that educators should not shy away from the conflicts that often accompany differences in values. At the same time, in schools and colleges where interdependence is increasing, we value skillful collaboration above competitive conflict and believe that collaborative goals can best be achieved through methods that emphasize trust building and open communication.

OD facilitators must convince participants that feelings—whether of attraction, anxiety, interest, or resentment—provide important information that a group needs if work is to proceed efficiently and effectively and that to feel emotion toward another person is a sign of relatedness and interdependence. Acknowledging one's own feelings and the feelings of others eliminates unnecessary guesswork and makes available energy that is otherwise spent in concealing emotions.

Of course, there is much more to eliciting personal resources than hearing another's feelings. It also is important to help others tell about their experience and ideas and make suggestions about courses of action. OD facilitators must convince participants that ideas, however incomplete they might be, must be articulated and discussed if grass-roots participation is to work. The facilitator's skill entails both showing understanding and appreciation for ideas and linking participants' ideas during group deliberations.

Trust. Being open, communicating during emotion, and offering one's personal resources entail taking risks, and risk taking depends in turn on the presence of interpersonal trust, which is in many ways the key to enhanced communication even where true differences exist. A fragile quality on which a single action can have profoundly destructive consequences, trust is built very slowly and in small increments, is established more by deeds than by words, and is sustained by openness in interpersonal relations. But it is very difficult to achieve this quality in interpersonal relations, because being genuinely honest when an existing level of trust is low entails taking a very great risk. Perhaps this helps to explain why trust develops slowly and incrementally; if only small risks are taken, only small amounts of trust are built.

McGregor (1967) defined trust as the confidence that the other person will not take unfair advantage of one, either deliberately or accidentally, consciously or unconsciously. Trust is built between two people when each person is convinced that the other is both motivated and competent to sustain the relationship. Binding responses that diminish the other person's autonomy are likely to destroy trust; freeing responses that increase a sense of equality are likely to promote it. At the same time, however, the amount of gain or loss in trust depends on the amount that was present at the beginning; that is, a binding response is less binding and a freeing response less freeing when trust is low. Following is a list of interpersonal effects of various responses:

FREEING RESPONSES

- Listening attentively rather than merely remaining silent
- Paraphrasing and checking your impressions of the other's inner state
- Seeking information to understand the other
- Offering information that is relevant to the other's concern
- Describing observable behaviors that influence you
- Directly reporting your own feelings
- Offering your opinions or stating your value position

BINDING RESPONSES

- Changing the subject without explanation
- Interpreting the other's behavior by describing unchangeable experiences or qualities
- Advising and persuading
- Vigorously agreeing or obligating the other with "how could you?"

- Approving the other for conforming to your standards
- Commanding the other or demanding to be commanded

Interpersonal Communication Skills

The six skills described in the following subsections are neither new nor unique; indeed, they are tried and true methods of helping openness, communication during emotion, and an exchange of personal resources to occur. Those who regard the skills as gimmicks and use them perfunctorily or mechanically should not be surprised when results are disappointing. Merely becoming aware of communication skills will not in itself improve the ability to communicate. The skills must be applied consciously and strategically if they are to help overcome some of the difficulties in communication, and they must arise out of a genuine desire to understand the other person as an individual.

Of the six skills, *paraphrasing* (checking your understanding of the other person's meaning) and *impression checking* (checking your impression of the other person's feelings) are ways of helping you understand the other person. *Describing the other's behavior, describing your own behavior, making clear statements of your ideas*, and *describing your own feelings* aim at helping others to understand you. The six skills shown in Figure 4–4 are highly interdependent, so much so that it is virtually impossible to imagine a relationship of trust in which all six are not used at one time or another. The term *public information* refers to that which should

Figure 4-4. Relationships Among Six Communication Skills

	When the Information Is Public or Visible	*When the Information Is Private and Concerns Inner States*
To Be Open	Tell what you did that might have affected others by *describing your own behavior.*	Tell what you think by clearly *stating your own ideas.*
To Be Candid	Tell what others did that affects you as a group participant by *describing another's behavior.*	Let others know as clearly and unambiguously as possible about your own inner state by *describing your feelings.*
To Be Receptive	Check to make sure you understand the ideas of the other person by *paraphrasing.*	Check to make sure how the other person feels by *impression checking.*

already be known to oneself and to others. *Private information* is similar; it refers to what Luft has called blind or hidden in the Johari Awareness Model (Figure 4–2).

Every message and behavior has both a public and a private component, and senders, receivers, or observers always have seven choices: to say nothing, to describe their own behavior, to state their own ideas about the task-content, to describe others' behavior, to describe their own feelings, to paraphrase, or to check an impression of what the other is feeling. Consider, for example, the question of whether it is normal to feel sad at the end of the school year. If a student asks that of an instructor on the last day of class, the instructor might wish to check an impression that the student is feeling sad, describe his or her own feelings at the time, or even describe his or her own behavior in the past in relation to taking final exams. If a student teacher asks the same question in a college methods class, the professor might paraphrase to determine whether the student teacher is considering a research problem, and later perhaps give his or her own ideas about the issue. If a colleague sticks his head in your office for the fifth time one morning to ask the same question, and if you are annoyed by the repeated interruptions you might describe his behavior and your own feelings about it.

To acquire the six skills, the key to success is practice. OD facilitators should introduce the skills early and reinforce their use at every opportunity. With continuing practice, participants will become more skillful, and increased clarity of understanding will result. There is no given point at which one finally becomes skilled at communication, however. Each new person, relationship, and situation calls for practicing the skills anew, and no one should be excused on the grounds that he or she has "had that" elsewhere.

Paraphrasing

Many people mistakenly assume that they understand what another person has meant to convey without troubling to check whether the remark means the same thing to both of them or without giving the sender any evidence that the remark has in fact been understood. As we use the word here, paraphrasing denotes any method of showing other people how you have apprehended their meaning. By testing your understanding against their intentions you show them that you want to understand and you invite them to clarify their meaning if you have not understood them correctly.

As the following example from Wallen (1972) demonstrates,

simply repeating another person's ideas in different words can result in a mere illusion of mutual understanding.

SARAH: Jim should never have become a teacher.
FRED: You mean teaching isn't the right job for him?
SARAH: Exactly. Teaching is not the right job for Jim.

Instead of trying to reword Sara's statement, Fred should have asked himself "What does this statement mean to me?" In that case the exchange might have gone this way:

SARAH: Jim should never have become a teacher.
FRED: You mean he is too harsh on the children? Maybe even cruel?
SARAH: No, I meant that he has such expensive tastes that he can't earn enough as a teacher.
FRED: Oh, I see. You think he should have gone into a field that would have ensured him a higher standard of living.
SARAH: Exactly! Teaching is not the right job for Jim.

A general statement may convey something specific to you.

LARRY: I'd like to own this book.
YOU: Does it contain useful information?
LARRY: I don't know about that. I meant that the binding is beautiful.

A very specific statement may convey a more general idea to you.

RALPH: Do you have twenty-five pencils I can borrow for my class?
YOU: Do you just want something for them to write with? I have about fifteen ballpoint pens and ten or eleven pencils.
RALPH: Great. Anything that will write will do.

The comments of another person may possibly suggest an example to you.

LAURA: This text has too many omissions; we shouldn't adopt it.
YOU: Do you mean, for example, that it contains nothing about the role of ethnic minorities in the development of America?
LAURA: Yes, that's one example. It also lacks any discussion of the development of the arts in America.

Skillful paraphrasing thus requires an ability to make generalizations, identify examples, and think of opposites. Developing these abilities requires trying out different ways of discovering the kinds of responses most helpful to you.

Checking Your Impression of Others' Emotions

Inferences drawn from the words, tone, gestures, or facial expressions of another person are often inaccurate, not least because we may unconsciously attribute to that person our own feelings, attitudes, or desires. "Impression checking" involves describing what you perceive to be the other person's emotional state in order to determine whether you have accurately decoded his or her expressions of feeling. That is, you transform expressions of feeling into tentative descriptions, such as, "I get the impression that you're angry with me. Are you?" "Am I right that you're feeling disappointed because no one commented on your suggestion?" "I'm uncertain as to whether your expression means that my comment hurt your feelings, irritated you, or confused you. Can you help me?"

Skillful impression checking requires observing nonverbal clues, drawing tentative inferences from them, clearly describing the inferred feeling, and indicating that you are at this point guessing. An impression check aims to convey the fact that you wish to understand the other person's feelings in order to avoid actions based on false assumptions about them; it does not express approval or disapproval of the feelings.

Describing Another's Behavior

For most of us it is not easy to describe another person's behavior clearly enough for that person to understand which actions are affecting us. Indeed, instead of describing observable behavior, we usually discuss internal states or processes such as attitudes, motivations, and personality traits, often unaware that our conclusions are based less on observable evidence than on our own feelings of affection, insecurity, irritation, jealousy, or fear. Accusations that impute undesirable motives to another, for example, are usually not descriptions at all but are rather expressions of the speaker's unpleasant feelings toward the other. Yet if we are to discuss the way we work together or what is occurring in our relationships, we must be able to talk about what each of us does that affects the other.

Behavior description means reporting specific observable actions of others without judging those actions as good or bad or right or wrong, and without making generalizations or accusations about the other person's motives, attitudes, or personality traits. As the following examples illustrate, it also means describing the actions clearly and specifically enough for others to know what you have observed. To remind yourself to describe specific actions, it is helpful to begin with "I see that . . ." or "I noticed that. . ., or "I heard you say . . ."

Example: "Jim, you've talked more than others on this topic. Several times you've cut off others before they had finished." (Not "Jim, you're too rude," which identifies a trait and gives no evidence, or "Jim, you always want to hog the center of attention," which imputes an undesirable motive or intention.)

Example: "Bob, you've taken the opposite position on nearly everything that Harry has suggested today." (Not "Bob, you're just trying to show Harry up," which is an accusation of an undesirable motivation, or "Bob, you're being stubborn," which is name calling.)

Example: "Sam, you cut in before I had finished." (Not "Sam, you deliberately didn't let me finish," which implies that Sam knowingly and intentionally cut you off. All that anyone can observe is that he cut in before you had finished.)

To develop skill in describing behavior you must sharpen your observation of what actually occurred, pay attention to that which is observable, recognize when you are making inferences, and be able to couch them in language that reflects both their tentative nature and your desire to check them out.

Describing One's Own Feelings

Reporting one's own inner state provides the additional information necessary if two people are to understand and improve their relationship; certainly, others need to know how you feel if they are to take your feelings into account. Unhappy feelings should not be ignored; they signal that something may be going wrong in a relationship and that the two parties need to check for misunderstandings or faulty communication. In describing your own feelings, however, your aim should be to open a dialogue that will improve the relationship; it should not be to coerce the other into changing so you won't feel as you do. Although the other person may behave differently on learning what distracts, distresses, or pleases you, you may also discover that *your* feelings are based on false perceptions and should themselves be changed.

To let others try to divine your feelings without a direct description of them is chancy. Emotions can be expressed in bodily changes, actions, and words; a specific expression can indicate myriad feelings (a blush may indicate pleasure, annoyance, embarrassment, or uneasiness, and what appears first to be an expression of anger may turn out to result from hurt feelings or fear); and a particular feeling is not always expressed in the same way (fright may result in widened eyes and mouth, in hugging oneself, or in leaving the room).

One way to describe a feeling is to name it and use *I*, *me*, or *my* to indicate that you own the feeling—for example, "I feel angry," "I feel embarrassed," or "I feel comfortable with you." Another way is to report the kind of action the feeling urges you to take: "I feel like hugging you," "I'd like to slap you," or "I wish I could walk off and leave you." A feeling can also be specified by means of simile ("I feel like a tiny frog in a huge pond") or of metaphor ("I just swallowed a bushel of spring sunshine"). Finally, as the following examples demonstrate, any one expression of feeling can actually represent a number of quite different descriptions of feeling.

EXPRESSIONS OF FEELING	DESCRIPTIONS OF FEELING
Person blushes and says nothing.	"I feel embarrassed." "I feel pleased." "I feel annoyed."
Person suddenly becomes silent in the midst of a conversation.	"I feel angry." "I'm worried about this." "I feel as if I've been slapped."
"She's a wonderful person."	"I enjoy her sense of humor." "I respect her abilities." "I love her but feel I shouldn't say so."
"Shut up!"	"I hurt too much to hear any more." "I feel angry at myself." "I'm angry at you."
"You shouldn't have bought me such an expensive gift!"	"I really like your gift." "I feel obligated to you and I resent it." "I feel inferior to you when I think of the cheap present I gave you.

Describing One's Own Behavior

This skill is similar to that of describing another's behavior. The actions described might have occurred previously in the same group or they might have occurred in another setting. The usual intent of the skill is to reveal weaknesses or inadequacies in one's own behavior that will help to establish empathy and understanding with the others.

We think of this skill under the more general label of openness. The speaker shows that he or she is aware of personal mistakes or errors of judgment and is willing to announce them publicly in the group. At times such revelations can be accompanied by humor as long as the receivers understand that the sender is also being serious. To use the skill is to say, "Look, I did some things myself in this group that weren't so helpful. Remember when I did _____." This indicates that to make an error is human and to be expected and that we should all be open to feedback and willing to change.

Sometimes, too, the skill of describing one's own behavior is used not to display a weakness, but simply to clarify what the sender is trying to convey. It stands as an example of the main message. By way of illustration, one might wish to check impressions of how another is feeling. In the course of such checking, it could be useful to present an example of one's own behavior and the feelings that accompanied it.

Stating One's Own Ideas

This skill might appear to be the easiest of all, but for many people it is difficult. The skill entails using words that are understandable to the receivers, putting the words together in a logical flow, and limiting the length of one's string of words. This calls for putting a check on one's jargon and use of special language, defining terms that might be misunderstood, thinking through the major points in the fashion of an outline, pausing to check impressions of others' understanding, and being succinct.

Giving and Receiving Feedback

Giving or receiving feedback is not a single skill in the way the six we have described above are. All six of the basic skills come into play when one is giving or receiving feedback. At the same time, many communicative acts using one of the six basic skills become feedback. Feedback is so intertwined with the six basic skills that we include it here as a kind of wrapping around them.

The concept of feedback originated in the field of cybernetics, the study of automatic control mechanisms in machines and living organisms. It refers to an error-correcting process in which information about a system's output is returned as input so that the system can control its own performance. Because of its circularity, the term *loop* is often used to describe the feedback process.

In human communication, feedback consists of information sent by the receiver back to the source of a message so that the original sender can gauge the effect of the message. By comparing this effect with the intention behind the communication, the original sender can adjust his or her subsequent message, which can serve as the stimulus for further feedback, which in turn can be used to modify the succeeding message, and so on. Ideally, sender and receiver will continue to use this circular mode of interaction until the desired level of accuracy is achieved.

The feedback process is a two-way endeavor and should not be regarded primarily as a way for the listener to aid the speaker. Mutual feedback, a cardinal feature of transactional communication, is achieved when the person giving feedback is also given information that will help gauge the effect of the feedback. Thus each communicator can help the other to become skillful in using feedback to the benefit of their mutual communication. To communicate transactionally with another person requires a great expenditure of time and energy, although limited evidence suggests that the need for great amounts of feedback diminishes with continued use (see, for example, Leavitt and Mueller, 1951).

Without mutual feedback, miscommunications—discrepancies between intended and received messages—occur frequently, partly because certain behaviors are more difficult than others for some persons to perform, partly because of the confusion that arises from an effort to express oneself authentically while attempting to perform in ways meant to be attractive to others. To try to impress others is not necessarily to be phony; it is a natural phenomenon that enables people to cope more easily with superficial social events. But superficiality and self-concealment are often detrimental to effective transactional communication.

Whether it is given or received, feedback can best be carried out if the following guidelines are observed:

1. *Noncoercive.* Feedback should be given so that it does not require the recipient to change his or her behavior.
2. *Consideration.* Feedback should be given after a careful assessment has been made of the recipient's feelings. This does not mean, for example, that you should avoid showing anger to the other person; it means that the other should be ready to deal with it productively.
3. *Descriptive.* Feedback should involve a clear report of the facts rather than an explanation of why things happened as they did.
4. *Recency.* Feedback should be given close to the time of the events causing reaction. "Gunnysacks" full of grievances are hard to carry and can burst at inopportune times.
5. *Changeability.* Feedback should be given about behavior that can be changed. It is not helpful, for example, to tell people that you are bothered by the color of their eyes.

Finally, mutual feedback must arise out of a true wish for the welfare of the other person. Each participant should want to find ways of moving psychologically closer to the other and of helping that person to grow, for without such concern transactional communication will be hollow. Even when caring is keenly felt by all parties, however, the decision of whether to give feedback is not easy to make, perhaps because feedback seems to imply a desire to change the receiver. To say, for example, "You've been quiet all through the meeting, and I feel anxious" is to imply that the receiver should speak up more often. To this, the receiver might reply, "I'm comfortable speaking no more than I do. Why don't you learn to accept my quietness?" If the same feedback with its implied demand for change had been given many times before, an irritated receiver might snap, "Get off my back! I like being quiet!"

In such a case, senders must decide whether to pursue a request for change or to accept the other person's behavior. If senders consider their own values, explore the possibility of accepting the other, and still experience the other's behavior as a violation of certain basic values, the receiver deserves to know that. If senders can widen the band of behaviors that they find acceptable, feedback can be withheld until something more important happens. Senders might also reexamine their own values to find reasons why the behavior initially appeared unacceptable and thereby change themselves instead of trying to change the receiver. In other words, feedback is not just a process of requesting another person to change, but can often begin the process of changing oneself.

Communication in the Subsystem

Although much of the work in educational organizations is accomplished through communication exchanges between two persons, the work of people in groups—cabinets, departments, committees, and teams—is very important as well. As groups increase in size, especially as they exceed three or four members, new issues and communication problems arise. Since only one person can speak at a time and since speakers must follow one another serially, it is inevitable that some members will have more "air time" than others. Indeed, group norms develop about the appropriate amount of talking time for each member of the group. When a norm supports speaking by the leader but by few others, for example, communication will be confined to a very small subgroup, with the rest of the group participating as a passive audience.

Group members who remain silent at formal meetings may nevertheless do a great deal of informal communicating with colleagues in clusters based on such factors as shared responsibility, personal attraction, and the physical location of the work space. Although informal communication often serves a social function rather than the function of promoting work, at most educational organizations, formal meetings are so poorly conducted that informal communication is necessary for tasks to be completed adequately.

Problems arise when informal communications run counter to formal communications. Most formal communication is followed by interactions in small informal groups that strive to achieve an adequate understanding of the original message. When the original message is distorted by these informal discussions, problems of coordination arise for the organization. When the most influential members of the informal networks disagree with the views and decisions of the formal leaders, the messages from the informal leaders often take precedence over the formal communications. A breakdown in authority then occurs and norms about decision making become ambiguous, leading to the development of distrust in a work situation, the more so when differences of opinion and belief are kept private.

OD facilitators should gather data on both formal and informal communication networks to help group members become more aware of the effects of these patterns. Examining how communication structures affect small-group performance, Leavitt (1951) found that differences in degree of satisfaction, accuracy, time spent at problem solving, and the emergence of a leader were all related to the type of network involved. The quality of performance in Leavitt's groups improved when one person or a subgroup in the group had communicative contact with all other members of the group, and the satisfaction of members increased as each gained some power through communication to influence the way the group performed.

The OD facilitator also gives attention to the type of information that passes through communication channels and networks: the amount of time that the group devotes to sharing information about a task, the methods to be used, the interpersonal feelings that emerge, as well as the situations, targets, and plans. Figure 4–5 shows these six kinds of information in a matrix of nine combinations. Examples of the kinds of statements that fall in each cell accompany the figure. The ultimate payoffs for groups result from high-quality work in Cell 3, although high-quality task proposals do not come out of thin air; groups must exchange information in all cells regularly.

The amount of energy a subsystem expends on each topic of communication is governed in part by communication norms. In

Figure 4-5. Content of Subsystem Communication

Aspects of problem analysis

		Situation	Target	Proposal
Level of analysis	Task	I	2	3
	Methods	4	5	6
	Interpersonal	7	8	9

Cell 1: There are more students in Class A than in Class B.
Mary doesn't like to teach large classes.

Cell 2: We ought to interest more students in taking Class B.
Mary should have a smaller class at least one semester of the year.

Cell 3: We can get more students to elect Class B by adding two field trips.
Mary can have the first chance at encouraging her students to transfer into that class.

Cell 4: Our staff meetings usually last two hours.
The principal observes in most classrooms only once or twice a year.

Cell 5: We should come to meetings prepared to discuss agenda items.
The principal should spend more time in classrooms before evaluating teachers.

Cell 6: We will start our meetings a half-hour later to give people time for preparation.
Teachers will rotate playground duty so that the principal is freed for observations.

Cell 7: I'm pleased that everyone participated at this meeting.
Only half of us feel influential regarding decisions about X.

Cell 8: We should always make sure that everyone who has something to say gets a chance to speak.
We should reconsider who is to be involved in decision making about X in the future.

Cell 9: The convener of the meeting will periodically ask if all who wish to speak have had a chance.
We'll give two days' notice before making another X decision so that interested persons can be contacted.

some groups, for example, no one expects anyone to exchange information about the interpersonal feelings that emerge from members working together. Other groups might exhibit a norm supporting regular interpersonal-process debriefings. Norms also specify rewards for openness, communicating during emotion, and eliciting statements of personal resources. Subsystem norms specifying what people should or should not talk about greatly influence the degree to which interpersonal communication skill will be displayed.

It should be noted, however, that information is always distorted to some degree as it passes from one person to others. When most group members distort a message in the same way, as when a majority of group members believes an untrue thing to be true, a condition of pluralistic ignorance is said to exist. In many groups, an effective strategy for dealing with pluralistic ignorance in relation to interpersonal matters is to use the Team-Expectation Survey described later.

The OD facilitator could collect interview or questionnaire data that illustrate pluralistic ignorance. By feeding these data back to the group and encouraging discussion of obvious discrepancies, the facilitator can help the participant group to improve the accuracy of information at its disposal. To facilitate clearer communication, the facilitator can also teach groups to use the following procedures or activities during their regular meetings. (For further discussion of some of these procedures, see chapter 5 under "Exercises and Procedures for Improving Meetings.")

1. *The Right to Listen.* Typically, faculty meetings are run so that members have their say without much regard to whether they are understood by others. A procedure that can help to ameliorate this situation is to require a member before speaking to paraphrase what the last person has said, both to indicate understanding of the previous speaker and to ensure some continuity in the discussion. If the speaker cannot paraphrase the previous speaker's remark, the remark was probably either too vague or too rambling. The remark should be repeated, but with amplification if it was too short and fewer words if too long. The convener or chair can assume the duty of ensuring each participant both the chance to be heard and the chance to listen or to paraphrase.

2. *Time Tokens.* To assure that members initiate no more than their share of comments, poker chips can be equally divided among group members with the stipulation that one chip be tossed into the "pot" when a member makes a statement. In addition to sensitizing the group to frequency of participation,

this procedure often leads members to make long speeches, so that the group also becomes aware of the negative effects of a series of prolonged monologues.

3. *High-Talker Tap-Out.* In this procedure, a group monitor notifies a speaker when he or she has exceeded a given time limit, either by giving a tap on the shoulder or by handing over a card on which an explanation has previously been typed. At the monitor's notification, the person notified drops out of the discussion by moving back a few feet. When only two people are left and have had their chances to contribute, the entire group discusses feelings and responses to the process. Such an activity often makes it easier to confront established patterns of discussion and decision making, offering an opportunity to discuss reasons for infrequent participation and perhaps to increase the number of persons involved in decision making.

4. *Thumbs Up.* It is often difficult for groups to carry on meaningful discussion while simultaneously monitoring their group functioning. If group members have trouble recognizing when they are ready to make a decision, for example, members might give a thumbs-up signal when they are ready to state their opinions and test whether others agree with them. If a group decides to monitor the use of a newly acquired communication skill, each member would display thumbs up when another member uses a skill effectively and thumbs down when an unhelpful comment is expressed. The use of this procedure can create stress, particularly when a unanimous thumbs-down signal is presented, but some of this stress can be productively harnessed if the group periodically discusses the procedure and its implications.

5. *Taking a Survey.* In a survey, one member of the group asks for the opinions of all others on a specific issue ("I'd like to know what everyone thinks of this proposal right now"); then some other member paraphrases the request until all members understand what they are being asked. All members in turn state their positions on the topic in one or at most three sentences. The members might also express uncertainty, confusion, a desire to hear more, or they might admit they have nothing to say. Each person must say something, however, and as soon as everyone has stated a position, someone summarizes the group's position—for example, "Only two people seem to have reservations about the proposal," or "Only the third, fourth, and ninth ideas seem to have captured our interest." Group members should not confuse a survey with a vote,

although a survey does sometimes become one. Sometimes a survey is used to test the water instead of as a way of ascertaining commitment. In any case, the person requesting the survey should make clear what it is intended to accomplish.

Generally, a survey should be taken at the time it is requested, superseding any other activity. If group members using this procedure for the first time find it too cumbersome or too mechanical, they might take a minute to plan their response before the survey starts, or flash thumbs up if they think a survey is a good idea at that time and thumbs down if they would prefer to wait. This procedure, like all others, should periodically be talked about by group members.

6. *Sitting in a Circle.* Although arranging group seating in a circle soon becomes automatic behavior for OD projects, group members sometimes forget the importance of this procedure when an OD facilitator is absent. Close circular seating has two advantages: nonverbal behaviors are more easily sent and received when each person has an unobstructed view of everyone else, and equal participation is encouraged when there is no podium or head of the table to suggest that any particular member should assume leadership. When it is desirable to record information on a chalkboard or on newsprint, the circle can be opened into a horseshoe arrangement so that all have an unobstructed view of the recorder.

7. *Fishbowls.* In large groups too much time may be used if everyone speaks on an issue. In this case the OD facilitator may institute a procedure whereby those in an inner circle talk while those in a concentric outer circle listen. Those on the outside may still contribute if there is an empty chair in the inner circle to which they can move when they have something to say, or if those in the inner circle occasionally turn around to confer with or receive coaching from them. A fishbowl is a kind of working through representatives in a rapid and responsive way.

8. *Video Taping or Audio Recording.* Video-taped and (the less dramatic) audio-recorded segments of a meeting can provide excellent feedback and stimulate a group to review its own functioning. But both techniques require a skilled technician who can judge what to record and can quickly find important bits of interaction to play back. Replaying a two-hour meeting is usually time-consuming and frustrating, while delaying the feedback until someone can edit the tapes could destroy part of the drama. Relying on transcription of tapes as the sole record of a meeting can cause frustrating delays when

important decisions are being made. Nonetheless, well-made tapes are extremely useful for teaching group members to observe communication and other group processes.

Organization-Wide Communication

Communication in the organization as a whole can best be observed by attending to the regularized procedures through which it occurs. The OD facilitator looks at regular and legitimate channels of communication among subsystems, the regularity with which information from the organization's environment is discussed, the time that elapses between problem identification and responsive action, the regularity with which extra resources in one task group are used by another, and the like.

By formal channels of communication we mean interactions that are sanctioned by the organization and that carry information of the officially relevant acts; examples are announcements in bulletins or newsletters, faculty or departmental meetings, and curriculum committee meetings. Informal channels—such as coffee-break conversations among departmental colleagues or parking-lot debriefings of faculty meetings—are not officially required; nor do they typically carry much of the kind of information that flows through the formal channels. Indeed, informal channels are kept alive precisely for the reason that they carry kinds of communication the formal channels reject.

When the official channels fail to transmit information important to the organization's functioning, or when useful information is crowded out by irrelevancies, the OD facilitator can sometimes help by examining the formal channels that are supplementing the official channels. Sometimes a new formal channel can be built on the model of an informal channel.

Likert (1961) has distinguished a form of organizing that he terms "link-pin structure." A link-pin function is performed by a person or subgroup that participates in two or more separate communication networks, carrying information up and down and across groups that would normally not otherwise communicate. To be sure, it is not unusual for a principal to attend teachers' meetings or student council sessions to report decisions of an administrative team; but it is very unusual for a teacher or student to sit with an administrative team or for a group of people (instead of an individual) from one level to engage in face-to-face communication with a group from another level. The OD facilitator should be alert to the possibility of building unique link-pin structures to promote an accurate flow of information within an educational organization.

As chapter 10 will explain, a cadre of part-time organizational specialists is an important link-pin structure, because its members work in and among different subsystems, thereby gaining access to much important information. Further, representatives of cadre intervention teams serve as link-pins to the cadre coordinator through a steering committee. Finally, another report of our work (see Schmuck et al., 1975) has shown how OD facilitation can create team-leader roles and how team leaders can serve as link-pins in schools with teams of teachers.

However laudable increased information flow may be, it is more helpful to identify specific organizational problems first and only then to introduce changes aimed at helping the organization solve the problems. An organized system implies a restricted number of channels that can be used to perform a specific function; to move from one organized state to another may require new norms supporting the use of only certain channels while omitting others or reserving them for organizationally irrelevant purposes. Changing norms requires much time and effort and should not be undertaken lightly.

A way of combining the link-pin idea with the need for dealing with specific organizational problems is to structure a college, for example, in the form of a matrix. For example, the columns of the matrix could be the academic departments. The rows of the matrix could represent some of the overriding tasks or problems faced by the whole college, such as consistency in grading, continuity from one semester to another or among subjects, student involvement, racial and ethnic integration, and the like. The key to our version of the matrix structure is for members from each of the departments to form the membership of a task force, thereby increasing the effectiveness of communication in the whole college.

The larger the educational organization, the more important it is to provide clarity about channels that carry task-related information. In a group of six persons, for example, each can communicate with all five others; there are only 15 channels to contend with altogether. An organization of 60 persons, by contrast, contains 1,770 possible pair-channels. Unless people in larger organizations know clearly to whom they should go for what kinds of information, the results are likely to include overloaded channels, pluralistic ignorance, and insufficient information to do the job. A matrix structure as we have used it in which every staff member takes part in at least two formal subsystems (an instructional unit and a collegewide task force) can be an effective form for facilitating communication in colleges.

Though we advocate clear designation of the channels to be used for formal organizational purposes, we also value freedom to use any channel for informal purposes. In our view, organizational life is better when hierarchical lines and specialized subsystems do not prevent people from reaching out to one another for support, comfort, or good times. Although teachers may have to go to administrators for information about budget procedures, for example, they should not be prohibited by either time or architectural constraints from interaction with one another.

Gathering Data About Communication

The first source of data about communication in colleges or schools is the facilitator's own informal observations. The facilitator should be alert to note how staff members talk to one another in meetings, in the hallways, and in the faculty lounge. Are people trying to make their positions known and to persuade others while actually talking past one another and showing an unwillingness to hear what others are saying? Are unpleasant feelings remaining hidden, are feelings of others being ignored, is little checking done to ascertain what others are thinking, are voices quickly becoming loud and emphatic regardless of the issue, and is there a lot of talk about trivial issues but little about important needs and issues? If so, the faculty's communication skills are probably weak, and a fair amount of conflict will probably come out before any real collaborative problem solving is possible.

On the other hand, the facilitator must keep in mind ideal staff communication and seek illustrations of it. For example, are there people checking to make sure they understand what others are saying? Are there instances when people seem to feel free to report directly to others the sorts of things that are bothering them? The facilitator could find such behavior in the very first meeting with a faculty committee. If so, he or she should make a special effort to comment on how helpful and difficult it is to be open during meetings in most educational organizations. The facilitator should also stay alert to the kinds of topics that come up for discussion. Do they entail instruction, the curriculum, the students' quality of life, citizens' responses to the target system, and the like? If so, the facilitator should tell the staff how unusual and special it is for groups of educators to collaborate on such critical issues.

All this observation and reaction to faculty members comes before a formal diagnosis. The questionnaires and observation forms that follow can be used to diagnose problems of communication in a much more formal and systematic manner. They can also be used, of course, by administrators and faculty members for gathering data from their own groups. In some cases, the data can be presented to the group immediately after they have been collected, or a questionnaire can be administered and scored during a single meeting. In other cases, the facilitator or participants can summarize lengthy questionnaires or the data from several observation periods and present the summary to the group later. Guidelines for feeding data back to the group are detailed in chapter 9.

The Knowledge and Use of Communication Skills

The questionnaire below was developed by Robert Crosby and John Wallen to assess a participant's recognition of communication skills (unpublished). Members of the group may wish to compare their answers and discuss their differences.

This questionnaire, as well as a good many others in this book, is not intended to show who is right or better than other people at communicating. There are no right answers; there is no scoring key. The questionnaire is intended to stimulate conversation about communication—not in the abstract, elsewhere, at some other time, but in the present among these actual people. It enables people to find out how they sound to one another when they talk in certain ways.

Concepts About Communication ─────────────────────

Communication is much more than words. It includes tone of voice, facial expressions, posture, gestures, and eye contact or lack of it. But words are also important. If they match the tone of voice, etc., one's communication message is clear and congruent. This questionnaire is about communication by words. Please do not infer tone, etc., but rather focus on the words.

Section I: Description of the speaker's feelings. Before each sentence below that represents a description of feelings, put an X.

1. _____ What a lovely day!
2. _____ I'm bored and confused!
3. _____ Cut it out!
4. _____ I feel like I'm on a pedestal.
5. _____ Why can't you ever be any place on time?
6. _____ You're a very interesting conversationalist.
7. _____ You shouldn't have bought me such an expensive gift.
8. _____ I feel that he didn't care if he hurt my feelings.
9. _____ Go jump in the lake!
10. _____ I feel this is an easy text.

Section II: Behavior description. Put an X before each sentence representing a description of behavior.

11. _____ Joe interrupted Harry.
12. _____ Harry was sincere.
13. _____ Harry misinterpreted Joe.
14. _____ Joe was discouraged.
15. _____ Harry's voice got louder when he said, "Cut it out, Joe."
16. _____ Joe was trying to make Harry mad.
17. _____ Harry talked more than Joe did.
18. _____ Joe was dismayed by Harry's statements.
19. _____ Joe said nothing when Harry said, "Cut it out."
20. _____ Harry knew that Joe was feeling discouraged.

Section III: Impression check. Put an X before each sentence representing an impression check.

21. _____ Are you angry with me?
22. _____ I can tell that you're embarrassed.
23. _____ Why are you mad at me?
24. _____ Did my statement cause you to feel put down?
25. _____ What Jim said obviously upset you.
26. _____ You seem unhappy.
27. _____ Your feelings get hurt pretty easily, don't they?
28. _____ Oh, heck, are your feelings hurt again?
29. _____ What is it about Bill that makes you resent him so much?
30. _____ You're not getting mad again, are you?

Section IV: *Personalness* in which the speakers reveal something about their private life versus *openness* in which the speakers tell their reaction to the other person. Put an X before each sentence expressing openness.

31. _____ I've enjoyed our time together tonight.
32. _____ I'm annoyed at your making fun of me.
33. _____ I've never been able to cope with authority figures.
34. _____ I'm seeing a counselor regularly.
35. _____ Sometimes I feel so discouraged and frightened that I'm afraid I'll commit suicide.
36. _____ I envy you.
37. _____ I'm beginning to tune out because you are telling me so much detail.
38. _____ I'm afraid people would disapprove of me if they knew my background.
39. _____ I'm very fond of you.
40. _____ I felt hurt and disappointed when you said you didn't want to hear about my difficult time with those students.

Cognitive awareness is insufficient in itself to ensure the use of communication skills. The observation form shown in Figure 4–6 can be used to provide information regarding the actual use of the skills by specific individuals and to obtain frequency counts for the use of each type of skill per unit of time. The latter measure can be used to compare use of the various skills by two different groups or by the same group on two separate occasions.

Figure 4-6. Instances of Use of Communication Skills

Name of group: _____

Time at start of tally: _____   Time at end: _____

Tally each instance of initiation of each skill by each person.

Names or symbols of participants	Para- phrase	Behavior description (other)	Behavior description (own)	Feeling description
_____	_____	_____	_____	_____
_____	_____	_____	_____	_____
_____	_____	_____	_____	_____
_____	_____	_____	_____	_____

Names or symbols of participants	Impression check	State idea (own)	Give feedback	Ask for survey
_____	_____	_____	_____	_____
_____	_____	_____	_____	_____
_____	_____	_____	_____	_____
_____	_____	_____	_____	_____

Actual and Perceived Participation

Participation in a group discussion may vary over the course of time because of differences in task involvement, in feelings about the group, or in such factors as fatigue or preoccupation with matters outside the life of the group. The facilitator must sample participation several times during a meeting, and perhaps at several different meetings, before arriving at an adequate measure of actual and typical participation. The form in Figure 4–7 can be used to sample actual participation in a task-centered group. The facilitator may also wish to have group members provide subjective estimates of member participation by means of the form in Figure 4–8, even though the objective and subjective measures will often be highly correlated. In any case, the subjective data can be compared with an observer's more objective tallies, or it can be fed back to group members as a stimulus for group self-analysis. The estimates should represent participation during a specific time period, usually the time just before the ratings are made. (See Figure 5–2, chapter 5, for another tallying method.)

Figure 4-7. Members' Participation: Observer's Form

(1) Take three ten-minute samples at early, middle, and late stages of each meeting observed. (2) Tally at ten-second intervals to indicate who is talking at that instant. (3) Write the times that observation begins and ends in the spaces provided.

Sample Observation Form

Observer: _____   Date: _____

                                        Page no.: _____

                                        Time begun: _____

                                        Time ended: _____

Persons in group
(Name or code number)   Tallies of participation

_____   _____

_____   _____

Norms About Communicating

If they are to perform effectively, all group members must know what behaviors other members expect. This section offers

Figure 4-8. Members' Participation: Estimate by Group Members

Each member should be given enough copies of the rating form to rate everyone in the group. After the ratings are completed, all members are given all the estimates of their participation so they can study and total their individual ratings.

Sample Rating Form

Name of member being rated: _____

Please rate other members in the group on the following scales. Circle the appropriate number from 0 (low) to 6 (high).

I.   How much did he or she participate?

0	I	2	3	4	5	6
None						A great deal

2.   How well did he or she listen to other members?

0	I	2	3	4	5	6
Little or none						Very well

three questionnaires that can be used to identify norms about communication in the group and to determine the amount of agreement that exists about a specific norm.

Do's and Don'ts

In any educational organization, there are informal "do's and don'ts." They are rarely written down anywhere, but they serve as a kind of code, making it clear what educators in the system should and should not do if they are to be accepted by others.

Below is a list of specific things that a person—an administrator, an instructor, a staff member—might do or say. We would like you to estimate what most people in your system would feel about each item. That is, we want you to tell us whether the predominant feeling of most of the people is that one should or should not do or say the thing in question. You can indicate your answer by placing a check mark in the appropriate column beside each item.

	Should publicly	Should privately	Should not publicly	Should not privately
I. Ask others who seem upset to express their feelings directly.	___	___	___	___
2. Tell colleagues what you really think of their work.	___	___	___	___
3. Look for ulterior motives in other people's behavior.	___	___	___	___

4. Always ask, "Why?" when you don't know.
5. Avoid disagreement and conflict whenever possible.
6. Question well-established ways of doing things.
7. Disagree with your superior if you happen to know more about the issue than he or she does.
8. Withhold personal feelings and stick to the logical merits of the case in any discussion.
9. Push for new ideas, even if they are vague or unusual.
10. Ask others to tell you what they really think of your work.
11. Keep your real thoughts and reactions to yourself, by and large.
12. Trust others not to take advantage of you.
13. Be skeptical about things.
14. Point out other people's mistakes, to improve working effectiveness.
15. Try out new ways of doing things, even if it is uncertain how they will work out.

The next questionnaire is excellent for checking the pervasiveness of pluralistic ignorance in a group. It also is excellent for showing people how ready (or unready) they are to talk openly with one another. People not only answer for themselves but estimate how others will answer. The content of the expectations can be changed to fit the situation. If, for example, English teachers were asked how many science teachers they would be willing to work with and how many science teachers would like to work with them, science teachers in turn would be asked how many English teachers they wanted to work with and how many English teachers wanted to work with them.

Team-Expectation Survey

Directions: In the blanks before each of the items below enter a number from the following rating scale that best expresses your opinion at this time.

Rating Scale

5 = All members of this group
4 = All members except one or two
3 = A slight majority of the members of this group

- -

2 = Slightly less than half the members of this group
1 = One or two members of this group
0 = None of this group

A. Others' Candidness

How many members of this group do you expect will candidly report the following information during future group sessions?

_____ 1. When they do not understand something you said?

_____ 2. When they like something you said or did?

_____ 3. When they disagree with something you said?

_____ 4. When they think you have changed the subject or become irrelevant?

_____ 5. When they feel impatient or irritated with something you said they did?

_____ 6. When they feel hurt—rejected, embarrassed, or put down—by something you said or did?

B. Your Candidness

With respect to how many members will you candidly report the following information during future group sessions?

_____ 7. When you do not understand something a member said?

_____ 8. When you like something a member said or did?

_____ 9. When you disagree with something a member said?

_____ 10. When you think a member has changed the subject or become irrelevant?

_____ 11. When you feel impatient or irritated with something a member said or did?

_____ 12. When you feel hurt—rejected, embarrassed, or put down—by something a member said or did?

C. Others' Interest in Directness

In your opinion, how many in this group are interested in knowing . . .

_____ 13. When you do not understand something a member said?

_____ 14. When you like something a member said or did?

_____ 15. When you disagree with something a member said?

_____ 16. When you think a member has changed the subject or become irrelevant?

_____ 17. When you feel impatient or irritated with something a member said or did?

_____ 18. When you feel hurt—rejected, embarrassed, or put down—by something a member said or did?

D. Your Interest in Directness

With respect to how many members are you interested in knowing . . .

_____ 19. When they do not understand something you said?

_____ 20. When they like something you said or did?

_____ 21. When they disagree with something you said?

_____ 22. When they think you have changed the subject or become irrelevant?

_____ 23. When they feel impatient or irritated with something you said or did?

_____ 24. When they feel hurt—rejected, embarrassed, or put down—by something you said or did?

Answers to the 24 questions from two teaching teams from each of two elementary schools are shown in Figures 4–9 through 4–12. The dotted lines show the average response to items 19–24: "With respect to how many members are you interested in knowing . . . ?" The lines made with short dashes show the average response to items 13–18: "How many in this group are interested in knowing (from you) . . . ?" The lines made with long dashes show the average response to items 7–12: "To how many members will you candidly report . . . ?" And the solid lines show the average response to items 1–6: "How many members of this group do you expect will candidly report (to you) . . . ?" The results in group after group in schools and colleges are like those shown here. The number of others to whom respondents say they are willing to tell their reactions (the long dashes) is almost always larger than the number of others respondents think are ready to return the favor (the solid lines). The number of others from whom respondents say they are interested in getting reactions (the dotted lines) is almost always larger than the number whom respondents think want reactions from them (the short dashes). The number of others from whom respondents want reactions (the dotted lines) is almost always dramatically larger, for items at the right side of the graph, than the number of respondents whom respondents think will actually tell their reactions (the solid lines). And so on—you can compare any two lines. Also notice that the discrepancies generally get larger with the items toward the

**Figure 4-9. Team-Expectation Survey
Elementary School I, Third- and Fourth-Grade Team**

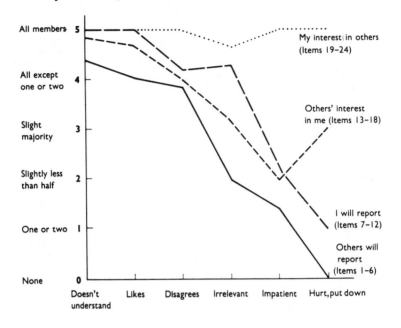

**Figure 4-10. Team-Expectation Survey
Elementary School I, Fifth- and Sixth-Grade Team**

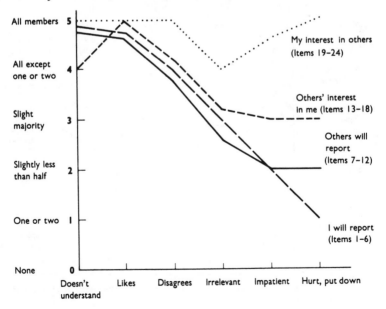

**Figure 4-11. Team-Expectation Survey
Elementary School 2, First- and Second-Grade Team**

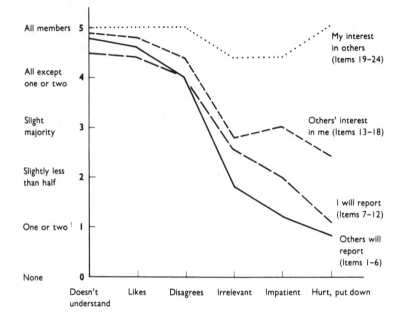

**Figure 4-12. Team-Expectation Survey
Elementary School 2, Third- and Fourth-Grade Team**

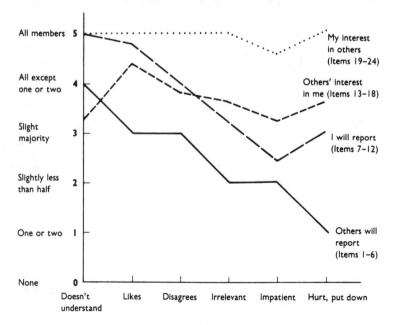

right side of the graph—the items that deal with the more emotional reactions. Those are the reactions most respondents want from almost everyone else but expect to get from very few. This graphic illustration of pluralistic ignorance about readiness for open communication can be useful feedback to teams of educators during an OD project.

In the questionnaire below, Questions 1 and 2 ask the respondent to predict the actions of others; Questions 3 and 4 ask the respondent to predict his or her own response. The facilitator may wish to write additional questions so that respondents provide both types of prediction for a single situation. The two predictions can then be compared to see how much the individual agrees with what he or she perceives to be a group norm and how much pluralistic ignorance exists in the group.

Communication in Problem Situations ——————————

1. Suppose Instructor X feels hurt and put down by something a colleague has said to him or her. In Instructor X's place, would most of the instructors you know in your department be likely to . . .

   1a. Tell the other instructor that they felt hurt and put down?
   ( ) Yes, I think most would.
   ( ) Maybe about half would.
   ( ) No, most would not.
   ( ) I don't know.

   1b. Tell their friends that the other instructor is hard to get along with?
   ( ) Yes, I think most would.
   ( ) Maybe about half would.
   ( ) No, most would not.
   ( ) I don't know.

2. Suppose Instructor X strongly disagrees with something B says at a faculty meeting. In Instructor X's place, would most of the colleagues you know in your department . . .

   2a. Seek out B to discuss the disagreement?
   ( ) Yes, I think most would do this.
   ( ) Maybe about half would do this.
   ( ) No, most would not.
   ( ) I don't know.

   2b. Keep it to themselves and say nothing about it?
   ( ) Yes, I think most would do this.
   ( ) Maybe about half would do this.
   ( ) No, most would not.
   ( ) I don't know.

3. Suppose you are in a committee meeting with Instructor X. The other members begin to describe their personal feelings about what goes on in the department, but Instructor X quickly suggests that the committee get back to the topic and keep the discussion objective and impersonal. How would you feel toward X?
( ) I would approve strongly.
( ) I would approve mildly or some.
( ) I wouldn't care one way or the other.
( ) I would disapprove mildly or some.
( ) I would disapprove strongly.

4. Suppose you are in a committee meeting with Instructor X. The other members begin to describe their personal feelings about what goes on in the department. Instructor X listens to them and tells them his or her own feelings. How would you feel toward X?
( ) I would approve strongly.
( ) I would approve mildly or some.
( ) I wouldn't care one way or the other.
( ) I would disapprove mildly or some.
( ) I would disapprove strongly.

Communication Networks

Questions like the following can be used to determine the number, size, and complexity of communication networks within an educational organization.

A. Perhaps there are some people in your organization with whom you talk rather frequently about matters important to you. Please think of people with whom you talk seriously about things important to you, inside or outside formal meetings, once a week or more on the average. Write their names below. (If there are fewer than six people, write down only as many as there are; if none, write "none." If there are more than six, list just the six with whom you feel your conversations are most satisfying.)

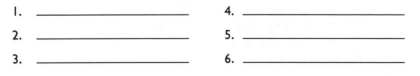

1. _____   4. _____

2. _____   5. _____

3. _____   6. _____

B. Now look back at question A. Each name is numbered. Listed below are all the pairs that can be made among six numbers. Perhaps you know whether some of the six people talk to each other about matters important to them. Please look at each pair of numbers below, look back to see what names they represent, and circle the pair of numbers if you have good reason to believe that the two people talk to each other once a week or more about matters important to them.

1–2				
1–3	2–3			
1–4	2–4	3–4		
1–5	2–5	3–5	4–5	
1–6	2–6	3–6	4–6	5–6

Feedback in the School or College

The following questions provide information about the availability of feedback. Question B is less direct than Question A, but if many participants indicate that they do not know whether others agree with them on important issues, the facilitator can be relatively certain that the level of interpersonal feedback is low.

A. Do you get any information from other professionals that helps you to tell whether you are doing an effective job?
( ) No, none.
( ) Yes, about once or twice a year.
( ) Yes, about once a month, maybe.
( ) Yes, about once a week.
( ) Yes, more than once a week.

B. Would you say there is some particular aspect of the college's or school's functioning where new ideas are especially needed?
( ) No, things are working about as well as they can.
( ) No, no particular aspect more than another. We just need things polished up a bit all over.
( ) Yes. If yes, please describe a feature of the organization's functioning that needs attention:

_____

_____

C. If you wrote in an answer above, how many people would you say agree with you?
( ) Many.
( ) Some.
( ) Only one or two.
( ) None.
( ) I don't know.

Communicative Roles

Communicative acts in work-oriented groups fall into two general categories. The task-centered category includes acts that promote getting a job done; the social-emotional category includes acts that lower tension and increase group cohesiveness. Figures 4–13 and 4–14 are observation forms for task-centered and interpersonal processes. Using these forms, an observer can tally all group interactions during a specified time period or focus on each member successively.

Figure 4-13. Categories for Task-centered Process

Tallies

I. Helps group collect data related to task

   A. Contributes data, defines terms, gives
      facts, states objectives and goals,
      gives opinions and generalizations   _____
   B. Asks questions, asks for survey   _____
   C. Suggests actions and alternatives   _____

II. Helps group use data

   D. Organizes, combines, compares, points
      out relations in data   _____
   E. Summarizes: identifies points of agreement
      and disagreement   _____

III. Tests for consensus

   F. Checks to see if group agrees   _____

Figure 4-14. Categories for Interpersonal Process

Tallies

I. Acts to increase shared understanding

   A. Paraphrases   _____
   B. Impression check   _____
   C. Helps others paraphrase or make perception
      checks   _____

II. Acts to provide data about interpersonal process

   D. Describes interpersonal behavior   _____
   E. Reports own feelings directly
      1. Positive feelings   _____
      2. Negative feelings   _____
   F. Helps others to describe interpersonal behavior
      or to report their own feelings directly   _____

An observer sometimes wishes to code unproductive communication processes as well. The following list, while not exhaustive, includes some of the unproductive procedures commonly seen in groups.

- Recognition seeking, claiming expertise because of seniority, etc.
- Self-confessing, apologizing repeatedly
- Pleading a self-interest that is irrelevant to the task
- Side talking; that is, talking with others while someone else is addressing the group
- Asking for special favors

Another useful observation and feedback tool can be created from the matrix of Figure 4–5. Observers can tally the incidence of communication about the situation of the convening tasks, target statements about methods, proposals for improving interpersonal relations, and so on. They can also record the kinds of contributions made by each group member to give feedback on the roles that are or are not being filled in the group.

The role-perception questionnaire below, which can be completed by group members near the end of a work session, provides subjective data to complement the data collected by an observer.

Directions: For each of the ratings below, imagine that the value of the contributions from all members equals 100 percent. Then, beside each member's name, show what percentage of the total effort you would attribute to that person. You may give any member a score from 0 to 100 on each question. Remember that the scores for all members must add up to 100. Be sure to list your own name and to score yourself.

Question A: Show how much each member has contributed to making this a smoothly working, friendly, comfortable group by such acts as encouraging others to participate, showing interest in the feelings of others, helping to resolve tensions and misunderstandings, providing support when members were feeling uneasy or upset, and, in general, showing concern for how well the members of this group got along together.

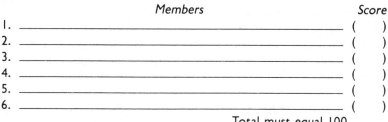

Question B: Show how much each member contributed to the group's achievement by such acts as providing good ideas, suggestions, and information, by keeping the group on the ball, by summarizing what had been accomplished and what still needs to be done, and, in general, by showing concern for productivity, or getting a lot of work done.

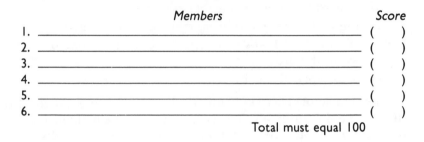

	Members	*Score*
1.		( )
2.		( )
3.		( )
4.		( )
5.		( )
6.		( )
		Total must equal 100

Again, the questions can be changed to reflect the observation scheme being used, as, for example:

A. Show how much each member contributed to clarifying the *situation* in which the group found itself by such acts as describing the purpose of the meeting, reporting an observation of how the meeting was going, or describing his or her own feelings toward another at the time.

B. Show how much each member contributed to making the *methods* used in this meeting effective by such acts as describing methods that were being used, suggesting better methods, or proposing that the group take a survey or meet in buzz groups.

Exercises and Designs for OD Projects

Basic Communication Skills

In practicing the following exercises, the facilitator should not only encourage correct use of the skills but should help group members learn ways of correcting one another. It is useful if participants identify their attempts to use the skills by stating, for example, "I'd like to paraphrase what I heard you say," and so on. Of course, all the exercises and designs presented at the end of this chapter will reinforce points discussed earlier, just as exercises and designs presented elsewhere in this book should highlight or otherwise encourage discussion of communication.

Paraphrasing. For the purpose of paraphrasing, members cluster into circles of no more than six persons. A facilitator or someone in the group suggests a topic that is relevant and important to the group, such as "What is the most important problem facing our department?" One member answers the question briefly; the next person in the circle accurately paraphrases this before giving his own answer, and so on around the circle. This exercise is also effective in two-person units, especially if the two join still another pair and each speaks from an understanding of his partner's answer.

A variation on this exercise can be particularly useful with a new group or with groups that have new members. Here, each person writes five to ten answers to the question "Who am I?" on either a 5" x 8" card pinned to the person's chest or on a piece of newsprint taped to the wall. All members mill around the room for a few minutes silently reading one another's answers. Then, in dyads or triads, individuals paraphrase items from the other persons' lists, perhaps limiting themselves to items that are most like or unlike items on their own lists.

Impression Checking. Two exercises are useful. In the first, the OD facilitator asks group members to take turns conveying their feelings to others by means of gestures, expressions, and nonsense language and then ask others to check to make sure that they read the emotion correctly. In the second, called the Alter Ego Procedure, half the group members sit in a circle while the other half take their places behind specific members of the circle. While those in the center discuss an agreed-upon topic, those in the outer ring whisper their impressions to their partners ("Are you upset because you can't get a word in edgewise?" or "Am I correct in inferring that you're slumping because you're uninterested?"). Partners in the inner circle respond only by nodding their heads yes or no to these questions.

Describing Behavior (Own or Other's). Nonverbal exercises (see the index) can provide content for practicing this interpersonal communication skill. After a five-member group completes the Five-Square puzzle, for example, members might begin their debriefing discussion by describing orally a behavior that was conspicuous to them. Members should be encouraged to start with descriptions of their own behavior and go on to descriptions of others' behaviors. If group members appear to be withholding significant oral reactions from one another, the facilitator might instead ask each person to write a behavior description. The facilitator then collects these statements and reads them aloud anonymously.

Stating One's Own Ideas. A simple exercise for practicing this skill is to arrange participants in pairs and to ask each pair to practice simultaneously the skills of stating their own ideas and paraphrasing. The topic for discussion can be far from or relate closely to the educational organization; for example, "Discuss what you consider the most important challenges facing education today," or "Discuss what you consider the most important problems in your department today." The facilitator should stress clarity of communication, not agreement among the participants. If the receiver can't paraphrase quickly and accurately, the sender must restate the idea again, using different words.

Describing One's Own Feelings. Many of the nonverbal exercises in this book arouse strong feelings that can later be described in an oral debriefing, a technique that works especially well when group members describe the nonverbal behavior that triggered their feelings. Written self-tests can also help participants learn this skill. In the following example, group members individually mark a *D* (for *describe*) by sentences that directly describe feelings and an *N* (for *not describe*) by sentences that convey but do not directly pinpoint a feeling. When all participants have marked Item 1, they discuss their responses in trios, and then check against explanations of what is correct. The explanations appear out of order, so that the eye is not drawn to the list of answers. After everyone in the trio understands the explanation, the trio marks Item 2, and so on. This self-test takes about 45 minutes to complete.

Self-Test ————————————————————————————

_____ I(a). Shut up! Not another word out of you!
_____ I(b). I'm really annoyed by what you just said.

_____ 2(a). Can't you see I'm busy? Get out!
_____ 2(b). I'm beginning to resent your constant interruptions.
_____ 2(c). You have no consideration for anybody else's feelings. You're completely selfish.

_____ 3(a). I feel discouraged because of some things that happened today.
_____ 3(b). This has been an upsetting day.

_____ 4(a). You're a wonderful person.
_____ 4(b). I really like you.

_____ 5(a). I feel comfortable and free to be myself when I'm around you.
_____ 5(b). We all feel you're a wonderful person.
_____ 5(c). Everybody likes you.

_____ 6(a). If things don't improve around here, I'll look for a new job.
_____ 6(b). Did you ever hear of such a lousy outfit as this is?
_____ 6(c). I'm afraid to admit that I need help with my work.

_____ 7(a). This is a very poor exercise.
_____ 7(b). I feel this is a very poor exercise.
_____ 7(c). I'm confused, frustrated, and annoyed by this exercise.

_____ 8(a). I feel inadequate when teaching that particular subject.
_____ 8(b). I am inadequate in teaching that particular subject.

_____ 9(a). I am a failure; I'll never amount to anything.
_____ 9(b). That teacher is awful. He didn't teach me anything.
_____ 9(c). I'm depressed and discouraged because I did so poorly on that test.

_____ 10(a). I feel lonely and isolated in my group.
_____ 10(b). For all the attention anybody pays to me I might as well not be in my group.
_____ 10(c). I feel that nobody in my group cares whether I am there or not.

Answers and Explanations_____

1(a): *N.* Commands such as these convey strong emotion without describing what kinds of feeling evoked the commands.

1(b): *D.* The speaker conveys feeling by describing himself or herself as annoyed. Thus, the statement not only expresses feeling; it also names the feeling.

7(a): *N.* This statement expresses a negative value judgment. It conveys some kind of negative feelings without describing them.

7(b): *N.* Although the speaker begins by saying, "I feel . . . ," he or she does not then tell the feeling. Instead the speaker passes a negative value judgment on the exercise. Note that merely tacking the words "I feel" onto the front of a sentence does not turn it into a description of feeling. People often say "I feel" when they mean "I think" or "I believe." For example, "I feel the Red Sox will win" or "I feel it will rain tomorrow."

7(c): *D.* The speaker specifies the feelings of confusion, frustration, and annoyance. The speaker describes feelings but does not evaluate the exercise itself.

Although we can disagree with value judgments expressed by another person, we should not deny that the person feels whatever he or she feels. If Joe says the exercise is poor and Jill says it is good, an argument may ensue about which it "really" is. However, if Joe says he was frustrated by the exercise and Jill says she was pleased and stimulated by it, no argument should follow. Each person's reaction is what it is. Of course, discussion about what causes each to feel as he or she does may provide important information about each person and about the exercise itself.

Many persons who say they are unaware of what they feel habitually express value judgments about others without recognizing that they are thereby expressing positive or negative feelings.

10(a): *D.* This statement conveys feelings by describing the speaker as feeling lonely and isolated.

10(b): *N.* This statement conveys negative feelings without telling whether the speaker feels angry, lonely, disappointed, hurt, or any other specific way.

10(c): *N.* Because it begins with "I feel," this kind of expression is often thought to describe the speaker's feelings. Notice, however, that the last part of the sentence really tells what the speaker assumes the others in the group feel about him or her and not what the speaker feels.
  Expressions 10c and 10a relate to each other as follows: "Because I believe or assume that nobody in my group cares whether I am there or not, I feel lonely and isolated."

4(a): *N.* This sentence states a value judgment. It conveys positive feelings toward the other without describing what they are. Does the speaker like the other, respect the other, or what? The expression does not tell us.

4(b): *D.* The speaker conveys positive feelings by describing it as liking for the other.

2(a): *N.* Strong feeling is conveyed by the question and accompanying command, "Get out!" but the feeling itself is not described.

2(b): *D.* The speaker's feeling is described as resentment.

2(c): *N.* The speaker makes charges and accusations about the other. The accusations certainly convey strong negative feelings. However, because the feelings are not identified we do not know whether the accusations stem from anger, disappointment, or hurt feelings.

6(a): *N.* This statement conveys negative feelings about the organization without specifying them. It alludes to the condition of things in this organization but does not clarify the speaker's inner state.

6(b): *N.* This is a rhetorical question that expresses a negative value judgment about the organization. It certainly conveys some kind of negative feeling but does not describe what it is.

6(c): *D.* This is a clear description of how the speaker feels in relation to his job:

> Expressions *6a* and *6b* are attacks or criticisms of the organization that could result from the kind of fear described in *6c*. Notice that expressions conveying anger result from fear. Many expressions of anger result from fear, hurt feelings, disappointments, or loneliness, but because the speaker's basic feelings are not described, the other person does not understand them.

9(a): *N.* This is another example of the subtle distinction introduced in Item 8. The speaker is conveying a strong negative feeling about himself or herself ("I am a failure"). The statement does not, however, describe the feeling. Is it dejection, fear, resignation, or what?

9(b): *N.* Instead of taking it out on himself, the speaker blames the teacher. His value judgment conveys negative feelings, but it does not describe what the speaker feels.

9(c): *D.* This conveys feelings by describing the speaker's emotional state as depressed and discouraged.

> Expressions *9a* and *9c* illustrate the important difference between labeling oneself and describing one's feelings. Feelings can and do change. To say that I am now depressed and discouraged does not imply that I will or must always feel the same. However, if I label myself as a failure, if I truly think of myself as a failure, I increase the probability that I will act like a failure.
>
> One person stated this important insight for herself this way, "I always thought I was a shy person. Now I have discovered that I am not shy although at times I *feel* shy." No longer did she keep herself from trying new things she wanted to by reminding herself that she was too shy.

5(a): *D.* This is a clear and specific description of how the speaker feels when around the other.

5(b): *N.* First, although this conveys positive feelings toward the other, it does not say that the speaker feels this way. To be a description of feeling, the statement should use "I," "me," "my," or "mine" to make clear the feelings are in the speaker. Second, "you're a wonderful person" is a value judgment which does not specify what feeling is behind it (see Item 4a).

5(c): *N.* The statement is not about the speaker's own feelings but refers to everybody. It is true that a feeling is named in the statement but the speaker does not make clear that the feeling is his or her own. A description of feeling must contain "I," "me," "my," or "mine."

Note how much more personal and warm you feel when another says to you that *he* likes you rather than *everybody* likes you. Do you find it more difficult to tell another "I like you" or "everybody likes you"?

8(a): *D.* This conveys feeling by describing the feeling as one of inadequacy.

8(b): *N.* Careful! This sounds much the same as *a.* However, it really says the person *is* inadequate. The person labels himself or herself as inadequate. It is true that a negative feeling about self is conveyed but the person does not describe the feeling.

This subtle difference was introduced because many people confuse *feeling* inadequate with *being* inadequate. A person may feel inadequate when teaching a certain subject and yet do an excellent job of it. Likewise, a person may feel adequate and competent in a subject and perform poorly. One sign of emotional maturity may be when a person functions adequately while feeling inadequate.

3(a): *D.* This describes the speaker as feeling discouraged.

3(b): *N.* Conveys negative feelings without describing what they are. The statement appears to be about the kind of day it was when, in fact, it is an expression of the way the speaker is feeling. We cannot tell from this expression whether the speaker is feeling depressed, annoyed, lonely, humiliated, or rejected.

Giving and Receiving Feedback. In this section we offer two exercises that enable people to practice giving and receiving feedback. In the first exercise, group members form trios in which one member is assigned to give feedback, the second to receive the feedback, and the third to observe both the giving and receiving. The giver describes two helpful and two unhelpful kinds of behavior he or she has seen in the receiver; the receiver paraphrases, and the observer sees to it that the two continue to use communication skills correctly.

The second exercise demonstrates the importance of giving and receiving feedback by showing that close-mouthed behavior is more often interpreted as disapproving than as approving. Participants select partners and decide which of them will be A and which will be B. The facilitator tells A privately, "Your partner was supposed to contact you for lunch yesterday but failed to do so, and you are disappointed. On a scale of feeling ranging from 1 (extremely distant) to 9 (extremely close), portray a feeling of 3 in the one-minute conversation that you'll be having soon." To B the facilitator says privately, "In the one-minute conversation that you'll soon be having with your partner, whom you like, respect, and value, pretend that you think it would be nice to share a ride to an evening meeting. You think the probability that your partner likes you is about 8."

The partners then come together to talk for one minute about whatever they choose. At the end of that time the facilitator tells all Bs to assign their partners a number from 1 to 9 based on the scale of feeling from extremely distant to extremely close. Before it is divulged that all the A partners had been asked to portray a 3, all the B estimates are recorded on newsprint. Almost invariably, the average B estimate will be less than 2. The facilitator can then initiate a discussion of why this is so, pointing out that silence or lack of candor about feelings can strain trust in even a one-minute interaction.

Unilateral and Transactional Communication

This section describes two exercises in unilateral and transactional communication (defined at the beginning of the chapter, under "Types of Communication"). The first exercise, commonly known as the One-Way, Two-Way Communication Exercise and adapted from Bass (1966), is designed to provide a group with a springboard for discussions of communication in the educational organization within a brief period of time (see Figure 4–15). In this procedure, one member is designated as the coordinator; another is asked to be the sender; the remaining members are receivers. The coordinator signals when to begin, keeps track of how much time is spent during each phase of the activity, and observes the nonverbal reactions of the receivers.

To commence the activity, the coordinator gives the sender two patterns of rectangles, being careful not to show them to the receivers. The first pattern is presented to the receivers as a unilateral communication during which they must remain silent and refrain from asking questions as they draw the pattern as accurately as possible. The second is given through transactional communication, during which the receivers are encouraged to break in at any time, to raise questions, and to interact orally with the sender.

Figure 4-15. Handout for Unilateral and Transactional Exercise

Phase I: Unilateral Communication

Handout for Sender:

Directions for sender:
1. Be sure that none of the receivers sees the overall design below.
2. Sit with your back to the receivers.
3. When you are ready to start, describe the diagram below so that the receivers can duplicate it on their own papers.
4. None of the receivers may communicate with you in any way at any time.
5. When you are through, take several minutes to record below your degree of satisfaction with the activity just completed.
6. Hand this sheet to the coordinator.

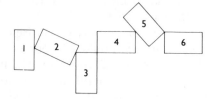

Satisfaction scale (circle one):

| Very dissatisfied | Rather dissatisfied | Rather satisfied | Very satisfied | Don't know |

What factors caused the reaction you circled above?

Handout for Receivers:

Directions for receivers:
1. Sit with your backs to the sender.
2. Your task is to reproduce on this paper whatever the sender instructs you to.
3. Only the sender can talk. You may initiate no communications and make no audible signals of any type.
4. It is best to use only your own ideas about what the sender is saying. A neighbor's understanding of the task may be wrong.
5. When the sender has finished, answer the two items below and give the paper to the coordinator.

Figure continued on next two pages

A. How many pieces of the diagram do you think you completed accurately?
Circle the appropriate response: 1 2 3 4 5 6
B. If you felt any frustration during the exercise, circle the number below that best
describes your feelings:

1	2	3	4	5
Not at all	A little	Some real	Very	Don't
frustrated	frustrated	frustration	frustrated	know

Handout for Coordinator:

Directions for coordinator:
1. Prior to the exercise
   A. Check back-to-back seating so that receivers cannot see the sender's paper.
   B. You may answer questions before exercise begins.
   C. Tell sender to begin when all are ready.
2. During the exercise
   A. Record starting time _____
      Completion time _____
      Elapsed time _____

   B. Record below apparent evidences (including nonverbal) of feelings such as satis-
      faction, frustration, interest level, high or low morale, and so on, of:

Sender	Receiver

3. After the exercise
   A. Note elapsed time for exercise completion in 2A.
   B. Complete your own notes in 2B.
   C. Collect completed papers in your group.
   D. Record on the back of this sheet any on-the-job implications of the exercise you
      have just observed.

Phase II: Transactional Communication

The handout for the *sender* differs from the one for unilateral communication in only two ways:

    1. Rule 4 now reads, "The receivers may interrupt your directions with questions or comments at any time."

    2. The diagram to be transmitted is this one:

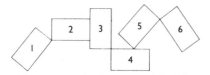

    The handout for the *receiver* differs from the one for unilateral communication only in Rule 4, which now reads, "You may question the sender about instructions at any time and as often as you wish."

    The handout for the *coordinator* is identical to the one for unilateral communication.

After the two episodes are completed, the coordinator assists the receivers in determining the number of correct placements in their drawings. A correct rectangle touches one or two other rectangles at the matching location on the sides of the other rectangles and should also be oriented vertically, horizontally, or diagonally as on the sender's page. One point is granted for each rectangle drawn correctly. Scores can range from zero to six for each communication episode. Or if you wish, you may count one point for each correctly oriented rectangle (maximum of six) and one point for each correct point of contact between rectangles (maximum of five) for a maximum of 11 points.

After the receivers score their own drawings, receivers and senders are asked to answer the following questions for discussion: With which communication were you most frustrated or tense? Which type would you prefer to use as a sender? Which type would you prefer to receive? (To each question, three alternative answers are possible: unilateral, transactional, or no difference.) When is unilateral communication efficient in our work, and how might we improve it? When is transactional communication necessary in our work, and what can we do to improve it? What are other implications of this activity for our work? What keeps us from using transactional communication more often in our work?

When using the exercise with multiple groups, coordinators are asked to report the primary outcomes of their teams to the entire staff so that all group members can discuss what they learned from the activity and recommendations can be made for continued work on improving communication clarity. Finally, before meeting with the total group, the facilitator may meet with the coordinators during a scheduled break and prepare summary charts of the time required, accuracy, and attitudes associated with each communication mode in each of the groups. These summaries can be used to supplement individual reports by the coordinators during the meeting with the entire group.

The Blind Walk

The Blind Walk is another exercise that highlights the differences between unilateral and transactional communication. In this procedure, each member of the group is asked to pair with a person whom he or she does not know well or would like to know better. One member of the team is blindfolded and is silently guided by the other through, over, or around things. After several minutes the roles are reversed, but during this second phase talking is allowed. When the walk is completed, participants share their mutual reactions about the two ways of communicating and about their relationship. In a variation of this exercise, half the members of the entire group are blindfolded, and the sighted members choose a partner. Each leads one blindfolded member around without identifying himself or herself, which seems to augment the impact of the nonverbal phase of the walk. In still another variation, no touching is allowed while leading the blindfolded partner around; this requires the sighted partner to give clear verbal instructions.

The Five-Square Puzzle

The Five-Square puzzle exercise (adapted from Bavelas, 1950) demonstrates cooperation in a group task characterized by nonverbal communication. It is administered to participants in groups of five. Observers are instructed to look for ways in which participants communicate nonverbally and for ways in which cooperation is helped or hindered.

Participants occupy five chairs around a table on which, before each person, are laid some flat, mostly irregularly shaped pieces of plastic or cardboard. In an unordered pile before one person are three pieces marked A; before another are four pieces marked B; before another, two pieces marked C; before another, two marked D; and before the fifth person are four pieces marked E. The participants are told that there are exactly enough parts distributed among them to make five complete squares (see Figure 4–16). The task is completed when a square has been composed in front of each member of the group.

Figure 4-16. The Five-Square Puzzle

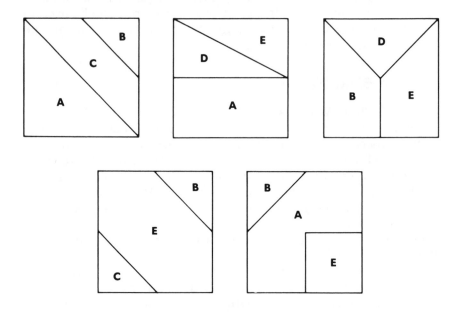

The procedural rules are as follows: (1) each member must construct one square at his own work place; (2) no member may talk, signal, or gesture in any way that would provide guidance, direction, or suggestions to any other member—for example, no member may signal for a piece from another member; (4) except for any piece given to another member, members' pieces must be in front of them at work places. Only giving is allowed, no taking.

Doing the Five-Square Puzzle is frustrating for individuals who are accustomed to managing others as well as for people who are accustomed to guiding themselves by watching for signals of the expectations of others. To the extent that rules are observed (and it is very difficult for most participants to apply this discipline to themselves), the exercise focuses participants' attention on discovering ways in which they can be helpful to one another. The most direct contribution members can make is to give appropriate pieces from their places to the appropriate people, but they must allow the others to find for themselves the way in which the desired pieces fit with those before them.

This exercise points up the great difficulty of allowing other people to do things in their own way and the great extent to which we rely on language to influence the behavior of others. At the same time, it provides very useful information about how group members act toward one another under the frustration the exercise produces. When the performance is completed, the ensuing discussion should focus on problems of coordinated effort and on the implications of the exercise for relations among group members in their daily work. To guide the discussion, the facilitator might ask the following questions: What were some of your feelings during the exercise? Do you have similar feelings when you are working in groups in your school or college? Under what circumstances do these feelings arise? What implications does this exercise have for our work in the school or college?

The Five-Square Puzzle also can be employed for giving practice in the communication skills. For that purpose, an observing group of five persons sits in a Fishbowl Arrangement around the group doing the puzzle. The inside group members are told to keep track of their feelings during the exercise and to note the behavior of others in their groups as accurately as possible. The observers watch behavior and make notes about their impressions of the insiders' feelings, and after the insiders have finished their work, the insiders paraphrase and verify or contradict the observers' impression checks. The facilitator might then ask if the behavior observed during this exercise is similar to or different from what typically goes on in the school or college.

Group Agreements

An exercise in making group agreements about communication not only encourages discussion about the behavior expected from group members but also serves to introduce the survey procedure. (We described taking a survey in the section headed "Communication in the Subsystem.") If it is feasible, educators who will continue to work as a team should be grouped together for this exercise (adapted from one by Hale and Spanjer, 1972). The exercise requires little preparation beyond providing each participant with a copy of the handout instructions (see Figure 4–17), although the facilitator may wish to point out that the outlined agreements are only examples.

Emotional Distance and Closeness

The purpose of this exercise is to heighten awareness of how degrees of distance and closeness in communication affect human

Figure 4-17. Handout for Group Agreements

Group functioning is improved when members have clear expectations of what kinds of behavior are expected of them as group members. Here are two examples of agreements that a group might accept.

1. *Directness:* If I am dissatisfied with the way the group's work is going, I will report my reactions directly to the group when it is in session. If, outside of a regular session, another member expresses to me dissatisfactions with the group, I will suggest that that member bring the matter before the total group at a regular session.
2. *Surveys:* Any member may request a survey at any time. The requesting member states what he or she wants to know from the total group; another member paraphrases or otherwise clarifies the topic until all concerned are clear about what is being asked of them; then each person in turn states his or her current position on the topic in two or three sentences. A survey is not a vote that will bind the group or its members. A survey must be taken at the time it is requested, with all other activity suspended.

You should now discuss and decide whether you wish to conclude any group agreements and, if so, what they are to be.

---

relationships. The exercise is most effective if group members are skilled at describing their own feelings, objectively describing the behavior of others, and checking their own inferences about the feelings of others. Groups form two-person units to engage in a series of three-minute conversations on one of the following topics:

1. A topic that is of interest to only one of you and is unrelated to this day or event.
2. A topic that is of interest to both of you and is unrelated to this day or event.
3. A topic that is of interest to only one of you and is closely related to your life today or to this event.
4. A topic that is of interest to both of you and is closely related to your life today or this event.
5. What is happening between the two of you right now—the way you are relating, your feelings, and your inferences about your partner's feelings. Emphasize your experience of this moment.

When the five conversations are completed, the facilitator can guide the debriefing using the following questions: How did your experiences change over the series of conversations? Did you find some conversations easier or more difficult than others? Why? What is happening between you right now? After the debriefing, the facilitator might give a lecturette highlighting the dimensions of closeness and distance or might distribute a handout similar to Figure 4–3. The exercise can be concluded with a discussion in quartets of the ways in which emotionally distant and emotionally close communication affects the everyday lives and relationships of people, groups, and organizations. It should be emphasized that close communication does not require intimate friendship between persons and that emotionally close communication cannot be achieved immediately but is based on a step-by-step increase of mutual trust.

Imaginary Situations for Giving and Receiving "Feedback"—for Giving and Receiving Information That Has Some Emotional Content

FIRST PHASE

Instructions: Each item below is typed on a card, and the cards are dealt out to the members of the group. One person reads aloud what is on a card and then says what seems suitable in a situation like the one described on the card. That is, the person "gives feedback."

Next, the same person picks out another member of the group to "receive feedback." The second person responds to what the first person has said, saying what he or she would feel urged to say in such a situation.

Then a few others volunteer some examples of what would be good and bad to say in such a situation. Then it is another person's turn to read a card.

The first item below is followed by an example of these instructions.

1. You are standing in a crowded lobby. Someone steps back and stands on your foot. What do you say?

   (Person A reads the above aloud and then says something to the offending person. Perhaps A says, "Get off my foot!" Then Person A picks another member of the group, say B, and asks something like, "What would you answer to that?" Person B might say, "Well, don't stick your feet out where other people can stand on them!" Then a few other people say things like, "It might make further conversation more friendly to say _____" and "It would certainly make the other person angrier to say _____.")

2. About five minutes ago, you proposed a plan of action to the group. You thought your proposal had merit. No one, however, said anything about it; the discussion went on as if you had said not a word. You are feeling angry at being ignored. What do you say?

3. Someone says, "You just got your doctorate a couple of months ago, didn't you? So I guess we can excuse you for having an opinion like that." What do you say?

4. After you speak, someone says, "That's exactly the right attitude! I'm certainly glad to hear that you are standing with me on this question. We need more people like you around here—people who can think straight." What do you say?

5. About three minutes ago, George proposed a plan of action to the group. Then three other people proposed plans of action, none of them commenting on George's plan or anyone else's. George now says, "I don't think anybody is listening to anybody else. I might as well be talking to a lamp post." What do you say?

6. Jim has been talking more than others. During the last five minutes, he twice raised his voice and cut off others in mid-sentence. You are annoyed at his behavior. What do you say?

7. During the meeting, most people have been proposing actions, and most people have been arguing for and against the various ideas. You have noticed, however, that almost every time you have proposed something, Amy has immediately or soon afterward found fault with it. What do you say?

8. During the meeting, almost everyone has wanted to talk a lot. The convener has been very active and very skillful in enabling everyone to have a fair share of the time and in assuring that everyone's contribution has been acknowledged. At the same time, no one has seemed to feel squelched. You admire the convener's skill, and you are grateful to her for keeping the meeting orderly and on track. What do you say?

9. An expert is present. He has pronounced several ideas put forward by members to be right or wrong. You think he is acting like a referee, and you don't think his rulings of "That's right" and "That's wrong" are helping the work to get done. The discussion seems to drop into a heavy silence after each of his rulings. What do you say?

10. An expert is present. She has explained several times some theory and some experimental findings about some of the topics that have come up in today's discussion. Though what she says is interesting, it doesn't seem to you to help move the

group toward solving its problem. It doesn't help you to know that most experimental groups do this or that. You want to know what *your* group can do. What do you say?

11. During a couple of recent meetings and again just now, Albert has made three or four statements such as "I don't think we are being very honest with each other in this group." You have not pursued the matter, because you thought Albert would get down to brass tacks in his own time. Now, however, you think Albert is asking for help. What do you say?

12. A possible client comes to a meeting of an OD cadre and describes his need for a consultant. As the conversation proceeds, the project begins to sound dubious to you. Then you hear a member of the group say to the potential client, "Of course, we want to help you in any way we can." What do you say?

SECOND PHASE

After all cards have been read, the group can turn from imaginary feedback to actual feedback. Here are three possible exercises for the second phase.

1. *Simple feedback.* The group breaks into pairs. The pairs can be used that have already played out the imaginary situations on the cards. Now, however, each member of the pair tells the other something the other has done—something pleasing, displeasing, or indifferent. The other says something in receipt. Both comment on the giving and the receiving. Rotate pairs if there is time.

2. *Helping trios.* The group breaks into trios. In each, one member is designated to give feedback, a second to receive the feedback, and the third to observe and comment on the giving and receiving. The giver describes two helpful and two unhelpful kinds of behavior he or she has seen in the receiver. The receiver paraphrases—no more. The observer is limited to seeing to it that the other two continue to use communication skills correctly and appropriately.

3. *Newsprint.* All participants list on newsprint some features of their own behavior that they regard as strengths or weaknesses, as helpful or unhelpful, in their joint work. They post the lists on the walls. Participants stroll from sheet to sheet, reading the sheets and then adding, where they can, helpful or unhelpful actions they themselves have perceived on the part of the person. Each person then takes time to read and think about what others have written on his or her sheet.

The facilitator or leader now tells the group that each person can choose one of three ways to use the feedback:

a. Think about the feedback without discussing it with others.

b. Request clarification from others if what is written is unclear, insufficiently specific, or otherwise inadequately informative about others' perceptions. Participants may ask what actions of theirs led to a particular perception or may request to be told a specific example of their behavior. Participants must try to be clear about the kind of information they want and from whom.

c. Contract for feedback in the future about a particular kind of behavior if others find the participant behaving that way: "Will you agree to tell me when you see me doing X?"

The duty of the facilitator is to facilitate and clarify communication and to urge a lot of paraphrasing. If what is said seems to attribute good or bad intentions to another, the facilitator should immediately remove the implication. The facilitator should also watch for signs of increasing stress to make sure that no one receives too much or too rapid feedback, whether unpleasant or pleasant.

Improving Communication Skills

With a facilitator's help, communication skills can be improved directly and indirectly. As an example of the former, the following sequence of events emphasizing the use of these skills helps a group to pinpoint issues and problems for additional work. The design takes about seven hours to complete and can be divided into morning and afternoon sessions.

The day begins with a general meeting introducing an overview of training goals and activities followed by an introduction to paraphrasing. The group is divided into small subgroups to discuss what should be changed to help their educational organization operate more effectively. Following this discussion, members concentrate on paraphrasing and attempt to pinpoint its difficulties and potentialities. After the unilateral and transactional communication exercise is introduced, participants discuss it within their subgroups, giving special attention to impression checking and describing one's own feelings. The total group is then reassembled, and the facilitator reviews all the skills introduced so far before the group adjourns for lunch.

The afternoon session begins with an introduction to the Five-Square puzzle, following which the group is again divided into small subgroups but of different participants. After completing the exercise, the subgroups discuss it using the skills of behavior description, impression checking, and describing one's own feelings. The total group reconvenes for an introduction to the Group Agreements Exercise, and participants are reassigned to new subgroups. Emphasis is placed on using communication skills correctly during the task and during discussion as well. The small groups then report their various discussions to the total assembly.

The final activity of the day is introduced by a lecturette on the Johari Awareness Model, and the subgroups form helping trios to practice giving feedback on helpful and unhelpful behaviors. If time permits, group members may redistribute themselves into new helping trios and continue practicing. The facilitator ends the meeting by reviewing the day's activities, distributing handouts on communication skills, and suggesting possible directions for future OD activities.

Occasionally a facilitator will discover that organizational processes other than those of communication are so seriously impaired that the target system's functioning is impeded. In this case initial training efforts must be directed to those processes if the training is to benefit the organization. For the facilitator who is designing a training sequence, however, this sequence poses a problem, because clear communication is essential to the success of other organizational training events. The solution to this dilemma is to plan the training activities in such a way that communication skills can be introduced even when the focus of the activities is elsewhere.

For example, Schmuck once worked with part of a community college in which conflict between administrators and instructors was so intense and goals so ambiguous that collaborative problem solving and decision making were impossible to initiate. To use the terms of Gibb (1961), the climate was defensive rather than supportive. The warring administrators and instructors were interested only in the amount and kind of communication skill training that would move them out of their strife rapidly. Schmuck decided to work separately with the two groups in a series of meetings distributed over four months.

At the first meeting individuals were asked to write on index cards behavior descriptions and statements of their own feelings about the situation in the college. Participants took turns sharing what they had written on the cards while others in their group practiced paraphrasing and impression checking. At other meetings Schmuck asked staff and parents separately to describe their behaviors and feelings when the college situation was as they wished it to be. Again they took turns sharing what they had written on index cards while everyone had a turn to practice paraphrasing and impression checking. At all these meetings Schmuck collected the index cards, eventually categorizing their content into five major areas including the grading system, advising new students, collecting post-course reaction data, and so on.

All participants were given handouts describing interpersonal communication behaviors characteristic of defensive and supportive communication. According to Gibb, defensive climates are characterized by evaluation, control, strategy, neutrality, superiority, and certainty; supportive climates are characterized by description, problem orientation, spontaneity, empathy, equality, and provisionalism. Both groups were encouraged to consider how their own behaviors contributed to defensive reaction by members of the other group.

After all participants had attended at least two meetings—in extra training events, the instructors worked on departmental issues not directly related to relationships with administrators—Schmuck brought the two groups together for a seven-hour meeting at which they performed the Imaging exercise described in chapter 8. This exercise required them to use the communication skills to give and receive feedback. The content of the feedback was then compared with the five kinds of problems participants had discussed earlier, and that comparison helped them choose problems for further work. Small problem-solving groups of administrators and instructors subsequently met for several months to generate proposals that were ultimately reported back to the total group. Throughout these meetings Schmuck continually urged people to use the communication skills and taught them how to coach one another when they used the skills improperly.

In contrast, we have also done OD with a number of educators who were unaware that communication in their departments needed improvement. They had simply not given much thought to their procedures for communicating. With such groups we have found that the exercise on unilateral and transactional communication is a good place to start. This exercise demonstrates the respective advantages and disadvantages of two organizational forms of communication. In discussing the implications of the exercise, most educators will seek ways of improving one-way communication and of increasing the amount of two-way communication. Their interest in the latter offers a good opportunity to introduce the practice of basic communication skills. Once the six communication skills have been rehearsed, the facilitators can ask participants to talk about strengths and weaknesses in the department's current communication patterns. While selecting strengths and weaknesses, participants are urged to practice the communication skills again. Finally, such a design leads to the identification of organizational problems in communication for future problem solving.

Improved communication is a fundamental objective of organization development. Because an educational organization's adaptability depends in part upon effective communication among individuals, within subsystems, and in the organization at large, most OD efforts in colleges and schools begin with practice in new forms of interpersonal communication and proceed to the use of new communication skills, norms, and structures within the target system.

Chapter Five

Improving Meetings

In colleges and schools, as in most other organizations, we spend a considerable portion of our time in meetings. Rarely, however, do we or our colleagues speak favorably of them. Most people speak of meetings as a burden to be endured.

That negative attitude is unfortunate. Although all channels of communication can be useful, formal meetings are singularly important for staff communication. Meetings give faculty members the opportunity to coordinate information about problems and decisions while satisfying motivational needs for achievement, affiliation, and power.

Meetings provide an opportunity for participation not found in memos, newsletters, loudspeaker announcements, and the like. They permit us to check reactions immediately to a speaker's contribution and to our own utterances as well. If managed effectively, meetings can be the principal channel for bringing faculty members into collaboration to reach common under-standings and for that reason can be highly productive and satisfying events in the life of the educational organization.

Yet most educational staffs and subgroups use meetings infre-quently and ineffectively, often inhibiting clear communication and

183

wide participation. Indeed, since many educators regard meetings as a dull waste of time or as a burden to be endured while more interesting work awaits elsewhere, it is not surprising that mismanaged meetings can arouse distaste and even hatred. There are many traps that prevent meetings from being effective: holding meetings merely because they are scheduled, clinging strictly to Robert's Rules of Order, failing to deal with feelings, blocking members' help in planning the meeting or compiling the agenda, failing to keep a record of things done, attempting to cover too many items on an agenda, allowing a few members to do all the talking, allowing only those with high status to conduct the meetings, and neglecting to carry the group's decisions into action. All these pitfalls keep meetings from realizing their potential.

OD facilitators, who conduct most of their OD projects in meetings and who are called on in the course of the academic year to give help at ordinary faculty meetings, should make their OD training sessions models of effective meetings. This chapter introduces methods that facilitators can use to help educators organize meetings for the most effective mobilization of human resources.

Purposes of Meetings

Most educators recognize the potential benefits of forming committees, departments, and teams for organizing curricula and developing policy. They see, too, that present trends in organizing for education, such as team teaching, curriculum committees, site-based management, and direct citizen involvement with instructors, will bring about a greater need for effective problem solving and decision making in groups. Although individuals working alone can often reach more efficient decisions, when you must depend at least partly on other people to carry out the decision that is made, you will almost always get better help from them if they get in on the decision (or at least the planning) itself.

Where issues with many alternative subtasks are involved, where elements are not easy to describe to others, where one person cannot perform a subtask without coordinating with others, and particularly where efficiency depends on the continued coordination and interaction of a number of persons, a group decision will almost always be more effectively carried out than will one produced by even the most capable individual. Groups can usually produce more ideas, stimulate more creative thought among members, pool ideas to develop more realistic forecasts of the consequences of decisions, and generally produce bolder plans than can the average individual working alone. Perhaps most important, group members can commit themselves to action in one another's presence.

In an educational organization that requires intelligent coordination among staff, one-way communication is not enough; the percentage of people responding constructively to messages must be high. It is important for an organizational member to know how many people have "bought" a message, who they are, and why they have found the message to be either inspiring or distasteful. Beyond getting a message accepted, it is often important for many people to know firsthand that the transmission occurred and that others know it occurred. The face-to-face meeting is the only setting in which all these functions can take place quickly.

Perhaps the greatest value of meetings is that they draw out and coordinate the staff's resources for a systematic exchange of creative ideas. Meetings can also be useful for planning action that will require the consistent coordinated effort of several faculty members. Even the simplest matters, such as using audio-visual equipment or art supplies, are often difficult for faculty members to coordinate and might be facilitated by faculty discussions. If, however, the transmission of simple information at meetings wastes valuable time, another mode of communication, such as a clearly written memorandum, would be more appropriate, require less time, and be available for later reference. Chapters 6 and 7 provide further discussion of the assets and liabilities of participative involvement in problem solving and decision making.

Finally, meetings provide one of the few means by which educators can come together to satisfy emotional needs. Observers such as Jackson (1968) and Lortie (1975) long ago noted the social isolation, the vagueness of outcomes, and the relatively low degree of power associated with teaching and working in schools. Colleges can be even more lonely places to work. The traditional self-contained classroom at any level requires instructors to work apart from their colleagues most of the time. Vague but demanding educational goals are often set by the larger society of which the school or college is a part but on which the faculty has little influence. Joining with other adults in meetings to solve mutual problems and share common frustrations can greatly improve the chance for educators to take initiative, feel successful, experience affiliation with others, and feel that they are exercising some influence over their own and shared fates.

Because meetings are confined in time and space and have limited membership, they bring many group processes that are elusive in the larger organization into full view for the OD facilitator to observe. Thinking of meetings as microcosms of the educational organization will enable the facilitator to anticipate many of the norms manifested outside meetings. Moreover, in initial contacts with participants, facilitators should make observations at regularly scheduled meetings in which real work is taking place. It is better to see participants in action than to hear them talk about how they work together, and meetings are among the most easily observable group actions in educational organizations.

By observing interaction at meetings, OD facilitators can discern roles and norms that reflect the organization's goals, approved procedure, and affective climate. The kinds of communication encouraged at meetings, for example, can reveal the expectations and skills that members use to coordinate their efforts. The amount of time devoted to goal setting can indicate the importance that members attach to this in relation to other activities. Shared assumptions about the functions of conflict can be noted in the ways in which opposing views are uncovered and handled. To understand how faculty members have organized to accomplish their tasks, comparisons of problem-solving and decision-making activities can be made at faculty meetings, smaller committee meetings, and informal sessions. Finally, facilitators can watch the degree to which participants comment on how they conduct their meetings and how they assess changes in their group processes.

Meetings that are handled ineffectively often have unfortunate repercussions elsewhere in the educational organization. For example, deans who receive a policy decision at a meeting convened by the provost without a clarifying discussion may misinterpret the policy and transmit wrong directions to their faculties. When educational goals are seldom discussed at site meetings, school teachers may find themselves working at cross-purposes. When small conflicts over grading students are not discussed at faculty meetings, they may grow into hostilities. When problem solving and decision making during meetings are confined to only a few faculty members, nonparticipants are likely to experience frustration and to tune out; those who stay out of the discussion may be unwilling or unable to carry out the action steps that others have developed. Finally, if faculty members fail to discuss changes occurring in the community and student body, their instructional programs will lose effectiveness.

Effective Meetings

Effectiveness at meetings is uncommon, especially when issues are not easily resolvable. But ineffectiveness should not be punished when it occurs. Instead, sometimes OD facilitators will encourage groups of educators to aspire to more productive meetings, but other times they will encourage groups to *lower* their expectations (about how much commitment can be elicited in one hour to a complex plan, for example).

Four Features

Effective meetings are characterized by at least four features: (1) a balanced mixture of task and maintenance functions, with an edge given to sticking to the task; (2) many more group-oriented actions than self-oriented actions; (3) wide dispersal of leadership roles; and (4) adequate follow-through to permit decisions made at the meeting to result in the expected actions.

A Balance of Task and Maintenance. To have effective meetings, groups must learn to fulfill both task functions, which carry forward the meeting's work requirements, and maintenance functions, which help group members develop satisfying interpersonal relationships. Task functions include initiating ideas on work procedures, seeking information or opinions from others, giving information or opinions, and summarizing what has occurred in the meeting. Maintenance functions include ensuring that others have a chance to speak, ensuring that listeners have a chance to check on what they have heard, reconciling disagreements, sensing group mood, and being warm and responsive toward others. Since most groups have difficulty staying on task, the facilitator will usually wish to emphasize task functions. At the same time, without maintenance functions the group will not continue to stay on task and to act as a group. The OD facilitator will have to perform maintenance functions in some groups and trust that group members will model some of their behavior after that of the facilitator.

Meetings are most effective when some members attend to how well the group is accomplishing each part of its work and others stop working on their tasks periodically to discuss the group's process. Symptoms of difficulty include excessive nitpicking, repetition of obvious points, ignoring suggestions for improvement, private conversations in pairs or subgroups, domination of discussion by two or three people, polarization of members, general inability to paraphrase others' points of view, attacks on ideas before they are completely expressed, and apathetic participation. When such symptoms are present, the group should set aside the original task and place emerging maintenance issues on the agenda. It must also learn to deal effectively with its processes and to shift easily back to its main work. Most if not all staff members should be capable of performing both task and maintenance functions.

Group Orientation. The second feature of effective meetings is the degree to which members engage in self-oriented rather than group-oriented behavior. Unproductive behaviors such as fighting, withdrawing, blocking, avoiding, depending on the formal leader, expressing indifference, sandbagging, and keeping agendas hidden are directed toward individual needs rather than toward the task at hand. Schein (1969) theorized that self-oriented behavior occurs when groups fail to recognize or to deal with any of four underlying emotional issues of members: identity, control, needs and goals, and acceptance of intimacy. Self-oriented behavior also probably reflects low trust in the group.

Self-oriented behavior may be a problem when it delays accomplishment of the main task and leaves members dissatisfied, but groups often allow individuals to take up everyone else's time for their own purposes. If this can be done aboveboard, the group should not avoid it, and an individual should not be afraid to ask. Everyone, however, should be clear that it is happening and be willing to delay the original group task so that a discussion of the individual's concern, like attention to group process, will pay off later.

Shared Leadership. The third feature of effective meetings is shared leadership—that is, any behavior that helps the group carry forward its work or satisfy members' needs in constructive ways. Leadership is needed for (1) planning and preparing for the meeting, (2) setting goals by building an agenda, (3) coordinating task business, (4) keeping records of what happens, (5) helping attend to group and interpersonal processes, (6) evaluating how well activities meet goals and how satisfying and helpful interpersonal processes are, and (7) planning ways of following through on plans.

In our view, these functions should be shared by all members of a group at the same time that individual members are assigned primary responsibility to see that certain special roles are performed effectively. These special roles—meeting organizer, convener, recorder, process observer, and follow-up monitor—are described later in this chapter.

Follow-through. The fourth readily observable feature of effective meetings, follow-through, occurs after the meeting. If requests pour into the secretary's or department head's office for information about items discussed at the meeting, the meeting was probably ineffective in relaying that information. If faculty members grumble in the coffee room about a decision made at a meeting, they probably did not feel free to contribute their own views. Tasks that are implemented with commitment and dispatch, however, give evidence of adequate preparation at the meeting.

The OD Facilitator's Roles and Functions

Two factors encourage facilitators to improve meeting skills at a very early phase of an OD effort. First, although most faculties cannot easily call off work, even for brief periods, to practice new group and organizational processes, facilitators can often gain admission to regularly scheduled meetings to help with the ongoing work of the educational organization. Second, any initial successes achieved at moving group members from chaotic to productive meetings can increase their trust in the facilitator's competence and encourage them to work toward resolving the larger issues confronting their organization. Four methods are available to the OD facilitator to improve meetings: (1) modeling an effective group member, (2) providing information about effective meetings, (3) providing training, and (4) providing consultation and feedback.

Modeling. By attending the meetings of a particular faculty group or other staff group within the target system, facilitators to some extent become temporary members of these meetings and, as such, may act as models of effective group members. If members seldom clarify one another's statements, for example, facilitators may repeatedly clarify what others are saying. If agendas are loosely described and facilitators are themselves on the agenda, they may insist that the purpose of their agenda topic be clarified and that definite time requirements be imposed for them. If a group leaves decisions dangling with no clear indication of who is to be responsible for follow-up actions, facilitators can ask leading questions that focus on this lack of specification.

For purposes of modeling, OD facilitators can sometimes assume important leadership roles as well. As convener, the facilitator can demonstrate assertive behavior, help the group warm up, organize its agenda, and encourage wide participation; in other roles, facilitators can exhibit the careful recording of events or demonstrate careful observations of group processes. Unless considerable trust exists between members and the facilitator, however, this type of modeling—assuming a key role at the center of the group's attention—should be avoided. The role of OD facilitators is not necessarily to furnish leadership functions for the group, although that might sometimes be the case, but rather to help the group establish effective meetings by passing on their own skills to group members.

Providing Information. If group members already perceive the nature of their problems, facilitators can often help by providing information about the characteristics and procedures of effective meetings, especially the guides for conveners, recorders, and process consultants described later in this chapter. After giving this information, they can lead discussions about the advantages and disadvantages of the recommended procedures or techniques and then coach members as they conduct their meetings in new ways. In this way, too, facilitators can help a group find resources that none of its members individually can provide by assisting in a search beyond the group for other people and materials.

Training. When group members are unhappy with their meetings and have committed themselves to improving them, the facilitator is in a good position to offer training in alternative modes and roles. Training events can be set up at which members practice the exercises and procedures connected with various leadership roles and functions described in this chapter.

Providing Consultation. Finally, group members are often unaware of how they are influenced by group norms and processes. Members of a faculty, for example, may know that their meetings are going poorly but may not understand why. Some members may be upset because the group cannot work effectively on its agenda in a brief period of time; others may criticize meetings because they are all work and no fun. In such instances, OD facilitators acting as process consultants can collect and feed back data about meeting processes so that members can perceive, understand, and act in ways that will improve their meetings.

Gathering Data About Meetings

The first source of data about meetings is the OD facilitator's own informal observations. The facilitator might keep the following questions in mind: Do meetings start late, with members straggling in? Or do the meetings start promptly, with most members ready to work? Is there an atmosphere of confusion and muddling through? Or is there a clear direction to the meeting guided by a publicly shared agenda? Do members compete and act coldly toward one another? Or do the members cooperate and act warmly toward one another? Do only a few members talk? Or do most members seem to be engaged and getting a chance to talk? Do members interrupt one another, talk at the same time, and use sarcasm, ridicule, or put-downs to express disapproval? Or is the communication open and direct, with favorable and unfavorable feelings being described explicitly?

Answers to such questions will help the OD facilitator to get an initial sense for what this staff is like. Subsequently, however, the facilitator will need to collect more formal data for purposes of diagnosis and feedback. In this section we present several questionnaires, interviews, and observation schedules that we have found useful for gathering data about meetings in colleges and schools. We describe the context in which we think each instrument works best and the settings in which many have been used successfully. Many of the instruments can be adapted to meet special situations. Items from the Meetings Questionnaire, for example, might become part of an interview schedule or might suggest behavior the OD facilitator can observe and report in a process-feedback session. You need not think of the questionnaires or interview guides you see here as indivisible "tests" or research devices. They are not meant to be used in the meticulously replicable ways you may have read about in books on research method. They are meant to bring you tentative information that you will check against other information and that you will use to stimulate discussion among participants about facts and problems. Feel free to use only a part of any data-gathering device you see here or to add something to it.

Instruments for Diagnosing Problems

Meetings Questionnaire. We have used the Meetings Questionnaire, developed by Matthew Miles for the Cooperative Project on Educational Development, in numerous school and college settings to diagnose the quality of participants' meetings (unpublished). In the normal procedure, each member of a group that meets regularly responds to the thirty-seven items on the questionnaire. The facilitator or steering committee can then tabulate and display these data on newsprint to present means and frequency distributions for each item. Participants can be encouraged to diagnose their own meetings by discussing items on which high agreement exists or items with mixed responses. In the questionnaire below, the introductory paragraph can be modified to suit the type of meeting to be described.

Meetings Questionnaire ————————————————

Educational organizations of all types hold a lot of meetings, and much depends on their quality. Please think specifically of the meetings you have in your educational organization.

How often are these meetings usually   How long is the typical meeting?
held? _____   _____

Now, please consider what usually or typically happens in these meetings. Some possible happenings in meetings are listed below. Before each item below, please write one of the following numerals to indicate how usual or typical it is in your group.

5 This is very typical of the meetings; it happens repeatedly.
4 This is fairly typical of the meetings; it happens often.
3 This is more typical than not; it happens sometimes.
2 This is more untypical than typical, though it happens now and then.
1 This is untypical; it rarely happens.
0 This is not typical at all; it never happens.

1. _____ When problems come up in the meeting, they are thoroughly explored until everyone understands what the problem is.
2. _____ The first solution proposed is often accepted by the group.
3. _____ People come to the meeting not knowing what is to be presented or discussed.
4. _____ People ask why the problem exists and what the causes are.
5. _____ Many problems that people are concerned about never get on the agenda.
6. _____ Participants have a tendency to propose answers without really having thought through carefully the problem and its causes.
7. _____ The group discusses the pros and cons of several different alternate solutions to a problem.
8. _____ People bring up extraneous or irrelevant matters.
9. _____ The average person in the meeting feels that his or her ideas have gotten into the discussion.
10. _____ Someone summarizes progress from time to time.
11. _____ Decisions are often left vague as to what they are and who will carry them out.
12. _____ Either before the meeting or at its beginning, any group member can easily get items onto the agenda.
13. _____ People are afraid to be openly critical or make good objections.
14. _____ The group discusses and evaluates how decisions from previous meetings worked out.
15. _____ People do not take the time to really study or define the problem they are working on.
16. _____ The same few people seem to do most of the talking during the meeting.
17. _____ People hesitate to give their true feelings about the problems discussed.
18. _____ When a decision is made, it is clear who should carry it out and when.

19. _____ There is a good deal of jumping from topic to topic—it's often unclear where the group is on the agenda.
20. _____ From time to time in the meeting, people openly discuss the feelings and working relationships in the group.
21. _____ The same problems seem to keep coming up over and over again from meeting to meeting.
22. _____ People don't seem to care about the meeting or want to get involved in it.
23. _____ When the group is thinking about a problem, at least two or three different solutions are suggested.
24. _____ When there is disagreement, it tends to be smoothed over or avoided.
25. _____ Some very creative solutions come out of this group.
26. _____ Many people remain silent.
27. _____ When conflicts over decisions come up, the group does not avoid them but really stays with the conflict and works it through.
28. _____ The results of the group's work are not worth the time it takes.
29. _____ People give their real feelings about what is happening during the meeting itself.
30. _____ People feel very committed to carry out the solutions arrived at by the group.
31. _____ When the group is supposedly working on a problem, it is really working on some other "under the table" problem.
32. _____ People feel antagonistic or negative during the meeting.
33. _____ There is no follow-up on how decisions reached at earlier meetings worked out in practice.
34. _____ Solutions and decisions are in accord with the chairman's or leader's point of view but not necessarily with that of the members.
35. _____ There are splits or deadlocks between factions or subgroups.
36. _____ The discussion goes on and on without any decision being reached.
37. _____ People feel satisfied or positive during the meeting.

Expectations about Meeting Behavior. The Team-Expectation Survey in chapter 4 (under "Gathering Data About Communication") enables participants in meetings to discover what kinds of information they want from others and what kinds of information they are willing to give to others. Fosmire and Keutzer (1968) discuss protocols collected from a wide range of educators showing that (1) meeting participants usually say they are receptive to interpersonal feedback but perceive others as unwilling to give it, and (2) meeting participants usually say they would report their feelings candidly but doubt that others would do so. Our experience confirms Fosmire and Keutzer's findings. This survey is useful not only for measuring and reporting data for discussion but also for showing meeting participants that attempts at openness might be safer than they had formerly believed. We have used this questionnaire with a variety of school staffs and college faculty subgroups that meet regularly. When each participant has completed the questionnaire, we calculate the mean scores for each item and feed the results back to the group for analysis and discussion during a regular meeting. Figure 5-1 illustrates how the data might be displayed for feedback.

Instruments for Process Observation and Consultation. The instruments in this section consist mainly of observation schedules that the OD facilitator can use in carrying out process consultation during meetings. With these instruments, an observer can record both descriptive and quantitative data during a meeting, and these can later be fed back to group members for their own analysis and discussion.

Observing Participation. Effective groups make use of their members' resources during meetings. All members participate

Figure 5-1. Displaying Results of the Team-Expectation Survey

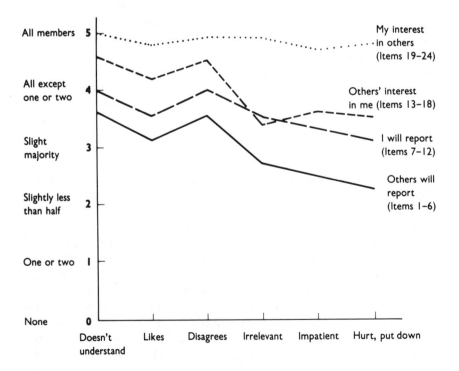

although in different and complementary ways. By means of the observation schedule illustrated in Figure 5-2, the facilitator can record the frequency with which individuals speak to other individuals, to the total group, or not at all.

Figure 5-2. Observer's Frequency Chart: Patterns of Communication

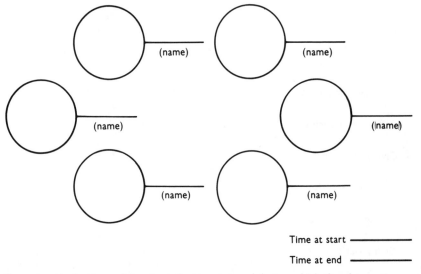

Time at start ─────────

Time at end ─────────

Record at the bottom of the chart the time interval during which the observations are made. Label the circles with the names of group members. The first time a person speaks to another person, draw an arrow from the speaker to the receiver of the message. The first time a person speaks to the total group, draw an arrow to the center of the cluster of circles. Indicate additional messages from the speaker to that individual or to the total group with tally marks on the arrow. Place an *X* in a person's circle if he or she interrupts another to speak. Place a check mark in the circle to indicate that the person's remark encouraged another to participate.

Observing Leadership Functions. The following observation schedule can be used to observe particular leadership functions in groups. In this instance, the observer makes a tally every time a member performs a leadership function in the specified categories listed in the schedule. At the end of the meeting, tallies can be counted and fed back to members. The numbers in Figure 5-3 illustrate how the tallies might turn out.

Figure 5-3. Leadership Functions in Meetings

While observing the group, make a tally mark every time you hear or see behavior (verbal or nonverbal) that approximates one of the following.

			Member			
Categories	S	W	E	R	J	O
I. Setting goals		3				
2. Proposing problems	8	2		20	3	12
3. Asking for information	3	8				2
4. Giving information		2	I	2		2
5. Proposing solutions	4			2		2
6. Asking for clarification	2	I				
7. Giving clarification	3	I		15	3	6
8. Testing for consensus		I				
9. Supporting				I		
10. Asking about group progress			I			
I I. Summarizing		I		2		
12. Evaluating	5	I		20	2	9

Interaction Process Analysis. Another way of observing and analyzing leadership functions in meetings is to collect information on the task behavior and socioemotional behavior of group members. Bales (1950) developed an instrument with categories similar to the task-maintenance functions described earlier in this chapter. His categories were as follows:

SOCIAL-EMOTIONAL: POSITIVE

1. Shows solidarity, raises others' status, gives help, rewards
2. Shows tension release, jokes, laughs, shows satisfaction
3. Agrees, shows passive acceptance, understands, confers, complies

TASK: NEUTRAL

4. Gives suggestions, direction, implying autonomy for others
5. Gives opinions, evaluation, analysis, expresses feeling, wishes
6. Gives orientation, information, repeats, clarifies, confirms
7. Asks for orientation, information, repetition, confirmation
8. Asks for opinions, evaluation, analysis, expressions of feeling
9. Asks for suggestions, direction, possible ways of action

SOCIAL-EMOTIONAL: NEGATIVE

10. Disagrees, shows passive rejection, formality, withholds help
11. Shows tension, asks for help, withdraws, leaves the field
12. Shows antagonism, deflates others' status, defends or asserts self

The OD facilitator can collect information on these categories using the observation schedule in Figure 5-4. The data can be reported to group members, who can discuss the task and socioemotional activities they usually perform or identify those they would like to practice to gain greater proficiency.

Instruments for Evaluating Meeting Effectiveness

The following questionnaires measure participants' reactions to meetings. The first three were developed to help a group analyze a single meeting; the fourth has been used to measure perceptions and expectations about a series of meetings.

Figure 5-4. Cumulative Interaction Form

Date _____   Group _____

Time _____ to _____   Observer _____

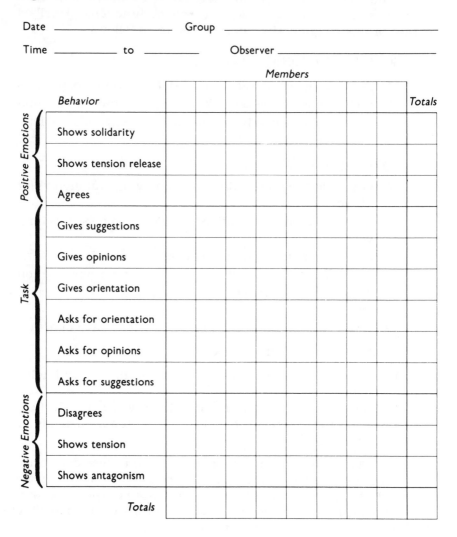

	Behavior									Totals
Positive Emotions	Shows solidarity									
	Shows tension release									
	Agrees									
Task	Gives suggestions									
	Gives opinions									
	Gives orientation									
	Asks for orientation									
	Asks for opinions									
	Asks for suggestions									
Negative Emotions	Disagrees									
	Shows tension									
	Shows antagonism									
	Totals									

Example 1. Several facilitators have used this questionnaire for feedback to groups of educators.

Directions: Mark an X in the space that best shows your reaction to this meeting.

Agreement		Disagreement		
Strong	Mild	Mild	Strong	
( )	( )	( )	( )	1. The results of this meeting
YES!	yes	no	NO!	were worth the time.

( )   ( )   ( )   ( )   2. I was given adequate oppor-
YES!   yes   no   NO!   tunity to state my beliefs
                                 about subjects discussed by
                                 the group.

( )   ( )   ( )   ( )   3. Our meeting was efficient.
YES!   yes   no   NO!

( )   ( )   ( )   ( )   4. I am satisfied with the atten-
YES!   yes   no   NO!   tion and consideration that
                                 others gave to my ideas and
                                 opinions.

( )   ( )   ( )   ( )   5. We wasted too much time in
YES!   yes   no   NO!   this meeting.

( )   ( )   ( )   ( )   6. The group effectively used
YES!   yes   no   NO!   my knowledge of the sub-
                                 jects discussed.

( )   ( )   ( )   ( )   7. The most important topics
YES!   yes   no   NO!   were never discussed.

( )   ( )   ( )   ( )   8. I had adequate opportunity
YES!   yes   no   NO!   to influence our conclusions
                                 and decisions.

Example 2. The following items were developed by Runkel.

1. Do you feel that anything of value happened during this meeting?

( )   Yes, quite a lot.
( )   Yes, something.
( )   Not much.
( )   Nothing.

2. If you found something of value in this meeting, does any particular happening or idea stand out in your mind?

( )   Nothing of value happened.
( )   It was a valuable meeting, but no particular thing stands out.
( )   Yes, something does stand out for me—namely,

3. If you found something in this meeting to be of *no* value, was there a particular happening or idea that stands out in your mind as being valueless?

( )   Most everything was of some value.
( )   Some parts of the meeting had no value, but no particular thing stands out.
( )   Yes, something stands out for me as having no value—namely,

_____

_____

4. Was there any feature about the way this group operated that you thought particularly effective?

( )   No   ( )   Yes—namely,

_____

_____

_____

5. Was there any feature about the way this group operated that you thought *ineffective?*

( )   No   ( )   Yes—namely,

_____

_____

_____

Example 3. This form is based on an instrument developed by Schein (1969).

Answer the items according to *your own opinions* about the meeting. There are no right answers. Circle the number on the scale that corresponds to your opinion.

1. Goals of the meeting

Poor_____1_____2_____3_____4_____5_____Good

(Conflicting; unclear;   (Clear; shared by all, en-
diverse, unacceptable.)   dorsed with enthusiasm.)

2. Participation in the meeting

Poor_____|_____2_____3_____4_____5_____Good

(Few dominate; some passive; some not listened to; several talk at once or interrupt.)

(All get in; all are really listened to; open and lively discussion.)

3. Leadership of the meeting

Poor_____|_____2_____3_____4_____5_____Good

(Group needs for leadership not met; group depends too much on one or a few persons; no direction or no leadership.)

(A sense of direction is in evidence; leaders are allowed to emerge as needs for leadership arise; everyone feels free to volunteer to lead.)

4. Decisions made during the meeting

Poor_____|_____2_____3_____4_____5_____Good

(No decisions were made; decisions were made to which I feel uncommitted; bad decisions were made.)

(Good decisions were made; everyone felt a part of the decision-making process; people feel committed to the decisions.)

5. Your feelings during the meeting

Poor_____|_____2_____3_____4_____5_____Good

(I was unable to express my feelings; my feelings were ignored; my feelings were criticized.)

(I freely expressed my feelings; I felt understood; I felt support from the participants.)

6. Organization of the meeting

Poor_____|_____2_____3_____4_____5_____Good

(It was chaotic; it was too tightly controlled; very poorly done; I felt manipulated.)

(It was very well organized; it was flexible enough to enable us to influence it; all went smoothly.)

7. Relationship among meeting participants

Poor___1___2___3___4___5___Good

(My relationship with them is the same as before; I feel antagonistic toward many of them; I don't trust them; there is little potential for a future relationship.)

(Our relationship is much improved; I trust them more than I did prior to the session; I feel I got to know and understand many of them better; there is good potential for the future.)

8. Attitude about the meeting

Poor___1___2___3___4___5___Good

(Boring; it was a waste of time; I don't like the way it was presented; I disliked it.)

(Interesting; was helpful; I liked it.)

9. Content of the meeting

Poor___1___2___3___4___5___Good

(Uninstructional; I did not learn much; not informative; too much process; not enough content.)

(I learned a lot; was informative; I'll be able to use the content; content was appropriate to our needs.)

10. Productivity of the meeting

Poor___1___2___3___4___5___Good

(Did not accomplish much; no useful ideas emerged; it got us nowhere.)

(Got a lot done; very fruitful; something will come of this session.)

Example 4. The following questionnaire can assist group members in analyzing members' contributions to meeting effectiveness. The information might be sensitive for groups with low degrees of openness and trust, so the facilitator should strive to accentuate the helpful and favorable aspects of the meeting.

Role-Perception Survey ————————————————————

Which members, in your judgment, contributed most to meeting effectiveness by:

Helping to get started on time? _____

_____ (names).

Sticking to the agenda? _____

_____ (names).

Performing acts of encouragement, warmth, friendly interest, and support?

_____ (names).

Bringing in ideas, information, and suggestions? _____

_____ (names).

Helping us to stay on the track, summarizing, checking to make sure we

understood one another? _____

_____ (names).

Exercises and Procedures
for Improving Meetings

This section offers exercises and procedures that OD facilitators can use either in formal training sessions or during regular meetings. Although some might prefer another scheme, we have categorized these exercises and activities according to their effectiveness in helping group members (1) warm up for meetings; (2) plan, conduct, and evaluate meetings; (3) broaden participation; (4) stimulate creativity; and (5) deal with hidden agendas and game playing. OD facilitators will want to adapt them to their own particular applications, although each has been successfully tried as described here.

Helping Members Warm Up

Fatigue, illness, or other preoccupations can prevent participants from becoming engaged in the tasks at hand. Procedures that help them to become attentive to the here and now will increase the efficiency of meetings. To this end, we have found the following five warm-up activities to be effective.

Naming. This activity enables strangers to learn the names of others in the group while their own names are being learned. One person states his or her own name; the next person to the left or right repeats this name and adds his own, the next person repeats the first two names and adds his own, and so on until all names are given. Because connecting names and faces (or whatever other aspect of appearance is mnemonic) requires alertness, the exercise has the effect of focusing eyes on people instead of on note paper or out the window.

Announcing Preferences for the Agenda. This activity, which is also designed to focus attention on persons and their directions of thought, can be used rapidly to yield a quick acquaintance with persons and their ideas, or it can be used thoughtfully, with deliberation, to get more depth. Each person addresses a particular other person, expressing what he or she believes to be a preferred agenda item that the two of them share. The person addressed is obliged to agree or disagree with the first speaker, and then turn to another person and announce another agenda item to be agreed on by both. The procedure continues in the same manner.

Milling. In this procedure, each person walks about the room looking at other members without speaking to them. After a few minutes, participants are asked to choose someone they would like to know better and to talk about their hopes for the meeting. After another few minutes the milling begins again and each person chooses someone else with whom to repeat the activity. After a while, all group members are asked to summarize their hopes for the meeting.

Billy Goat. This activity is helpful for loosening people up in preparation for some creative task. The group stands in a close circle; the facilitator steps into the center of the circle and says, "When I point to someone and say 'billy goat,' that person must place her hand beneath her chin to resemble a goat's beard and bleat *baa*. The persons to her immediate left and right must at the same time form a goat's horns by each holding an index finger to that person's head. The last person of the three to do this must then step to the center of the circle and choose the next billy goat." After a few rounds the OD facilitator may introduce variations such as Elephant (middle person makes a trunk by holding two fists to his nose while neighbors form floppy ears) or Kangaroo (middle person makes a pouch by cupping hands while neighbors hop up and down). There are endless variations, and the group should be encouraged to create a few of its own.

Walk Across the Circle. In this exercise, eight to twelve persons are seated in a circle and, at a signal from the facilitator, all walk across the circle and sit in the chairs of the persons opposite them. But only one step may be taken at the first signal, only one step at the second signal, and so on. After each single step, participants must hold their positions until the next step is called. As soon as everyone has taken one step, call the next step promptly, although not while someone is still off balance. Keep calling until the last person has reached a chair and is seated. You may join the exercise yourself while calling the steps. After the first step, participants will get in one another's way and will have to choose whether to circumnavigate or to plow through the scrimmage. Those who prefer bodily contact will get it; those who do not will easily avoid it. This exercise requires only an average feeling of friendliness and good will among group members. During the debriefing, some of the participants will quickly offer descriptions of behavior and feelings.

Helping Members Plan, Conduct, and Evaluate Meetings

We have already noted the leadership functions needed for effective meetings and the several leadership roles that should be assigned to individual members in rotation. Here we discuss how OD facilitators can help members plan, conduct, and evaluate their meetings and how they can strengthen the ways in which leadership functions are managed and leadership roles assumed.

Planning and Preparing. Before a meeting is called, the convener should give thought to clarifying goals, to issues of appropriate membership, and to matters of time scheduling and physical facilities. If the purpose of a meeting is not clear to everyone present, prepare relevant contributions beforehand to accomplish that purpose. If goals are unstated or unclear, some people whose presence is necessary may not be invited; some will discover that their presence is unnecessary; others may feel little desire to attend the meeting at all; and many who attend will present concerns irrelevant to the major purpose.

Goals are also important to consider with respect to scheduling. A group that wants to generate fresh ideas for teaching should probably not plan to meet in the late afternoon after a hard day's work. And time allotments must be considered as well. Too often educators spend hours discussing a five-minute report only to find themselves forced to make a major decision in a few minutes. Finally, most meetings for problem solving and decision making require physical arrangements that encourage participation. Chairs should be placed in circles or around tables so that face-to-face communication can occur, and materials such as newsprint and felt-tip pens should be available for illustrating and recording members' contributions.

As simple as these items appear, in many colleges and schools they are ignored by those responsible for meetings. Facilitators can help to improve meetings by going over the planning prerequisites and by encouraging an individual member, not necessarily the formal leader, to assume responsibility in guiding the meeting. Meeting organizers can use the three planning sheets displayed in Figures 5-5, 5-6, and 5-7 (developed by Schindler-Rainman, Lippitt, and Cole, 1975, pp. 23–25) to increase the effectiveness of their efforts.

Organizing an Agenda. Most meetings entail several topics or activities that vary in their respective time requirements. Some items will be presented for information only; others will require longer discussion and planning for action. A group can greatly improve efficiency by spending a brief time at the beginning of the meeting to set priorities, designate time allotments, and decide what kind of action each item requires. Unfortunately, many people are inexperienced at running meetings in a disciplined way. Those accustomed only to the free-for-all style will need repeated explanations of the disciplined step-by-step method and will learn faster if others in the group help to model and explain this style.

The following procedure allows everyone to contribute to building an effective agenda. (1) Ask group members to name the items they want to deal with at this meeting. (2) When you are reasonably sure that all members understand each item, order the items according to their similarities and place them in homogeneous clusters. (3) Select the order by asking group members for their priorities, trying

Figure 5-5. Diagnostic Planning for Designing Participatory Meetings

Thinking about the participants or members (e.g., how many, subgroups and individual differences, needs, readinesses, interests, expectations)	Some desirable outcomes of the meeting (e.g., skills, information, values, concepts, actions, plans, recommendations, decisions)	Ideas for activities, experiences, resources, to facilitate the outcomes (e.g., exercises, projects, resources, facilities, work groups)
*Star most important characteristics and differences among participants to keep in mind when designing	*Star highest priority outcomes	*Star what seem to be most appropriate, effective, feasible ingredients of design

Summary statement of desired outcomes:

Source: Eva Schindler-Rainman, Ronald Lippitt, and Jack Cole, *Taking Your Meetings Out of the Doldrums*, San Diego, CA: University Associates, Inc., 1975.

Figure 5-6. The Meeting Design

Time estimate	Activities, methods, groupings	Who is responsible	Arrangements of space, equipment, materials

1. Premeeting and start-up of the meeting

2. Flow of session after start-up activities

(continue on additional sheet as needed)

Source: Eva Schindler-Rainman, Ronald Lippitt, and Jack Cole, *Taking Your Meetings Out of the Doldrums*, San Diego, CA: University Associates, Inc., 1975.

Figure 5-7. Commitments, Follow-ups, Supports

1. *Plans for ending the meeting* (e.g., closing activities, evaluation, reports of back-home plans, deadline commitments, etc.)

2. *Follow-up:* Who will do what? When? Where?
(e.g., often a directory of names, addresses, telephone numbers of participants is very important at this point; make sure any follow-up dates are recorded in everyone's calendar)

3. *Clean-up and other immediate commitments*
(e.g., what has to be returned, thank-you calls made, bills paid, etc.)

Source: Eva Schindler-Rainman, Ronald Lippitt, and Jack Cole, *Taking Your Meetings Out of the Doldrums*, San Diego, CA: University Associates, Inc., 1975.

at the same time to establish rough time estimates for each agenda item. You can accomplish some of this before the meeting begins by posting an agenda sheet in a central location and encouraging group members to write items for the next meeting's agenda on it. In this way participants can both contribute their own items for the group's consideration and think about other people's items in order to offer informed questions and decisions.

The best strategy we have found for helping groups improve their ability to organize an agenda is to assign that responsibility to the convener, gain the group's agreement to follow that procedure, and then coach the convener over several meetings. OD facilitators can recommend that the convener use the meeting format exhibited in Tables 5-1 and 5-2 or some modification of them.

Table 5-1. Sample Agenda Format (School)

Agenda Item	Order	Time	Person	Required Action
United Way	4	5	Sue	Information only
Hall passes	2	10	Lee	Discuss, appoint study committee
Selection committee for new vice principal	1	15	Lynn	Advise principal on membership criteria
New science textbook	3	35	Task force	Decision
Debriefing	5	10	All	Discuss

Table 5-2. Sample Agenda Format (College)

Agenda Item	Order	Time	Person	Required Action
Course evaluations	2	15	Pete & Mary	Brainstorming
Curriculum changes	1	20	Committee	Decision
Exam schedule	4	5	Mark	Information only
Search for new faculty member	3	30	Committee	Discuss
Office changes	5	5	Mark	Information only
Debriefing	6	15	All	Discuss

Convening. Using a chairperson or convener to lead the discussion and rotating the role throughout the membership are common procedures for providing some of the leadership functions previously discussed. Conveners have the legitimate authority to conduct the meeting. They should facilitate discussion by gatekeeping (seeing that others have a chance to speak), asking brief questions, and summarizing concisely. They should move groups efficiently through their tasks, steering discussions to group processes when that appears helpful. They should bring hangers-back into the discussion, though remaining conscious of the necessity of moving the group along. They should see to it that someone is recording minutes, writing on the chalkboard, and assigning tasks to individuals and subgroups. Although they should be forceful and definite, not hesitant and apologetic, conveners should be aware that their role is to facilitate, not to dominate, and they should avoid arguing down others or writing on the board only that which meets their approval.

The convener's primary duty is to remind the group of its pact to discuss certain items during the meeting and to stop at a stated time (although this pact can be altered by common consent). If the group is taking too much time on one item, the convener should point this out, asking something like, "Do you wish to subtract time from other items, cancel one or more items, extend the meeting, or what?" Some conveners appoint a timekeeper if someone is willing to keep an eye on the clock. Conveners should not choose or even suggest a solution but should demand procedural decisions from the group. When the group is not capable of making such decisions, it is useful to discover the fact.

Over a series of meetings, each group member can practice guiding the group. This procedure is most helpful if group members give the convener feedback after the meeting about how well this individual met their needs. The following guide for the convener has proved very easy to use for those with a fair amount of previous experience at conducting deliberative meetings. Conveners should think about all these tasks but should not try to use them all if the meeting is brief or attended by very few.

GUIDE FOR THE CONVENER

Before the meeting:

• Review the agenda.
• Make sure a recorder is assigned to document proceedings at the meeting.

During the meeting:

- Get it started promptly.
- Lead the group to establish priorities among items on the agenda and to specify the time to be spent on each item.
- Keep the group at the task (i.e., monitor discussion and inform the group when it strays from the agenda at hand).
- Keep the group to its time commitments for each agenda item.
- Be attuned to feelings of confusion and try to clarify them.
- At the end of each agenda item:
  Check to be sure that everyone who wanted to has had a chance to contribute to the discussion.
  Check to see whether everyone understands where the matter now stands.
  Summarize or ask someone else to summarize. Be sure the recorder records the summary.
- Take process checks whenever they seem appropriate: if a process observer is present, employ that person's services (see the guide for the process observer below).
  Check to see whether group members are satisfied with their participation.
  Check the decision making being done.
- Conduct or ask someone else to conduct a debriefing session during the last ten minutes of the meeting.

Recording Activities and Decisions. Activities initiated at a meeting are seldom completed at the same meeting, because most such issues require some sort of procedure for storage and retrieval of information at a future time. Since groups cannot rely on individual memories, recording and distributing minutes are crucial for continuity. Effective groups assign recording tasks to one individual but rotate the role throughout the membership just as the convener role is rotated. The following guide is appropriate for most college or school meetings but can be adapted for brief informal meetings attended by few people.

GUIDE FOR THE RECORDER

Before the meeting:

- Review the agenda and the record of previous meetings for unfinished agenda items.
- Gather materials necessary to record what happens at the

meeting (e.g., pencil and paper, large newsprint and felt-tip pens, and perhaps a video or audio recorder).

During the meeting:
- Describe the setting for the meeting (place, date, time) and list the participants.
- Copy down the agenda in the order finally agreed upon.
- During each agenda item, record the major views expressed and points of information shared.
- At the end of each agenda item, record a short summary containing decisions made, understandings achieved, and action to be taken.

After the meeting:
- Collect any newsprint used by group members during the meeting (e.g., for brainstorming ideas) and prepare to attach a typed copy to the record.
- Meet with the convener to check the clarity and completeness of the record.
- Have the records typed, duplicated, and transmitted to group members.
- Make sure a debriefing item gets on the agenda.

Facilitating Process. A group can usually improve its meetings by appointing one of its own members as process observer with functions that complement those of the convener, and if the OD facilitator has been successful in transferring to group members the skill and responsibility for observing and analyzing their own process. The facilitator can coach the process observer over several meetings by using the guide below and by helping this person become proficient in using the instruments for process observation and feedback described earlier in this chapter. Groups new to process observation and discussion might take a look at how they are doing every 20 to 30 minutes, with the observer leading a brief discussion at each process break about how satisfying and productive the meeting has been so far. The following guide suggests important tasks for the process observer. That individual should not attempt to squeeze all these tasks in at once, however, but should choose among them in accordance with the size and type of meeting.

GUIDE FOR THE PROCESS OBSERVER

Before the meeting:

- Collect and practice using appropriate observation schedules for gathering data on meetings.
- Ask the group the kind of information it would like you to look for and when you could make a process check or report back observations.

During the meeting:

- Attend to the group process rather than to the content of the work.
- Record your observations and impressions about why the meeting is going as it is. Look at communication patterns, breadth of participation, atmosphere of the group, apparent satisfaction of group members, decisions being made.
- Organize your observations so that you can convey them to the group. Coding similar observations may help to make sense out of a clutter of notes.
- Report your observations to the group when appropriate, and make sure you describe observed behavior to support your interpretations of what was happening in the group.
- If the group gets bogged down at any point, ask members to stop and discuss what is preventing them from accomplishing their purposes.

At the close of the meeting:

- Conduct a debriefing session during the last few minutes of the meeting, asking members to consider the following:
  Did we accomplish our goals for this meeting?
  Did we use our resources effectively?
  Did we avoid pitfalls such as wasting time?
- Ask members for feedback about how well you served as their process observer.

Group Agreements. Rewards and punishments come into play when groups have definite but inexplicit norms about behavior. If people believe that they will suffer rejection or punishment by failing to conform to these norms, it will be difficult for them to practice new behavior or to take creative risks unless doing so is explicitly encouraged. Hence, norms controlling collaboration, use of power, and especially openness about feelings should be made explicit if they are to have a beneficial influence on meeting effectiveness. If, for example, group members deal with feelings of boredom or frustration when they arise, the conditions that produce these feelings can be changed to create a better climate for accomplishing the tasks at hand. The following procedures are helpful for clarifying norms.

1. *Forming group agreements.* Each member states a norm or custom that he or she would like others to practice. The group discusses each proposal until it reaches consensus on several of them. Because it is important to describe the behavioral content of a proposed norm, the facilitator may wish to provide samples like the two that follow.

   a. For directness, I will report dissatisfactions with the way the group is going during the meeting. I will not discuss these dissatisfactions with nonmembers. If outside a regular session another member tells me of his dissatisfaction with the group, I will suggest bringing the matter before the total group at the next meeting.

   b. Any member may ask for a survey at any time. The member will state what he or she wants to know from the total group, and someone else will paraphrase the request. Each person will state a position in two or three sentences. A survey is not a vote and will not bind us. A survey must be taken when it is requested and all other activities will be suspended for it.

New norms are made by establishing group agreements. Members discuss the explicit ways in which they have been rewarding and punishing one another for certain behavior in the past. They say that they want to give up some of the behavior that was maintained in that way, that they want certain other behaviors to be rewarded, and that they will join in new common patterns of encouraging and discouraging one another's behavior. It's as simple and as difficult as that.

2. *Continuing group agreements.* Periodically a group should review its agreements and discuss whether they are being kept. Agreements should not be regarded as sacrosanct. An effective group will change its agreements often and will plan actions to build commitments for new agreements. Above all, the group should be clear and explicit about what kinds of behaviors are expected.

3. *Listing inhibited and induced behaviors.* Each group member answers the following questions in writing:

   a. What have I wanted to do in this group but have not done because it seemed inappropriate?

   b. What have I done in this group that I didn't want to do but to which I couldn't say no?

After sharing the answers aloud, the group looks for common patterns that suggest norms. The members then make consensual agreements about which existing norms are dysfunctional and which new norms would be better. In the final step, members plan for instituting the new agreements by stating steps and dates for actions that will reflect them.

Broadening Participation. Most meetings could be more effective if all group members were encouraged to participate actively. Accurate communication demands active listening, and effective decision making requires at least minimal participation by those who will carry out decisions. Members should not have to guess what others think of their ideas; if they are to improve the way they participate in the group, they must know the effects of their remarks on others. The following procedures are useful for broadening participation.

The Chance to Listen. By time-honored democratic tradition, the right to speak is everyone's basic right at a meeting. But parliamentary rules and procedures do not ensure our right to understand what has been said. To ask a question for clarification, you are first required to "get the floor," and getting the floor is hedged about with numerous rules, restrictions, protocols, customs, and protections. By the time you have fought through the channels to be allowed to ask your question, you have had a 10-minute debate with the meeting's chairman or parliamentarian, three other speakers who were awaiting their turn at the floor have made long speeches, and the earlier speaker of whom you wished to ask your question has gone out to lunch.

One way to alter this situation is to insist during crucial periods that before someone speaks, he or she must paraphrase the person who just finished speaking. Before a proposal is decided upon, several people should paraphrase so that everyone is clear about what is being decided. The chance to listen means that you are allowed at any moment to interrupt a speaker for clarification. This procedure works, however, only when the group as a whole genuinely values mutual understanding.

In the other situations, particularly those in which the OD facilitator is taking a strong role, the facilitator can require that before one contributes to the discussion the contributor must paraphrase what the last person said. Also, it can be beneficial to ask subgroups reporting on their discussions to paraphrase or summarize the last subgroup report before making their own.

High-Talker Tap-Out. It is not uncommon to find during small-group discussions that only a small percentage of the group is engaged in a large percentage of the interaction. The High-Talker Tap-Out, described in chapter 4 under "Communication in the Subsystem," deals with this problem by evening out participation. Appoint someone to watch for anyone seizing more than a reasonable share of the discussion. When that happens, give the person a note requesting that he or she refrain from further comments on content (comments on group process may still be permitted).

Time Tokens. The Time Token, also covered in chapter 4, is another device for dealing with people who contribute too little or too much. Distribute tokens to participants, each token to be redeemed for a specific amount of discussion time—say 15 seconds. Participants who use up their tokens may say nothing more unless other members are willing to give some of their own. This less obtrusive procedure has certain advantages over the tap-out. It allows an exceptional contributor to overcontribute with the consent of the other group members; it makes each member's degree of participation obvious and salient, and it encourages participants to make their contributions more concise. Participants monitor their own talking and need not wonder at the meaning of certain other members' silence.

Beach Ball. Still another procedure for dealing with those who contribute too little or too much is the Beach Ball. Only the person holding the ball is permitted to speak. Others who wish to contribute must nonverbally attract the attention of the person with the ball and induce the speaker to toss it to them. Instead of a beach ball, a wad of newspaper or another harmless object can be used.

Fishbowl. Another procedure discussed earlier that employs some of the advantages of the small-group discussion within the setting of a larger meeting is the Fishbowl. As noted in chapter 4, in this procedure a small group forms a circle within a larger group to discuss whatever is on the agenda as the other participants observe. To allow wider participation, the arrangers can provide empty chairs in the central group so that any observing members can join the discussion, with the understanding that their visits will be only temporary. The onlookers are themselves arranged in a circle so that they can all see and hear the inner group clearly and also get to a visitor's chair quickly.

This procedure is useful when those in the encircling group can see an obvious reason why those in the interior circle were selected—if, for example, they are a regularized group within the educational organization, if they are temporary or regular representatives of segments of the onlookers, or the like. If members of the inner group are not obviously different from the rest, assigning them special seating will usually seem unjustified.

Fishbowl seating can also be used during OD exercises on leadership or group process. Each member of the outer circle pairs with a member of the inner circle. The outsider observes the group behavior of the insider. At planned intervals, the pair gets together to discuss what is happening in the group. The outsider gives feedback while the insider makes plans about new behavior to be tried in the group.

Buzz Groups. Buzz groups are effective in diffusing participation in a large group, especially when important decisions must be made and some members hesitate to express opposing views before the entire assembly. Suppose, for example, that a faculty is at the point of setting priorities among several goals. Some faculty members have stated their preferences, but most have remained silent. The chairperson may interrupt the meeting temporarily while groups of four to seven persons form to discuss the issue briefly, seeking to discover whose opinions are opposed and whether they are ready to reach agreement. When opinions are difficult to bring out, have reporters from each buzz group summarize the ideas and feelings of their subgroups without indicating who expressed them. Such summaries also discourage any one subgroup of members from dominating the flow of interaction.

An Exercise to Encourage Participation. The following eight-step exercise* shows the importance of maintenance functions in a decision-making group, emphasizes the necessity of engaging all members in group decision making, and gives practice in observing leadership behavior in a group. It concentrates on encouraging group members to become engaged in group activities.

I. Introduce the exercise by reviewing the task and maintenance functions in a group and by telling participants that the exercise focuses on leadership behavior in a decision-making group. Inform them that there is a "best" solution to the problem, based on research, which they will learn after they have completed the first six steps.

*Originally created by Hall (1969); here adapted from Johnson and Johnson (1975, pp. 39–40 and 351–54). A similar exercise appears in Johnson and Johnson's second edition (1982, pp. 68–71, 473).

II. Form groups of 10 to 14 members—large groups are essential in this exercise—with two additional observers for each group. Distribute copies of the following case study.

Overcoming Resistance to Change

In American industry, competition makes change necessary—like changing products and the way in which jobs are done. One of the most serious production problems at the Sleep-Eze pajama factory has been that production workers have resisted necessary changes. The upshot has been grievances about the piece rates that went with the new methods, high job turnover, low efficiency, restriction of output, and marked aggression against management. Despite these undesirable effects, methods and jobs must continue to change at the Sleep-Eze company if it is to remain a competitor in its field.

The main plant of the Sleep-Eze Manufacturing Corporation is in a small town in a southern state. The plant produces pajamas and, like most sewing plants, hires mostly women; there are about 500 women and 100 men employees. The workers are recruited from the rural areas around the town, and they usually have no industrial experience. Their average age is 23, and their average education is 10 years of formal schooling. Company policies in regard to labor relations are liberal and progressive. A high value has been placed on fair and open dealing with the employees, and they are encouraged to take up any problems or grievances with the management at any time. Sleep-Eze has invested both time and money in employee services, such as industrial music, health services, lunchroom facilities, and recreation programs.

The employees of Sleep-Eze work on an individual-incentive system. Piece rates are set by time study and are expressed in terms of units. One unit is equal to one minute of standard work: 60 units per hour equal the standard efficiency rating. The amount of pay received is directly proportional to the weekly average efficiency rating achieved. Thus, an operator with an average efficiency rating of 75 units an hour (25 percent more than standard) would receive 25 percent more than the base pay. The rating of every piece worker is computed every day, and the results are published in a daily record of production that is shown to every operator.

The average relearning time for workers who are transferred to a new job is eight weeks. The relearning period for experienced operators is longer than the learning for a new operator.

The company now recognizes that the time has come to make changes again. Although they are to be minor ones, changes heretofore have been met with extreme resistance by the employees involved. Such an expression as "when you make your units [standard production], they change your job" is heard all too frequently. As in the past, many operators will refuse to change, preferring to quit.

Some examples of the changes to be made are:

1. Eighteen hand pressers have formerly stacked their work in half-dozen lots on a flat piece of cardboard the size of the finished product. The new job calls for them to stack their work in half-dozen lots in a box the size of the finished product. An additional two minutes per dozen will be allowed (by the time study) for this new part of the job.
2. Thirteen pajama folders have heretofore folded coats with prefolded pants. The change calls for the pants to be folded too. An additional two minutes per dozen will be allowed.
3. Fifteen pajama examiners have been clipping threads and examining every seam. The new job calls for pulling only certain threads off and examining every seam. An average of 1.2 minutes per dozen will be subtracted from the total time.

What is the best procedure for management to take to make sure the least amount of resistance results from these needed changes? Listed below are several different ways of handling this problem. Rank these alternatives in terms of their effectiveness for bringing about the least resistance to change. Place a 1 by the most effective alternative, 2 by the second most effective, and so on through 5, the least effective. Remember that after the exercise you will be told what researchers have found to be the "best" ranking.

_____ By written memo, explain the need for a change to the employees involved, and allow extra pay for transfers to make up for the usual drop in piece rate after a change.

_____ Before any changes are made, hold meetings with large groups of the employees involved, and give a lecture explaining that the change is necessary because of competitive conditions. Have the time-study man thoroughly explain the basis of the new piece rate. Then put in the change as planned.

_____ Before any changes take place, hold meetings with large groups of the employees involved. Using demonstrations, dramatically show the need for change. Present a tentative plan for setting the new job and piece rates, and have the groups elect representatives to work with management in making the plan final.

_____ By written memo, explain the need for the change, put the change into operation, and make layoffs as necessary on the basis of efficiency.

_____ Before any changes occur, hold meetings with small groups of the employees involved. Employing demonstrations, dramatically present a tentative plan for setting the new job and piece rates, and ask everybody present to help in designing the new jobs.

III. Meet with the observers and give them copies of task- and maintenance-functions observation sheets. Explain that their role is to give their attention to the leadership and decision-making behavior of the group.

IV. Give the groups thirty minutes to arrive at a decision on the case study, indicating that their decision should be based upon accurate information and facts.

V. At the end of the thirty minutes, have every group member fill out the form below, circling the number in front of the answer chosen.

1. How much did you participate in making the decisions reached by your group? I participated:

7 Completely or thoroughly
6 A lot more than others
5 More than others
4 About as much as most others
3 Less than others
2 A lot less than others
I Not at all

2. How satisfied did you feel with the amount and quality of your participation in reaching a joint decision? I felt:

7 Completely satisfied
6 Generally or mostly satisfied
5 A little more satisfied than dissatisfied
4 Neutral, as satisfied as dissatisfied
3 A little more dissatisfied than satisfied
2 Generally or mostly dissatisfied
I Completely dissatisfied

3. How much responsibility would you feel for making the decision work? I would feel:

7 Completely responsible
6 Generally or mostly responsible
5 A little more responsible than irresponsible
4 Neutral, as responsible as irresponsible
3 A little more irresponsible than responsible
2 Generally or mostly irresponsible
I Completely irresponsible

4. How committed do you feel to the decision your group made? I feel:

7 Completely committed

6 Generally or mostly committed
5 A little more committed than uncommitted
4 Neutral, as committed as uncommitted
3 A little more uncommitted than committed
2 Generally or mostly uncommitted
1 Completely uncommitted

5. How much frustration or fulfillment did you feel during the work on the decision? I felt:

7 Completely frustrated
6 Generally or mostly frustrated
5 A little more frustrated than fulfilled
4 Neutral, as frustrated as fulfilled
3 A little more fulfilled than frustrated
2 Generally or mostly fulfilled
1 Completely fulfilled

6. How good was the decision your group made? It was:

7 Completely accurate
6 Generally or mostly accurate
5 A little more accurate than inaccurate
4 Neutral, as accurate as inaccurate
3 A little more inaccurate than accurate
2 Generally or mostly inaccurate
1 Completely inaccurate

7. How much influence did you have on the group's decision? I influenced:

7 Completely or thoroughly
6 A lot more than others
5 More than others
4 About as much as others
3 Less than others
2 A lot less than others
1 Not at all

8. When members had differences of opinion, to what extent were all sides carefully listened to and the conflict directly faced and resolved?

7 Completely listened to
6 Generally or mostly listened to
5 A little more listened to than not listened to
4 Neutral, as listened to as not listened to
3 A little more not listened to than listened to

2   Generally not listened to
1   Completely not listened to

9. To what extent are you willing to work effectively with this group in the future?

7   Completely willing
6   Generally or mostly willing
5   A little more willing than unwilling
4   Neutral, as willing as unwilling
3   A little more unwilling than willing
2   Generally or mostly unwilling
1   Completely unwilling

Questions 1 through 9 above are phrased to make lessons in the exercise explicit. Examining those dimensions of group functioning, however, is also useful in diagnosing decision making in actual working groups. A Personal Reaction Index suitable for use with intact groups is available from Teleometrics International, 1755 Woodstead Court, The Woodlands, Texas 77380.

VI. On the basis of the response to question 1, divide the reaction forms from all groups into two categories as follows: place in the high-participator category any person who responded 5 or higher on the first question and in the low-participator category anyone who responded 4 or below. For each category, determine the mean response to the rest of the questions by totaling the responses for each question and dividing by the number of persons in the category. Enter the mean response in the table below.

	High participators	Low participators
Amount of satisfaction obtained from participation	_____	_____
Feelings of responsibility for making the decision work	_____	_____
Feelings of commitment to the group's decision	_____	_____
Amount of frustration felt during group meeting	_____	_____
Appraisal of decision quality	_____	_____
Influence felt on the group's decision	_____	_____
Direct dealing with conflict	_____	_____
Willingness to work with the group in the future	_____	_____

Present the results to the participants, ask each group to discuss them, and propose a theory concerning both the effects of participation in group decision making on the implementation of a decision and the effects of maintenance functions (especially encouraging participation) on group decision making. Give each group up to thirty minutes to formulate its theory.

VII. Gather all into one meeting and ask that someone from each group describe orally the group's theory. Encourage a general discussion about the importance of maintenance functions in groups. Only after this discussion, present participants with the correct ranking of alternatives presented in the case study, as below:

This case study was an actual situation studied by Coch and French in the late 1940s. From the results of their study, they considered the correct ranking to be 4, 3, 2, 5, 1. The two principles involved are (1) group discussion is more effective than lectures and memos in influencing change, and (2) belief that one is participating in making the decision leads to commitment to putting the decision into practice.

VIII. Have each group analyze the leadership behavior in its group using the information gathered by the observers. Review the leadership behavior of group members in terms of the theories just formulated in step VI. Of special interest should be information on who encouraged the participation of other members.

Stimulating Creativity

Brainstorming. Members of groups have a wealth of ideas about most problems, but their ideas too often remain untapped. The purpose of this technique is to get as many ideas as quickly as possible and to elicit ideas that would remain hidden in free-for-all criticism. The OD facilitator can help group members select a topic to be brainstormed and then discuss the following principles with them. (1) Groups will be more productive if they refrain from evaluating ideas at the time they are proposed; critical judgment should be suspended until all ideas are out. (2) Group production of ideas can be creative. Wild ideas should be expected, and people should build on one another's contributions. (3) The more ideas the better. Quantity is more important than quality during brainstorming.

The Self-Inquiry Method. Schindler-Rainman, Lippitt, and Cole (1975) have used the self-inquiry method to help members think through those problems that might inhibit open communication and inquiry during meetings. The steps include explaining the purpose of the activity and having members spend a few minutes alone answering these questions:

- What are some of the factors in this meeting that will inhibit free and open exchange?
- What might a member like yourself propose to reduce the barriers to openness' and creativity?

The final step is having members share the results of their self-inquiry with others at the meeting. If certain factors are repeatedly identified, or if group members want to find ways of carrying out their individual proposals, group problem solving might follow.

Dealing with Hidden Agendas

OD facilitators will sometimes observe behavior that has nothing to do with the immediate goals of the group or with the agenda posted before the meeting. Perhaps two faculty members have had a running feud for years and delight in putting each other down at every opportunity. The department head may have information members need but may be withholding it, afraid of some or other consequence. Two members may be carrying on a flirtation with each other. When these relationships are played out in meetings, we say that people are dealing with hidden agendas, and the energy that goes into these agendas saps energy from the public agenda of the group.

The following exercise is designed to create an awareness of hidden agendas and how they affect the accomplishment of group goals.* The exercise requires a minimum of five role players and two observers; it can be done within an hour.

1. Introduce the exercise as a way to think about differences between individual and group goals. Select five role players and two observers (or sets of seven with large groups).
2. Present the following instructions to all role players. Read your instructions alone, and do not reveal them to other role players. When thinking about how you will play your role, think of ways to emphasize the role while remaining natural and not

*Adapted from Johnson and Johnson (1975, pp. 91–92 and 365).

overacting. You are all actors at a meeting of a special fact-finding committee of the Community Action Program (CAP) Governing Board in Middleburg. Your committee was established to study the suggestion that CAP revise its procedures for electing board members. At present, representatives are elected for three-year terms and must run in a general-area election. Your committee is to consider two questions: (1) What would be the best electoral basis? The general-area election? Smaller District elections? Even smaller neighborhood elections? (2) How long should representatives serve? The chairwoman of your committee is LaVerne Turner; she will make your recommendations to the city council.

3. Present the following instructions to individual role players:

(a) Instructions for Carol Stone: You are a social worker with the Middleburg Department of Welfare and would like some of your welfare clients to become active in CAP. You want some of your clients elected to the CAP governing board so that your department head will be impressed with your efforts and you will have more power in CAP. Because your assignment and those of other social workers are determined by districts, you want board members to represent districts and the terms of board representatives to remain at three years.

(b) Instructions for LaVerne Turner: You own and operate a store and are an ambitious community leader. You think poor people are lazy and want their representatives on the CAP governing board to be divided about goals so that business and professional members can run things their own way. You support citywide elections for board members so there will be more representatives without support from small-interest groups, and you support one-year terms so as to minimize continuity among members from poverty areas.

(c) Instructions for Roberta Stevens: You are a mother of five on a federal benefit called Aid to Dependent Children and want a greater role for poverty representatives on the CAP governing board. You support the concept of neighborhood elections and one-year terms for board members so that more people from poverty areas get a chance to serve. You want more poverty representatives on the board so as to minimize the influence of business and professional members.

(d) Instructions for Lou Haber: You are a dentist who is also on the city council. You feel that government officials and professional people know what they are doing and should have a greater voice on the CAP governing board. Your objective is a weaker group of poverty representatives on the board, so you would support general-area elections and one-year tenure for board members.

(e) Instructions for Ed Simon: You are vice president of the chamber of commerce and are not really interested in this committee. You joined only to meet Carol Stone so you could ask her for a date. During the meeting you plan to agree with and support every point she makes. Your behavior is guided by your desire to impress her.

4. While individual role players are studying their individual instructions, tell the observers that they are to answer the following questions:

- What is the basic goal of the group? How did each member contribute to or hinder goal accomplishment?
- Toward what goals were the individual members working?
- What task and maintenance behaviors were present and absent?
- What was the group atmosphere like? Did it change from time to time?
- Was participation and influence distributed throughout the group? If not, who dominated?
- How far did the group get in attaining its goal?

5. Set the stage for role players by reviewing the situation and setting up the space for the meeting of the fact-finding committee. Instruct them to begin.

6. End the role playing after fifteen minutes whether or not the group has come to a decision about what to recommend to the city council. Ask observers to report, and encourage role players to join in a discussion of the observers' questions.

7. Have role players read their individual instructions with Ed reading his last. Then ask role players and observers to discuss answers to these questions:

- How do hidden agendas affect the group; how do they affect each group member?
- What are some of the indications that hidden agendas are operating?
- Is the recognition of hidden agendas necessary to understand what is going on in the group?
- How can hidden agendas be productively handled to help in accomplishing the group's goals?

Good skill in conducting meetings is the foundation for skill in the special tasks educational groups undertake such as making decisions, solving problems, and resolving conflicts—matters to be discussed in later chapters.

Chapter Six

Solving Problems

Problem solving is the heart of OD. All else is preparation, follow-up, or recycling.

When we speak of problems, we mean problems that concern the group or organization—as for example, when members of a community college come to believe their departmental organization is not working well. Individuals have problems, too—for instance, when a history instructor puzzles over the best way of describing the economy of colonial America or the best way to bring a student's attention back to academic matters. But in this book we deal with problems that require cooperation in a faculty group or in the college or school as a whole.

This chapter lays out the steps of the systematic problem solving we call (following Fred Fosmire and John Wallen) the S-T-P. The basic idea is that a problem is the gap between an unsatisfactory present situation (S) and a more desirable goal or target (T). The problem is solved (or at least reduced) when we find a path (P) from S to T.

An Illustration*

The following is an instance of problem solving carried out by a very skillful group—a team of first-grade and second-grade

*Quoted from Schmuck, Murray, Smith, Schwartz, and M. Runkel (1975, pp. 89–90).

teachers in a school we will call Spartan School. The episode began when two members of the team visited another school, Palmer, and saw there a reading program they liked. We quote a memorandum written by a member of the team:

> Two members of the 1–2 teaching unit visited Palmer School on November 30, 1970, and returned very excited about their reading program. Others in the school became interested in learning about it, too. This type of reading program was discussed at unit meeting. It was thought that this type of program would improve the reading in the low grades and would also bring the unit closer together. A survey was taken to see if everyone in the unit was willing to participate in planning and operating this program. Everyone was eager to begin.
>
> The entire unit worked out a schedule of classes which half the children would attend for forty minutes while half the class had reading with their classroom teacher. After a schedule had been worked out the unit broke into four subgroups to plan a scope and sequence for each class (art, PE, questioning strategy, guidance, reading games). Each teacher joined the subgroup in which she was most interested or felt she could contribute the most. We also listed some of the problems we would have to face. They were (1) extra personnel would be needed; (2) would the children be able to move? (3) we would have to switch gym periods with the 3–4 unit; (4) music schedule would have to be changed because it conflicted with the new gym schedule; and (5) auxiliary personnel would have to be willing to participate in the program.
>
> At the next meeting, we attempted to solve some of these problems. The 3–4 teaching unit was contacted and they agreed to change gym times if we could change the music schedule. The principal—through the leadership team—scheduled ways in which needed art and ditto work would be completed for the 1–2 unit.
>
> To find the extra rooms we needed, we listed all possible choices and decided to have a first-and-second grade teacher move to the rooms next door, sharing the room with the teachers there. Because of the lower class numbers this was possible. This left two classrooms free to hold Art, reading games and two other groups. This also answered the question of whether children can move to other parts of the school. The classes they would move to will be right next door, and it was felt that the children could handle this.
>
> To find the extra personnel, parents were contacted and enough volunteered to cover the classes. The classes would be on questioning strategies, group counseling, reading games, art, and PE. The principal agreed to take part in the PE program. A meeting for everyone engaged in the program was held on Friday (workday) at 10:00 A.M. The entire program was explained and the group was then divided into subgroups to discuss different subjects each would cover.
>
> In essence, this new 1–2 program, which came to be known as the *back-to-back reading program*, allowed each teacher to focus on

reading with one half of the class, while the other half was engaged in another, interesting activity with a large group. The program made use of the previously untapped resources of teachers, parents, auxiliary staff, and the principal. An article describing this program, complete with a picture of the principal teaching PE to six- and seven-year-olds, appeared in the local newspaper.

That episode illustrates several features of good problem solving. It illustrates collaborative goal setting and commitment: "A survey was taken to see if everyone in the unit was willing to participate in planning and operating the program." That is, the group determined whether every individual accepted the goal of putting the new reading program into effect. The writer of the memorandum noted the result: "Everyone was eager to begin." The next sentence indicates commitment: "The entire unit worked out a schedule of classes . . ."

The episode illustrates how the team gathered information and other resources, one of the metaskills described in chapter 1. The 1–2 teaching unit gathered information from outside when two of its members visited Palmer School to see what was going on there. The unit used resources from outside again when "the program made use of previously untapped resources of . . . parents. . . ." And the unit called upon resources outside itself but within the school: "The 3–4 unit . . . agreed to change gym times." In general, the teaching unit made use of the "untapped resources of teachers, . . . auxiliary staff, and the principal." The unit also made discriminating use of its own internal resources: "Each teacher joined the subgroup in which she was most interested or felt she could contribute the most."

The episode illustrates how an effective group explicitly anticipates obstacles: "We also listed some of the problems we would have to face." And it shows how the unit acted to deal with those obstacles: "we attempted to solve some of these problems. The 3–4 unit was contacted. . . ."

The episode illustrates collaborative coordination: The "program was discussed at a unit meeting." The tasks necessary to reduce obstacles were planned in the group. Then, though the memorandum does not say so, the various tasks were assigned to individuals. The unit used its meeting on the Friday workday to be sure everything was ready to go. The writer of the memorandum shows the group's explicit attention to maintaining its collaborative norm when she writes, "It was thought that this type of program would . . . bring the unit closer together."

The episode illustrates skill in conducting meetings (see chapter 5): "After a schedule had been worked out, the unit broke into subgroups to plan a scope and sequence . . ." and "a survey was taken. . . ."

The episode illustrates another metaskill: mobilizing synergistic action. The memorandum says the unit "attempted" to reduce obstacles, and it is clear that its actions succeeded in doing so. "The 3–4 unit . . . agreed . . .," "the principal agreed . . .," "the principal . . . scheduled ways . . .," "parents were contacted and enough volunteered . . .," and rooms were rescheduled.

The episode illustrates the group's attention to motive satisfaction; it celebrates its achievement: "An article . . . appeared in the local newspaper."

The episode also shows that a problem is not solved at one sitting. The unit's solution took shape as it planned its adaptation of Palmer's reading program to Spartan School, as it took sequential actions to reduce the obstacles it foresaw, and as it moved the new program into actual operation.

Finally, the episode shows that problem solving does not always begin with a formal review of "what problems do we have?" In this case, when it sent two of its members to Palmer School, the group was simply exhibiting its routine (but lively) metaskill of gathering information that might be useful. These two members liked the reading program they saw at Palmer better than the one they had been using at Spartan. Upon discussing the discrepancy between the existing program's results and those they expected from the Palmer program, the members of the 1–2 teaching unit decided that the improvement would be great enough to justify considerable effort. They then chose the discrepancy as a problem and Palmer's program as their target.

Theory

Let's begin our theoretical discussion with a very brief description of the *S-T-P* procedure for solving problems in groups. We will go into detail later in the chapter.

1. *Agree on the problem.* Effective problem processing demands attention to two kinds of questions at the outset: Where are we now (the situation, *S*)? and Where do we want to be (target, *T*)? An effective group of educators must reach a working agreement early about what it chooses to take as its *S* and *T*. At the same time, the effective group realizes that agreements about both the *S* and *T* are inevitably temporary. Situations do not stand still; targets move into new definitions as they are approached. Further, as a group reaches new clarity about the

problem that brought it together, its members become aware of problems they had not thought about earlier. The process is a natural one in human awareness and thinking.

2. *Generate alternative paths.* The group chooses a target and tries to think of steps or paths or plans (*P*) to get from the existing situation (*S*) to the target (*T*). Brainstorming is often used in this phase. This is the phase (though it may also occur earlier or later) in which a group typically envisions a benefit from reaching deeper into its members' personal knowledge and resources or from reaching outside itself for information and resources. A skillful group of educators can begin at any point and then oscillate among *S*, *T*, and *P* in its discussions.

3. *List helping and hindering forces.* Once the group has agreed firmly on the desirability and feasibility of a target (and by considering *P*s helps to clarify the desirability and feasibility), it can move into considering the forces that will work for and against its efforts. Among the kinds of helping forces groups sometimes name are publicly announced support from certain authorities, support from interfacing groups, some available money, some time already set aside for problem solving, some people already committed to the target, and some necessary skills already existing in the group. Among the kinds of hindering forces sometimes named are a debilitating history, political blocks, anticipated lack of support, anticipation of too much cost of change, and lack of knowledge or skill.

4. *Choose action steps.* The group next chooses the hindering forces that seem feasible to reduce and generates ideas for reducing them. The group agrees on the forces to be attacked first and on the best steps to use from among those proposed. Again, brainstorming is useful to generate ideas.

5. *Act.* This is the phase of mobilizing for committed action. The group assigns people to the various agreed-upon actions and assigns schedules.

6. *Monitor and recycle.* Meetings are scheduled at which progress will be reviewed. Working toward a target tests how well the situation has been understood.

That is the scheme in brief.

All colleges and schools deal with problems in one way or another, but our observations convince us that most educational organizations use up a great deal of energy unproductively. Colleges often flounder through problems instead of using systematic procedures that save time. Schools sometimes put the wrong people to work: they give a problem to a faculty committee when almost everyone is willing to accept a solution chosen by the principal or the school's secretary, or, conversely, the principal imposes a solution that actually requires the initiative and commitment of groups. Colleges sometimes undertake to solve a problem within the college that cannot be solved there. They sometimes expect to solve a problem once and for all when in fact work on the problem must be recycled year after year. Schools sometimes use methods that alleviate one problem only to make others worse. Finally, colleges often engage in "fire-fighting"—they try to cope with a great many very difficult problems at the same time by trying to paper over one after another. All those ways of coping are understandable, but the waste of effort is prodigious. A sustained problem-solving capacity requires ways of working that avoid the waste and that enable educators to devote most of their energy to the rewarding parts of their jobs.

Converting Frustrations into Problems

A problem is more than a frustration. Some frustrations go away by themselves, and some remain but only as minor irritations. Part of the problem-solving skill is the judicious selection of frustrations to be treated as problems. In our view, educators are likely to flounder in frustration interminably until they explicitly conceive a problem as a gap between a specified undesirable present situation (What do I want to get away from?) and a more desirable specified state of affairs (Where do I want to go?).

When we listen to educators discuss their frustrations, we hear them say or imply that they would prefer something to be different. They sound as if they find something unpleasant about the current state of affairs and as if they believe some alternative state of affairs would be more pleasant. Often, however, they are not able to specify the features of that improved state of affairs. From our point of view, educators who primarily complain about the present without conceiving a better alternative have not yet conceived a problem and are therefore not ready to solve a problem.

Life is full of frustrations. You may not enjoy driving 10 miles to the college every morning, but if you accept the commuting as a reasonable price for living in a neighborhood you want to live in, it is not a "problem" in our sense, not something you are motivated to *solve*. Since our topic is solving problems, we want a concept that opens the door to doing something that is new.

We use the word *problem* to mean a discrepancy between a present state of affairs and a more preferred state of affairs— sufficiently more preferred that one is ready to spend some energy to get there. Without the two parts—the current situation and the more desirable one—no problem has been specified. Frustration, irritation, anger, or confusion is often a feature of a problem—part of the present state of affairs—but it is not in itself a problem.

Usually, people feel frustration, irritation, or anger before they can put a discrepancy into words, because those feelings are typical symptoms of underlying problems. But not all disgruntlements are worth converting into problems. Most of us, almost without thinking, make a judgment about whether a frustration is worth the energy required to remove it or whether the frustration will remove itself in the natural course of events.

Often, a frustration does indeed signal a problem worth working on. It is a profitable habit to give at least a little thought to any feeling of frustration that does not go away in a few minutes or an hour to see whether an important problem might be lurking under it. It may be that the source of the frustration is not the condition most evident to the eye when the frustration arises. It may be that a problem more worth working on lies elsewhere. For instance, if an instructor feels frustrated by the application of a college policy and is unwilling to discuss it with the department head or dean, the problem worth working on may be not the instructor's unwillingness to confront the appropriate head, but rather the absence of a college norm enabling the instructors to feel free to describe their frustrations to someone in authority. That is, while the feeling of frustration itself, being a psychological condition, lies within the instructor, the proper place to conceive and solve the problem may lie in the interpersonal skills and norms of the college faculty.

Finally, it should be clear that in our view the problem lies inside people's heads, not in the real world. When someone says that a college has problems, to us that means some people in the college react to the state of affairs there by wishing they were different. But different individuals in the college may have very different images in their heads of the present state of affairs, the more desirable state, and the steps necessary to move from the one state to the other. The implication is obvious; one of the first steps in problem solving is to ascertain with some precision the images the people concerned have of the present state of affairs and the alternatives.

Educators perceive a problem—in our use of the term—when they perceive a discrepancy between what they diagnose to be actually happening in the here and now and what they would prefer to be happening in the future. Whatever the degree of discrepancy, optimal problem solving occurs as those who perceive troubles are motivated to do something productive about them by designing proposals and then taking action. Along with awareness of a discrepancy, "having a problem" also means contemplating change and taking action. The person or group with a problem is energized to move from the present state of affairs to a happier, more satisfying state.

The S, T, or P may be unclear when educators first feel a frustration. A problem begins to take shape when educators begin to conceptualize situations and targets and explain their images of them to one another. They become energized when they can conceive alternative proposals to bring the situation closer to the target. Achieving clarity about the three aspects of problem solving is necessary for effective group action.

We said earlier that problems lie in people's minds. We mean that the discrepancy between what you want and what you are getting lies in your head. But your conceptions of what you want and what you are getting usually depend a great deal on what actually exists out there. What most of us want, most of the time, has some sort of existence in the world that is independent of our minds. And what we experience to be happening to us does have some origin or counterpart, for most of us most of the time, in that outer world. Accordingly, we do not imply that a problem is "merely" in your head or that it is "all in your mind" or that the solution to it lies merely in taking a different view of the matter. Once in a while, it is true, a problem is solved after re-examining the logic or the evidence, but most of the time, for most of the people engaged in problem solving, some action is required in the outer world. Although the discrepancy lies in your head, the solution that will reduce the discrepancy almost always requires a changed pattern of action in the world outside your head—a changed pattern of action among the people in the school or college.

Rationality and Creativity

Many observers of human problem solving are impressed with individuals' insights—the sudden leaps to valid solutions that seem to short-cut all logic. Indeed, the brain seems to work in two fairly distinct ways. One is logical, analytic, systematic, rational, and usually verbal. The other is the intuitive, insightful, quick apperception of relationships, patterns, and recombinations, usually in a nonverbal mode—the kind of cerebration we usually associate with art and invention. It is not much of an overstatement to say that we would waste the creativity and speed of half the brain if we required *individuals* to work at problems only systematically, rationally, and verbally. For that reason, a systematic procedure for solving problems in a group should allow some time for individual intuition—for example, a period for brainstorming.

In educational organizations, problem solving that affects them can benefit immensely from the intuitions and insights of participants. If those capacities are to be brought out, individuals must be given time to be creative without being held down to rationality, ritual, or "reality." If those capabilities are to be salvaged for use by the group, interpersonal skills and group skills must be used delicately to prevent the creative ideas from being submerged in conformity to whatever thinking is most evident in the group at the moment.

But solutions that depend for their success on the group or the educational organization as a whole cannot be reached merely by bringing out individual creativity, no matter how brilliant it may be. Chaos results when one person wonders aloud whether there is a problem worth working on, another says the problem is how to oil the present mechanism, another urges throwing away that mechanism, another advocates an action step she thinks is likely to have pay-off regardless of what the problem is, another asks whether there is consensus on a goal, another asks whether the right people are represented at the meeting, and so on. Chaos grows when all those cross-currents occur while participants are unaware that they are occurring. Often, many members of a meeting assume that all the others are talking about the same part of the problem-working process without checking whether that is true. The result is that many of the remarks sound like nonsense.

At some point, individuals must be able to direct their actions toward a common goal, taking steps in unison toward it. At some point, therefore, there must be time for every group member to come to understand the images others see and to feel familiar with them. There must be time for members of the group to compare images and explore their potentialities. There must be time to agree on the advantages and disadvantages of proposed solutions and on the best bets. There must be time, too, to ascertain the willingness of every member to commit the energy and take the risks necessary to make the adopted solution work.

A Vicious Circle

Many educational organizations encounter frustrations and impediments to their work: low achievement scores, uninspired teaching, unproductive research, decreasing tax bases, poverty in the community, desegregation, demographic shifts, ethnicity mixes, mobility and attrition among students and faculty, over-large districts and colleges, decay of facilities, politicization of the trustees, crime among youth, dropouts, drug abuse, and so on. But some educational organizations are burdened with more of those difficulties at any one time and in more severe degrees than others. Many urban high schools, for example, contain larger stockpiles of troubles from which their members can extract problems than do most nonurban high schools.

When troubles pile up and the stew of difficulties becomes so constant, intrusive, and demanding that it tears out the vitals of the educational organization's work, administrators and faculty members become distraught, anxious, and bone weary. Even the constant perplexity about the difficulties that should be chosen as problems is anxiety-provoking and wearing. Instructors' energies are drawn away from their teaching into worrying and fire-fighting. They have little energy left for the demanding task of reconceiving their stresses as problems about which something might be done.

Under stress and enervation, educators often turn in one of two directions. One reaction is to stop taking action and to become deeply pessimistic and cynical about the possibility of fruitful change. It is not surprising that instructors, in particular, should react that way. Often, they have suffered from too much fruitless upheaval. Superintendents and provosts declare new policies, programs, and procedures and appoint new functionaries. Consultants come in and demand faculty members' time for a myriad of projects. Faculty associations and unions make demands for new rules they think will reduce stress on instructors, but the new rules often add other stresses. Citizen groups add their demands, and so it goes. And too often the efforts make no difference. Faculty members come to look upon any new proposal as almost certain to add to their burdens and to drain their energies without any benefit. They want desperately to be left alone. Posing a problem to be worked on becomes a threat, not an opportunity.

The other frequent response to stress and enervation is to demand miracles from outside helpers. Some educators still believe that a half-million-dollar project will cure their woes with little effort on their own part. Or they may hire in consultants, but, mindful of consultants in the past who have drained their energies to no profit, say to the new consultants, in effect, "Show results quickly or leave." The attitude is understandable, but unrealistic nevertheless.

Both reactions to stress and enervation lead to further abortive efforts. Neither sluggish participation in a new project nor unrealistic demands upon it improves the likelihood of its success. And the projects that fail simply add to the burden of difficulties educators suffer. The vicious circle feeds upon itself; the difficulties mount and become harder and harder to alleviate.

This is not the place to paint all the details in their terrible colors.

Still, we take space for one brief example of the vicious circle. In the more stressful school districts, superintendents often have rather brief tenure. They burn out and look for easier jobs, or they make enemies during their heroic efforts to improve matters, and those enemies engineer their expulsion. (In Oakland, one superintendent's tenure was cut short by assassination.) When a superintendent goes, the school board looks for a new superintendent who can clean the Augean stables that the previous one could not. The new superintendent declares a new policy, reorganizes the district's personnel, and imposes new programs of work—typically curricular improvement programs. Many of the teachers, however, have seen all this happen before. They remember putting in a lot of hard work in the past only to find their jobs as difficult as ever. Or perhaps they remember a program that was improving matters along with their dejection when a new superintendent came in, threw out the program underway, and started a new one. The teachers protect themselves against a repetition of that experience. They obey the new superintendent superficially, but spend the least energy possible. The new program is not their idea anyway, and they have little stake in its success. Many teachers, intentionally or unintentionally, sabotage the program by doing too little too late. Some teachers persuade others to join the resistance. The program fails. Some teachers who were in favor of the program decide, "You can't do anything worth while around here. There are too many old fuddy-duddies." They look for jobs elsewhere. Some who must stay retreat to their classrooms and join the resistance when the next new program comes along. The superintendent leaves, and a new debilitating cycle begins. Colleges, too, often suffer from similar debilitating cycles and similarly demoralized faculty members with little appetite for constructive problem solving.

Breaking the Vicious Circle

Luckily, colleges and schools are loosely coupled systems. That is, action in one part of the organization does not immediately or necessarily produce a specified action in another part. Connections are only probabilistic. Some probabilities are rather high, such as the probability that absence lists will reach the office by 9 A.M. if the principal orders them to be there by then. Other probabilities are rather low, such as the probability that college instructors will observe one another's teaching and give advice for improvement even if the dean suggests that it would be a good idea. Some probabilities are rather high if a time lag is allowed. For example, some time usually elapses in both colleges and schools between the decision to adopt a new curriculum and its first actual use in a class. The result of the loose coupling is that not all members of an educational organization get caught in the vicious circle to the same degree or at the same time. At any one time, some members of the organization may be enjoying a respite off at the edge of the vortex of turmoil.

Adding to the dispersing effect of the loose coupling is the natural variability in the amount of threat that different individuals perceive from the vicious circle. Persons who perceive less threat will be less immobilized than persons who perceive more. Some faculty members may even perceive more opportunity than threat, finding stimulation where others find incapacitating confusion. In sum, though aspects of the vicious circle may immobilize some or even most, others may remain able to act with deliberation, and still others may be aroused to new energy.

Even though a college or school as a whole may be unready to begin energetic problem solving, smaller efforts can begin with subsystems containing individuals who are more ready. Here is a list of some signs to look for:

1. Look for educators with some time and energy who are willing to discuss their troubles and to discuss whether fruitful problems might be built from them.

2. Look for administrators, in particular, who realize that short projects will only continue to waste their energy and who are ready to plan at least a year or two ahead and to bear their troubles as best they can in the meantime.

3. Look for faculty members who have not yet succumbed to pessimism and cynicism and who still have energy. Often they are the newer members.

4. Look for those who can be motivated by a vision of joint achievement, greater control over their work, and camaraderie.

5. Look for those who understand that colleges and schools are complex systems with complex dynamics and that the norms in work groups are the key to productivity and change.

6. Look for those who have faith that there must be a better method of dealing with difficulties than blundering through.

7. Look for those who know that educational improvement will require extra and sustained energy, that some kinds of change will require skills they do not now have, and that some ways of doing things now disapproved must become approved if they are to shake loose from an old way and lay the basis of a new one.

Those seven signs reveal opportunities for change within the target system. They indicate places where problem solving can usually start with a fairly good chance of gaining a beachhead, even though the educational organization as a whole may be unready to muster all its members for a sustained and concerted attack upon a major problem. If a small project by one subsystem succeeds, it can do a good deal to counter pessimism in other parts of the college or school.

Gathering Data About Problem Solving

Because picking the right problems and finding solutions to them is the heart of OD, every skill we describe in this book helps in problem solving. Gathering data about any of the skills is a way of gathering data about an aspect of problem solving. For that reason, the methods of gathering data offered in other chapters are good diagnostics for problem solving. Chapter 4 gave ways of ascertaining whether the communicative norms in the college or school are appropriate to support good problem solving, chapter 5 described ways of gathering data about a group's effectiveness in problem-solving meetings, chapter 7 describes ways of assessing the decision-making skills necessary to choose paths toward targets, and chapter 8 presents ways of assessing a target system's readiness to deal with the conflicts that arise as coordination is sought.

It will suffice here to present two more problem-solving aids. The following is another set of interview questions. You might use them for a quick reconnaissance among members of a college or school.

Interview Questions for Finding Problems ————————

1. What are some things you would like to see this college or school working toward that it isn't doing now?

   _____

   _____

2. [If named something:] Which faculty members do you think could help accomplish these things?

   _____   _____

   _____   _____

3. Have you received any information recently about your work or about the college or school that you found surprising? [Yes, no] [If yes] Please describe one or two such kinds of information:

---

4. To make things operate more effectively, which people do you think ought to work together more closely? [Write names. Show each cluster of names the respondent says should work more closely together by encircling that cluster.]

---

5. What are some aspects of the current situation in the college or school that need changing?

---

6. What are some target conditions that you would like to see your staff attempt to achieve?

---

7. Do you have any proposals for action in mind right now for moving toward those targets?

In the heat of solving problems, groups often become strongly task oriented. The following is a brief questionnaire that might be useful to help a group stand back and examine its group dynamics.

Questions to Check on Group Effectiveness ————————

You have been working on a task. Like an automobile, a group needs maintenance. While working on a task, a group needs to stop occasionally to be explicit about its *interpersonal processes*. Please circle one number in each of the following scales.

What I say is prized and valued here.	6	5	4	3	2	I	What I say is being ignored here.
Our group is falling into traps.	6	5	4	3	2	I	Our group is avoiding traps.
I have participated often.	6	5	4	3	2	I	I have participated very little.

Discuss your responses on the three scales with the group. Try to be helpful. You will tend to be *helpful* when you are specific (e.g., "I felt valued by you, John, because you often asked me to say more when I spoke," or "An example of when I thought we fell into a trap was . . .," or "I felt put down when you . . ."). You will tend to be *unhelpful* if you are general and evaluative (e.g., "You're the kind of person who puts people down," or "This group isn't working well," or "This group is the greatest I've ever been in").

Two Examples of Systematic Problem Solving

This section presents two examples of how groups of educators use systematic problem solving. We reproduce here actual records of group work made by faculty members who had received five days of OD training, mostly in communication skills, group and intergroup exercises, and problem solving. About half of the five-day period was devoted to the problem-solving procedure. We reproduce the participants' own words so that you can see how ideas come out in actual instances.

Clarifying the Department Head's Role

This example is taken from the newsprint records kept by a team of instructors and their department head in a community college. Although the statements below are just some of those the group wrote on the newsprint, they do include the agreements that enabled the group to move from stage to stage.

Stage 1. Specifying the Problem
Where we are: Lack of clarity in the role of the department head. Where we want to be: We (the faculty) know where the head stands, and he knows where we stand.
Our task: To clarify the role of the department head.

Stage 2. Listing Helping and Hindering Forces
Forces that are helping us move toward our target:
1. Many of the faculty are open and want to know about the head's philosophy.
2. The faculty's willingness to be open is enhanced by our new communication skills.
3. The head is willing to clarify his philosophy and his role.

Forces that are hindering our movement toward where we want to be:
1. Lack of time.
2. Some faculty members' willingness to be the head's "mouthpiece" and the feeling that she does nothing to discourage this.
3. Lack of complete openness of the faculty, including the head.
4. Confusion about our own roles.

Stage 3. Specifying Multiple Solutions
The most important ideas that we brainstormed were as follows:
1. We need more time for process and problem-solving meetings.
2. We need to practice openness.
3. We should let the head know if we like something she is doing.
4. We should let the head know if we do not like what she is doing.
5. We want the head to give us feedback.
6. We need to clarify roles and expectations of each other and with our upper-class students.

You must do some hunting to find the correspondences between the items in one stage and those in earlier stages. For example, Item 1 in Stage 4 (below) says, "The head will make a statement to the faculty . . . ." That plan for action takes advantage of Helping Force 1 under Stage 2 above: "Many of the faculty . . . want to know about the head's philosophy." By getting the word directly from the head, the plan reduces Hindering Force 2 in Stage 2: "Some faculty members' willingness to be the head's 'mouthpiece'. . ." Because it says the staff will "interact with" the head, it offers a chance for Solution 2 in Stage 3 to operate: "We need to practice openness." And it carries forward the task the group set for itself in Stage 1: "To clarify the role of the department head."

In Stage 4, you will note that the group permitted discussions of the head's role to arise several times. Members were realistic about recycling.

Stage 4. Planning for Action
Our intended actions, developed from elaborations on our brainstormed ideas, are as follows:

1. The department head will make a statement to the faculty about her educational philosophy and role expectations, and the faculty will have a chance to interact with her. Observers [names specified] will record the interaction and check on the communication processes between the head and faculty. All will evaluate the process and progress at the meeting. These actions will occur during our forthcoming retreat.

2. During the last week before classes start, we will go to Dick's place on the Hood River for a debriefing and planning session after the leaders' workshop. The whole staff is invited.

3. A departmental handbook will be written with everyone participating. It will contain:
   a. Role descriptions.
   b. A statement of how we hope to operate (openness).
   c. The head's philosophy and expectations.
   d. Each group's summary of what it did and felt during this workshop.
   e. Operational procedures.
      It should be flexible and changeable and written in behavioral terms.

4. A faculty retreat workday in the fall will be used to do follow-up debriefing with the whole staff in communication with the help of a few outside OD facilitators.

5. During the first week of classes we will conduct a two-hour orientation for our majors, and

a. Introduce all the staff to students.
b. Provide some student-faculty discussion groups about our department.
6. For all faculty meetings, communication and procedural matters will be checked by:
   a. Having a couple of people observe the meeting and report back on how we did.
   b. Including total faculty in all meetings, at least for the next four months.
   c. Setting aside at least 15 minutes for debriefing near the end of each meeting.
7. One faculty meeting a month will be set aside for sharing ideas, innovations, and failures. Seating will be arranged to prevent faculty cliques from isolating themselves.

Stage 5. Anticipating Obstacles
[The faculty discussed ways in which the plan could go wrong.]

Stage 6. Taking Action
[The faculty implemented Action-Plan 6 (evaluating faculty meetings) immediately. They also formed several small ad hoc groups to develop the other plans and to try them out.]

Stage 7. Evaluating
[Most of the ideas for action had built-in evaluation plans. The faculty was careful to allow time for evaluation as each sequence of actions unfolded during the academic year.]

Sharing Strengths and Encouraging Variety

This example is taken from the problem-solving activities of a group of elementary teachers attempting to move from teaching in self-contained classrooms to teaching in teams. The experience of this group reinforces our admonition not to give up when things don't seem to be going according to plan. For a time, the group seemed to have stalled after Stage 5, but outside OD facilitators helped the group proceed to action and evaluation.

Stage 1. Specifying the Problem
Situation: Lack of established procedures for sharing innovative ideas and supporting one another in experimentation.
Target: We shall have adequate procedures for developing, sharing, supporting, and protecting educational innovations.

Stage 2. Listing Helping and Hindering Forces

Facilitating forces: (1) physical plant conducive to sharing within units, (2) staff is willing to try new things, (3) principal encourages innovation, (4) new staff is willing and enthusiastic, (5) young staff has good ideas, (6) interns and others have experiences that will bring in outside ideas, (7) experienced staff is supporting changes and participating in them, (8) there is ready access to equipment that can be used for innovations, (9) there is willingness to know and communicate because of our new staffing arrangements (esprit de corps), (10) shared experiences brought us together during planning weeks, (11) kids serve as communication channels for ideas, (12) kids are very open to new experiences and sharing them, and (13) some parents are very supportive.

Restraining forces: (1) noise carries, (2) units are physically cut off from one another, (3) three of four units (or unit rooms) are separated, (4) some kids resist sharing, (5) facilities are overcrowded, (6) procedures for flexible use of space have not been worked out, (7) there is limited access to outside OD facilitators for planning and execution, (8) failure to pass budget threatens many contracts (e.g., aides and interns), (9) funds are lacking for supplies and field trips, and (10) the fear of a lack of supplies sometimes leads to hoarding. [In addition to the above, the group listed the most important restraining forces in this order:]

1. Lack of procedures for sharing knowledge between and within units about what each teacher has done, can do, and wants to do regarding innovations.
2. Competition and a lack of procedures for seeking support result in feelings of inadequacy, mistrust, and failure among staff members.
3. Teachers feel inadequate to innovate and are forced to fall back on traditional methods when confronted with large groups of students.
4. Some parents lack a view of the total picture at the school, and they feel apart from what we are doing; consequently, teachers fear parental nonacceptance.

Stage 3. Specifying Multiple Solutions
[The group brainstormed ideas for overcoming each of the most important restraining forces.]

Stage 4. Planning for Action
[The group reviewed its list of solutions, discarding many ideas and categorizing the rest as follows.]

1. Procedures for sharing knowledge:
   a. Ideas for immediate action: (1) take a survey at a staff meeting of each person's desires and strengths, (2) set up a card file of past and future ideas for innovations, and (3) set up tours. Ensure that staff members get to walk through the building to all rooms regularly.
   b. Ideas for future committee action: (1) make a list of strengths and have staff members put a check by the ones they feel they possess, (2) release each teacher once each week to go around and visit other classes (i.e., observe and interact), (3) have everyone tack a big sheet of newsprint up with his own strengths and hopes, (4) allow each person to add to other lists by writing perceptions of others' strengths, (5) put the lists into a file of "resources" in our building, (6) share lists stating "what I feel like doing today," (7) keep a record of what is being done (include critiques), (8) update the outside resource file, and (9) use outside resource people more often.
   c. Ideas for future individual or team action: (1) inform your team leader about what you have done, can do, want to do, (2) establish time at each team meeting for sharing such information, (3) set up memory refreshers throughout the year, (4) send your students to find out what is going on elsewhere in building, (5) use intercom to invite others to visit your lesson, (6) create central displays about what is going on in your team, (7) tape-record events and let others listen, (8) make posters advertising all events, (9) encourage classes to visit other classrooms, and (10) set up and exchange student programs within and between teams.
2. Procedures for seeking support, decreasing competition, and reducing feelings of inadequacy, mistrust, or failure:
   a. Ideas for immediate action: (1) use direct expression of feelings, (2) acknowledge own or others' feelings, (3) hold brainstorming sessions on these problems, (4) wear signs saying how you are feeling, (5) keep signs saying "I need support," and wear them when you do, (6) wear button with smile on one side and frown on the other, and (7) help staff to share crazy ideas.
   b. Ideas for future committee action: (1) arrange staff parties, (2) arrange demonstrations by faculty (e.g., of lessons), (3) plan a trust-building day, and (4) use student questionnaire on feelings and evaluation.

   c. Ideas for future individual or team action: (1) establish positive reinforcement outside building, (2) eat right, get sleep, (3) survey periodically for feelings, (4) know own strengths and limitations, (5) give positive reinforcement to your colleagues, (6) accept others' limitations, (7) work together in unit groups, (8) let others accept you—be open-minded, (9) openly express feelings, (10) try to get success from apparent failure, (11) talk about your failures and weaknesses, (12) avoid secrecy, (13) share feelings with your team leader, (14) paraphrase, describe behavior, and check impressions, (15) share long-range plans across units, (16) establish as a goal the expression of a certain number of statements about your feelings, and (17) share your feelings with principal and auxiliary staff.

3. Ways to facilitate innovations with large groups and overcome teachers' feelings of inadequacy:

   a. Ideas for future committee action: (1) set up a committee to implement the use of student helpers, (2) set up procedures for using parent volunteer groups, and pass them around the building for additional information, (3) talk to people at other schools doing similar things, (4) enlist help of student teachers, university students, and high-school students for large meetings, and (5) observe other large groups.

   b. Ideas for future individual or team action: (1) use the skills of a partner, (2) plan with auxiliary staff to cooperate during large meetings, (3) use rooms as research centers, (4) strive to use new materials, (5) forget that you are a teacher, (6) use district coordinators, (7) try one new method each week, (8) visit the Curriculum Materials Center more often, (9) look for successes, point them out to your colleagues, and praise one another, (10) appreciate individual differences among teachers (e.g., let some work with large groups and some with small), (11) value student concerns and student feedback, (12) use large groups to free staff, (13) remove or rearrange furniture, (14) have principal help teachers, (15) use machines, (16) read, (17) lengthen school day, (18) innovate in area where you are comfortable, (19) teach outdoors, and (20) have a problem-sharing session each week.

4. Ways to increase the support of parents:

   a. Ideas for immediate action: (1) evidence a lack of

phoniness, (2) complete parent questionnaires, and (3) consider the parent knows something about his or her child.

b. Ideas for future committee action: (1) set up newsletters, (2) set up conferences (have parents come to school for feedback about students), (3) use room helpers, (4) hold an open house, (5) establish a teacher-parent social time (parents bring nonparents), (6) present precise information about student progress to parents, (7) hold parent workshops, (8) work cooperatively with Education Center in framing news items for the press, (9) plan carefully for meeting with parents (e.g., work in role-playing situations with others and critique, meet with public during staff meeting, and establish sessions in which teachers role-play parents and parents role-play teachers), (10) keep school facilities open for community use during nonschool hours, (11) do not combine too many activities in one parent-teacher meeting, (12) plan for greater informality at PTA meetings, and (13) plan Dad's Night and Mom's Night.

c. Ideas for future individual or team action: (1) invite parents to observe special projects, (2) encourage school visits any time and at special times, (3) make phone calls to children's homes when all is going well, (4) ask parents for suggestions and use them, (5) plan teacher-parent-team potlucks, (6) send room newsletters home, (7) send notices about new team planning, (8) be open with children, (9) have kids write letters to parents, (10) establish school newspaper, (11) take an interest in parents' interests, (12) have a parent "share day," (13) learn to live with parental nonacceptance, and (14) encourage team mothers to meet.

Stage 5. Anticipating Obstacles
[Unfortunately, members of this group neglected to anticipate the barriers to carrying out their plans. Excited and committed to following up their ideas, they did not recognize the many constraints that would hold them back when school began, with the result that most of the ideas they developed were either lost or placed in suspended animation. As it happened, they had written their ideas in a form they could retain, so later in the school year they were able to recapture many of these plans and use them effectively.]

Stage 6. Taking Action

[The group wrote out its plans on ditto masters, assembled a booklet for each staff member, and described its work to the rest of the staff at a special meeting.]

Stage 7. Evaluating

[This stage received scant attention. During the follow-up OD meeting in the fall, the group reconvened to assess the current state of its problems. Several members were too busy to attend; the remaining members attempted to act on some of the simpler plans, but they, too, soon abandoned the task. Seven months later, however, the school staff was ready to recoup many of the resources they had discovered during the summer. Staff members spent a good part of one Saturday in April reaffirming the goals they felt to be most urgent and finding other members with whom to collaborate in planning for action. For a description of the microdesign used on that Saturday, see the section headed "The Charismatic Day" in chapter 3.]

Solving Problems with the *S-T-P*

Good problem solving requires readiness. Before starting actual problem solving, you may wish to use survey-data-feedback to provoke discussion and focus attention, thereby heightening readiness. The technique is explained in chapters 3 and 9.

The group should have reasonable skill in communicating, some skill at watching its own processes in meetings, and some hope of agreeing on goals. Before asking the group to undertake systematically to solve a serious problem, you may find it advantageous to improve some of those conditions or skills (already discussed in chapters 4 and 5). Systemic problem solving will certainly go badly if the group is split into distrustful or hostile factions. If it is, you will probably want to use one of the methods described in chapter 8 for reducing conflict. With reasonable readiness, however, and a little luck, systematic problem solving can be successful, invigorating, and fun.

In our previous problem-solving examples we labeled the stages, and for convenience we will use the same labels here. But be warned that problem solving is not neatly sequential. As we go along, we will call attention to the recycling—the oscillating between one subtask and another—that is likely to occur. Working on problems is a juggling act that has been nicely described by Cohen, March, and Olsen (1972, p. 2): "An organization is a collection of choices looking for problems, issues and feelings looking for decision situations in which they might be aired, solutions looking for issues to which they might be the answer, and decision makers looking for work."

Nevertheless, the stage labels help participants to stick to one part of the task at a time. Participants can use the labels to help one another answer such questions as "Are we clear about what the problem is?" "Are we talking about helping forces, or are we planning action steps?" "Do you want to shift now from planning for action to anticipating obstacles?"

Stage 1. Specifying the Problem

To reiterate, by a problem we mean a gap between a present situation and a desired target. We specify a problem by describing the existing situation (S) and the desired target state (T). In our first example in the preceding section, the participants specified the S as a "lack of clarity in the role of the department head" and the T as a state in which norms and procedures in the college would enable faculty to say at almost any time, "We know where the head stands, and she knows where we stand." As we noted, a solution is a procedure, plan, or path (P) that will enable participants to get from S to T.

When people state something they do not like about the present situation (S), they are also likely to think of how things might be better (T) and of actions (P) that might move in that direction. When people state something they think the college ought to do (P), they are also likely to think of something about the present situation (S) that they think might be improved by the action, and they are likely to think of how things might get better (T) after the action is taken. When people describe a state of affairs they wish existed (T), they are also likely to think of how the present state (S) fails and of something they might do (P) to move toward the better state. That is the way our minds work, and it is how we ordinarily discuss problems with others—cycling among S, T, and P. That is what Cohen, March, and Olsen meant when they said that an organization is full of choices (Ts) looking for problems (gaps), issues and feelings (about S) looking for an airing, and solutions (Ps) looking for issues (problems) to which they might be the answer.

In this first stage, we deal with S, T, and P all at once—that is, cyclically.

A group may come together to discuss a problem that is already pretty well delimited in their minds—for example, the gap between an existing method in a high school of assigning students to classes that generates a lot of reassigning during the first two weeks of classes (S) and a more desirable method that would settle all students in their classes during the first couple of days (T). Group members may also come together to survey all significant problems they feel and pick the most pressing for immediate work. We treat here the case in which the precise problem has not been picked. For the more limited problems, the procedure can be compressed.

Step 1. Put up three sheets of newsprint and label the one at the left S, the one at the right T, and the one in the middle P. You can write on the newsprints yourself or appoint a recorder. Have more sheets ready.

If you think the important thing is to get the participants working as fast as possible, don't start with a lecture about S, T, and P. Simply get the discussion going and write down on the appropriate sheet what people say. They will understand the S, T, and P better after they see all the examples you have written down.

If part of your purpose is to teach the participants how to use the problem-solving procedure themselves, then you might spend three minutes explaining the S, T, and P before starting the discussion.

You can start the discussion at any of the three places. Use simple language and perhaps a question, such as one of these:

- (S) What's wrong with the way things are now?
- (T) What would you like to be doing in your work that you are not doing now—or doing too little of?
- (P) What would you like to do to improve things?

When you get a statement that seems to be a clear instance of S, T, or P, write it on the proper sheet. If someone wants to argue about wording, remind the group that the sheets are not for publication, that they are only a beginning stage. The words are there only to remind the group of what has been talked about. There will be plenty of time for careful wording in later stages.

In this first step, get everybody's ideas onto the newsprints. Try to get statements that fit clearly into one of the three classifications, but don't work so hard for clarity that you slow down the generation of ideas. If two or three short questions don't clarify what a participant is saying, write whatever you have on the sheet that seems best at the moment. Alternatively, you could put up a fourth sheet for unclassifiable statements and return to them later.

Don't let a discussion start about whether an idea is good or bad. Write down everything.

When the contributions are slow, ask whether anyone wants to change an item from one sheet to another. If you have not yet done so, you can explain now the labels S, T, and P. The important thing here is not to get the group to agree on where the statements best belong, but to generate additional items. If someone thinks that having a group discussion with the department head about her role is a T, and someone else insists it is a P, write it down on both sheets. The group can agree in a later stage on how to classify the item. Being flexible here is a good introduction to the cycling in Step 2.

Step 2. Tell the group you now want to use the ideas on each sheet to generate ideas for other sheets. It is not yet time for participants to agree on what they want to take as Ts and build toward with action steps. You want everyone to hear all the group's ideas about how the statements on the newsprints are connected. Talking about the connections will clarify for everyone how the group is coming to think about the present situation, about what would be a happier state, and about how to get there.

The ideas here for cycling among S, T, and P are taken from a handout written in 1971 by Fred Fosmire and John Wallen. The questions we use below are adapted from theirs. Much of the handout has been put into print by Pilon and Berquist (1979).

You might begin by generating more ideas for the shortest list, or you might want to add more specific ideas to the list containing the vaguest items.

To get more Ts, you can point to an item on the S list and ask questions like these:

- If you could change this feature of the present situation, what would you want to accomplish?
- What would be your goal in improving this feature of the situation?
- What does this fact make you think is missing? What is it you want?

To get more Ts, you can also point to an item on the P list and ask,

- What will that accomplish?
- What goal does that aim at?
- What will this bring that you really care about?

To get more Ps, you can point to an item on the S list and ask,

- What might be done to improve that?
- What kind of action would you say that requires?
- What kind of plan would use that resource?

To get more Ps, you can also point to an item on the T list and ask,

- What might be a possible way to get started toward that?
- What steps might move toward that goal?

To get more Ss, you can point to an item on the P list and ask,

- What would that improve about the present situation?
- What would that deal with, or take account of, that is part of the present situation?
- What resources do we have that will help do that?

To get more Ss, you can also point to an item on the T list and ask,

- In what ways does the present situation fall short of that goal?
- What in the present situation is holding us back from that goal?
- What in the present situation can help us move toward that goal?

If your participants are at all lively, they will begin to volunteer translations among S, T, and P. If they are not so lively, you can ask them to join the game: What do you see in one list that gives you an idea for another list?

When contributions slow, begin cleaning up the lists. In each list, cross out the duplicate items or items that are clearly included in others. Add a few words to clarify items you wrote too fast. If the group seems in the right mood, appoint a committee to do this work. If there is time, ask them to copy everything neatly to make the list more legible. Because of the rush to get everyone's ideas written down, newsprints often get very messy, and it becomes hard to read words that are squeezed hurriedly into small spaces.

Step 3. Now the group focuses on the target statements. Ask participants to delete target statements that are simply not feasible in the reasonable future or that are the least urgent. Use consensus to reach the choices if at all possible. (By consensus, we mean getting everyone's view with sufficient clarity to show that it is plain no one will work against the decision. For a full explanation of consensus, see chapter 7 under "Group Decision Making.") If full consensus does not seem feasible, use voting, but set the necessary vote closer to 80 percent than to 51. Give time—five seconds instead of one—for persons in the minority to voice serious objections. If they do so, point out that the objections should be remembered for Stage 2. Make a note.

The group now examines the remaining target statements. The members discuss the statements to clarify them. "Joe, did you mean by Number 6 that _____?" "Amy, does your statement overlap with Joe's?" Members give their opinions on the desirability and feasibility of the targets. Sometimes it helps to have the group write numerical ratings beside the targets, calculate the totals or averages, and then resume the discussion. Urge the group to envision (and talk about) what their working lives will be like after the target is reached. Rewrite any targets the group wants rewritten.

The goal of Step 3 is to come out with at least one target, but not more than, say, four that everyone agrees are both urgent and feasible. Copy the agreed-upon targets onto a fresh sheet.

Helping the Group Through the First Steps

Start with participants' own problems, not the problems you think they have. Action can spring only from the reality the participants perceive.

Help participants to loosen their thinking about causes. When they think of things that are wrong with the present situation (S), their Ps will spring from their ideas about what *causes* the bad things. When they think about how to get to a target (T), their Ps will also spring from their ideas about what causes human action. Most people's ideas about why things go wrong fall into three types: (1) it's the way things are (it's fate, that's the way people are built); (2) it's somebody's fault (make Joe behave properly); and (3) it's the system (we're all in this together).

You won't have to do much about "it's fate." Somebody else will think of something that can be done.

You may have to help now and then with "it's somebody's fault." Some difficulties certainly do center upon one or a few persons—or on a group. Some people are bottlenecks, at least sometimes, and changing the behavior of a particular person or group may be key to solving the problem. The key person may be at a point where work flows converge, or the key person may be an administrator. The person may be one of the participants present. But if difficulties seem to center upon a particular person or group, it is important to get a lot of information about what is going on in the neighborhood of that person or group.

The danger in blaming a person or group is that it is easy to take it for granted that the problem, and its solution too, lies solely with that person or group. It is too easy to say, "We've just got to put the pressure on Joe," or "Somebody's got to go in there and straighten that bunch out."

You can remind the group about systems and norms. If a problem hasn't faded away of its own accord, it is likely that some regular routines somewhere in the organization are holding it in place. When you take this view, you are thinking about the whole *system*—all the ties and expectations and norms and communication links that keep things going—both the things you want kept going and the things you don't.

If your cuckoo clock squeaks, it squeaks *because* the pendulum is swinging, the gears are going around, and the clock is keeping time. Both what you want it to do (keep time) and what you don't want it to do (squeak) come from the whole system. The clock repairer's task is to find a way to stop the squeak *without stopping the time keeping* and without introducing a squeak in another part of the clock. Think how much more complicated your organization is than a cuckoo clock.

In the short run, maybe the cheapest thing you can do is nothing—just accept your fate. But that could be the most expensive thing in the long run. It's not very expensive in the short run to scold somebody or even to fire somebody, and if you are lucky the work may even go better for a while after you've taken those actions. In the long run, however, you may find yourself chasing the squeak all over the district.

Dealing with the system is usually more expensive, at least in the short run, than dealing with a few individuals. But if you can avoid merely pushing a squeak from one person to another and instead rearrange roles or work flows so that squeaks become rare everywhere, you won't have to go on paying for that same squeak the rest of your life.

Most problems can be categorized according to whether they reside predominately within one person (intrapersonal), among a few people (interpersonal), within a group, between two or more groups, throughout a subsystem, or among several subsystems. But most organizational problems in colleges actually exist at several levels at once. When a faculty is concerned about a discrepancy between its current and an ideal set of instructional procedures, for instance, the discrepancy exists not only at the level of the entire educational organization but also among various subgroups, among several sets of individuals, and within many individuals. In addition, this problem can involve institutional policy and discrepant expectations among faculty, students, and non-academic staff.

Although a problem can be categorized chiefly within a particular issue such as goal setting or conflict management, each content area is interrelated with all others. Goal setting, for example, overlaps with issues of communication, managing conflict, running meetings, and making decisions. Since educational organizations are multifaceted and their organizational problems are multi-determined, solutions will necessarily be multiple.

Stage 2. Listing Helping and Hindering Forces

Now the group chooses one of its highest priority targets (listed in Step 3 of Stage 1) and lists both the existing forces that will help it reach the target and those that can hinder its efforts. It lists forces within individuals (attitudes, feelings, values, typical behavior); within the small groups (norms, roles, interpersonal skills); within the whole college or school (norms, roles, rules, procedures, organizational "climate"); and within the larger community or society (economic trends, political "climate," pressure groups).

The group can choose to work toward a single target until reaching it before beginning work toward another. Or the group can choose to work toward several targets simultaneously. If the group makes the first choice, it carries the first target through the remaining stages of problem solving, including action and evaluation, and then returns to its list of highest priority targets. If it makes the second choice, it carries the first target at least through Stage 5 (anticipating obstacles) before turning to the next target.

Put up a newsprint bearing the diagram shown in Figure 6-1. Have extra newsprint ready.

The vertical line in the diagram represents the current state of affairs (S). There are forces at the left pressing toward the target (T) and forces at the right resisting that movement. Listing the

Figure 6-1. The Force Field

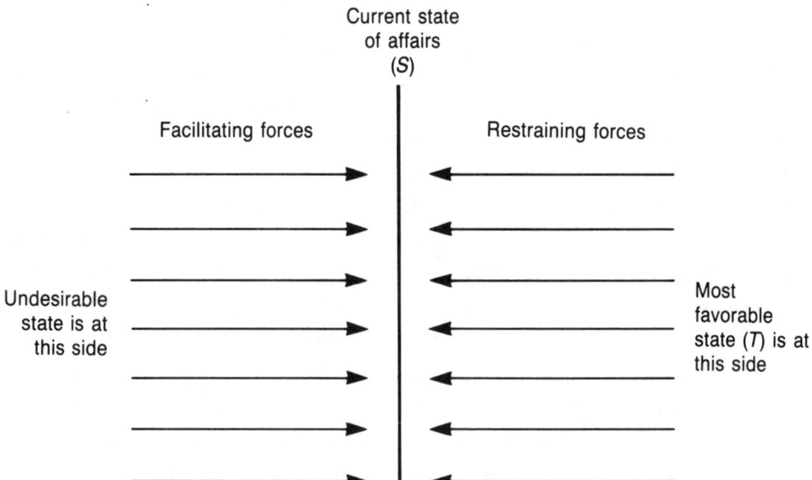

helping forces at the left will remind the group of valuable resources and allies. Listing the hindering forces at the right will remind the group of obstacles to be surmounted. It is usually easier to move into action by weakening the hindering forces than by increasing the helping forces.

Step 1. List all the forces anyone can think of. Avoid argument and evaluation. Suspend critical judgment, but encourage paraphrasing for clarity. Strive for an accepting, inventive mood.

Work back and forth. A force of one sort named by one person will remind someone else of a force of the other sort. A force can have both helping and hindering aspects. List such a force on both sides of the diagram.

This is the time to recall any objections voiced by outvoted persons during Step 3 of Stage 1.

Step 2. Ask group members to agree on the forces they think can hinder their efforts the most. Try to keep the number to six or fewer. If the hindering forces are insightfully chosen, reducing only a few of them will almost always suffice to get the group moving toward its target. Choosing too many hindering forces to overcome will make the task seem too formidable, and trying to keep too many forces in mind will be confusing.

Rate the forces according to how feasible it will be to reduce them. You will end with a few hindering forces that the group believes are both important and possible to reduce.

It is not necessary to choose and rate the helping forces. The group will recall them easily as the need arises.

Sometimes there will be disagreements about the fact. Is there or is there not some loose money in the budget? Does the law prohibit certain action or does it not? Will a certain community organization or pressure group see our change project as something they'd like to help with, or won't they?

Avoid arguing about fact. Delegate someone to get on the telephone immediately and find out. If finding the answer is likely to take more than half an hour, write down the uncertainty as a hindering force: "We don't know whether . . ." Finding the answer can become an action step later.

Sometimes pluralistic ignorance gets confused with fact. A member of the group may say it is not feasible to reduce a particular hindering force because of something "everybody knows." Maybe "everybody knows" that the counselors will have a certain opinion, or that the dean won't permit a certain action. Often, "everybody" goes on believing something for months or years because each takes the others' word for it without testing the matter. It is usually a good idea to ask for evidence or go get some.

Stage 3. Specifying Multiple Solutions

The purpose of this stage is to generate as many ideas as possible for reducing the hindrances selected in Stage 2. It is easy, in this stage, for people to get bogged down in arguing about the feasibility of actions or their likely efficacy. It is important to tell participants at the outset, therefore, that they will get their chance to be critical later on. The important thing now is to be inventive. Some very good ideas seem crazy at first glance.

This stage is a time for creativity and fun. Now is the time for brainstorming. Withhold critical judgment and evaluation; rather, encourage one another to be creative, playful, even wild.

Consider each hindering force in turn, and think of ways to reduce its strength. Use the following ideas to increase your creativity:

1. *Get ready.* Loosen up. Stretch your body; reach for the ceiling. Try some warm-up activity such as Billy Goat described in chapter 5.

2. *Get set.* Have lots of newsprint tacked to the wall. Appoint a recorder who can hear well and write rapidly. If it will speed the recording, appoint two recorders.

3. *Go.* Brainstorm ideas for eliminating the first hindrance. Be silly and wild, and pool your wildness. Don't say no to any idea. Don't even take time to express approval beyond exclamations like "Hurray!" "Hear! Hear!" "Wow!" or "Go! Go!" Proceed to the next force in the same way.

Limits

Either in this stage or the next, some people will have worries about particular points of feasibility. They will worry that some of the ideas for action might push them into untenable positions. Likert and Likert (1978) remind us that people do face limits to their actions. It is a good idea to find out the limits on individuals before getting very far into serious planning for action.

A principal might need to make it clear that he or she cannot violate certain laws or is constrained by district policy not to delegate certain responsibilities. A department head might point to the state's requirements for certain curricula. A counselor might insist that no plan is acceptable that reduces the hours available for personal counseling with students. Others might demand that their ethical, moral, or religious values not be violated. They might require that any plan show promise of increasing their freedom to make choices about their own work. In short, one or more participants might have nonnegotiable requirements—Likert and Likert call them "essential conditions"—that any solution must satisfy. It is better for the group to learn those requirements sooner instead of later.

Usually, no one will name a condition that brings the problem solving to a halt. Should that occur, however, it is usually possible to plan a solution that gives the objector limited participation that does not violate his or her essential condition. If that is impossible, only two courses of action remain: (1) ask the member to withdraw from the problem-solving group or (2) cease trying to solve the problem as a group and turn it over to an administrator to solve by fiat.

As essential conditions are listed, it will sometimes happen that people forget to restrict themselves to essential, nonnegotiable conditions and will name a few that they actually hold only as desirable. After the list is made, therefore, it is a good idea to ask a question such as, "Are these now the conditions which, if violated, would cause you to withdraw from the project?" Once the essential conditions are settled, the group should take them as given and not to be questioned.

Use your own judgment about the best time to list the essential conditions. If you list them just before brainstorming possible solutions in Stage 3, you will forestall possible anxieties on the part of the people who might see violations of their essential conditions appearing on the newsprints, but you might also put a damper on the group's freedom to be creative. If you wait until after the brainstorming in Stage 3, it will be easier to generate playfulness in the brainstorming, but a few people could be anxious and therefore reticent, and it might be more difficult to draw them out later.

Stage 4. Planning for Action

Now is the time to be critical and hard-nosed.

Step 1. Pick out the solutions from Stage 3 that seem most feasible—likely to bring good results for a reasonable amount of effort. Make a new list of those ideas that seem within the capacity of the group and its allies to carry out. Use consensus if possible.

(For the characteristics of consensus, see chapter 7 under "Group Decision Making.")

In Step 3 of Stage 1, we chose targets—states in which a problem would no longer exist. In Stage 2, we listed hindering forces whose removal would allow us to move toward the targets. In Stage 3 we listed actions (solutions) that would put us in motion toward the targets. Those solutions were large chunks of action—large actions, so to speak. The large actions we choose in this step of Stage 4 can be thought of as subtargets. We must now think of smaller actions that will move us into the larger actions (solutions). Just as the solutions called for more specific and immediate actions than the targets, so now the smaller actions we will list in Step 2 will be more specific and immediate than the solutions. These smaller actions will be so specific, immediate, and clear that everyone will be able to take action tomorrow morning.

You can see that in effect we are recycling the first three stages, but now with the subtargets. Indeed, Stage 5 will be part of the recycling.

Step 2. Specify dates and persons:

1. For each solution selected, put its necessary steps of action into a time sequence.
2. Designate the groups or persons who will take each step.
3. List the materials and other resources needed.
4. Plan to begin the sequence as soon as possible.
5. Estimate specific dates on which each step will be taken.
6. Make plans for periodically evaluating the effectiveness of the actions as they are taken. Agree on criteria where they are not obvious: "We will know this action is successfully completed when we see (or hear) that. . . ."
7. Be prepared to revise the plans as the action sequences unfold. Specify dates for review.

Stage 5. Anticipating Obstacles

Now we recycle to hindering forces, but new ones. We anticipate what might go wrong with our plans. The step-by-step planning in Stage 4 will have revealed some possible difficulties not apparent when we were generating hindering forces in Stage 2.

Step 1. Once more, weigh the probabilities of success against the probable effort required. Do that for each proposed action.

Step 2. Try to imagine all possible things that might go wrong. Remember to anticipate barriers in the environment (university regulations, economic trends, political "climate," pressure groups) as well as in individuals, the group, and the college or school.

Simulate the actions by asking friends to role-play persons who will be affected by the planned actions and to tell you their reactions.

Step 3. Go directly to the actual persons who will be affected and ask them how well they think your plans will work.

The steps in this stage are arduous, and you will be impatient to get on with the planned actions. It is easier to deal with obstacles that are realistically anticipated, however, than to deal with obstacles that come as surprises.

Stage 6. Taking Action

Do not delay taking the first step. The best time is tomorrow morning, even today. Many of the forces affecting the problem are changing from day to day. Your solutions may not remain appropriate for long.

Under Stage 5, we urged you to ferret out every possible obstacle. Now we temper that advice. Do not overplan. A group sometimes gets so fascinated with the planning or so anxious about the obstacles that it seems to want to leave not the slightest detail to chance. It seems willing to go on planning forever (see "Mobilizing Synergistic Action" in chapter 1). But the current of events flows on while you are planning. You cannot anticipate everything. You must leave a good deal to the skill and judgment of the people who will carry out the action steps. Indeed, too much planning sometimes indicates too little trust in the group.

No plan can be perfect. Have the courage to go forward with an imperfect plan.

Stage 7. Evaluating

Things can go wrong. Something usually does go wrong. Without tracking, monitoring, and evaluating, the finest plan can founder when no one is looking. Planners should establish criteria for evaluating the effectiveness of their actions (see Item 6 under Step 2 of Stage 4). They should review their progress (or appoint someone to do so) as each action step occurs.

Working toward a target tests not only how well a plan has been conceived but also how well the original situation has been understood. New information brought to light while a plan is being carried out may call for a change in the plan itself, a modification of target, or revised ideas about the desirability of the target as first conceived. As people approach their target and form a clearer picture of what living in the ideal state might actually be like, they may not find it as desirable as they had originally thought. Or perhaps reaching it will have come to seem too costly. This does not necessarily mean that they planned poorly or chose the wrong target. It means that no plan or target stays good for very long, and that if the group's vision does not change, circumstances will.

For that reason, participants should tackle concrete problems first, pick targets of moderate scope, and avoid the trap of overplanning. The danger of large-scale planning is that after devoting an immense amount of effort to it, people feel reluctant either to "waste" any of it or to put still more effort into reconceiving the goal or changing the plan. If they succumb to the temptation to carry out the plan to the last detail even though the facts show that things are going badly, they face the worse danger of losing the norms and skills of openness. Thus, instead of planning on the grand scale, we advocate incremental planning informed by regular feedback and replanning. Educators should build their new world in moderate steps, repeatedly surveying both the wider horizon and the immediate path.

Promoting Effective Problem Solving

Here are some admonitions and ideas that can be useful at various stages of solving a problem.

1. At intervals, as the group goes through the stages, it should take time out to discuss how well the problem solving itself is going. Doing this will ensure that the systematic process is serving the group well instead of becoming a burdensome ritual. As a group becomes skillful, it looks at its own process, briefly or at length, whenever someone comes to feel that a step should be short-cut, lengthened, or conducted in a more fruitful way.

2. The group should attend to the feelings of its members as they work at the task.

3. Because disagreement can be a valuable tool for creative problem solving, encourage respect for its use as a stimulant for new ideas. The convener should help group members distinguish among disagreements over beliefs about facts (S), disagreements that involve different value positions (T), and

disagreements concerning different proposals for action (*P*).

4. Because conveners have great power even when they lack formal authority, be aware of your domination as a convener and try to limit it.

5. Because leadership is a set of functions, the convener should encourage the group to share responsibility for the functions.

6. In describing a systematic problem-solving procedure for groups, we do not mean that the procedure will be serviceable only where individuals all conceive the problem in exactly the same way, agree wholly on the strengths of the facilitating and restraining forces, and so on. Nor do we mean that every individual must be enthusiastically committed to the steps agreed upon. The procedure is serviceable whenever no one is so opposed to the conception or so fearful of the action steps that he or she will take action to sabotage the sequence of action. Part of the skill of solving problems in groups is the ability to ascertain whether anyone feels that sort of opposition. Success in ascertaining whether there is opposition requires that participants have sufficient trust in the convener.

7. When we say that getting work done requires coordination and agreement on how to do things, we do not mean that people must swear undeviating commitment to long-term goals, short-term goals, and all the myriad small steps for reaching them. We mean only that there is inevitably some minimal orderliness in what people expect from one another today, next week, and next month. Planning in a group, for example, probably yields its greatest benefit when it enables people to test the trustworthiness of those expectations. Dowling (1978) interviewed Fletcher Byrom, chairman of the board and chief executive officer of the Koppers Company. Byrom said:

> We do quite a bit of [long-range planning] . . . but to us, it's a discipline more than it is a guide to future decision making . . . If you have taken the trouble of anticipating something, you should at least be able to recognize that it hasn't happened that way. If you hadn't done the planning, you wouldn't have realized that what happened was unexpected. As a regimen, as a discipline for a group of people, planning is very valuable. My position is, go ahead and plan, but once you've done your planning, put it on the shelf. Don't be bound by it. Don't use it as a major input to the decision-making process. Use it mainly to recognize change as it takes place (p. 40).

Chapter Seven

Making Decisions

Solving problems requires that proposals for action be generated. Because educators have different values, see the same circumstances in different ways, and think differently about different plans, choices among alternatives become necessary. Making decisions can be defined as choosing among alternatives.

The preceding chapter described problem solving as bringing together information about situation and target and generating proposals to move educators from their present state to an ideal state. Problem solvers become decision makers when they determine the validity of situational information, select their preferred targets, or choose among alternative plans of action. In other words, decision making follows problem solving whenever a choice arises. Problem solving requires gathering, filtering, and processing information; decision making requires assigning priorities and acting on them.

Although problem solving and decision making are often viewed as a single process, we have chosen to distinguish them for four reasons. First, we believe that increased awareness of decision-making methods can alleviate the tensions and frustrations that arise when the methods are imperfectly understood, when decisions are made by default, or when decisions are made but not implemented. Second, we believe that people who are aware of how decisions are made can participate more effectively in making those that require their aid and that such decisions will more likely be carried out. Third, we think that a group of educators that has been trained to employ multiple decision-making modes effectively can better select the mode most appropriate to the kind of decision to be made. Fourth, we believe that educational resources will not be adequately shared unless educators in all important roles can at least sometimes take part in collaborative decision making.

Although an educational organization's ability to maintain access to resources, to act responsively, and to assess its movement toward goals is critically linked to the clarity and explicitness of its decision making, few colleges or schools regularly examine their norms, structures, or procedures for exerting influence or making decisions. This chapter describes concepts and skills that can clarify these processes for achieving shared influence and collaborative decision making in colleges and schools.

Making Decisions in Educational Organizations

Traditional theories of organization located the major sources of power at the top of the organizational hierarchy and consequently limited the power and influence of those at lower levels. Early organizational and management theorists believed that workers were motivated primarily by economic incentives and job security, that efficient organizations developed rational rules and procedures to keep subordinates under control and protect the organization from human caprice, and that participation in decision making and shared influence were incompatible with organizational effectiveness.

For many organizations now, however, those traditional views are mistaken. In particular, there are school districts in which power is not located exclusively at the top but is shared among principals, teachers, students, and even parents. And there are colleges with very active governing boards that include educators and citizens in equal numbers. Indeed, there is a good deal of evidence that a wider distribution of influence yields measurable benefits. In addition, problem solving and decision making are not always sequential, deliberate, orderly, rational processes carried out by people tightly connected with one another. We support the view of Weick (1976), who described educational organizations as systems that are loosely coupled rather than "coupled through dense, tight linkages." Using Weick's imagery, consider the implications of this view.

> Imagine that you're either the referee, coach, player, or spectator at an unconventional soccer match: the field for the game is round; there are several goals scattered haphazardly around the circular field; people can enter and leave the game whenever they want to; they can throw balls in whenever they want; they can say "that's my goal" whenever they want to, as many times as they want to, and for as many goals as they want to; the entire game takes place on a sloped field; and the game is played as if it makes sense.

> If you now substitute in that example deans or principals for referees, instructors or teachers for coaches, students for players, citizens at large or parents for spectators, and education for soccer, you have an equally unconventional depiction of educational organizations. The beauty of this depiction is that it captures a different set of realities within educational organizations than are caught when these same organizations are viewed through the tenets of bureaucratic theory.

> Consider the contrast in images. For some time people who manage organizations and people who study this managing have asked, "How does an organization go about doing what it does and with what consequences for its people, processes, products, and persistence?" And for some time they've heard the same answers. In paraphrase, the answers say essentially that an organization does what it does because of plans, intentional selection of means that get the organization to agree upon goals, and all of this is accomplished by such rationalized procedures as cost-benefit analyses, division of labor, specified areas of discretion, authority invested in the office, job descriptions, and a consistent evaluation and reward system. The only problem with that portrait is that it is rare in nature. People in organizations, including educational organizations, find themselves hard-pressed either to find actual instances of those rational practices or to find rationalized practices whose outcomes have been as beneficent as predicted, or to feel that those rational occasions explain much of what goes on within the organization. Parts of some organizations are heavily rationalized, but many parts also prove intractable to analysis through rational assumptions (p. 1).

If entire states, universities, or school districts are unlikely to be moving in the same direction at the same time, it is important for groups solving problems and making decisions to be substantially independent of other subsystems while they marshal their commitment and take their first steps. It is unrealistic to believe that people in loosely coupled systems are able to commit themselves to one another over long periods of time. For this reason, problem solving and decision making must occur in brief cycles in which people take small first steps, assess progress, and only then move on to further action.

Influence and Decision Making

In an organization, a decision is a directive, a promise, or an agreement asserting that particular people will carry out particular acts. A decision, therefore, is a channel of influence. When an administrator makes a decision that certain other people will do something, the administrator is seeking to influence those people. When a group decides that it will do something, the group members are seeking to influence themselves as a collectivity.

Many writers have speculated about the sources of social power or influence. We believe that thought about influence, aided by a good deal of empirical research, has begun to converge.

French and Raven (1959), from whom we have borrowed some of our ideas about power sources, postulated five potential sources of power that people can use to influence others in social settings:

1. *Reward power:* The control and distribution of rewards valued by others
2. *Coercive power:* The control and withholding of rewards valued by others
3. *Legitimate power:* Authority legally vested in or assigned to a position
4. *Expert power:* The expertise of special knowledge, skill, or experience
5. *Referent power:* Personal attractiveness or membership in someone's primary reference group

Subsequent to the classical publication by French and Raven, Raven and Kruglanski (1975) added a sixth base of influence, i.e., informational power and Hersey and Goldsmith (cited in Hersey, 1984) introduced a seventh, i.e., connection power. They were described as follows:

6. *Informational power:* The amount of insider information a person has about the history, culture, and customs of the group.
7. *Connection power:* The number of close relationships that a person has with other key members of the group.

In general, the more such sources people can marshal, the more powerful they will be, although expert and referent power tend to be especially important. Bachman, Smith, and Slesinger (1966) have shown, for example, that the satisfaction and performance of subordinates improve as organizational leaders rely increasingly on expert and referent power bases. According to Hornstein and his colleagues (1968), teachers find more satisfaction working under principals who employ expert or referent power than those who impose legitimate or coercive power. These findings supported Weick's position that reward, coercion, and legitimacy are less tightly coupled to action than are expert and referent power.

Foa and Foa (1974) wrote that there are six kinds of resources we exchange with one another: goods, money, information, status, love, and services. We gain influence over another person by giving (or offering to give) or withholding (or threatening to take away) one or more of those six resources. Harrison (1978) identified four styles of influence: reward and punishment, assertive persuasion, participation and trust, and common vision or charisma. Here are some ways in which those ideas and some others come together.

Reward and Punishment

In one circumstance or another, people find many kinds of things rewarding or punishing. The Foas made that clear when they point out that you can reward or punish by giving or taking away any of the six interpersonal resources. French and Raven (1959) also listed reward and punishment (coercion) as sources of power. In the same vein, Longabaugh (1963) wrote about dominance versus submission, and Boulding (1978) wrote about the polity and the "threat system."

McClelland's (1958) concept of power emphasized the negation of punishment—not being subject to punishment or threats from others, being in control of one's own destiny. When you are not at the mercy of others, you can bargain from a position of strength. Similarly, Harrison and Kouzes (1980) listed disengaging as a form of power, saying that it enables us to avoid emotionally draining involvements and to conserve energy. DeCharms (1968a, 1968b, 1976) pointed to the same positive and negative faces of power when he wrote of being an origin (making one's own initiatives) or being a pawn at the mercy of others.

Information

"Knowledge is power," we often hear. Harrison's (1978) influence style of "assertive persuasion" includes using information when proposing courses of action and arguing about them. Having special information is an important part of Raven and Kruglanski's informational power and French and Raven's category of expert power. The Foas made information one of their six interpersonal resources. The power of having information comes not only from knowing facts that others do not have, but also from how we are able to connect the facts to matters at hand and from our persuasiveness in doing so.

Affiliation

McClelland referred to our immemorial need for bonds of affection with others. Harrison and Kouzes called this joining. The Foas include it in their category of love. Maslow (1954) included it when he wrote about social relations, Longabaugh when he wrote about love versus hostility, Alderfer (1972) when he wrote about relatedness, and Boulding when he wrote about the integration of society. It is an integral part of Hersey and Goldsmith's connection power. When we affiliate ourselves with others, when we join them to do work, we must to some extent put ourselves at their mercy. We take a risk that others will not have our welfare in mind. Influencing others to work both for our benefit and their own, therefore, requires cooperation and trust. Developing a group in which work is shared, participation is widespread, trust is high, and personal ties are strong is a way of magnifying our own powers through the powers of the group. Working with a cohesive group of that sort is the style of influence that Harrison called participation-and-trust. French and Raven called this referent power—power through being an attractive figure, one with whom people can identify. Goldman, Dunlap, and Conley (1993) have described it more recently as facilitative power. It is the kind of influence or power that is implicit, and sometimes explicit, when we write in this book about the following topics: effective sub-systems, group maintenance, participation, interdependence, trust, openness, sharing resources, using conflict constructively, emotional closeness, two-way communication, third-party helping, consensus, and similar matters. It is the sort of influence that the OD facilitator hopes will become normative in colleges or schools.

Status

Status includes, among other things, the common notion of authority (but not authoritativeness, which belongs better with informational or expert power). French and Raven called this concept legitimate power. The influence that accrues to status comes from the culture, customs, or laws of society; from the norms or regulations of an organization; or from the agreements within a group. The influence that goes with status is bestowed by others. To persons in certain positions, we delegate, so to speak, the use of one or another of the kinds of influence we described above.

When we put a person into a position of authority, we grant that person the use of certain kinds of influence with us. Educational administrators can reward educators with money, goods (materials), services, information, and status (recognitions of merit) or punish them by withholding these. Instructors can reward (or punish) students with information, services, status, and affection.

But status can come from positions other than those of formal authority. A person of high achievement (a captain of industry, say) can attract the allegiance of others who hope for a share in the achievement. An expert can command deference because of the information or know-how he or she has to give or withhold. Status can come through respect prescribed by culture or custom, as when we give respect to age. Status can even accrue to sheer munificence of love, as in the case of Eleanor Roosevelt.

A special case of status comes not as much from position, expertness, or control of resources as from personal qualities and leadership skill. It is the status of the charismatic leader. The charismatic leader articulates our yearnings and inspires us to action. Harrison called this the influence style of common vision. French and Raven included personal attractiveness under referent power. Although charisma brings the emotional ties that also arise in what we called affiliation or facilitation, the ties are not a network in the group, but are usually focused on one person. Still, charisma need not reside solely in a leader. Berlew (1974) has argued that charisma ("organizational excitement") can characterize an entire organization. Indeed, the phenomenon of organizational excitement is part and parcel of the OD change process.

Many people grow up thinking of power and influence as attached to authority and position. As we have seen, however, influence arises from many sources, and all of us can reach out to some of them. Furthermore, as Harrison and Kouzes wrote, "Many people now recognize that the authority of an office is not sufficient to get things done in organizations and in society. We see people at all organizational levels having to use their skills of persuasion, negotiation, personal charisma, and trust building in order to influence others" (1980, p. 44). The industrial literature is full of reports substantiating Harrison and Kouzes's claim. The empirical literature in education on the point is meager, but Hornstein and his colleagues (1968), as noted above, did report that teachers find more satisfaction working under principals who employ expert or affiliative power than under those who impose positional or coercive power. We have found that the same is true of instructors and department heads in higher education.

Participative Decision Making

The OD facilitator can help participants to pinpoint the sources of power at their disposal, to develop sources they do not have, and to rely more often on those that have strong intended effects and few undesirable side-effects. For example, the facilitator can help a student council gain legitimacy by getting them school-board approval to give feedback to the faculty of a school. Or college faculty members can describe one another's resources and rewarding behavior to become aware of those sources of influence. The facilitator can also help those in positions of legitimate power—deans or principals, for example—to begin distributing part of their power to others. Forming new organizational structures such as special decision-making bodies or ad hoc steering committees can encourage faculty members to assume leadership and responsibility for what goes on in their college or school. Particular problems in moving toward more facilitative power and shared influence are discussed later in this chapter.

It is not necessarily true that if some people become more influential, others must become less so. Powerful people who subscribe to this view often fear an OD project as a threat to their power. In effectively functioning educational organizations however, educators of all hierarchical levels can gain in power and influence as the power and influence of their subordinates increase. In other words, influence is reciprocal in effective educational organizations.

March and Simon (1958) theorized that expanding the influence of lower echelons not only increases the power of those members but also allows management to participate more fully. According to Likert (1961, 1967) who described much the same phenomenon in connection with his link-pin model for organizations, more influence is given to subordinates by communicatively linking all organizational levels. Researching the relationship between organizational power and effectiveness, Tannenbaum (1968) found it feasible for more influence to be exercised at every hierarchical level in what he called *polyarchic organizations*, and has shown that when more people exert influence, the extent to which they are influenced by others increases as well.

The creation of management or leadership teams and interdisciplinary structures are attempts by educators to organize themselves according to these principles. The multiunit elementary school developed by the Wisconsin Research and Development Center for Cognitive Learning, for example, provides procedures for teachers to work with students of various ages in teams rather than in isolation, and it creates the position of team or unit leader.

Regular meetings between the principal and unit leaders provide a forum for broader involvement in decision making and a communicative link between unit teachers and the principal. The total organization becomes more integrated as information goes directly from its source to where it is needed, and all levels gain more actual operating power from the increased interaction.

Likewise, many colleges are organized with division heads or department chairs acting as communicative links between the dean and the teaching faculty. Such structures work best when the intermediary linkers self-consciously assume the function of communicating important messages openly both up and down.

Indeed, there is a definite trend for educational organizations at all levels to exhibit increasing formal collaboration and cooperation among staff members. Such changes in the social structure of colleges and schools are driven by an assumption that innovative curricula and instruction will flourish in group arrangements that facilitate greater interdependence among the professionals. Increasingly, educators are expected to work together and to share their resources to provide a broadened range of learning opportunities for students. We have shown how an OD project might facilitate the development of such relationships among teachers in elementary schools (see Schmuck and Schmuck, 1992), and among instructors, department heads, and deans in community colleges (See Schmuck, 1994). In those projects we also learned a great deal about striking the right balance between high interdependence and loose coupling. Close collaboration can be overdone in educational organizations; increased influence should not be unremittingly exercised from everyone to everyone every hour of every day.

It is better, for example, to place a leadership team between the faculty members and the administration than to have the total body of faculty members making demands on the head every week. In the latter case, the head, learning too much about every week's details, would be tempted to get into the faculty members' roles, which would destroy necessary differentiation. For the same reason, it is better for deans or principals to meet the provost or superintendent with serious demands every month or two instead of every week. The OD facilitator can help educators explore how influence is distributed in their organization and compare this to their images of ideal distributions. By helping them learn to exert and receive influence, give and receive feedback, and recognize the existence of interdependencies, the facilitator can help participants create more effective and satisfying decision-making structures.

A number of empirically oriented organizational theorists have challenged the traditional notion that participation deters rather than enhances organizational effectiveness. Lewin (1951) and Coch and French (1948) indicated how participation satisfies social needs; Maslow (1954), Schein (1965), and McGregor (1967) suggested that participation satisfies growth needs as well. Research carried out in industry, voluntary organizations, and schools alike has demonstrated that the satisfaction of organization members increases when they can influence decision making.

Our experiences with OD in education lead us to believe that people in schools and colleges not only want but need to offer critical input and to participate in decision making. Like members of other organizations, educators who have access to powerful people in the larger educational organization feel better about their jobs and their departments and are more willing to display their capabilities to others. Faculty members in both colleges and schools report greatest satisfaction with administrators when they perceive some degree of mutual influence. There is even a positive correlation between student satisfaction and their perceptions of mutual influence with their instructors.

But organizational effectiveness means more than satisfied people; it means improvement in the quality of decisions and increased likelihood of implementation as well. Maier (1970) provided some of the best evidence that shared decision making produces more acceptable decisions of higher quality than those made by individuals alone. Participative decision making enhances organizational effectiveness, because people who feel the support of a group are more willing to take risks in pursuit of creative solutions. Another reason is that the possibility of finding the best solution is greater in a group than with an individual. In short, decision-making procedures that allow more people to risk sharing their good ideas can yield decisions that are worth implementing. To this end, OD facilitators can help participants explore the kinds of decisions made in their educational organization, pinpointing those that must be of high quality and that require high acceptance for implementation, and calling attention to situations in which participative decision making is especially important.

One of the most significant obstacles to participative decision making is the size of a large organization. Katz and Kahn (1978) suggested solutions to the problem of size. We can apply their ideas to big schools. Virtually all colleges and most large schools—those with more than 40 faculty members—can profitably experiment with decentralizing decision making in substructures such as areas, departments, divisions, or "houses." Feedback about decisions in the substructures can be communicated through unit heads, who function as links between the substructures. Job enlargement is often possible within existing structures so that, for example, regular faculty members can take on some of the functions of administrators and vice versa. Committee or team responsibility for a set of tasks can ensure greater psychological engagement of individual staff members in the college or school. The key idea in managing a big educational organization is to conceive of it as composed of groups working on specific tasks and linked by members of more than one group.

Group Decision Making

Three Modes

How influence is distributed in an organization depends upon how decisions are made in face-to-face groups. Although groups vary considerably in their composition and procedures, three decision-making modes occur most often: (1) decisions made by a single person or by a minority, (2) decisions based on the ability of a majority to overrule a minority, and (3) decisions based on acquiescence and support of the total group after discussion and debate (here called *consensus*). Although it is difficult to obtain these patterns in their purest forms even under controlled laboratory conditions, behavioral studies indicate that each affects a group's performance differently.

Although many kinds of educational decisions are best made by one person or by a small committee, these are either about matters that do not require committed action by all or most of the members of the educational organization, are not so complex as to require subtle coordination and understanding among those implementing the decisions, or are those whose outcome is a matter of indifference to most people. Examples include the form on which to report absences, the date on which a particular colloquium will be held, the time to call a committee meeting, or the advice to give architects of the new wing of science labs. The efficiency of such decisions is widely understood and does not require discussion here.

Relegating discussions to a minority subgroup is the method most frequently practiced in the everyday life of educational organizations. This method is the least effective in using members' resources, obtaining their commitment, or in achieving high quality. Decisions made by one or a minority of persons may be welcome when contestants find strife so unpleasant that merely resolving the matter is more attractive than the quality of the solution. It is nevertheless true that when only a few members contribute to making a decision, the final decision will depend upon the limited resources of only those few.

When problems are too complex to be solved by simple sequential decisions, a minority does less well than the total group, partly because it lacks the total group's resourcefulness and partly because the mutual probing and stimulation of the total group are missing. The inferiority of minority decision making is especially evident in complex organizations like colleges and large schools, whose central organizational tasks cannot be carried out in face-to-face groups containing most of the members.

Because it allows more resources to be introduced into discussion, decision by majority vote is superior to minority decision making in producing decisions that require wide commitment for implementation. Where commitment by everyone is not required, a majority vote can also serve very well. If, for example, a faculty decides to hold a picnic on a certain day with the understanding that not everyone will attend and that there will be no penalty for nonattendance, a majority vote will enable the picnic to be held with no damage to the undertaking by those in the minority.

It should be remembered, however, that a majority vote ascertains only those alternatives that people find more or less preferable; unless there is extended discussion, it does not uncover the alternatives that certain people find insupportable. To the extent that the outvoted minority is unable to use its resources to influence the decision, some resources are still not being brought to bear on the decision. Indeed, when nonsupport or sabotage by one or more members could seriously damage an undertaking that requires total group support, a decision by majority vote could be dangerous.

Group consensus is, for us, a process in which (1) all members can paraphrase the issue under consideration to show that they understand it; (2) all members have a chance to voice their opinions on the issue; and (3) those who continue to doubt the decision or disagree with it are nevertheless willing to try it for a prescribed period without sabotaging it. Consensus is therefore different from a unanimous vote. It does not mean that everyone agrees or even that the decision represents everyone's first choice. It means that enough people are in favor for it to be carried out and that those who remain doubtful nonetheless understand the decision and will not obstruct its implementation.

Because consensus requires fairly advanced skill in two-way communication, in coping with conflict, and in the use of para-phrasing and surveying, it is more difficult to achieve than majority vote, although its emotional benefits in many ways outweigh the cost. Majority vote hides pain. Members who may be hurting silently vote one way or another without having to reveal their dismay, with the result that the group is unaware of their pain and is surprised by subsequent foot-dragging and sabotage. But pain is far more likely to find expression and to be dealt with during the consensual process. Thus, majority rule sacrifices pain to efficiency, while consensus takes pain into account but at the expense of considerable time and discomfort.

Where there are pronounced status differences among staff members, a minority decision is often employed in the hope of short-circuiting conflict and saving time. For avoiding conflicts that arise from differences of opinion the majority vote holds great attraction for many. Consensus, however, is designed neither to avoid conflict nor to overcome group resistance in the short run. Perhaps for that reason consensus is often discounted as impractical or unfeasible. Although consensus usually results in more resourceful decisions for complex tasks, it is a form of decision making seldom employed in educational organizations.

For our part, we are convinced that decisions about instructional matters, for example, can be made more effectively when faculty members are able to stimulate and encourage use of one another's resources during decision making. To this end, a number of procedures described in this book are extremely useful for uncovering minority views that might otherwise not surface easily. Surveying, for example, can be carried out by tactfully inviting silent members to express their views. Paraphrasing, summarizing, and checking the feelings of others can also be used to elicit responses. Those who hold the majority position can assume the role of the minority and express this view to the rest of the group, asking minority members to say whether the expression of the role player was accurate.

Alternative Structures

Members of instructional teams or departments and small faculties with common values can readily learn to use the consensual mode of decision making. But techniques and procedures that facilitate consensus in small groups are difficult to apply successfully when value orientations are pluralistic or when the group is too large for easy interaction in face-to-face discussion. In such educational organizations, the OD facilitator and steering committee members may wish to create alternative structures that allow for different modes of decision making. Three alternative arrangements that have been used in large organizations include the management team, the decision-making body, and ad hoc groups.

The Management Team. We know of a senior high staff of 70 teachers that was engaged for several years in an OD effort. The administration team, composed of the principal and three vice principals, found that some staff did not wish to be involved in shared decision making. The latter viewed the process as too complicated, time-consuming, and frustrating. After considerable experimentation, the administrative team agreed to continue providing overall leadership to the staff.

Each member of the team now holds certain fixed responsibilities related to student services, physical plant, curriculum, and so on, but avoids making unilateral decisions about matters that have ramifications for someone else's responsibility. For example, the vice principal in charge of student services does not decide whether students can hold an assembly in the gym without first conferring with the vice principal in charge of physical plant to see that the gym is available. The group still meets regularly, any member can suggest items for the agenda, and all decisions are made by consensus.

The Decision-making Body. In this same educational organization, most decisions are made by a group called the DMB (decision-making body). Composed of all department chairpersons, head teachers, the principal, and the three assistant principals, this body meets regularly to make schoolwide policy, make curriculum decisions that affect more than one department, and allocate the staff's total budget. Any staff member or student may initiate agenda items and speak on any issue during open meetings. The positions of convener and recorder are rotated every nine weeks or less so that almost everyone shares in leadership roles. The principal counts only as one member of the group unless he clearly states in advance that he will take responsibility for making a unilateral decision; otherwise decisions are made by consensus.

Ad hoc Groups. In the same senior high, staff or students who think that the administrative team and DMB are inadequate forums for particular issues have the right to form ad hoc groups, whose proposals are placed before the total staff for a majority vote. This arrangement, while seldom used, is nevertheless always present as a backup when consensus for decision making appears to be too costly to someone involved. We also know of a large college that used an ad hoc group when it was faced with a major policy decision about its mission and organizational staffing pattern. The creation and use of this group entailed a four-stage activity spread over two days.

First, the provost described the issues and problems facing the college. A representative group of faculty members, assisted by two OD facilitators, discussed this presentation and the extent to which any means of resolving the issues would affect the faculty, continuing until all were able to report clear understanding. In a method approximating consensus, they used a survey to agree that no solution would be acceptable until everyone in the group could vote 3 or 2 on a scale in which 3 meant wholehearted support, 2 meant support with some reservations, and 0 meant no support for any part of the solution.

Second, an ad hoc group was formed of faculty members who stated either that they had special resources or expertise to contribute to decision making or that they cared greatly about the decision's ultimate outcome; a survey identified these persons among the total group. Third, the ad hoc group met in a Fishbowl until its members agreed consensually to recommend a single proposal to the total group. An open chair in the Fishbowl allowed persons in the outside circle to make process observations or comments about the proposal being developed. The facilitators monitored reactions of other group members, occasionally providing feedback to members of the ad hoc group.

Fourth, the ad hoc group presented its proposal to the total group. When a survey of the total group indicated that several people were still reluctant to support the proposal, the ad hoc group reconvened to refine it and to plan a way of taking the reservations into account. Again, all other group members could occupy the empty chair in the Fishbowl or otherwise observe the meeting. A second presentation was followed by a survey indicating that the proposal now had sufficient support to become the basis of a new policy statement for the college.

Readiness for Joint Decision Making

Changing the norms and procedures associated with decision making is not easy for facilitators or participants. Discussions of how influence is exercised and received are often the most prolonged, painful, and conflict-producing parts of an OD project. Indeed, as influence becomes more widely dispersed through collaborative decision making, more rather than less conflict can occur. This does not mean that facilitators should avoid dealing with the decision-making process, but only that they should be aware of several potential difficulties.

Leadership. The amount of participation in joint decision making by people in colleges and schools is determined in part by the leadership style of the formal leader—for example, the dean, principal, team leader, or department chairperson. Schmidt and

Tannenbaum (1958) listed six leadership styles that recur again and again in the writings of more contemporary social psychologists:

Telling: The leader makes the decision autonomously, announcing only its substance.

Selling: The leader makes the decision autonomously but provides rationale to encourage others to go along with it.

Testing: The leader makes a tentative decision and elicits reactions before deciding finally and autonomously.

Consulting: The leader elicits input before making the decision and explains how input was used or why it was ignored.

Joining: The leader asks others to take an equal part in decision making and agrees to go along with what the group decides.

Abdicating: The leader lets others make the decisions either by delegating the responsibility or by default.

Evidence from OD projects in colleges and schools indicates that unless the formal leader is willing and able to join with others, efforts toward joint decision making are likely to fail. In one college that was moving toward new faculty teams, for example, decision-making authority was to rest within each new team. The teams were to be coordinated by a special leadership team composed of the dean and three team leaders. But satisfaction with the dean and the college declined over the course of the OD project, primarily because of the dean's unwillingness to allow others to exert influence on decisions affecting the college. Unfortunately, the faculty teams never got off the ground and were dissolved a year after the trial run.

In an elementary school pursuing a similar goal, on the other hand, the principal valued joint decision making. Initially lacking the skills to join effectively with others, he went through a period of indecision that led to staff frustration and dissatisfaction, but by the second year he had gained enough skill and confidence for himself and the staff to work out a way in which decisions could be made to their mutual satisfaction.

OD facilitators must carefully assess the readiness and capability of formal leaders to join others in decision making, and they might arrange a variety of special experiences to help them become more comfortable and skillful in doing so. These experiences might include special skill-practice sessions, opportunities to discuss leadership behaviors, or coaching. The facilitator can also serve as a counselor merely by being supportive or by actually helping a leader link with other leaders in a peer-support system.

In one project with a middle school in which parents were forcing a principal to share influence, we not only helped the principal plan meetings and develop interpersonal communication skills, but we also arranged for her to talk with the principal of a neighboring middle school about the problems of sharing influence and of joining with others in decision making. In another project, we brought principals from several elementary schools together in monthly meetings to share their concerns and to role-play difficult situations that they were facing. We gave special coaching to some of these elementary principals, sitting with them as they convened decision-making meetings, explaining our observations of the group's dynamics, and making suggestions about what they might do to improve participation and performance.

Motivation and Skill. Since few instructors at any level of education are trained to make decisions outside their classrooms, it is not surprising that many members of a college or school faculty may themselves lack the motivation or competence needed to make shared decision making work. Some faculty members might lack commitment to institutional goals, be uninterested in certain decision issues, distrust the formal leader's motives, or otherwise have little investment in finding solutions or taking action. Since the spread of influence is likely to increase conflict, some faculty members may be unwilling to pay the cost of involvement in time and energy. Finally, some faculty members simply prefer being at home with their families to participating in long decision-making meetings.

Many of the instruments presented in the next section of this chapter can be used to assess the readiness of faculty members to participate in joint decision making. Several of the exercises presented in the final section can be used to build this readiness when it is low. Faculty members can see the advantages of using the consensual process by participating in one or more of the consensus exercises described later in this chapter. They can specify the areas of decision making that are the most important to them by helping to develop a decision-making matrix. Procedures such as surveying can alleviate many of their fears about inability to handle conflict.

Environment. Several factors within the larger educational organization or larger environment may impede movement toward joint decision making. Members of colleges or school districts that exhibit highly diverse goals, unsupportive polarized subgroups, and a history of continued conflict or management by crisis may hesitate to change their decision-making norms and structures. In such cases, the OD facilitator might provide evidence that groups in the environment are not invariably obstructive, or might collect data from these groups to help in designing a new decision-making structure. The Imaging exercise described in the next chapter can help to clarify real environmental constraints and reveal those that are only imagined.

Gathering Data About Decision Making

An important source of data about decision making is the OD facilitator's observation of group processes. The facilitator watches, for example, for signs that the decision-making responsibilities are unclear and for instances of decisions made without appropriate amounts of staff involvement. The facilitator also looks to see how much consensus is used and evaluates the faculty members' understanding of who is to do what and when. The facilitator is particularly concerned when faculty members express frustration over not being heard, or even being ignored, by the leader or by a minority. Such instances are hints of alienation and powerlessness in the college or school.

The facilitator keeps in mind a few ideal targets when making initial observations. Such targets might be decision making by those with the necessary information, the formal specifying of decision-making responsibilities so that faculty members understand them, and wide recognition by faculty members that several decision-making methods exist and that different procedures are useful for different issues or circumstances.

Certain questionnaires and observation schedules can help in assessing an educational organization's ability to make group decisions. By using the instruments provided here, the facilitator can design OD strategies or gather information to feed back to participants.

Actual and Preferred Decision Making

The following questionnaire reveals how respondents think decision making is handled and how they think it should be handled by three levels of the organization—the team or department level, the school or college level, and the overall district or university level. Discrepancies between what is and what ought to be provide a focus for group problem solving about decision-making processes and procedures.

Instructions: Circle one number at the left and one number at the right.

The way things are	**The way things should be**

Always · · · · Never   Always · · · · Never

Always					Never		Always					Never
1	2	3	4	5	6	1. Decisions are made through teamwork.	1	2	3	4	5	6
1	2	3	4	5	6	2. Facts from those who know are used to make decisions.	1	2	3	4	5	6
1	2	3	4	5	6	3. You take a part in making decisions that affect you.	1	2	3	4	5	6
1	2	3	4	5	6	4. You or your peers help make decisions.	1	2	3	4	5	6
1	2	3	4	5	6	5. When decisions are made, they are based on information that you think is right and fair.	1	2	3	4	5	6
1	2	3	4	5	6	6. Decisions are made by those who know most about the problem.	1	2	3	4	5	6
1	2	3	4	5	6	7. The people who make decisions that affect you are aware of the things you face.	1	2	3	4	5	6
1	2	3	4	5	6	8. Decisions are made in such a way that you do not mind carrying them out.	1	2	3	4	5	6
1	2	3	4	5	6	9. Leaders work with their peers and people below them to make the decisions.	1	2	3	4	5	6

The way things are   **The way things should be**

Always   Never   Always   Never

1 2 3 4 5 6   10. Things are   1 2 3 4 5 6
                       organized so that
                       you or your peers
                       can help make
                       decisions.

Actual and Preferred Influence

The first question below measures the amount of influence a faculty member believes occupants of different positions in the larger educational organization now exert. The second question measures how much influence the respondent thinks each occupant ought to have. Results from the two parts can be compared and used for feedback to members of the target system. Discrepancies between the two parts can stimulate discussion and problem solving to reduce the differences. Other phrases can be substituted for "in determining what innovations get attempted in your college or school." For example, the facilitator might ask about influence in determining curriculum policy, influence in determining codes of conduct, or influence in determining what library supplies and equipment will be purchased.

1. In general, how much actual influence do you think each of the following groups or persons has now in determining what innovations get attempted in your college or school? Please indicate how much influence each person or group has by circling the appropriate number.

	None	A little	Some	Con-sider-able	A great deal
The governing board	1	2	3	4	5
The president or superintendent	1	2	3	4	5
Dean or principal of your school	1	2	3	4	5
You yourself	1	2	3	4	5
A small group of faculty members	1	2	3	4	5
Faculty members in general	1	2	3	4	5
Curriculum personnel (supervisor, director, or coordinator)	1	2	3	4	5
Students	1	2	3	4	5
Citizens or parents	1	2	3	4	5

	None	A little	Some	Con- sider- able	A great deal
Teacher associations or unions	1	2	3	4	5
Alumni or PTA	1	2	3	4	5
Other (specify)	1	2	3	4	5

_____

_____

_____

_____

2. How much influence do you think these groups or persons *ought to have* in determining innovations attempted in your college or school?

	None	A little	Some	Con- sider- able	A great deal
The governing board	1	2	3	4	5
The president or superintendent	1	2	3	4	5

[and so on, as in 1 above]

Participation in Decisions

Answers to the first three items below help to draw a picture of influence structures and networks of interdependence. Item 4 elicits perceptions of the power of various people in the college or school and helps assess how autocratic, democratic, or polyarchic the influence structure is perceived to be by the faculty. Item 5 elicits the faculty's perceptions of the dean or principal's sources of power. Is the dean or principal influential because of his or her expertise, or what?

1. Please mark an X before the one statement below that best describes your part in deciding upon the instructional methods you use.

_____ I choose my own instructional methods without assistance or direction.

_____ The final choice of instructional methods is left to me, but there are others whose job includes making recommendations or suggestions.

_____ Within certain limits I can choose my own instructional methods.

_____ As a member of a group or committee, I share with others the job of deciding the instructional methods to be used.

_____ I do not choose my own instructional methods. They are laid down for me by others.

2. If you chose answer 2, 3, 4, or 5 in the question just above, you were indicating that some other person or persons were somehow involved in deciding upon the instructional methods to be used in your classroom. If you chose answer 2, 3, 4, or 5, please write below the names and positions of the other persons involved.

_____   _____

_____   _____

3. When you want to receive approval in your college or school for an idea you are proposing, it is sometimes helpful to enlist the support of certain individuals in the organization. Please list below, by name and position, the individuals whose support would help most in obtaining approval for your ideas.

_____   _____

_____   _____

4. Please check the column that indicates your best estimate of the influence of instructors and heads on the areas of college or school life listed at the left.

	None	A little	Some	Consider- able	A great deal
In general, how much influence . . .					
Does the head have on how the organization is run?	____	____	____	____	____
Do faculty members as a group have on how the organization is run?	____	____	____	____	____
Does the head have with faculty members when it comes to activities and decisions that affect the performance of their instructional duties?	____	____	____	____	____
Do faculty members have on the head's activities and decisions?	____	____	____	____	____

5. Listed below are five reasons commonly given when people are asked why they do what their superiors suggest or want them to do. Read all five, then number them according to their importance to you as reasons for doing what your head suggests or wants you to do. Write 1 by the most important factor, 2 by the next, etc., using each of the numerals 1 through 5 only once.

I do what the head suggests or wants me to do because:

_____ I admire the head's personal qualities and want to merit his or her respect and admiration.

_____ I admire the head's competence, good judgment, and experience.

_____ The head can give special help and benefits to those who cooperate.

_____ The head can apply pressure or penalize those who do not cooperate.

_____ The head has a legitimate right, considering his or her position, to expect that suggestions will be carried out.

Exercises and Procedures in Decision Making

The exercises presented here can be used to highlight influence patterns, decision-making procedures, the behavior of decision makers, or some combination of these. Ideas for sequencing or combining these exercises with those in other chapters appear in the final section of this chapter.

Nonverbal Procedures and Exercises

The following procedures and exercises work only with people in pairs. Repeating them with a sequence of partners can generate data for considering how individual influence in decision making varies in different situations.

Hand Mirroring. Spread out so that their outstretched arms do not collide, participants face their partners and present their hands palms out and fingers up about two inches from the other's hands. When they have agreed who will lead the first round, the leader moves his or her hands and arms while the partner follows as in a mirror image. After three minutes the partners reverse roles. For the final round, roles are left unspecified, and partners discover nonverbally who will lead and who will follow. At the end of each round, partners describe their feelings and check their impressions of the other's thoughts and feelings. At the end of the exercise, all describe thoughts and feelings.

Influence Line. Participants nonverbally arrange themselves in rank-order according to the amount of influence each one has. The rank-order can be recorded on newsprint before the group debriefs its experience. Questions to guide the debriefing might include the following: In what ways does the rank-order surprise or not surprise anyone? What are the consequences of this particular influence structure on the way the group makes decisions? How did it feel to be where you were in the line?

Exercises on Influence Styles

The following two exercises can be used in training designs to expose participants to alternative styles of influence and to help them explore both their own preferred styles and the styles of others.

Role-Playing Three Leadership Styles (Democratic, Authoritarian, and Laissez-faire). The goal of this exercise is to help participants recognize different styles of leadership and their effects. It should lead participants to become more aware of influence processes and help them talk about leadership in staff discussions. This exercise attempts to replicate the spirit of the classic experiment of 1939 by Lewin, Lippitt, and White.

The facilitator arranges the seats so that participants are sitting face to face in pairs. Three pairs are closely clustered. Half the participants are called leaders and half are called followers. The followers must have available to them another room where they can go while the facilitator coaches the leaders about their roles. Another facilitator can help with the logistics by taking the followers to the other room.

Before the followers leave, give each a copy of the sheet headed "Interaction I" (see Figure 7-1). Ask them to rank the traits while they are waiting to be called back. Tell them they will be interacting with three different leaders in three different decision-making tasks, and that the first task will deal with this sheet. Tell them also that after each task, they will fill out a questionnaire about what happened during the task.

After the followers have left the main room, give each leader three copies of the sheet headed "Reaction to Leadership Exercise" (Figure 7-2), one copy of the sheet headed "Interaction I," and one copy of the sheet headed "Instructions for Leader I" (Figure 7-3). Tell the leaders briefly about the experiment by Lewin, Lippitt, and White. Tell the leaders that this exercise will replicate the leadership styles used in that experiment, beginning with the democratic style.

Success in the exercise does not depend on your knowledge of the experiment by Lewin, Lippitt, and White. It should suffice that you have a clear understanding of the three leader styles as described on the three sheets of instructions.

Figure 7-1. Interaction I

Rank the following eight traits in the order of their importance for being a competent parent. Place a 1 by the most important trait, 2 by the second most important trait, and so on down to 8, which will be the least important trait.

_____	Tact	_____	Compassion
_____	Honesty	_____	Energy
_____	Ambition	_____	Intelligence
_____	Courage	_____	Sense of humor

Figure 7-2. Reaction to Leadership Exercise

Check one: Discussion 1 ___ 2 ___ 3 ___ Check one: Leader ___ Follower ___ For each question, please circle the number that best summarizes your opinion.

1. Who led in the interaction?
   9 Superior led completely.
   8
   7 Superior led somewhat more than the subordinate.
   6
   5 Leadership was shared; each led about equally.
   4
   3 Subordinate led somewhat more than the superior.
   2
   1 Subordinate led completely.

2. How much satisfaction did you derive from the discussion?
   9 Completely satisfied
   8
   7 Moderately satisfied
   6
   5 Neutral: neither satisfied nor dissatisfied
   4
   3 Moderately dissatisfied
   2
   1 Completely dissatisfied

3. How much responsibility do you feel for the ranking you made as a pair?
9 Feel complete responsibility
8
7 Feel some responsibility
6
5 Neutral
4
3 Feel very little responsibility
2
I Feel no responsibility

4. How much hostility did you feel toward your partner?
9 Felt completely hostile
8
7 Felt somewhat hostile
6
5 Neutral
4
3 Felt somewhat friendly
2
I Felt completely friendly

5. Rate the quality of the ranking you made as a pair.
9 Best possible ranking
8
7 Moderately good
6
5 Average
4
3 Moderately poor
2
I Worst possible ranking

Figure 7-3. Instructions for Leader I

This interaction is a joint undertaking. Develop an acceptable basis for working together before you start into the rankings. For example, you and your subordinate might set the goal of agreeing first on the items that lie at the extremes of the scale and then resolving any differences in the intermediate categories. Be sure every item gets a reasonable amount of consideration. Give your subordinate a full chance to participate. Even though you are the leader, you have high respect for the quality of your subordinate's thinking and ability; your goal, therefore, is to weigh his or her opinions and your opinions equally. Discourage the use of chance, like coin tossing, in any doubtful cases.

Keep in mind that after you finish you will be asked to evaluate the efficiency of your subordinate in helping your pair develop the most adequate list. At the same time, your subordinate will be asked to evaluate *your* efficiency in acting according to these instructions. You are both responsible for getting a good list by working together in the manner described.

Remember, it is your responsibility to use the authority of your leadership to ensure that you and your subordinate come up with a ranking of the list that represents your collaborative thinking and that matches in quality the best ranking of the list. In the final analysis it is a joint effort.

Ask the leaders to read "Interaction I," "Instructions for Leader I," and "Reaction to Leadership Exercise," in that order. Give them any further explanation you think they need, and answer their questions.

Call the followers back. Each follower sits with one leader. Ask the pairs to begin deciding upon the best ranking of the traits.

After the pairs have made their decisions, distribute sheets headed "Reaction to Leadership Exercise" to the followers. Ask both followers and leaders to fill out those sheets. Collect them.

Then give sheets headed "Interaction II" (Figure 7-4) to the followers. Ask them to go to the other room, rank the items on the sheet, and wait to be called.

After the followers have left, give each leader copies of "Interaction II" and "Instructions for Leader II" (Figure 7-5). Let them read the sheets, give them any further explanation you think they need, and answer their questions.

Call the followers back. Ask the followers to sit with leaders they did not sit with before. After the pairs have made their decisions, distribute reaction sheets to the followers. Ask followers and leaders to fill out the sheets.

Then give sheets headed "Interaction III" (Figure 7-6) to the followers, and send them to the other room. Give each leader copies

Figure 7-4. Interaction II

Rank the following eight items in order of importance for being a competent principal. Place a 1 by the most important, a 2 by the second most important item, and so on down to 8, which will be the least important item.

_____ Has a good understanding of the structure of the organization
_____ Is able to give clear-cut understandable instructions
_____ Keeps all parties who are concerned with a decision fully informed on progress and actions taken
_____ Is willing to change own viewpoint when it proves to be wrong
_____ Is able to make decisions based on facts rather than personal feelings, intuition, hunches, etc.
_____ Is able to make good decisions under time and other pressures
_____ Is able to delegate effectively
_____ Is able to resist making a decision before all the facts are in

Figure 7-5. Instructions for Leader II

In this interaction *you* are responsible for the activities and procedures followed by your pair. Assume that you have more knowledge, background, and skills than your subordinate. Take into your own hands whatever responsibility you consider necessary to get the job done. Your goal is to give greater weight to your own opinions than your partner's. You tell your subordinate the procedure you wish him or her to follow in working for you. As the supervisor in this situation, you have a better grasp of things, and it is perfectly proper for you to bring the subordinate around to your point of view. In the final analysis *you* are responsible for the list. You will receive the criticism if your list is not good. Discourage the use of chance, like coin tossing, in any doubtful cases.

Keep in mind that after you finish you will be asked to evaluate the efficiency of your subordinate in helping you develop the most adequate list. At the same time, your subordinate will be asked to evaluate *your* efficiency in acting in accordance with these instructions.

Remember, you are responsible for using the authority of your leadership to ensure that you come up with the best ranking of the list. In the final analysis this is a situation of authority-obedience.

Figure 7-6. Interaction III

Rank the following eight items in order of importance for being a competent teacher. Place a 1 by the most important, a 2 by the second most important item, and so on down to 8, which will be the least important item.

_____ Communicates effectively
_____ Treats each student as an individual with unique abilities, interests, etc.
_____ Improves himself/herself by continuing formal education, reading current journals, attending workshops, training programs, etc.
_____ Relates well with colleagues, superiors, and subordinates
_____ Does research in his or her specialized field
_____ Takes an active part in community affairs concerned with education
_____ Is able to effectively handle the "administrative" aspect of teaching
_____ Is willing to try new teaching techniques and methods

of "Interaction III" and "Instructions for Leader III" (Figure 7-7). Proceed as before.

At the end of the third Interaction, display to the total group the responses on the reaction sheets. You can shorten the task of compiling the responses at the end if you compile what you have after each interaction.

Finally, ask questions for discussion: (1) What are the helpful and unhelpful aspects of each style of leadership? (2) Under what circumstances in the school is it good for the principal to be democratic, autocratic, or laissez-faire? (3) What about the staff members in the school—when should they use one leadership style or another?

Figure 7-7. Instructions for Leader III

In this interaction your goal is to avoid active participation in the content of the discussion as much as possible. You are, however, to see that the work is done efficiently. If discussion gets off target, bring your subordinate back to the task. As much as you can, avoid giving your opinions beyond expressing agreement when you feel it. You don't really care what order is produced, as long as your pair can establish an order or priority for the items. Your goal is to weigh your follower's opinions much more heavily than your own. Discourage the use of chance, like coin tossing, in any doubtful cases.

Keep in mind that after you finish you will be asked to evaluate the efficiency of your subordinate in helping your pair develop the most adequate list. At the same time, your subordinate will be asked to evaluate *your* efficiency in acting in accordance with these instructions.

Four Styles of Influence. * People influence one another in many ways, and various authors categorize the ways variously. David E. Berlew and Roger Harrison have put styles of influence into four categories that we find especially useful. The descriptions of the styles require only common language, and participants can quickly connect the styles and substyles to their own experience. After only about half an hour of explanation and discussion, most participants can begin using the categories.

The purposes of this section are to help participants to (1) become more aware of the extent to which they and others use the four styles of influence, (2) practice watching for influence styles that people use in groups, and (3) make conscious choices of influence styles that are suitable in various circumstances.

The activity can be conducted with any number of people, though the minimum is six.

Begin by passing out copies of the sheet headed "Influence Styles" (Figure 7-8).

Point out to the participants that they all know what assertive persuasion is. Teachers, managers, and others who work through words spend most of their time using assertive persuasion. Beyond reminding the participants of how dull meetings full of proposing and reasoning can get, you won't need to say much about *AP*.

---

* This section was composed from ideas in Harrison (1978) and Harrison and Kouzes (1980), from conversations with Harrison, and after using the influence categories in our own OD projects.

Figure 7-8. Influence Styles

Assertive Persuasion (AP)	*Charisma (CH)*
Proposing: Giving your ideas; proposing what should be done; asking questions that show where you stand.	*Articulating the vision:* Finding the common goal and describing the common yearning simply and clearly.
Reasoning: Telling why your ideas are good or others' are not as good; agreeing or disagreeing with others' arguments.	*Inspiring confidence:* Convincing people they can themselves do what is necessary. *You* can do it.
	The time is now: We don't have to wait. You can do it *now.*
Reward and Punishment (R&P)	*Participation and Trust (P&T)*
Approving and disapproving: Showing your values; making moral judgments.	*Openness:* Describing own emotions; admitting mistakes, lack of knowledge, uncertainty.
Setting standards: Telling what you expect from others; setting goals; setting forth requirements; making demands.	*Trying to understand:* Paraphrasing; describing others' behavior; checking your perceptions of others' emotions.
Offers and threats: Offering rewards; threatening punishments; offering to bargain or negotiate; invoking power, authority, or status.	*Appreciating others:* Inviting others to contribute; using what they offer; showing you value others as whole people.

You won't have to tell them much about reward-and-punishment, either. We all get it and give it. You might give some examples. You might also remind the participants that one style can wear the clothes of another. When an administrator interrupts someone and says in a loud voice, "I think the money is the first thing to think about," the words seem to have the form of making a proposal—AP. But in the ensuing silence the listeners may hear a threat: ". . . and you'd better do it my way or else!" The kind of influence a communicative act conveys depends less on the speaker's phrases or even on the speaker's intentions than on the way the listeners interpret the message.

Charisma will take a little explaining, because many people believe it to be a mysterious quality beyond analysis. If charisma is to be effective, there must actually be some common yearning in the group. (You often discover a common yearning during diagnosis.) The job of the person who wants to use charisma is to find that common yearning and then express it simply and clearly so that participants exclaim, "That's it! That's the way it is! You hit the nail on the head! Right on!" The capacity to use language simply and directly can be developed; you don't have to be born with it. The next job is to show the group members (or remind them of) their capacities—to show them that their present abilities can move them in the direction they want to go. The final part is to inspire action. With the common goal and the capability, the time is now. You don't have to wait until you die to find a better life. It is here for you to grasp.

You use participation and trust when you use the power of the group—when you use the influence of all upon all to carry the work forward to a cherished goal. Two prime features characterize a group that works through participation and trust: (1) the group draws out from its members all the resources of individuals that can be used to do the work better and (2) the group does not allow the task to become a juggernaut that grinds individuals under its wheels. The group values individuals for *all* their capacities and qualities—not only those that are useful now, but also those that may be useful in the future. If a group is to work that way, its members must openly make known their strengths and weaknesses, constantly check their understanding of one another's intentions and commitments, and repeatedly invite and use everyone's skills.

Because very strong interdependence arises in such a group, every member's fate is to a great degree in everyone else's hands. That means that members feel more willing to take risks than in a more formal and hierarchical group. Members know they will get help from others during periods of difficulty, because their troubles are the troubles of all. The willingness to take risks enables the group to carry out tasks that a more hierarchical and bureaucratic group would not attempt, but the strong interdependence also requires more time for group maintenance. It takes time to develop a strongly interdependent group, and it takes time to maintain it in that condition. This book contains many exercises and procedures for helping participation and trust to develop in a group.

The next step is to give participants practice in observing influence styles. Pass out the "Influence Tally Sheet" (Figure 7-9).

Participants should get practice very soon after hearing about the four influence styles. You can ask them to observe actual workaday groups or you can set up a simulation.

If there is going to be a break of a few days in your OD work with the participants, you can ask them to observe an actual group and make tallies. For good practice, participants need to observe a group discussion in which a variety of influence styles will be shown. Some actual working meetings exhibit a variety and some do not. Some faculty meetings, for example, exhibit almost unrelieved assertive persuasion, with the dean doing most of it. Other kinds of meetings show more variety. In a meeting of department heads, for example, the members might show approval and disapproval, tell what they expect of one another, make promises and threats, reveal their uncertainties, check their understanding of one another, show excitement about common purposes, and so on. Other meetings might serve—a curriculum committee, a facilities committee, the governing board. If a group of that sort will allow non-members, you could send some of your participants to its meetings.

Figure 7-9. Influence Tally Sheet

Write one person's name over each of the columns. Make a tally when someone exhibits one of the influence categories. Sometimes you will make more than one kind of tally for one utterance or act. But do not make extra tallies just because someone takes a long time to say something.

Influence category

Reward and punishment (R&P)							
Approving and disapproving							
Setting standards							
Offers and threats							
Participation and trust (P&T)							
Openness							
Trying to understand							
Appreciating others							
Charisma (CH)							
Articulating the vision							
Inspiring confidence							
The time is now							
Assertive persuasion (AP)							
Proposing							
Reasoning							

You can also ask participants simply to make tallies in gatherings they attend as part of their regular work. Many participants will belong to committees, for example. Further, participants who are instructors may have classes in which they encourage some talk among the students. If so, they can observe some variety there. Young students are often very free, for example, with approval and disapproval, telling their expectations, their sense of urgency, and the like.

Many exercises in this book occasion a good deal of attempting to influence others: Planners and Operators, the Five-Square puzzle, the various consensus exercises, and the several simulations (see under "Exercises" in the index). During debriefing, the activities below can be employed to heighten understanding of the four influence styles and to encourage self-examination or the making of group agreements.

To commence the debriefing, ask participants to gather in groups in which all members have worked together before. Groups of four are best, but three or five are acceptable. Ask everyone to draw a diamond like that in Figure 7-10 (a). Then explain that the corners of the diamond represent the greatest frequency possible of using the four influence styles. A person who uses reward and punishment all the time would be located at the corner marked "*R&P*," and so on.

But situations differ in the amount of opportunity they offer for using the various influence styles. Any of us may use more *R&P* in one setting and more *P&T* in another. Ask every group, therefore, to agree on an imaginary setting to keep in mind as they mark their diagrams—the curriculum committee, the last exercise they did, or whatever.

Now each person should estimate the amount of each style he or she has been using in the agreed-upon setting. A person who has been using none of the styles would mark the very middle of the diagram. Someone who has been using nothing but a particular style would mark a corner. Figure 7-10(b) shows how a person might mark the diagram.

Now ask the participants to connect the marks and shade in the inside area, as shown in Figure 7-10(c). The shaded area shows the portion of the influence domain the person has been using. The unshaded area is the portion that person might want to explore in further work with the group.

And now ask the participants to make a similar diagram for all the others in their group. Each person makes a diagram to show the kinds of influence he or she has felt from each group member. Then each person hands out the diagrams about the others to the members the diagrams describe. All will then have in hand the diagrams they made about themselves and those the others made about them. They can then compare their perceptions of themselves with the perceptions others have of them.

If the perceptions from others agree with the self-perceptions, participants will feel that their own perceptions have been verified. If perceptions from others agree among themselves but differ from the self-perceptions, participants can conclude (1) that they have been using more or less of a particular style than they thought or (2) that their skill is low, and they have been "coming across" in

Figure 7-10. The Influence Diamond

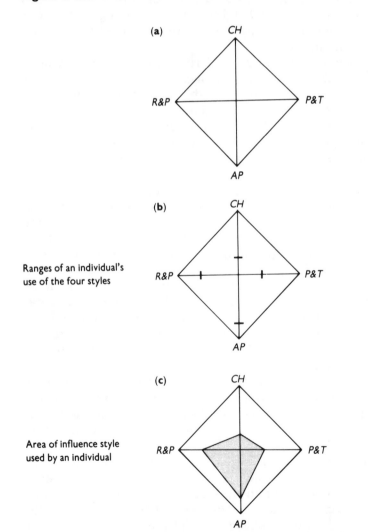

(a)

CH

R&P   P&T

AP

(b)

CH

Ranges of an individual's use of the four styles

R&P   P&T

AP

(c)

CH

Area of influence style used by an individual

R&P   P&T

AP

a way they did not intend. If perceptions from others do not agree among themselves, then (3) participants can conclude that their ways of using the influence styles affect some people some way and other people another. For the last two outcomes, participants could ask others for more paraphrasing to help them grow more sure of the effects they are having.

Finally, participants will inevitably get into a discussion of the uses of the four styles. They will say that a particular style works better in one setting or for one purpose than another. And they will be right. You might want to pass out copies of "When to Use the Four Influence Styles":

WHEN TO USE THE FOUR INFLUENCE STYLES

Assertive Persuasion

Use it when

1. Getting the task done depends on having the facts and on getting the technical detail properly ordered.
2. The task is so complex that more than one person's information or judgment is necessary.
3. Others *want* to have influence on the decision or solution. (Don't ask a group to argue about what brand of pencils to buy.)
4. The norms of group process permit all to put forth their ideas and all to be honestly heard.
5. The group is ready to judge proposals on their technical merit.
6. You are not simply giving a persuasive speech, but want full participation from the group, and when the group is reasonably small—say, three to twelve members.

Do *not* use it when

1. Almost everyone agrees that the task or decision is simple enough for one person to do it or to make the decision.
2. Most people prefer that you do it yourself. (If they want you to do it yourself but you think it would be better done by having more ideas than your own, then you need a meeting in *P&T* style to get more ideas.)
3. The norms within the group are competitive or strongly *R&P*.
4. The group will judge proposals chiefly by who makes them. (In this case, use *R&P* or *P&T*.)

Benefits

1. Puts attention on technical detail.
2. Brings to bear a range of facts, proposals, and chains of reasoning beyond what any single member is likely to bring: expands resources.

By itself, it *won't* usually bring you much

1. Energizing or inspiration.
2. Quick action.
3. Trust or commitment.
4. Long-term influence or predictability.

Reward and Punishment

Use it when

1. Time is short.
2. You have set standards for others, and you will not change them.
3. You actually have rewards or punishments that are in your power to give or withhold, and you are ready to do so. (Promises or threats not carried through have very temporary effect.)
4. You actually cannot get what you want unless others get less than they want—that is, when the situation is objectively win-lose.

Do *not* use it when

1. You are searching for the best standards to apply. (Then use *AP* or *P&T*.)
2. The rewards or punishments you might apply are weak or will be considerably delayed.
3. You need creativity, initiative, and risk taking from others. (Then use *P&T*.)

Benefits

1. Puts attention on the immediate task.
2. Usually makes decisions and effects quick—though not in complex negotiations and bargaining.
3. Locates the sources of *R&P* simply. Bureaucratic controls can be built in for the long term.
4. Maximizes getting what you yourself want, at least in the short term.
5. Useful with one person or ten thousand.

By itself it *won't* usually bring you much

1. Benefit of others' ideas, creativity, or risk taking. (Use *AP* or *P&T*.)
2. Solidarity, esprit de corps, or trust. (Use *P&T*.)
3. Long-term organizational resourcefulness. People will wait to find out what will bring them rewards and punishments. (Use *P&T*.)
4. Carry-over to the next leader.

Participation and Trust

Use it when

1. You need the continuing commitment of the group to follow through and get the task done.
2. You want initiative, creativity, a range of resources, or risk taking.
3. There is enough mutual trust and acceptance in the group so that members will make some personal disclosures, will want to involve one another, and will want to understand one another at some depth.
4. The group is no larger than, say, twenty, or the task is such that the people needed can be organized into separate but linked small groups.
5. There is ample time.

Do *not* use it when

1. Immediate action is necessary; when time is very short.
2. You do not need initiative, creativity, risk taking, trust, solidarity, or a range of resources.
3. Trust in the group is low.
4. The group is too large to be brought together face to face, or too large for everyone to participate even if the group is in one room (say, larger than twenty, or if the task cannot be done by separate but linked small groups).
5. You yourself are not ready to self-disclose, etc.

Benefits

1. Solidarity, trust, long-term commitment to group and task.
2. Generates creativity, initiative, risk taking, drawing-out of members' resources (synergy).
3. Flexible use of members' abilities. Members can move from one role to another as needed.
4. When combined with *AP*, groups can solve their own problems.

5. Maximum carry-over of leadership skills through turnover of membership and official leaders.

By itself, it *won't* usually bring you much

1. Clarity of control from the top (because members will make decisions and take action on their own or in small groups; you will hear about it *after* it is done).
2. If skill in *P&T* is low in your school, it may take you a year or more to develop it to the point where it is an effective way to get things done.

Charisma

Use it when

1. There is a clear possibility of a common vision (also called "superordinate goal").
2. You can articulate the vision clearly and simply.
3. It is within your power and that of others to take significant steps toward realizing the vision.
4. You want to energize people (though if you are doing it by yourself, you have to do it repeatedly).

Do *not* use it when

1. Visions within your staff are in conflict—when people are not merely in disagreement about how to get there, but when one faction can move toward its vision only if another is prevented from doing so.
2. You are not skillful at articulating the vision. (Get someone else to do it, or brush up your charismatic skill before you depend on it.)

Benefits

1. Energizes. Gets things moving.

By itself, it *won't* usually bring you much

1. Detailed problem solving.
2. Long-term clarity about the direction of the group's movement.
3. Solidarity within subgroups. (*CH* brings allegiance to the leader who articulates the vision. The only kind of solidarity it brings is that common allegiance. But through the use of *P&T*, *CH* can become a method of influence used *within* groups *by* groups as well as a method used by you.)

4. Carry-over to the next leader when you leave. (Followers of the charismatic leader develop little leadership skill of their own.)

A Resource-sharing Exercise

Many of the exercises in this book enable participants to observe the extent to which they use the resources in the group, including their own. The card-discovery problem, however, is especially effective in showing the use of resources. Unless the group succeeds in drawing out accurate information from every member in the exercise, fatal errors are almost inevitable. The card-discovery problem will go well with five to seven persons in the group. The facilitator prepares a deck of 30 cards for each group of participants. Each card has printed upon it a 12 x 12 matrix of points, and each point is designated either *X* or *0*. If each of the 144 points is randomly assigned either an *X* or an *0*, the problem is very difficult and time-consuming. The problem is simplified if you assign the same symbol to all the points in a small area. For example, the 12 x 12 matrix can be divided into 36 smaller 2 x 2 squares, with all four points in a given square containing the same symbol. Or the 12 x 12 display can be divided into 3 x 3, 4 x 4, and 6 x 6 squares. The examples in Figure 7-11 show that the complexity of the display diminishes as the size of the squares increases. You can further reduce the difficulty of the problem by labeling one edge of the card as its top. We strongly recommend doing so, because not knowing which way is up, so to speak, can slow the solution. You need not use the word *top*; any symbol in the same place on every card will serve.

The deck contains varying numbers of duplicate cards at the several levels of complexity. Below is the list of pattern types to use in making up the deck. Notice that the deck contains more than one card of every pattern except one; one card with a 2 x 2 pattern is unique.

LIST OF TYPES

Two cards of a 6 x 6 pattern
Two of another 6 x 6 pattern
Two of a 4 x 4 pattern
Three of another 4 x 4 pattern
Two of a 3 x 3 pattern
Two of another 3 x 3 pattern
Four of still another 3 x 3 pattern
Two of a 2 x 2 pattern

Figure 7-11. Several Levels of Display Complexity

```
O O O O O O X X X X X X        O O O O O O O O O O O O
O O O O O O X X X X X X        O O O O O O O O O O O O
O O O O O O X X X X X X        O O O O O O O O O O O O
O O O O O O X X X X X X        X X X X X X X X X X X X
O O O O O O X X X X X X        X X X X X X X X X X X X
O O O O O O X X X X X X        X X X X X X X X X X X X
O O O O O O O O O O O O        O O O O O O X X X X X X
O O O O O O O O O O O O        O O O O O O X X X X X X
O O O O O O O O O O O O        O O O O O O X X X X X X
O O O O O O O O O O O O        X X X X X X O O O O O O
O O O O O O O O O O O O        X X X X X X O O O O O O
O O O O O O O O O O O O        X X X X X X O O O O O O

        6 × 6                          3 × 3

X X X X X X O O O O O O        X O X O O X X X X X X O
X X X X X X O O O O O O        O X X O O X O O O X X X
O O O O O O X X O O X X        X X O O O O O X O O O X
O O O O O O X X O O X X        X O X X X X O O O X O
X X X X X X X X X X X X        X O X X X X O O O X O
X X X X X X X X X X X X        X O X O O X X O O O X X
O O X X O O O O X X X X        O O O O O O O X X X O
O O X X O O O O X X X X        X X X O X O O X O X O O
O O X X O O X X X X O O        X X O X X X O X O O O
O O X X O O X X X X O O        O X O X O O O X X O X X
O O X X X X O O O O X X        X X X O O O X X O X O
O O X X X X O O O O X X        O O X O X X O O O O X X

        2 × 2                        Random
```

Two of another 2 x 2 pattern
Three of still another 2 x 2 pattern
One card of yet another 2 x 2 pattern (the unique card)
Two of a random pattern
Three of another random pattern

Total: Thirty cards

The OD facilitator introduces the exercise by reviewing the instructions below with the group and, if desired, passing out copies of them. The facilitator then mixes the cards and distributes them, as equally as possible. Forty minutes is an average time for solving the problem.

The Card Discovery Problem

Instructions: A set of cards will be distributed among you. One card in the set is a *singleton*; it is unique. In other words, each card in the entire set has one or more duplicates except the singleton card. Your task as a group is to discover the singleton card in the set. When your group indicates that the unique card has been identified, the task is ended whether or not your answer is correct, so be sure that everyone is confident of your choice before you declare.

You may organize yourselves any way you wish to complete this task, except for the following restrictions:

1. You may not show your cards to another member.
2. You may not pass cards to another member.
3. You must not look at another member's cards.
4. You may not draw pictures or diagrams of the designs.
5. Do not pool your discards. Keep your own discards in your own separate pile.

While it is very important that you do not make an error in selecting the unique card, you will be scored also for the amount of time it takes you to complete the task.

After participants reach a decision, they should discuss the influence and decision making that occurred during the exercise, compare their way of working on this problem with the way they usually work as a group, and give their ideas about the barriers that reduced the effective use of group resources. Fosmire (1970) has noted four common errors among groups that try to solve this problem: (1) failure to agree on a common language for describing the displays, (2) attempting to work in pairs or trios instead of remaining in a single group, (3) passive listening, and (4) silent acceptance of nonunderstanding. The two latter errors he describes as follows:

> If one member describes a card and another replies, "I've got one; let's throw it out!" the group may be making two mistakes. First, the member may not be hearing the description correctly, but he does not paraphrase, so no one catches the error. Second, there may be a third card in the set. If a more passive member has the third card, he may fail to speak up to double-check his suspicion that he holds the card, silently accepting his nonunderstanding, only to run the risk of erroneously identifying that card as the singleton later in the task (pp. 21–22).

Facilitators should watch for those errors, but should not prevent them from happening and should present their observations to the group for discussion during the debriefing phase of the exercise.

Consensus Exercises

The exercises in this section allow participants to practice consensual decision making. The first exercise is described in complete detail, but we have condensed others by eliminating some information about procedures. Using the first exercise as a pattern, the facilitator can create handouts and scoring sheets for the others.

Grievances of Black Citizens. In the long form of this exercise, participants predict the order in which a large group of mostly black citizens identified the most significant grievances of American blacks in 1968. Distribute to participants the instruction sheet headed "Grievances of Black Citizens." Participants first rank-order the items individually and then discuss them to achieve a consensual order. Use the instructions [or consensus and guided debriefing given below; see also the section "Group Decision Making" earlier in this chapter. The ordering of the grievances given by the National Advisory Commission on Civil Disorders (1968), from most to least grievous, is as follows. The letters are those used on the handout.

1. (D) Discriminatory police practices
2. (H) Unemployment and underemployment
3. (E) Inadequate housing
4. (A) Inadequate education
5. (G) Poor recreational facilities
6. (L) Unresponsive political structure
7. (B) Disrespectful white attitudes
8. (I) Discriminatory administration of justice
9. (J) Inadequate federal programs
10. (C) Inadequate municipal services
11. (K) Discriminatory consumer and credit practices
12. (F) Inadequate welfare programs

Grievances of Black Citizens————————————————

During the fall of 1967 the research staff of the National Advisory Commission on Civil Disorders (the Kerner Commission) studied conditions in twenty cities that had experienced riots during 1967. The group consisted of nine cities that had experienced major destruction, six New Jersey cities surrounding Newark, and five cities that had experienced lesser degrees of violence.

A majority of the interviewees in each city were black residents living in or near the disorder areas. Also interviewed were people from the official sector (mayors, city officials, policemen and police officials, judges, and others) and the private sector (businessmen, labor leaders, and community leaders). Altogether, more than 1,200 persons were interviewed.

Using the answers to the interviews, the investigators identified and assigned weights to the four types of grievances that appeared to have the greatest significance to the black community in each city. For each city they made judgments about the severity of particular grievances and assigned ranks to the four most serious. Their judgments were based on the frequency with which a particular grievance was mentioned, the relative intensity with which it was discussed, references to incidents exemplifying the grievance, and estimates of severity obtained from those interviewed.

Four points were assigned to the most serious type of grievance in each city, three to the second most serious, and so on. When the point values were added for all cities, a list of 12 rank-ordered grievance types emerged. The type of grievance considered the most serious in the most cities was number 1. The one that seemed generally least serious was number 12. Following are the 12 grievance types reported by the Kerner Commission. Your task is to guess how they were ordered by the commission staff.

Put a 1 beside the type of grievance you believe the staff judged that black citizens felt to be the most serious to them across all 20 cities. Put a 2 beside the second most serious and pervasive, and so on down to a 12 beside the least widespread and least serious.

_____ A. Inadequate education: de facto segregation, poor-quality instruction and facilities, inadequate curriculum, etc.

_____ B. Disrespectful white attitudes: racism and a lack of respect for the dignity of blacks.

_____ C. Inadequate municipal services: inadequate sanitation and garbage removal, inadequate health care facilities, etc.

_____ D. Discriminatory police practices: physical or verbal abuse, no grievance channels, discrimination in hiring and promoting blacks, etc.

_____ E. Inadequate housing: poor housing-code enforcement, discrimination in sales and rentals, overcrowding.

_____ F. Inadequate welfare programs: unfair qualification regulations, negative attitude of welfare workers toward recipients.

_____ G. Poor recreational facilities: inadequate parks and playgrounds, lack of organized programs, etc.

_____ H. Unemployment and underemployment: discrimination in hiring and placement by organizations or by unions, general lack of full-time jobs, etc.

_____ I. Discriminatory administration of justice: discriminatory treatment in the courts, presumption of guilt, etc.

____ J.   Inadequate federal programs: insufficient participation by the poor,
          lack of continuity, inadequate funding.
____ K.   Discriminatory consumer and credit practices: blacks sold inferior-
          quality goods at higher prices, excessive interest rates, fraudulent
          commercial practices.
____ L.   Unresponsive political structure: inadequate representation of
          blacks, lack of response to complaints, obscurity of official griev-
          ance channels.

The short form of this exercise, which takes less time, offers
participants only eight grievances to rank instead of 12. The same
instructions can be used, but all designations of 12 should be
changed to eight. The eight items we have used and their correct
ranking are as follows:

1. (C) Discriminatory police practices
2. (F) Unemployment and underemployment
3. (D) Inadequate housing
4. (A) Inadequate education
5. (H) Unresponsive political structure
6. (B) Disrespectful white attitudes
7. (G) Inadequate federal programs
8. (E) Inadequate welfare programs

To begin, instruct participants to work individually, without
conferring, and to rank-order the items according to the instructions
they read on their sheets headed "Grievances of Black Citizens."
Next, give the participants "Instructions for Consensus." After they
read this sheet, instruct them to come to a consensual decision on
the best rank-order for the 12 items (or eight in the short form).

INSTRUCTIONS FOR CONSENSUS

Consensus means general agreement and concord. For
consensus to exist, it is not necessary for every participant to
agree in full, but it is necessary for every person to be heard
and, in the end, for none to believe that the decision violates
his or her convictions. It is not necessary that every person
consider the decision the best one.

Consensus is a decision process for making full use of
resources and for resolving conflicts creatively. Consensus is
difficult to reach, so not every ranking will meet with
everyone's complete approval. Complete unanimity is not the

goal—it is rarely achieved. But each individual should be able to accept the group rankings on the basis of logic and feasibility. When all group members feel this way, the group has reached consensus as defined here, and the judgment may be entered as a group decision. This means, in effect, that individuals can block the group if they think it necessary; at the same time, they should use this option in the best sense of reciprocity. Here are some guidelines for achieving consensus:

1. Avoid arguing for your own rankings. Present your position as lucidly and logically as possible, but listen to the other members' reactions and consider them carefully before you press your point.
2. Do not assume that someone must win and someone lose when discussion reaches a stalemate. Instead look for the next most acceptable alternative for all parties.
3. Avoid simply voting; don't try to resolve differences arithmetically. Through discussion, try to find a decision that has an objective and logical foundation.
4. Differences of opinion are natural and expected. Seek them out and try to involve everyone in the decision. Disagreements can help the group's decision because, with a wide range of information and opinions, there is a greater chance that the group will find a better solution.

Allow groups approximately 45 minutes to reach consensus about their rank-orderings, and then ask them to tabulate the results. In each group let one person act as recorder. As members of the group call out their private rank-orderings of the twelve (or eight) items, the recorder writes them on the scoring sheet shown in Figure 7-12. When each person's rank-ordering has been recorded, the recorder sums the ranking for each of the items and rank-orders the sums, thus arriving at an average rank-order for the group. (This is the rank-order that might have been obtained had the group merely voted and not held a discussion.) The recorder also writes down the rank-order that the group has reached by consensus.

It is best if all groups work in one large room in circles that are separated to minimize mutual distraction. When the recorders in each group have completed their work, the correct answer to this exercise according to the Kerner Commission is announced. The recorders also record this rank-ordering on their sheets. Each group then computes three scores by summing the differences (ignoring whether the differences are plus or minus) between the correct rank-order and (1) the rank-order obtained through consensus, (2) the

Figure 7-12. Scoring Sheet for "Grievances of Black Citizens"

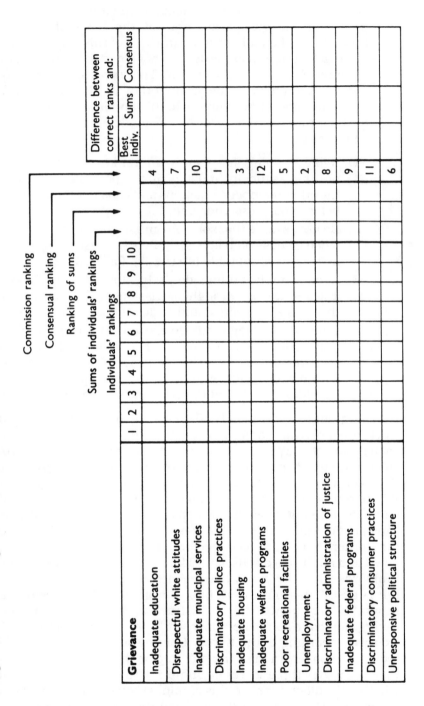

Grievance	Individuals' rankings										Sums of individuals' rankings	Ranking of sums	Consensual ranking	Commission ranking	Difference between correct ranks and:		
	1	2	3	4	5	6	7	8	9	10					Best indiv.	Sums	Consensus
Inadequate education														4			
Disrespectful white attitudes														7			
Inadequate municipal services														10			
Discriminatory police practices														1			
Inadequate housing														3			
Inadequate welfare programs														12			
Poor recreational facilities														5			
Unemployment														2			
Discriminatory administration of justice														8			
Inadequate federal programs														9			
Discriminatory consumer practices														11			
Unresponsive political structure														6			

average rank-order of the group before discussion, and (3) the individual rank-order that came closest to the rank-order. Each group then sees whether its "best" individual, its average produced before discussion, or its consensual product is superior. The smaller sums of differences are the superior scores.

After the participants have inspected and informally discussed the charts for a few minutes, each group should discuss three questions. The highlights of these discussions should be made known to the total assembly of participants.

1. What were my reactions to the exercise? How did I feel? What was I thinking?
2. How similar was our behavior here to our usual behavior in our educational organization? How different? What are the implications of this exercise for our faculty?
3. How well did we use our group resources? What prevented us from using them better? How could the obstacles to better use of resources have been avoided?

Occupational Prestige in the United States. The following instructions can be used in the same way as the foregoing as an exercise in consensus. The numbers in parentheses are the correct rankings and should not appear on the instructional sheet given to the participants.

Occupational Prestige in the United States ——————————

Instructions: In 1963 the National Opinion Research Center at the University of Chicago conducted a study of the prestige accorded ninety occupations. A national sample of the American adult population was interviewed, and all interviewed were asked their personal opinions of the general standing of each job. Below is a list of fifteen occupations included in this study. Your task is to rank them in the same order of prestige as did the sample of the American public. Place a 1 by the occupation that you think was ranked as most prestigious by the national sample; place a 2 by the second most prestigious occupation, and so on, through the number 15, which will be your estimate of the least prestigious of the fifteen occupations.

_____ Priest	(8)
_____ Nuclear physicist	(2)
_____ Author of novels	(11)
_____ Banker	(9)
_____ Member of the board of directors of a large corporation	(7)
_____ Carpenter	(15)

_____ Owner of a factory that employs about 100 people   (10)
_____ Physician   (1)
_____ Electrician   (13)
_____ Lawyer   (5)
_____ Architect   (6)
_____ College professor   (4)
_____ Official of an international labor union   (12)
_____ State governor   (3)
_____ Undertaker   (14)

Below is an alternate list of occupations taken from the same source as the one above.

_____ Banker   (6)
_____ U.S. representative in Congress   (2)
_____ Public school teacher   (8)
_____ Railroad engineer   (11)
_____ Sociologist   (7)
_____ Musician in a symphony orchestra   (10)
_____ Dentist   (3)
_____ Radio announcer   (14)
_____ Insurance agent   (15)
_____ Minister   (4)
_____ U.S. Supreme Court justice   (1)
_____ Farm owner and operator   (12)
_____ Policeman   (13)
_____ Airline pilot   (5)
_____ Building contractor   (9)

Lost at Sea. Pfeiffer and Jones have collected a great many exercises, including consensus exercises, into two very useful series of books: the *Handbook of Structured Experiences for Human Relations Training* (1969 to present) and the *Annual Handbooks for Group Facilitators* (1972 to present). Volume 4 (1973) of the *Handbook of Structured Experiences* collects eight consensus exercises into one section. A consensus exercise we particularly like is "Lost at Sea"; it appears in the 1975 *Annual Handbook*. Because "Lost at Sea" is easily available in the Pfeiffer and Jones volume at no cost for educational purposes, we do not reproduce it here.

Characteristics of a Successful Instructor. The following can also be used as an exercise in consensus. Although there are no correct rankings, the topic is of real relevance to people in schools, and reaching consensus on the most important characteristics of a successful instructor often brings out major value differences useful as foci for discussion.

Characteristics of a Successful Instructor

The following is a list of 11 characteristics of a successful instructor plus one space for adding a characteristic you think has been overlooked. Rank-order the characteristics according to your opinion of their importance in contributing to successful instruction.

Your rank-order		Group's rank-order
_____	Encouraging creativity among students.	_____
_____	Maintaining an orderly and focused student group.	_____
_____	Enriching the course of study or curriculum of the subject being taught.	_____
_____	Giving individual attention to students.	_____
_____	Experimenting with new instructional techniques.	_____
_____	Diagnosing learning problems of students.	_____
_____	Coordinating classroom activities with other parts of the school curriculum.	_____
_____	Ensuring that students learn basic skills.	_____
_____	Solving personal problems of individual students.	_____
_____	Developing student ability in analytical reasoning and problem solving.	_____
_____	Developing the aesthetic potential of students.	_____
_____	Other (specify): _____	_____

Intergroup Exercises

The exercises that follow show the effects of hierarchical decision making. Both require that more than one group work together in the same organization. Suggestions for forming the groups are included in each description.

Planners and Operators. By simulating problems that arise when one team makes decisions about another team's work, this exercise demonstrates the difficulties of using a formal hierarchy in group problem solving. Participants learn about the processes of team planning, about communication problems between a planning and an implementing group, and about the problems an implementing group confronts when carrying out a plan that is not its own.

The exercise is performed by clusters of nine to 12 persons divided into three subgroups of four planners, four operators, and one to four observers. The planners decide how they will carry the task through as best they can; and the observers watch the process, making notes of efficiencies and difficulties. The task consists of joining 16 puzzle pieces designed to form a 12-inch square, leaving an empty 1-inch square in the center. The diagonal lines on the diagram given to the planners (see Figure 7-13) are made thicker than the others to hint to the planners how they might organize their instructions for the operators.

Each member of the planning team is given four pieces of the puzzle; the planning team has the diagram shown in Figure 7-13. In placing the pieces in four piles, the exact distribution is not of great importance; the following combinations are possible—(1) A, B, I, G; (2) A, C, D, H; (3) A, D, F, J; (4) A, E, J, G—although the actual pieces should not be labeled. The key restriction on the planning group is that its members may not move the pieces, put the puzzle together, or give a drawing of the design to the operating team; they may only tell the operators orally or in written words how to fit the pieces together.

Figure 7-13. Planner's and Operator's Puzzle

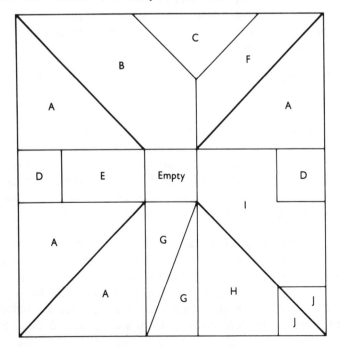

The facilitator explains that this is a simulation in which planners instruct operators to carry out a task, and divides the group into four-person planning teams, four-person operating teams, and observers. Observers leave the room to be briefed by a facilitator later. Operators go to another room. Planners gather around their tables to get acquainted.

Out of hearing of both the planning and operating teams, the facilitator briefs observers on what to look for in the planning, communicating, and implementing stages of the exercises, giving each a copy of the "Briefing Sheet for Observing Team" (see Figure 7-14).

Figure 7-14. Briefing Sheet for the Observing Team

You will be observing a planning team decide how to solve a problem and give instruction to an operating team so that they can carry out the solution. The problem consists of assembling sixteen flat pieces into the form of a square containing an empty square in its middle. The planning team is supplied with a diagram of the assembled pieces. This team is not to assemble the pieces itself, but is to instruct the operating team how to assemble the parts in minimum time. You will be silent observers throughout the process.

Suggestions

1. Each member of the observing team should watch the general pattern of communication but give special attention to one member of the planning team (during the planning phase) and one member of the operating team (during the assembling period).

2. During the planning period watch for the following behavior:
   a. Is there a balanced participation among planning team members?
   b. What kinds of behavior block or facilitate the process?
   c. How does the planning team divide its time between planning and instructing? (How early does it invite the operating team to come in?)
   d. Does the team decide that certain members should do one thing during the instructing and other members other things? If so, how do they decide?

3. During the instructing period, watch for the following behavior:
   a. At the beginning of the instruction, how do the planners orient the operators to their task?
   b. What assumptions made by the planning team are not communicated to the orienting team?
   c. How effective are the instructions?
   d. Does the operating team appear to feel free to ask questions of the planners?

4. During the assembly period, watch for the following behavior:
   a. What evidence do the operating team members exhibit that instructions were clearly understood or misunderstood?
   b. What nonverbal reactions do planning team members exhibit as they watched their plans being implemented or distorted?

To planning teams the facilitator hands out briefing sheets (Figure 7-15) and puzzle materials, reads the briefing sheets aloud, and emphasizes that the planning must end in 40 minutes. The planning now gets under way.

The facilitator next goes to the operating teams to distribute briefing sheets (Figure 7-16) that explain their task during the waiting period. Essentially this task is to discuss how they feel while waiting to be instructed and how they can prepare themselves for an unknown task. They are told that their planning team may summon them at any time but that if they are not called by five

Figure 7-15. Briefing Sheet for the Planning Team

Each member of the team sits by a packet containing some pieces of a puzzle. When all the pieces from all four packets are properly assembled, they will form a large square containing an empty place in the middle. A sheet bearing a diagram of the completed puzzle is provided for your team.

Your task is to do the following

1. Plan how the sixteen pieces distributed among you can be assembled to make the puzzle.

2. Decide on a plan for instructing your operating team how to assemble the puzzle.

3. You may call the operating team and begin instructing them at any time during the next forty minutes.

4. The operating team must begin assembling the puzzle forty-five minutes from now, and you are required to give them at least five minutes of instruction.

Before you start, read these rules

During planning:

1. Keep the pieces in your packet and in front of you at all times.

2. Do not touch the pieces nor trade any with other persons, either now or during the instruction phase.

3. Do not assemble the square; that is the operators' job.

4. Do not mark on any of the pieces.

During instruction:

1. Give all instructions in words. Do not show the diagram to the operators; hide it. Do not draw any diagrams yourselves, either on paper or in the air with gestures. You may convey your verbal instructions either orally or on paper.

2. The operating team must not move the pieces until the signal is given to start.

3. Do not show any diagram to the operators.

4. After the signal is given for the assembly to begin, you may *not* give any further instructions; stand back and observe.

Figure 7-16. Briefing Sheet for the Operating Team

1. Your team of four people will have the responsibility of carrying out a task according to instructions given you by your planning team.

2. Your task will begin forty-five minutes from now.

3. Your planning team may call you in for instruction at any time during the next forty minutes.

4. If they do not summon you during the next forty minutes, you must report to them at your own initiative at the end of the forty minutes.

5. While you wait for a call from your planning team, do the following:

   a. Individually, write on a piece of paper the concerns you feel while waiting for instructions.

   b. As a group, think of anything you can that might help you follow instructions or hinder you in doing so. Write the things that are working for you on one sheet of paper and the things that are working against you on another.

   c. How can the four of you organize as a team to receive and follow the instructions? Make notes on a sheet of paper.

   d. Keep handy the sheets on which you have written your ideas. You may find them useful during the discussion that takes place after you have completed the task.

6. You may send notes to the planners, and they may send notes in reply. Give notes to the game leader or to an observer to be carried to the planners.

7. Once you have begun the task your planners give you—forty-five minutes from now—your planning team will not be allowed to give you any further instructions.

8. Finish the assigned task as rapidly as possible.

minutes before the task is to begin, they are to report for work anyway. If the participants ask about visiting the other groups or passing notes, some facilitators will carry notes between groups and allow planners to visit operators (but not vice versa).

When the planning is completed, whether in 40 minutes or sooner, the planning team calls in the operating team and gives instructions.

The facilitator now calls time to begin, instructing planners to step back from the table and to remain silent as the operating team begins its work.

Operators complete the task according to their instructions, taking as much time as necessary.

Discussion includes reports from the observers, planners, and operators and observations of similarities between the exercise and other organizational and group experiences.

Planners and operators both experience several kinds of learning in the course of this exercise. Planners learn that it is frustrating to plan a task that someone else has to carry out and that they are themselves prohibited from performing. They frequently spend so much time planning the activity that they do not allow enough time to communicate their plans adequately to the operators, with the result that a good deal of the planning effort is wasted. In addition, planners often place limitations on themselves that are not in their instructions and fail to use all the resources at their disposal. Indeed, their very preoccupation with giving information under pressure often reduces the efficacy of the communication. They sometimes use geometric or other terms that the operators do not understand, and they frequently give cumbersome instructions in writing instead of taking the time to give them aloud. At the same time, planning is a very seductive task, which so absorbs the interest and attention of planners that they often forget what the operators are experiencing, and fail to take into account their anxieties, their need to feel physically comfortable in the environment, and so forth.

For their part, operators often feel anxiety about performing an unknown task and usually develop some antagonistic feelings toward the planning team. This is particularly true when several groups are engaging in the exercise in one large room and one operating team is called by its planners after seeing other teams called in earlier. Sometimes an operating team sets up its own organizational structure, selecting a leader to receive their instructions and give them guidance; but this structure is typically ignored by the planners, who usually never suspect that such an organization exists.

When the exercise is completed, the ensuing discussion may be guided by questions such as the following: Did you feel that your behavior during this task was typical, or were you surprised by some of your behaviors or feelings? Which actions of the planners and operators surprised you? What was most frustrating about the task, and what do you think is the key to its successful completion? What could planners or operators have done to improve their own or the other group's performance? What occurred during the exercise that was like or unlike what occurs at our college or school? Did any ideas arise that might be used to improve our college or school's organizational functioning? If no one else does, the facilitator may summarize the important points raised during the discussion.

Examining Influence and Participation

The next three procedures can be used in sequence to examine influence and group-participation patterns. Like High-Talker Tap-Out, Beach Ball, and such instruments as Communication Roles (see chapter 4), these procedures provide good transitions from communication skill to decision-making process.

Influence Group. Participants form three groups of equal size composed respectively and exclusively of high influencers, moderate influencers, and low influencers. The members decide among themselves by consensus who is to be in which group. Consensus on the final grouping is very important and ends the active part of the procedure. Debriefing can begin in a Fishbowl arrangement, with each group taking a turn in the center to discuss how it feels to be in this group and how its members feel toward the other two groups. The total group then explores the likely effects of the grouping on the functioning of the subgroups and total group.

Self-assessment of Participation. Group members form three groups of equal size composed of high talkers, moderate talkers, and low talkers, each group to discuss a regular item on the agenda in the presence of the two other groups. The Fishbowl arrangement allows all members to see how persons of high, middle, and low talkativeness deal with issues and also to see what the problems of communication are in these three groups.

Knutson (1960) demonstrated that highly loquacious persons get the greatest attention from others, including their own kind; that worthwhile contributions from low talkers are often inhibited or buried by the garrulousness of high talkers; and that high and low talkers alike come to believe that low talkers have little to offer. Asking high talkers to be quiet while low talkers speak can expand possibilities for both listening and interaction.

After every subgroup has had its turn in the center, the entire group discusses what has happened (Knutson's points will usually emerge in the discussion). Finally, the entire staff proceeds with the rest of the agenda. At the end of the meeting, members are asked whether the exercise had any effect on the later portion of the meeting.

Influence Roles. Two kinds of influence on group functions must be present for meetings to be effective: task functions, which answer the work requirements of the meeting; and the maintenance functions, which help the group with its interpersonal feelings and internal cohesion. Ideally, all staff members should be capable of performing both of these functions. Usually, however, only a few perform task functions and even fewer perform maintenance functions. In this exercise, group members individually nominate one person as the one who most often performs one or the other function in their group. Below, we have itemized each of the two functions into six subfunctions. On newsprint, write the 12 italicized words and phrases below; after them, write the nominations made by participants.

INFLUENCING TASK

1. *Initiating:* proposing tasks or goals; defining a group problem, suggesting a procedure for solving a problem, suggesting other ideas for consideration.
2. *Information or opinion seeking:* requesting facts on the problem, seeking relevant information, asking for suggestions and ideas.
3. *Information or opinion giving:* offering facts, providing relevant information, stating a belief, giving suggestions or ideas.
4. *Clarifying or elaborating:* interpreting or reflecting ideas or suggestions, clearing up confusion, indicating alternatives and issues before the group, giving examples.
5. *Summarizing:* pulling related ideas together, restating suggestions after the group has discussed them.
6. *Consensus testing:* sending up trial balloons to see whether the group is nearing a conclusion or whether agreement has been reached.

INFLUENCING MAINTENANCE

1. *Encouraging:* being friendly, warm, and responsive to others; accepting others and their contributions; listening; showing regard for others by giving them opportunity or recognition.
2. *Expressing group feelings:* sensing feeling, mood, relationships within the group; sharing one's own feelings with other members.
3. *Harmonizing:* attempting to reconcile disagreements; reducing tension by oiling troubled waters; getting people to explore their differences.
4. *Compromising:* offering to compromise one's own position, ideas, or status; admitting error; disciplining oneself to help maintain the group.
5. *Gatekeeping:* seeing that others have a chance to speak; maintaining group discussion rather than one-, two-, or three-way conversations.
6. *Setting standards:* expressing standards that will help the group to achieve; applying standards in evaluating group functioning and production.

Debriefing can focus on individual feelings and behavior either causing or resulting from the nominations, or on consequences for the group of the centralized or dispersed structure described by the nomination pattern.

This exercise can also be combined with the self-assessment of participation described earlier. After the group has divided into equal subgroups of high, moderate, and low talkers, there will be twice as many observers as participants in the Fishbowl. Each inside participant can have one outside colleague watching for task functions and another outside colleague watching for maintenance functions. The pairs of outside colleagues can give the inside participants feedback on the functions they did or did not carry out during group discussion.

If this procedure is repeated several times, persons being observed can tell the observers about several functions they would like to try to perform more, and the observers can give feedback in later meetings on the frequency with which they see their colleagues performing those functions. One of the most important conclusions to be drawn from such an activity is that many contributions are influential and helpful to the group even when not focused directly on the task. In addition, the dispersion of influence is likely to increase as more members learn how to keep the discussion circulating throughout the group.

Decision-making Roles

This exercise provides a vehicle for achieving group agreements about the roles each member should assume in decision making. In the matrix that follows, the columns represent different jobs or status levels within the organization; the rows represent functions about which decision making occurs. Participants use their own jobs and functions to head the columns and rows.

	Principal	Assistant principal	Coun-selors	Teachers	Service personnel	Students
Determin-ing goals	_____	_____	_____	_____	_____	_____
Ordering materials	_____	_____	_____	_____	_____	_____
Sequencing procedures	_____	_____	_____	_____	_____	_____

Next, the facilitator describes six kinds of influence that persons can have on a decision and tells the group to complete the matrix by discussing the kind of influence appropriately exerted on each function by each position. The kinds of influence are as follows:

KINDS OF INFLUENCE

Blank: May recommend or suggest. Because it is understood in a healthy educational organization that any person in any position may make recommendations to the person who can authorize action, we enter no special symbol for recommending and suggesting.

    I: Must be informed. *I* means that, to take appropriate coordinating action, position holders must know the results of a decision. *I* usually shows that a position will be affected by a decision or that the position holder will have to implement the decision.

    C: Must be consulted. The position must be given an opportunity to influence the decision making by presenting information, demonstration, or proof. Those with *C* power should be consulted early enough so that their information can make a genuine difference in the final decision.

    P: Must participate. *P* means that position holders must take part in making the decision and that at least a majority vote of all those with a *P* is necessary before the decision can be final.

    V: Veto power. *V* means that position holders have veto power over the function and that their agreement must be obtained before the decision can be made.

    A: Authority to make decision. *A* represents the greatest power of all. Those with *A* can make the decision, and others must go along with it.

Macrosequences for Decision Making

In designing macrosequences from the exercises in this chapter, four guidelines will be helpful: (1) begin with feedback, (2) sequence according to the social-psychological level of emphasis, (3) move from exercises to closer approximations of the group's real world, and (4) repeat or provide similar experiences to assess progress.

To help a group of educators move toward discussion of decision-making processes, first collect systematic data on meetings using the meetings questionnaire or observation categories presented earlier in this book. Next, report a summary of the data to the faculty. Finally, the faculty might do the self-assessment of participation exercise to highlight their own contributions or lack of contributions to decision making at meetings.

Two sequences are useful for informing participants firsthand about how the dilemmas of power and decision making look at the interpersonal, group, and organizational levels. One sequence starts with an interpersonal exercise such as Grievances of Black Citizens or Lost at Sea and ends at the intergroup or organization level with the Planners and Operators exercise. Another sequence moves in the opposite direction, beginning with the organizational emphasis, proceeding to the face-to-face group, and ending at the interpersonal level.

The sequence chosen depends upon the level of interaction that participants are most eager to explore at the beginning of a training event and upon the goal toward which the facilitator wishes to lead them. Generally, we believe that moving from the interpersonal to the organizational level is the more effective procedure. Participants can easily think about interpersonal influence at the beginning of training and, by proceeding from small group to organization, can be encouraged to analyze more carefully the issues of power and decision making in their organization.

Moving from exercises to procedures helps a group make use of the lessons learned from the exercises. After a consensus exercise such as Grievances of Black Citizens, for example, the facilitator can give the group a comparable period of time in which to reach consensus on some actual group issue that requires clarification and decision. In the course of the real decision making, the facilitator can ask them to take a self-assessment of participation. After the group has had ample time to reach a decision, participants can discuss how well they used members' resources, diffused participation, and made decisions. Occasional comments on processes by the facilitator help participants become more aware of their actual methods of making decisions.

Presenting two or more of the five exercises on consensual decision making one after the other can be particularly useful when participants can meet for only two or three hours at a time and the times are spread over several months or more. Desert Survival, Grievances of Black Citizens, and Characteristics of a Successful Teacher, for example, can be presented sequentially, each followed by a discussion of how well the group used its resources in making the decisions. The repetitive pattern encourages group members to remind one another of the new norms about discussion and decision making that these exercises expose. In addition, a series of exercises makes improvement visible. By seeing how well they perform in subsequent exercises, group members are less likely to deceive themselves about the difficulty of making effective decisions consensually.

Chapter Eight

Working with Conflicts

Conflicts are ubiquitous within educational organizations; they occur continually, arise for many reasons, appear in a variety of forms, and affect the educational process both favorably and unfavorably. The presence of conflict is in itself neither good nor bad; it simply exists and should be expected. Educators and students not only react differently to conflict but react differently from case to case and from time to time. Thus, the most effective strategies for dealing with conflicts must also vary according to the conflict, the organization, and the parties involved. That is, an appropriate conflict-management strategy will depend on the type of conflict, the intensity of the disagreement, the persons participating in the conflict, the seriousness of the issue for them, and the authority, resources, and knowledge they possess.

Conflicts range from disagreements over important matters to intensely emotional struggles over cherished resources. Conflicts of all varieties do create tension, anxiety, and unpleasantness. But unpleasant experiences in themselves are not always bad for the college or school. They can supply the punch and push needed for growth and development. Indeed, bringing conflicts into the open can provide a creative tension that inspires problem solving.

Moreover, open discussions of conflicts can enhance individual or group performance.

OD facilitators must know how to seek out conflicts, how to conceptualize them and make them known, and how to help educators generate creative solutions to them. The nature of the conflict-management strategy will depend in part on a careful analysis of the conflict itself and in part on the facilitator's own skill in working with educators in conflict. This chapter is intended to serve as a guide for diagnosing and analyzing organizational conflicts in educational organizations, for determining when it is appropriate for facilitators to intervene, and for selecting designs and specific consultative techniques for managing conflicts among educators.

One of the primary demands on any college or school is that its various parts should be linked to achieve overall objectives. To accomplish common tasks and achieve goals generally requires collaboration, and for most educational tasks the need for participant interdependence is great. Instructors in teams must work together; experts in curriculum must work with instructors; indeed, to facilitate a more open college or school, groups of instructors and administrators must work interdependently on committees and instructional teams that span academic levels.

Conflict is likely to arise when particular educational goals are perceived as being mutually exclusive (as when instructors believe that counseling is not benefiting students' cognitive learning); when activities undertaken to reach goals are regarded as interdependent (as when instructors and counselors alike believe that student self-concept is the key to cognitive learning); or when two or more parties draw upon the same limited resources to accomplish their goals (as when instructors and coaches compete for time with students).

More specifically, conflict occurs between two people when the goals of each are frustrated by the other, when each is competing for some reward at the other's expense, when they misunderstand or disagree with one another's expectations of conduct, or when they approach a problem from different points of view. Conflict occurs between groups for many of the same reasons, and it occurs between organizations when they compete for scarce resources or when, as in the case of revolutionary movements, the legitimacy of an organization is challenged.

For the OD facilitator, conflict should not denote individual distaste, disappointment, frustration, anger, or any of the common forms of miscommunication discussed in chapter 4. In these pages, conflict refers to a social condition in which two or more persons or groups cannot have the same thing at the same time. Further,

OD facilitators should regard conflicts between educators as natural, unavoidable occurrences that cannot be expected to vanish of their own accord. Instead, they should be brought out into the open and managed by means of channels or occasions through which adversaries can introduce their conflicting claims into the business of the educational organization.

If conflicts are legitimated, then compromises, trade-offs, and other negotiations can be conducted openly at problem-solving meetings; more realistic educational policies can be achieved, and anxieties diminished as outcomes are more clearly foreseen. If conflicts are not uncovered and managed, informal groups and underground networks (which often greatly distort the truth) will arise to cope with them, often increasing destructive tension and personal hostility between conflicting parties. Thus in many educational organizations, instructors cluster to criticize the work of counselors; counselors stay away from instructors, preferring to keep to their own offices and to enjoy informal breaks with one another; and only rarely do criticisms become public enough for problem solving to occur.

Before conflict among educators can be brought into the open for public discussion, some degree of interpersonal trust and constructive openness must exist. Most educators, however, are unaccustomed to expressing open disagreement directly to those with whom they disagree. In many colleges and schools, direct discussion of conflict is experienced as unpleasant and undesirable both by those engaged in the conflict and by those only observing it. This is especially true when staff members find it difficult to distinguish between disagreeing with a colleague's opinion and "putting down" or rejecting the colleague. Indeed, in addition to personal predilections, the norms of many educational organizations militate against the open expression of differences. The OD facilitator should strive to encourage new norms of constructive openness and open confrontation. Educators will be more willing to discuss conflict openly when a facilitator, whose own skill in dealing with conflicts can serve as an important model, is present to support and legitimate the process.

The facilitator should first look for signs of hidden conflict among individuals and subgroups. In some cases, different parts of the organization may be unaware that they are competing for scarce resources; in other cases, competitors may be aware of conflict but unwilling to communicate about it publicly or officially. Second, the facilitator should ascertain tentatively to what extent the conflict may be obstructing educational goals, making procedures inefficient, and frustrating the personal needs of staff members.

Conversely, the facilitator should also ascertain to what extent the conflict satisfies the power and achievement needs of some members and demonstrates qualities of inventive resourcefulness in the organization. Third, if the facilitator decides that the macrodesign should include steps for bringing the conflict into the open, procedures precisely suited to the nature of the conflict, the school, and the educators involved should be devised to make the conflict accessible to direct and constructive dealing.

Types and Sources of Conflict

To reiterate briefly, in the S-T-P procedure for problem solving, the S (situation) refers to the essential features of a current condition, the T (target) to a desired condition toward which an individual or group is striving, and the P (path) to specific action-plans aimed at bringing about the desired condition. The S is commonly associated with facts, opinions, explanations, perceptions, and feelings; the T, with goals, aims, ends, values, purposes, and objectives; and the P, with paths, plans, strategies, and implementation. The S-T-P points us to three kinds of conflict.

Factual conflict (type S) entails argument about the realities of a current situation—either debate over easily discoverable facts, such as the number of square feet in a classroom, or over facts more difficult to gather, such as the opinions of math and science instructors about current curricula. *Value conflict* (type T) encompasses argument over values, goals, or objectives ranging from highly specific phenomena, such as students' behavior or achievements, to more general events, such as debates between essentialist and progressive educational philosophies. *Strategy conflict* (type P) entails argument over the best way of moving from a present condition to a valued future condition with respect to either the major stages of a macrodesign or the microaspects of a specific action-plan.

Conflicts can also be sorted by using the concepts of closeness versus distance, which we discussed in chapter 4. Disagreement over facts, values, or strategies usually stems from topics or issues that are personally distant from both parties. Stronger conflicts—those conditions we typically call conflict—get down to things personally close to both parties. The question arises, "Can you and I both get what we want?" Those two types of conflict call for different OD strategies. Talking things through, voting, and agreeing to disagree can be applied successfully to disagreements, while negotiation, bargaining, and finally taking action are often necessary to resolve intense conflict.

The sources of conflict among educators, whether mild or intense or of fact, value, or strategy, can also be categorized as (1) differentiation of function among parts of the educational organization, (2) power struggles between persons and subsystems, (3) role conflicts, (4) differences in interpersonal style among educators, and (5) stress imposed on the educational organization by external forces.

Differentiation of Function

Effective adaptation to the community requires educational organizations to communicate with their environments through a number of specialized units, and this differentiation of function is often a major source of conflict. Members of different departments or subgroups who have access to different kinds of information from that of their counterparts in other departments are likely to take a different view of the facts of a situation and to entertain different strategies for accomplishing their primary tasks. When the same problem is tackled from widely diverging points of view, the presence of various cognitive, emotional, and attitudinal differences will produce interpersonal and intergroup conflict. All too often, however, conflicts arising from functional differentiation are misunderstood as arising from someone's personal incompetence. This happens because educators who interact every day are too close to their own parts of the organization to understand easily the parts others work in, and it is only natural for them to associate the source of the conflict with the person toward whom the frustration or irritation is directly felt.

An example of this type of misunderstanding once occurred in our work with a college faculty. Over a period of months faculty members had repeatedly complained that the head of student services was doing such an inadequate job that they had begun to question his competence, although the provost and a health-service counselor thought that he was doing a fine job and could not understand the faculty's dissatisfaction with him. At a faculty retreat designed by a couple of outside OD facilitators, the issue was raised and dealt with as it had been many times before. Defensive, bewildered, and frustrated, the head of student services knew that he worked hard but could somehow not get this across to the other faculty members.

After listening to the discussion and asking several questions, the OD facilitators realized that the problem had less to do with the head of student services as a person than with the fact that his position and functions caused his primary energies to be directed toward community, the college's governing board, and other outside agencies. Because of the way their own tasks were organized, the instructors had little contact with either the head of student services himself or with those in the college community with whom he worked, and for this reason they were largely unaware of the effects of his actions. The provost and counselor, on the other hand, had considerable contact with the student service's head and his work and were well aware of the effects of his actions. On the basis of this understanding, the facilitators were able to educate the staff about the effects of differentiation of function and clear the way for improved communication and understanding between the instructors and the head of student services.

In their work on industrial organizations, Lawrence and Lorsch (1967) concluded that success in achieving both high differentiation and a high quality of collaboration is determined by the organization's processes for resolving conflict. When organizational mechanisms for resolving conflicts are ineffective, the conflicts caused by differentiation can be destructive. When conflict is openly confronted and resolved, both differentiation and collaboration are effectively promoted.

Power Struggles

A common cause of conflict among educators, power struggles typically arise when some participants attempt to gain advantage over others. This can occur when adversaries compete for a commonly desired reward, such as a promotion or merit pay for good teaching; when self-interests conflict; when resources are scarce; and when opinions differ on the relative autonomy or interdependence of individuals or subgroups.

In one of our projects, for example, conflicting self-interests and the scarcity of a resource brought about a power struggle over a scheduling problem in an elementary school. One team comprising teachers of the first and second grades, another comprising the third and fourth grades, and still another comprising the fifth and sixth grades all wanted a late-afternoon PE schedule. All had good reasons, but, as only one gymnasium was available for the afternoon periods, the conflicting self-interests developed into a full-scale power struggle.

The lower grade units accused the upper grade team of having dominated the afternoon schedule in the past, claimed that this domination had been typical of numerous other faculty interactions, and coalesced to demand a schedule change, in part because they wanted to exercise their right to a share of schoolwide power. Feelings were heated, the upper grade team resisted, and the ensuing conflict took six hours to resolve. We describe this episode in more detail under "Tactics for Conflict Management" below.

Power struggles also developed over conflicting views of the appropriate power relationships between members of the school organization; that is, who should be accountable to whom, or who should tell whom what to do and when and how to do it? In a college Schmuck worked in, a conflict arose between the provost and the instructional staff over a new department-head role. The provost intended for the department head to begin urging faculty members to do more research, while the faculty members thought that they had been doing research adequately without external supervision and believed that the provost was treating them unprofessionally and unfairly.

Finally, power struggles can result from certain educators' desire to gain more personal influence over educational goals (value conflict) or over the instructional program (strategy conflict). Some faculty members may wish to put their own stamp on the college's philosophy and curriculum; others may wish to gain influence in order to be seen as more effective professionally. Whatever the particular social-psychological dynamics may be, such desires are typical in many colleges and schools.

Role Conflict

Insofar as an organization comprises persons interacting in roles, much organizational behavior can be understood by understanding role relationships. Thus, on becoming an educator, new instructors usually attempt to learn what others expect of them by meeting with the department head, the experienced staff, colleagues in the same unit, expert specialists, the counselor, the custodian, the secretary, and students. These others constitute role senders, and the behavior of new instructors will be strongly influenced by what those people expect of them. It should be noted, however, that as some jobs allow more leeway than others for individual differences, neophytes have the power to conform to these expectations, to resist them, or to comply with them only partially.

Individuals may fail to conform to expectations of role senders for a variety of reasons. First, they may receive from role senders conflicting or contradictory expectations about how they are to perform. Following the provost's or principal's expectations, for example, might mean violating important norms of a teaching team. Persons among the role senders might hold diverse expectations among which the individual will have to choose, as new instructors have sometimes to choose between the faculty's various goals and those they were themselves taught at the university. These examples of *intrarole conflict* illustrate conflicting demands that an individual acting in a single role cannot satisfy simultaneously.

Second, *interrole conflict*—conflict between roles—sometimes prevents individuals from conforming to expectations. Because most persons perform multiple roles within an educational organization, the individual will often have to choose among the expectations from different role senders. For example, an individual may simultaneously be an instructor, the head of a curriculum committee, a member of a planning committee, a representative of the faculty association, and the faculty member to whom most students express their dissatisfaction about how the educational organization is run. If this individual is firm about leaving an important curriculum meeting early, members of the committee may express disapproval, while to stay past the stated closing time without special arrangement for extra pay might elicit disapproval or even disciplinary action by the faculty association.

A third obstacle arises when the role expectations held by others conflict with an individual's own values, perception of the facts, or professional orientation; when they seem merely uninteresting; or when they accumulate to a greater amount of work than the individual alone can discharge. This condition can come about when recruiters overemphasize the favorable aspects of a job and underplay its unfavorable aspects, when recruits interpret the recruiters' messages to suit their own needs, or when there is a strategy on the part of new instructors to change the expectations of others by redefining the role once they are in the educational organization.

During one of our projects, a role conflict emerged when an elementary school staff sought to redefine the role of the school counselor. The three teaching teams in the school presented three sets of targets and action proposals for the counseling role, none of which appealed to the counselor, who maintained that the role, goals, and strategies she had adopted were based on her training as a counselor and offered a more responsible and useful version than those presented by the teaching teams. Hurt and angry, she finally mustered supporters to defend the ways in which she was currently carrying out her functions.

The problem in this case was threefold. First, the goals that the various subgroups held for counseling were themselves in conflict. Second, at the district office the counselor was considered to be performing well and meeting the expectations of that part of her role senders. Third, the counselor disapproved of the action proposals made by the teaching teams, believing that her graduate training had prepared her well for what she was doing, that the values articulated by the teaching teams were unimportant, and that the suggested new roles would not be personally fulfilling to her.

Role conflict is a common cause of conflict in educational organizations, bringing together organizational, interpersonal, and personal factors as the individual and the role senders try to find expectations that will be acceptable to all. If the expectations of new instructors conflict with those of others in the college or school, their own expectations are likely to go unfulfilled. As time elapses, neophyte instructors will conform to the expectations of members of their role set, try to change the expectations, or create tension within themselves and within the educational organization. If the conflict remains strong, they will usually move to another kind of job within the field or leave the field altogether.

Differences in Interpersonal Style

Every participant brings to an educational organization a unique set of needs and experiences, of styles of coping with stress, and of rhythms for getting things done. At times these interpersonal styles can work against one another, creating friction and conflict that may destroy productive collaboration. Several strategies can be effective in reducing or resolving these differences. As the following example demonstrates, encouraging open feedback between the parties involved may suffice to alter work patterns or interpersonal behavior for the better.

During an OD project with the staff of a college department in which we were working, it became evident that, with one exception, all the faculty members had developed highly collaborative and flexible team-teaching relationships, while one instructor remained closed off from collaboration with the rest. While the latter was uncomfortably aware of the others' anger, he nevertheless did not know how to change the situation. An exercise encouraging open feedback revealed that this man habitually responded to serious matters with a joke. No one ever got a straight answer from him, and many had become so frustrated that they had stopped trying to communicate with him altogether. Bringing this feedback to light enabled him to begin to change his behavior and opened an opportunity for future exchanges of feedback between him and the rest of the staff.

Another strategy for resolving conflict is to arrange the duties of contending individuals in such a way that they need communicate only seldom and then only in very precise and objective terms. When it is feasible, this method often works well enough in the short run, although in the long run the reduction of communication may only increase hostility and cause it to spill over into communication with others. Still another strategy is to capitalize on the different styles, extracting complementary and mutually supportive styles that will strengthen the capacity of the group as a whole.

External Stress

What educational organization in America has not been in conflict with groups of citizens over new bond issues, controversial curricula, or issues of tuition increase? Although some external stress may be induced intentionally, as when militant groups strive to produce revolutionary change in a college or school, some stress inevitably accompanies social change, and the demands made by external forces and groups often create conflict for the educators.

Disagreements will arise within the educational organization over the methods to be used in coping with external demands and assuaging external pressure groups, while diverse inputs from the community that lead to increased differentiation within the organization will not only increase tension in the college or school but exacerbate conflicts already in existence. Perhaps the most typical external stress comes from the public that wishes for improved conditions in American education. OD facilitators can help educational organizations cope with such stress by working to develop communication channels with the community and by involving citizens as aides and facilitators within the educational organization. The most ardent critics in the community can become energetic contributors to educational programs.

Organizing for Conflict Management

Some conflicts are inevitable, and may even provide a creative tension that has the effect of improving educational performance; others, although not helpful to the educational establishment, are not so destructive as to require the services of an outside OD facilitator. Still others, however, can significantly weaken the instructional program of an educational organization and for that reason should receive a facilitator's attention.

As they uncover conflicts between role takers or units in the educational organization, facilitators should answer two questions. First, are the conflicting parties required to work together to accomplish an important mission? A teacher in a school with self-contained classrooms, for example, is not required to work much with other teachers on matters of instruction; similarly, the faculty of an academic department may have little to do with some of the personnel of the provost's office. Second, how interdependent are the parties who must work together? If a great deal of collaboration is required among them, the OD facilitator should work toward making any conflicts accessible to problem-solving processes.

Whether conflicts should be uncovered at all depends upon the nature of the tension that is present. Some tensions enhance productivity, motivate change, and improve organizational functioning. If extremely high tensions can be reduced through clear communication or effective problem solving, uncovering conflict is likely to have constructive consequences. On the other hand, where tensions can be reduced only over a long period of time, uncovering conflict may have debilitating or even destructive effects.

The likelihood of a destructive outcome is greater when participants exhibit low readiness for dealing with conflict. A low level of communication skill can cause the issues in conflict to become increasingly confused. A low level of skill in problem solving can leave people who feel inadequate in dealing with conflict even more distant and alienated than before the conflict was uncovered. A low level of mutual trust among participants can have similar consequences, especially if the OD facilitator fails to realize that lack of trust and openness is not always the result of ignorance or lack of skill but is sometimes a realistic attitude on the part of individuals. In this case, a participant who is invited by the facilitator to state the conflict orally may be punished in some way by the others for doing so. In such a case, the level of trust would decline even more, defensiveness would increase, and the facilitator would be in a poor position to help resolve other conflicts.

Uncovering conflict, then, entails a certain risk for the facilitator and educators alike. The faculty's attitudes toward conflict, the existing degree of openness and trust, the faculty's skill in communication and problem solving, and its experience with conflict in the past are all indicators of whether the risk is worth taking.

In addition to exhibiting staff readiness, schools and colleges should themselves be structured to manage conflicts productively. Lawrence and Lorsch (1967) suggest that relatively simple organizations such as elementary schools need only a well-articulated, overlapping hierarchy for managing conflicts, but that more complex organizations such as colleges should have special formal structures alongside the regular managerial hierarchy for this purpose. In our view, two very productive structures for managing conflict are the multiunit structure for elementary schools and the cadre of OD specialists for universities and school districts.

How the multiunit school is organized to manage conflict has been described in Schmuck et al. (1975). The key to this structure is that it offers a communicative link among hierarchical levels and formal subsystems. Thus, for example, on the leadership team is the principal, who connects with the school's central office, and team leaders, who connect the leadership team with teachers and students. Everyone in the school knows someone who can communicate directly with the leadership team, and this arrangement permits direct managerial contact with those who may be in conflict. To be most effective, multiunit structures must have administrators who are not only competent at conflict management but who communicate accurately about mundane matters by means of memos and bulletins to forestall or resolve minor day-to-day disagreements.

As chapter 10 will document, our research and development activities have shown that a cadre of OD specialists can make a major contribution toward managing both university-wide and district-wide conflict. We describe the work of several OD cadres in that chapter.

Derr (1971) found in one big-city school district, which relied on a highly differentiated hierarchy for managing conflicts, ineffective coordination between subsystems. Little direct contact occurred among administrators to deal with differences, and those in positions of authority were perceived by many personnel as incompetent to handle conflict. Clearly, such a district could benefit from an internal cadre of organizational specialists.

Effective universities and school districts should have within them persons who are skilled at working with conflict and should provide for direct contact between these persons and the contending parties. They should have in addition a well-coordinated hierarchy, an effective formal procedure for settling small disputes, and the ability to build appropriate conflict-management components—such as roles, teams, and departments, depending upon the degree of differentiation—into their own fabric.

Tactics for Conflict Management

Many times, when people get into disagreements and arguments about what to do, they find themselves worrying not about what *is* happening to them, but about what *might* happen to them. Dragons that might spring upon us in the future are always more frightful than those we are holding at bay today. To reduce the threat from frightful future dragons, we advocated in chapter 6 choosing clear, near, reachable goals and clear, orderly steps of problem solving, with clear specification of who is to do what. Clear communication (chapter 4), productive meetings (chapter 5), and crisp decisions (chapter 7) also help. For more ideas on how to deal effectively with conflict in academic settings, see Birnbaum, Begin, and Brown (1985).

Often people with opposing views about a proposed action are imagining different future dragons. And frequently when more information is brought to bear, when the goals of individuals and of the organization are brought closer and clarified, when several paths to the goals are accepted as alternatives, and when clear arrangements are made for monitoring the steps of progress, the dragons shrivel and vanish. We came across an example when we worked with a school counselor who, unknown to most of the teachers, had been spending most of his time working with community, parents, and other outside agencies. We facilitators explained the counselor's work to the staff and conveyed some ideas about differentiation of function that helped them understand the usefulness of the counselor's work, and their worries about the counselor's future behavior dwindled. Many of the techniques we give in this chapter for uncovering conflicts will reveal situations of that sort—oppositions that have grown out of incomplete or wrong information.

Another example occurred in a senior high school in which the principal had been accusing the staff of five counselors that they were disorganized, were not using their time to the best benefit of the students, and so on (see Francisco, 1979, for an account). We spent three days making an actual minute-by-minute count of how the counselors used their time. We interviewed all the counselors, the principal, and several teachers who worked frequently with the counselors. It turned out that the counselors were very conscientious, and that the things bothering the principal about the way they worked were the very things bothering the counselors. Neither the principal nor the counselors, however, had been able to see their agreement, because both parties had taken an embattled stance. The accusations and defenses had created an opposition—a dragon—that really wasn't there. When we fed back our information and then helped the counselors forge a new way of working together—a way they found more satisfying and productive—the dragon vanished.

We think that most seeming conflicts in schools, and in most places, are of that sort—worries about what is going on that isn't, or worries about what might go on that doesn't have to. But some conflicts are more refractory than that sort.

Some conflicts stem from limited resources—limited materials, space, money, or time. If two secretaries fight over time at the copying machine, no amount of added information or of explaining each to the other will reduce the demand on the machine. You could conceive the conflict as a shortage of materials, and you could resolve it by buying a second copying machine. You could conceive the conflict as a shortage of time, and hire an aide to do the copying. You could conceive the conflict as a shortage of money, and ask for money to buy a second machine or to hire an aide. When a conflict comes down to the matter of limited resources, the solution must deal with the resources in a new way. There are several ways of dealing with limited resources. The parties to the conflict can use one of the following methods or some combination of them.

Reorganize Duties

If two secretaries fight over the copying machine, let one of them do all the copying or hire an aide. Or, if there is no shortage of time, require one secretary to copy in the morning, the other in the afternoon. Rearranging the flow of work is called the *sociotechnical solution*.

The cadre of organizational specialists (or *peer cadre*—see chapter 10 for its description) is a way of reorganizing duties. If a school district's funds are too limited to hire a succession of outside consultants or to hire some permanent inside consultants to help with organizational problems (including conflict resolution), the district can reorganize the duties of a couple dozen of its present employees so that they can devote, say, 10 percent of their time to helping with organizational problems throughout the district. That arrangement, as we explain in chapter 10, can be made at very small cost, both in universities and school districts.

Increase the Resources

You can ask for more money. You can apply to the federal government for funds for special purposes. You can campaign for a special tax levy. And so on.

In one school where we once worked, teachers were in conflict because of demands on their time. They resolved a great many of their conflicts by recruiting parents to take over some of their duties. In their letter to parents, they gave as examples "observing . . . working one-to-one with a student . . . teaching a specialty . . . using handicraft skills . . . typing . . . and leading small group discussions." During one year, that school of a couple dozen teachers had more than 50 parents working as volunteers.

Where budgets for materials and equipment are tight, many colleges have reduced conflicts over money by obtaining equipment or materials from federal grants that can be used in science, business, and technical arts courses, as well as for faculty research.

Trade Kinds of Resources

In a senior high school, if the English teacher needs new books and the science teacher needs new equipment but there is not enough money for both, the science teacher might relinquish enough money for the English teacher to get the new books, and the English teacher might help canvass local businesses for gifts of equipment that the science teacher could use.

Compromise

Sometimes both parties can agree to give up a little. The English teacher could agree to get new books for only one course, and the science teacher could agree to get new equipment for only one course. Often, principals in schools and department heads in colleges avoid conflicts of this sort between faculty members by making the allocations themselves.

Change the Schedule

Often a conflict arises because two or more parties wish to use the same equipment or the same space at the same time. Sometimes a discussion of respective needs and a negotiation can lead to a trade-off with each party using the scarce resource at different times.

We ran an OD project in Gaynor Elementary School when its staff was converting to team teaching and making itself into a multiunit structure. The teaching teams got into a conflict over scheduling the gymnasium (see pp. 218–225 of Schmuck et al., 1975). The team comprising the teachers of the fifth and sixth grades, a forceful and highly vocal group, had been dominant for some time. To resolve the conflict over the use of the gymnasium, we OD facilitators decided not to use a problem-solving mode, because it "might only help the highly vocal 5–6 unit to achieve its own objectives at the expense of the others. The facilitators also wanted the Gaynor staff members to realize that trying to gain power and acting on one's own behalf are realistic dimensions of any complex organization" (p. 219).

The facilitators arranged a negotiation procedure that emphasized "selfish bargaining." After the first part of the procedure, "The 1–2 unit got the message that they would have to take a stronger stand to get their desired schedules. Also, the 5–6 unit was somewhat shocked to discover that their hegemony was being questioned and that they would really have to bargain to get their way" (p. 221).

In the next part, the teaching teams tried compromising and trading one kind of resource for another:

> *Initial Intransigence.* At first the teaching teams reiterated their positions and tried to convince the other teams that their cause was the most just. When they saw that nobody would win at this game, the various units began searching for alternatives. Many of the unit members passed notes to their team leaders making suggestions and proposing alternatives.
>
> *Giving a Little.* The proposals and counterproposals advanced during this stage were not very significant but represented some give-and-take. For example, one unit which had originally requested an hour for PE was willing to take 35 minutes. Another group said it would also take a shorter period if it could simultaneously use one of the vacant classrooms.
>
> The 5–6 grade unit, as represented by its team leader, continued to ask for prime time and was unwilling to bend.
>
> Feelings were running high. The 5–6 unit members thought they owned this prime time; they had always had it. The other two groups thought that the 5–6 unit had usurped the schedule so long that now it was their turn (p. 222).

Finally, the three teams managed to agree on a schedule. It wasn't pleasant. When resources are scarce, it often happens that some people get less than they want:

> After lunch, the three units regrouped to discuss their alternative positions and to make counterproposals. The 1–2 and 3–4 grade units met together and decided to form an alliance that would force the 5–6 grade unit to adopt a morning PE schedule. The negotiators returned to the table after about 45 minutes of deliberation.
>
> The discussion became very heated as the two lower-grade units pushed their position and the upper-grade unit resisted. Two events finally enabled us to arrive at a settlement. One chair at the negotiation table had been left free for the use of any unit member. One member of the 3–4 grade unit used it effectively to confront the logic of the 5–6 grade team leader's position. Second, the facilitator suggested that the team leaders change roles and negotiate for the other side in an attempt to use both perspectives in reaching a solution.
>
> It was finally agreed that the 5–6 grade unit would have a morning PE schedule and the other grades would take the gym for PE in the afternoon. The unit leaders checked with their units and all agreed that they could abide by this agreement. The 5–6 grade unit added, "We can live with it but we surely don't like it" (p. 223).

Appeal to Authority

When contending parties believe they cannot find a solution on their own, they can turn over the solution to an arbitrator or an authority. Instructors can say to the department head, or the department head can say to the dean, "All right, you decide."

The decision is not always turned over to a single person. Sometimes it is given to a committee, one that might have been formed especially for that purpose. One elementary school where we worked had a wing that had been built in 1890. The district had almost promised to remodel the wing, but a tax levy failed at the polls, and the expected money was unavailable. The school staff was very disappointed, and conflicts arose over who would be assigned to teach in the old wing. At a meeting, the staff considered various ways of allocating rooms to teachers:

1. Committee composed of representatives from each teaching unit, principal, and vice principal. Staff agrees to abide by decision of this committee.
2. Total group decision by consensus.
3. Planning within teaching units—plans submitted, evaluated, and differences resolved by compromising.
4. Decision on allocation made by principal and next year's vice principal.
5. Decision made by principal.

In the end, the staff agreed that each teaching unit would meet and discuss its needs, then the principal's leadership group would meet and make several proposals. Next, the entire staff would react to the proposals and try to reach consensus, but if that failed, the leadership group would finally make the decision.

Get What You Can

If all the above methods fail, you are left with having to fight for what you want as best you can. Or, if you are in a position of power, you are left with having to use coercion. Schmuck et al. (1975, pp. 98–99) described a conflict among teachers of the fifth and sixth grades over the performance of a paraprofessional:

> But effective meetings did not serve to ward off all organizational difficulties for the 5–6 unit. In October, unit members argued about the role of their paraprofessional. One-half of the team supported what the paraprofessional was doing, the other half was opposed. The conflict centered on the amount of responsibility that the paraprofessional should have for actual teaching. Some team members believed

the paraprofessional should teach; others did not. The ones that did not were angry when the paraprofessional refused to carry out routine tasks. The team leader was also concerned because often she herself ended up doing the menial tasks of the paraprofessional.

Throughout the fall, the 5–6 unit tried a variety of schemes to change the situation. They published a time schedule of expected duties, confronted the paraprofessional when she was not carrying out her tasks, and had a special debriefing session once per week in the unit on the role of the paraprofessional. When these attempts did not work, the team leader took the problem to the leadership group. The leadership team spent several hours discussing possible actions. After gathering information and having the principal interview the paraprofessional, the leadership team decided to ask her to resign.

Resolving conflicts over scarce resources is often stressful. But most people do not resent going through a stressful negotiation if they succeed in getting what they want, or at least not losing as much as they feared. Sometimes a negotiation leaves rancor behind it, but it need not do so if each party believes the other is tempering its demands to reduce the loss to the first party. Participants can have confidence in one another's good intentions if they have developed openness and trust before entering the negotiation. The only method of resolving conflict that guarantees resentment is the last—that of fighting to get what you can with all claws bared.

Gathering Data About Conflict

Uncovering Conflicts

Collecting data through questionnaires, interviews, observations, or preferably some combination of all three and checking their validity by feeding them back to participants is a highly effective method for uncovering organizational, group, and interpersonal conflicts in colleges and schools. While data should be collected in a formal, systematic manner, it is not always important that they give a complete or balanced picture of the target system. In some instances the only data necessary are those that allow the facilitators or steering committee to produce a picture of significant disagreements.

In giving data feedback the facilitator should include interesting quotations from interviews together with tables of quantitative data derived from questionnaires, interviews or observations. Participants will tell whether the data are correct and whether they agree with the weight the facilitator is attaching to them. Data feedback may in itself engender meaningful conflicts that will help to move the OD project along, and the interaction that occurs within the target group may mirror organizational conflicts that can be discussed at once.

Evaluating Collaborative Relationships

Conflicts can also be uncovered by asking educators to describe the quality of collaborative relationships among them. Below is a question adapted from Lawrence and Lorsch (1967). The same sort of grid might be compared in other ways. For example, the names of individuals might be used if one is concerned about interpersonal relationships within a unit with high interdependence, or the titles of groups both within and outside the target organization might be used to study possible conflicts between the target organization and the larger organization in which it is embedded. Thus relationships might be assessed between a college and its university or between a school and its district office.

We would like to know about relationships that exist between various units in your organization.

Listed below are eight descriptive statements. Each of them might be thought of as describing the *general state of the relationship* between the various units. We would like you to select the statement you believe best describes each of the relationships shown on the grid and to enter the corresponding number in the appropriate square.

We realize you may not be directly involved in all of the possible relationships about which you are being asked. Probably, however, you have impressions about them. We hope, therefore, that you will put in every box a number corresponding to one of the eight statements. Here are the eight kinds of relationships:

1. Sound—a fully sound relationship is achieved
2. Almost full relationship
3. Somewhat better than average relations
4. Average—sound enough to get by even though there are many problems of achieving joint effort
5. Somewhat of a breakdown in relations
6. Almost complete breakdown in relations
7. Couldn't be worse—bad relations—serious problems exist which are not being used
8. Relations are not required

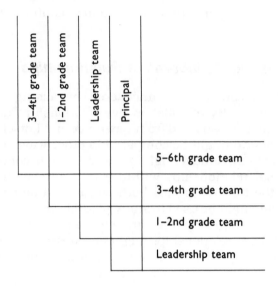

Ascertaining Interdependence

To determine the importance of conflicts to the educational organization, OD facilitators need information on the degree to which conflicting parties must work together to accomplish educational tasks. (Even serious conflicts may not need attention if they arise between relatively autonomous parties.) The following questionnaire adapted from Lawrence and Lorsch (1967) gives examples of items that help to determine the amount of interdependence required by various units in a college.

Questionnaire for Opinions About Others' Interdependence

We are interested in the degree of coordination required between the various units in your college.

1. Make an X by the statement that most nearly describes the extent to which the dean is able to carry out his or her job and make changes in it without having to bring others into the decision.

   The dean is able to choose his or her own job activities:

   ( )   to an extreme extent
   ( )   to a very great extent
   ( )   to a considerable extent
   ( )   to some extent
   ( )   to a small extent

( ) to a very little extent
( ) not at all

How about the English department? It is able to choose its own job activities:

( ) to an extreme extent
( ) to a very great extent, etc.

The Science department? Its members are able to choose their own job activities:

( ) to an extreme extent
( ) to a very great extent, etc.

One might continue to ask this question until all key departments have been covered. Afterwards the questioner might move to other major working groups:

The management team (dean and department heads):

( ) to an extreme extent
( ) to a very great extent, etc.

The counselors:

( ) to an extreme extent
( ) to a very great extent, etc.

2. Make an X by the statement which most nearly describes the extent to which the dean is influenced by:

The work of the English department (or science or math, etc.):

( ) to an extreme extent
( ) to a very great extent, etc.

The work of the management team:

( ) to an extreme extent
( ) to a very great extent, etc.

The work of those in the university administration:

( ) to an extreme extent
( ) to a very great extent, etc.

Actions of external citizens' groups:

( ) to an extreme extent
( ) to a very great extent, etc.

Actions of alumni:

( )   to an extreme extent
( )   to a very great extent, etc.

Actions of external funding agencies:

( )   to an extreme extent
( )   to a very great extent, etc.

Actions of professional associations and groups:

( )   to an extreme extent
( )   to a very great extent, etc.

We'll give an abbreviated version of the rest of the questionnaire to present general ideas about the kinds of questions that are
asked. It is possible in every case to ask similar questions for any
particular group.

3. Make an X by the statement which most nearly describes the extent
   to which the various departments are influenced by:

   The work of the dean:

   ( )   to an extreme extent
   ( )   to a very great extent, etc.

   The work of the management team:

   ( )   to an extreme extent
   ( )   to a very great extent, etc.

4. Make an X by the statement which most nearly describes the extent
   to which the management team is influenced by:

   The work of the dean:

   ( )   to an extreme extent
   ( )   to a very great extent, etc.

   The work of those in the university administration:

   ( )   to an extreme extent
   ( )   to a very great extent, etc.

One can also use an interview schedule to find interdependencies, as follows:

Interview About Interdependence with Others ───────────

[To interviewer: Read aloud words in parentheses only if necessary
for clarity. Do not read aloud words in brackets; they are instructions to
you.]

1. To achieve the school's (or college's) goals, is it necessary for you to work closely with others? [yes, no] [If yes,] which people? [Try to get names.]

————————————————   ————————————————

————————————————   ————————————————

2. Are there any important things that you do in your teaching (things important to you) that you think run counter to the school's (or college's) goals? [yes, no] [If yes,] what things are those?

————————————————   ————————————————

————————————————   ————————————————

3. [If yes on item 2:] In achieving these important things in your teaching, is it necessary for you to work closely with any others? [yes, no] [If yes,] what people work closely with you?

————————————————   ————————————————

————————————————   ————————————————

4. Upon whom, inside or outside your school (or college) (not students), do you depend most to perform your job effectively? [Write names.]

————————————————   ————————————————

————————————————   ————————————————

————————————————   ————————————————

5. [Taking each name separately:] Does [name] work closely with you? [Circle each name above working closely.]

6. Now I want to ask you about the sorts of help you get from these people [taking each name separately:] What is the chief kind of help

that ———————— gives you? ————————————

that ———————— gives you? ————————————

that ———————— gives you? ————————————

that ———————— gives you? ————————————

Finally, the questionnaire below can be used to measure interdependence in the organization.

Questionnaire About Own Interdependence with Others

Please circle the response that best describes your job:

5 = *Very* characteristic of the job
4 = *Quite* characteristic of the job
3 = *Moderately* or *fairly* characteristic of the job
2 = *Not very* characteristic of the job
1 = *Not at all* characteristic of the job
NA = Does not apply or don't know

1. Other people have to come to me for decisions.	5	4	3	2	1	NA
2. On my job I meet pretty often with my boss.	5	4	3	2	1	NA
3. On my job I meet pretty often with my subordinates.	5	4	3	2	1	NA
4. On my job I am expected to help other people.	5	4	3	2	1	NA
5. If I have to get help from someone, it's an indication I can't do the work well.	5	4	3	2	1	NA
6. My job requires a good deal of cooperation from others.	5	4	3	2	1	NA
7. On my job I have to interact with a lot of other people.	5	4	3	2	1	NA
8. My job depends on how well others do their work.	5	4	3	2	1	NA
9. On this job (assignment) you get to know other people really well.	5	4	3	2	1	NA
10. I work almost exclusively with other people.	5	4	3	2	1	NA
11. I am frequently in contact with other people.	5	4	3	2	1	NA
12. My ability to influence others has to be used on this job.	5	4	3	2	1	NA
13. I spend most of my time managing people.	5	4	3	2	1	NA

Assessing the Organizational Climate

In determining an educational organization's readiness to deal with conflict, it is important to know whether the organizational climate supports open confrontation of differences, supports receiving and giving feedback, and generally fosters an atmosphere of two-way interaction and discussion. Several questionnaires are useful for assessing these characteristics. One, entitled "Do's and Don'ts," was presented in chapter 4 and is described in greater detail in Fox et al. (1973). The following questionnaire also helps to evaluate the informal norms or the organizational climate with respect to how they help or hinder faculty members in uncovering and working with conflict:

Organizational Norms ————————————————————

1. Suppose educator X feels hurt and "put down" by something another educator has said to him or her. In X's place, would most of the educators you know in your school (or college) be likely to . . .

... tell the other educator that they felt hurt and put down?

( ) Yes, I think most would.
( ) Maybe about half would.
( ) No, most would not.
( ) I don't know.

2. ... tell their friends that the other educator is hard to get along with?

( ) Yes, I think most would do this.
( ) Maybe about half would do this.
( ) No, most would not.
( ) I don't know.

3. Suppose educator X strongly disagrees with something B says at a faculty meeting. In X's place, would most educators you know in your school (or college) . . .

... seek out B to discuss the disagreement?

( ) Yes, I think most would do this.
( ) Maybe about half would do this.
( ) No, most would not.
( ) I don't know.

4. ... keep it to themselves and say nothing about it?

( ) Yes, I think most would do this.
( ) Maybe about half would do this.
( ) No, most would not.
( ) I don't know.

5. Suppose educator X were present when two others got into a hot argument about how the school (or college) is run. Suppose X tried to help each one understand the view of the other. How would you feel about the behavior of educator X?

( ) I would approve strongly.
( ) I would approve mildly or some.
( ) I wouldn't care one way or the other.

( ) I would disapprove mildly or some.
( ) I would disapprove strongly.

6. Suppose educator X were present when two others got into a hot argument about how the school (or college) is run. Suppose X tried to get them to quiet down and stop arguing. How would you feel about the behavior of educator X?

( ) I would approve strongly.
( ) I would approve mildly or some.
( ) I wouldn't care one way or the other.
( ) I would disapprove mildly or some.
( ) I would disapprove strongly.

7. Suppose you are in a committee meeting with educator X and the other members begin to describe their personal feelings about what goes on in the school (or college). Educator X quickly suggests that the committee get back to the topic and keep the discussion objective and impersonal. How would you feel toward educator X?

( ) I would approve strongly.
( ) I would approve mildly or some.
( ) I wouldn't care one way or the other.
( ) I would disapprove mildly or some.
( ) I would disapprove strongly.

8. Suppose you are in a committee meeting with educator X and the other members begin to describe their personal feelings about what goes on in the school (or college). Educator X listens to them but does not describe his or her own feelings. How would you feel toward educator X?

( ) I would approve strongly.
( ) I would approve mildly or some.
( ) I wouldn't care one way or the other.
( ) I would disapprove mildly or some.
( ) I would disapprove strongly.

Determining the Seriousness of Conflict

The OD facilitator should attempt objectively to measure the seriousness of a dispute by asking participants, for example, to choose the position on the following scale that represents their perceptions of its seriousness:

1. Not at all serious
2. Not serious
3. Average
4. Serious
5. Very serious

A similar scale could be used to ascertain whether the conflict breeds creative or destructive tensions:

1. Makes me work much better
2. Offers encouraging competition
3. Doesn't affect me
4. Prevents me from being as effective as I could be
5. Is destroying our working relationships

Using an interview method, the facilitator can gain a sense of the degree of conflict by asking participants to describe the worst thing that could happen if the conflict were worked on openly. Later, when resolution proposals are being presented, those opposed to particular proposals can be asked to describe their worst fantasies of what would happen if the proposals were undertaken.

Procedures for Managing Conflict

The procedures introduced in this section are designed to serve a variety of purposes related to conflict management. The purposes include uncovering conflicting expectations between individuals and their role sets, managing role conflicts, reducing individual conflicts and other disagreements, bringing subsystem differences into the open, testing the intensity of conflicts and obtaining a quick resolution of those that are easily resolvable, causing perceptions to be verbalized in order to dispel misperceptions and manage real differences, and suggesting structural changes for the effective management of organization-wide conflicts.

Checking Expectations

This procedure is designed to reveal discrepancies between the expectations of individuals and their role set. Focal individuals are asked to write what they expect to be doing in their jobs in one year, five years, and ten years. Members of their role set are asked to write their expectations of what the focal persons should do to make the educational organization more effective. Facilitators may then organize the data and feed them back to the participants to reveal any discrepancies between the two; or they can group the parties together to read their expectations aloud—the focal individuals first and the others second—and then react together to the discrepancies revealed. This procedure is also useful when two parties have differing expectations regarding a third party's role.

Imaging

Because it sets the stage for future problem-solving sessions and provides a good setting for the introduction of communication skills, Imaging can be the introductory activity in a sequence of training events. Depending upon the number of groups engaged, Imaging typically requires a day and a half to two days. If more than two groups are engaged, it is best to work with them sequentially in pairs of groups until all the combinations have had a chance to meet.

In introducing this procedure, the OD facilitator should emphasize that its purpose is to clarify both the character of the relationship between the two groups and the problems that are contributing to their conflict. Participants are grouped into circles of six to eight persons, with both groups represented in each circle unless strong antipathies are evident. The skills of paraphrasing and behavior description are introduced, and all participants practice them with the others in their circle.

When intergroup conflict is particularly strong, the groups should meet separately during this first stage. Each group is instructed in the skills of paraphrasing and behavior description. Also, the facilitator strongly emphasizes the importance of resolutely continuing to use the skills during the confrontation yet to come between groups.

The groups are then given a four-part assignment. Each group, meeting separately, is to develop descriptive images, both favorable and unfavorable, of itself and of the other group. On the basis of observed behaviors, the descriptions are to be recorded on newsprint sheets that will later be displayed for the other group to see when the two groups reconvene. In sum, each group prepares four newsprints. The newsprints can be headed as follows:

- Helpful Things We (the _____ Group) Do, as we see it.
- Unhelpful Things We (the _____ Group) Do, as we see it.
- Helpful Things They (the _____ Group) Do, as we, the _____ group see it.
- Unhelpful Things They (the _____ Group) Do, as we, the _____ group see it.

As participants develop the images, one or two facilitators work with each group, encouraging it to focus on its relationship with the other group and to find behavioral examples that verify their images, reminding members that the newsprint sheets will be shown to the other group later.

When the images are completed, the two groups convene, post their sheets of newsprint, and share their images with the total group.

Members of the two groups sit in rows facing one another. The facilitator who is convening this part of the meeting stands at the end and between the two rows. The first member in one row reads a statement from a newsprint that row wrote about itself, and the first member in the row opposite paraphrases. Then the member in the first row (or the next member in that row, if you wish) reads a statement that row wrote about the other row, and the member directly opposite in the other row paraphrases. As paraphrases are given, the people in the first row accept or reject the paraphrases in the usual fashion.

The reading moves down the row. When the end of the first row is reached, the reading moves to the members of the second row, and the first row paraphrases. If there are many items written on the newsprints and if they arouse emotion, this session can be long and wearing. Participants will often feel the urge to defend themselves against what they take to be accusations, and the OD facilitator will have to act strongly to discipline the communication.

Next the two groups are again divided into several circles of six to eight people to review and practice the skills of checking one's perceptions of another's feelings and describing one's own feelings. Then the two groups are again asked to meet separately to accept the feedback they have been given and to recall examples of their behavior that support the favorable and unfavorable impressions of the other group. Group A takes the sheets Group B has written about it. For each point Group B has written, Group A tries to think of evidence—things its members have done or features of their behavior that would lead Group B to hold the opinions it does. Group A writes the evidence it thinks of on newsprint.

When this task is completed, the groups reconvene to share behavioral evidence with the total group. This time, inner and outer circles are used in the Fishbowl technique and again participants are urged to use communication skills. The group giving evidence sits in the inner circle. Each member in turn reads off one piece of evidence, and any member of the outer group immediately paraphrases it. The reading and paraphrasing continue until all evidence has been read. Then the other group takes the inner circle, and the process is repeated.

The inner circle includes an empty chair for outer-circle participants who want more information from the inner circle. As their admission ticket, they must describe their perception of the present feeling of someone in the inner circle and ask for a check of this perception. Only after their perception has been verified or corrected may they ask their question or make a contribution.

After each group has given the evidence supporting the opposing group's impressions, the two groups can work jointly with the facilitators to specify the issues that require further examination, discussion, or resolution. This work can be followed by a commitment to meet again to work on specific problems. Or representatives may wish to confer with their constituents before making any agreements. Although it is unlikely that Imaging will bring about a complete resolution of existing differences, it does set the stage for future problem-solving sessions, which, if carried out in good faith, can lead to increased trust and the development of a more collaborative relationship.

A Short Version of Imaging

1. Have each group (or person if the target system is a one-to-one relationship) meet separately to consider helpful and unhelpful on-the-job behavior in the other group. At the end of an hour or so, all agreed-upon descriptions of behavior in the other group are to be written on sheets of newsprint. Remind participants to use paraphrasing and behavior description skillfully.

2. Next, bring the two groups together. One group surrounds the other, more or less, in the form of a Fishbowl. Participants sitting in the outer ring read aloud the descriptions they wrote of the inside group. A member of the inner circle paraphrases the description to make sure the others understand it. Participants in the center group are not allowed to defend— their work is to make sure they understand.

3. Reverse the Fishbowl.

4. Next, the groups meet separately again to find evidence that will support the descriptions received. Members should recall examples of their own behavior that could have given the other group its impressions.

5. The two groups come together again and are asked to tell the insiders what they came up with that proves the insiders to be correct. As these descriptions are presented, an OD facilitator attempts to record on newsprint the genotypic issues that seem to be involved (e.g., poor communication, hierarchical

decision making, unclear or restrictive norms, ineffective group process at meetings, covered-over conflict, etc.).

6. Problem-solving groups are formed of members from both role groups, or of both individuals in strife if you are dealing with two people.

Role Negotiation

Assuming that most educators will prefer a fairly negotiated settlement to a state of unresolved conflict, and assuming that bargaining and negotiation are effective methods for helping adversaries change their behaviors, it is possible to help resolve some role conflicts through role negotiation. This technique also can be applied to one-to-one role relationships.

In this procedure each person writes three lists addressed to every other person. In the lists, the writers tell what they would like the others to do more often or better, less often, and about as often as they do now:

To: _____

Here is what I would like you to do more often or better:

_____

_____

_____

Here is what I'd like you to do less often:

_____

_____

_____

Here is what I'd like you to continue doing as you now do:

_____

_____

_____

The "letters" are then given to the addressees. Recipients are allowed to question those who have sent messages but not to argue about the information received. "Communication is controlled in order to prevent escalation of actual or potential conflicts" (Harrison, 1972). It is important at this stage to prevent the occurrence of any hostile, hurtful, or defensive expressions.

When the messages are clearly understood, both sides choose issues to negotiate, with each prepared to offer the other something of equal value in return for a desired behavior change. The OD facilitator can urge that a list of negotiable issues be compiled, asking each side to state its issue priorities and to rank-order the items from most to least important (ordering the agenda is itself a negotiable issue). The items can then be discussed in the order of preference. The negotiation takes the form of an exchange: If A does _____, B will do _____ in return. When all parties are satisfied that they will receive a reasonable return for what they are to give, the negotiation on one issue comes to an end, the agreement is recorded in writing, and another issue is negotiated.

Interpersonal Feedback

Interpersonal feedback is an important process for resolving conflicts that arise from differences in interpersonal style. *Feedback* is information on how close the recipient's behavior is to achieving its desired effect. Feedback must contain information about progress toward a goal chosen by the recipient, and it will not be effective unless the recipient specifically requests it. The following technique is designed to give recipients maximum control over requesting feedback.

As the procedure begins, all participants list on newsprint features of their own behavior that they regard as strengths or weaknesses, or as helpful or unhelpful, in relation to their work situations. The lists are posted on the walls, and participants mill around, first reading and then adding as feedback helpful or unhelpful behavior they have perceived. In this fashion all participants end with a list of their own helpful or unhelpful behavior as others see them. They then take time to read and think about this feedback.

Next the OD facilitator explains that individuals may choose one of three options in deciding how best to use the feedback. First, individuals can choose to consider their feedback personally, to see whether any of the information will be useful to them for future behavioral change. (If everyone chooses this option, there will be no need to discuss others in the group context.) Second, an individual can request clarification from others if the feedback is unclear, insufficiently specific, or inadequately informative about others' perceptions. In this case, participants may ask what actions of theirs led to a given perception or may request a specific example of behavior. In addition, a person may want feedback from one or two others.

When participants choose to ask for clarification, it is their responsibility to initiate the request and to be clear about precisely what information they want and from whom. Third, the participant can contract for future feedback about a particular behavior if that behavior occurs. This is a useful technique for helping people change behavior they are unaware of and for clearing up interpersonal misunderstandings on the spot.

Throughout this procedure, the facilitator's role is to clarify and facilitate communication. When one person asks another for clarification, for example, the facilitator might help the former to state the request clearly and ask the latter to paraphrase it. When the clarification is provided, the recipient might be asked to paraphrase it in turn, to describe specific instances when such behavior occurred, or to check with others to confirm that the behavior in question occurred in these instances.

Facilitators should also be concerned with the group's emotional climate during this procedure. Realizing that people might be sensitive to feedback about unhelpful behaviors, they should intervene to ensure that it is given clearly and constructively, and in a way that ascribes neither good nor bad intentions to the recipient. Facilitators should be aware, too, of each person's level of receptivity to the feedback and should intervene to regulate the process if too much feedback is given at one time.

Third-party Facilitators

The educational organization can make available to its members a list of organizational specialists who are qualified to serve as facilitators to individuals or groups in conflict. When a conflict develops that members believe will be difficult to resolve, or when they deal with a conflict but are unable to resolve their differences, they can call on one of these OD specialists for help.

Such specialists act as objective, neutral facilitators. They use communication skills, probe for concrete clarification, suggest role negotiation or problem solving, lead the parties toward agreements about new actions, and urge the parties to select a follow-up date to check on how things are going.

Structural Changes

Conflicts arising from differentiation require an appropriate organizational structure to be resolved. In particular, those in the upper echelons of the hierarchy should have direct contact with subordinates to work out their disagreements together. In highly differentiated organizations such as colleges and senior high schools that require a complex articulated structure, cadres of OD specialists specially trained to manage conflicts and facilitate group processes can help in achieving integration. See chapter 10 for a description of cadres of organizational specialists.

We have found that too much structural integration within a school or college can create tensions and conflicts, especially when the philosophies and instructional styles of faculty members are highly varied. In such educational organizations, conflict can be managed successfully by allowing for planned pluralism or organizational structures in which there are several teams, houses within colleges or schools, even schools within schools or colleges within colleges. During the past decade we have observed a number of schools and colleges containing several different structures for carrying out effective instructional programs. For schools and colleges seeking the qualities of self-renewal, deliberately decreasing interdependence and increasing differentiation is sometimes the best path to follow.

Microdesigns for Managing Conflict

This section offers possible intervention strategies for resolving problems common to educational organizations. When a conflict arises between two interdependent co-workers, determine whether the difference can be quickly resolved by using the communication skills described in chapter 4, since much of what appears to be interpersonal conflict can be due to miscommunication. If value or strategy differences are uncovered, test the intensity by using questions of the sort we gave earlier in this chapter under "Determining the Seriousness of Conflict." If the conflict cannot be resolved by one person acceding to the stronger feelings of another, try methods of negotiation, bargaining, and compromise. A third-party facilitator can be brought in to clarify the conflicting issues and help the co-workers proceed through the role-negotiation procedure. Finally, the facilitator should get the parties to formally agree to reducing their interdependence, and should see that the new circumstances are tested for a defined period of time. The third-party facilitator should later check to see how the relationship is going. See also the section above on "Tactics for Conflict Management."

The Imaging procedure is most useful for uncovering and working with conflicts between interacting individuals or groups such as one faculty member versus another or one department and another or between the administration and the professional association. In one very effective OD project, we used this procedure to help bring warring parents and educators at an elementary school into collaborative problem solving and decision making. Before a seven-hour meeting at which the parents and educators moved through most of the steps of the Imaging procedure, each group received training in communication skills. After that, each group offered its images of the helpful or unhelpful things that members of the other group were doing in relation to the school program.

At the meeting itself, the group followed six steps: (1) verifying the images, (2) presenting the images, (3) thinking of behavior that gave evidence of the images, (4) presenting the evidence, (5) determining issues for problem solving, and (6) choosing key problems for future work as well as forming groups to solve them. In Step 1, both groups examined lists of cross-group images created by the facilitators, and modified these images until they found the lists acceptable. In Step 2, the two groups were brought together within a highly structured format to show each other their lists. In Step 3, the two groups spent an hour apart; participants described examples of their own behavior that might have contributed to the other group's image of them. In Step 4, the two groups met again to show each other the behaviors they had each listed during Step 3. This step completed a round of generating and validating factual data, and the participants were ready to move on to identifying targets.

In Step 5, the facilitator presented a tentative summary of the kinds of targets parents and staff had been advocating. Then the participants divided into groups to list issues for problem solving, making use of the facilitator's summary and their own ideas as well. Finally, in Step 6, a list of seven major issues for collaborative problem solving was developed at a general meeting. For the next several months, seven problem-solving groups, composed of five to eight parents and one or two staff members, met for five three-hour sessions each. Each group spent time carefully clarifying its problem, considering the forces that prevented its solutions, and locating resources that might be brought to bear. The *S-T-P* problem-solving steps they followed were described in chapter 6.

Chapter Nine

Microdesigning

*Macro*designing refers to the overall structure, sequence of parts, and the large events of OD projects. *Micro*designing refers to particular elements within the structure, specific events in the sequence, and the minute-to-minute steps and activities within any event. Although all those activities are interrelated, microdesigning is more concerned with the *logistical*, *substantive*, and *methodological* details of an OD effort.

By logistical details, we mean the organization of materials and physical facilities before an OD event begins. For some events this might involve merely providing enough newsprint, masking tape, and felt-tip pens. For others it might require preparing materials for an exercise or simulation, writing and practicing lecturettes, arranging tables and chairs, assigning participants to groups, providing a timepiece, bringing refreshments for activity breaks, or preparing to take telephone messages so participants will not be interrupted in their work. Choosing a location in advance is also part of microdesigning. If furnished with tables and adult-sized chairs, a classroom or the school library is suitable. For very large groups, a school's cafeteria or a college's gymnasium can be used if its acoustics permit both small-group and individual work.

The substantive and methodological details of a microdesign include the particular content of a training event, the interview data to be collected for data feedback, the context of an intergroup confrontation, and certain special conditions to which the OD facilitator must attend during process observation and feedback. The nature of the details will depend upon the facilitator's goals for the event and the requirements for producing significant and lasting change. As facilitators turn from macro- to microdesigning, attention to ultimate goals and a perspective on what is needed to achieve them are the only matters that should not be allowed to become "micro."

Distinctions between macrodesigning and microdesigning appear in the facilitator's use of the S-T-P paradigm. In the large, diagnosis assesses S and T, and the macrodesign embodies the P. In the small, the S-T-P guides the specific, concrete, detailed steps of the problem solving within a microdesign.

This chapter focuses on microdesigns—that is, on the details and guidelines—within the four classical macrodesigns: survey-data-feedback, training, confrontation, and process observation and feedback. We assume here that the reader is acquainted with macrodesigning (see chapter 3) and with some of the skills, exercises, and procedures presented in chapters 4 through 8. The descriptions that follow highlight (1) the distinguishing micro features of the classical macrodesigns, (2) some important considerations for microdesigning, (3) guidelines for carrying out OD projects, and (4) examples of effective microdesigns within each macrodesign. The chapter also describes a complex macrodesign with elements drawn from all four classical designs. Finally, we list the most important characteristics of successful microdesigns.

Survey-Data-Feedback Designs

Designs for survey-data-feedback assume that collaborative functioning can be enhanced if organizational members have a common understanding of what is happening in a group, of what they think ought to be happening, and of which proposals will move the group to its goals. A survey-data-feedback design elaborates the first stage of the S-T-P (see chapter 6). Rather than assuming that participants already have sufficient information or that they can quickly get it (as we did in chapter 6) facilitators and steering committees using a data-feedback design begin by collecting data themselves. Facilitators elicit and organize information from individual group members, emphasizing discrepancies between what is actually occurring in the target group, what group members think is occurring, and what members would like to see occurring. The survey-data-feedback does not bear full fruit, however, until the participants go through the steps of problem solving. In the full sequence, the facilitators (1) collect the data, (2) organize the data for feedback, (3) create the behavioral setting in which feedback will occur, (4) present the feedback and help members choose the discrepancies upon which problem solving will subsequently focus, and (5) facilitate the actual problem-solving effort.

Just as experiential learning is important in the work of the OD trainer, inquiry learning is crucial for the facilitator using data feedback. Inquiry learning seems complicated, because it requires that participants learn particular concepts while simultaneously developing their skills for inquiring into other, discrepant data. Basically however, data-feedback strategies are rooted in a simple principle: don't tell or interpret for participants what you can get them to tell or interpret for themselves. You can encourage participants to examine and interpret data by using questions that ask Why? What theory do you have to explain this? or What evidence can you present to back up that assertion?

Guidelines for Survey-Data-Feedback

There is no question about the importance of collecting and feeding back data to educational organizations. Because of the extraordinary skills required, however, it is not surprising that this method poses a major challenge to most OD facilitators. First, the consultants must be clever enough to collect relevant, valid data and to put the information into a form that is at once understandable, engaging, stimulating, and tension producing—but without distorting the facts. Second, the facilitator must raise the mundane facts to a level of significance so that participants regard them as worthy of notice. Third, and perhaps most important, the facilitator must introduce the data into the ongoing ebb and flow of organizational life at opportune times. The more naturally and spontaneously the facilitators can do all that, the more helpful they will be.

Collecting Data. Scientifically trained facilitators may well envy the skill with which the world's great novelists make perceptive observations about human behavior, transform them into word pictures of brilliant clarity and detail, and at the same time create a sense of universality that is larger than the lives of their characters. Amassing relevant data but overcoming the scientific penchant for distant, abstract, and general phenomena are major challenges for OD facilitators, who, like anthropologists, must perceive the relationships between highly particularized organizational events and discern in them the organization's present manner of functioning and some feasible changes.

To assist participants in solving their unique problems while helping them recognize that their problems have, nevertheless, some points of similarity with problems in other organizations, the facilitator should continually collect data, by both formal and informal means, that will yield insights into the operation of the organization. Self-report questionnaires, interview schedules, and observational categories are the primary formal methods for survey feedback. At the same time, however, organizational letters and memos, informal conversations with organization members, and observations made during even the most casual visits yield important information as well. Ideally, facilitators allow their first impressions, however they are obtained, to guide their selection of formal questionnaires, interviews, and observations, the results of which will be embellished by insights gained from more informally collected data.

The following principles help formal data collection and feedback.

1. Interviewing some participants of the target system before collecting data via questionnaires helps to establish rapport and trust between participants and facilitator, which in turn supports more authentic responses by participants on self-report questionnaires.

2. Within an interview or questionnaire, ask general questions before specific ones. For example, ask "To achieve the college's (or school's) goals, is it necessary for you to work closely with others?" before asking "With whom is it necessary for you to work closely?" and ask that before you ask "What is the chief kind of help you get from Dr. Abernathy?" Going from general to specific gets you the respondent's salient, unprepared answer to the general question and helps you form context for the later specific questions. Going in the reverse order often brings back to you only the ideas you put into the respondent's head through your specific questions.

3. Modeling the communication skills of paraphrasing, describing behaviors objectively, checking impressions of the participant's feelings, and describing your own feelings when appropriate during the interview will facilitate the introduction of these skills later.

4. When using questionnaires, collect some data that can easily be quantified and other data that render quotable phrases. Though many educators prefer numbers, many are captivated,

too, by the catchy phrases of their colleagues. Ideally, numbers and phrases will support similar themes.

5. Employ the same open-ended questionnaire item several times throughout a sustained OD project in order to engage participants in discussions about how things are changing within the target system. Force-field analyses of the same phenomena, for example, might be drawn several months in succession (See chapter 6 for details about force-field analysis).

6. Use only a few categories for feedback. Ten are plenty; but it is better to use even fewer and to keep the tallying simple. Participants' arguments over a complicated instrument typically siphon off energy and motivation better used for self-analysis.

7. Carefully sift data before presenting them, give only small amounts at a time, and try to elicit discussion about their meaning for the target system.

8. After observing a formal feedback meeting, interview a few of the participants about which events were usual or unusual to give yourself a more balanced understanding of typical interaction in the group's meetings.

9. Finally, observe the participant group as it discusses the meaning of the data, voice your observations to encourage the group to discuss its interactions during the data feedback, and ask how typical these interactions are.

Making Feedback Significant. In addition to these principles for increasing the validity and usefulness of survey-data-feedback, there are several ways of giving concrete items in the feedback more significance for participants.

First, the feedback activity should be guided by a simple theory that applies to other social settings as well. "Gunny sacking," for example, is likely to apply wherever two or more persons become reasonably intimate, whether in the home or on the job. This term refers to an accumulation of pent-up and hidden frustrations, irritations, and resentments that participants rehearse only to themselves, afraid that exposing them would be emotionally overwhelming. Built-up interpersonal tensions lead to ineffective collaboration, but they can be reduced in open and direct discussions about them, especially if the facilitator points out that interpersonal irritations are inevitable and characteristic of all educational organizations, including the most cohesive faculty. Such a clear, reasonable, simple theory can be used during data feedback to emphasize the importance of exposing even the most trivial on-the-job frustrations and irritations.

Second, the facilitator can sometimes increase the significance of variables being measured by clustering them under a label that is interesting to the participants—for example, "Five Features of Organizational Health" or "Three Facets of Organizational Climate." The educational organization's productivity, its morale, and its use of human resources are other useful summary designations.

Third, particular data sometimes take on higher significance if they are compared with data from similar organizations. Pressures for understanding and action seem to be strongest when members of the target system view themselves as lying somewhere between the worst and best of the comparison systems.

Incorporating Feedback into Macrodesigns. To incorporate data feedback into the natural flow of an OD endeavor, facilitators should have two basic capabilities. First, they should have (both in their mind and in their file) a large and diverse collection of formal questionnaires, interview items, and observation categories. The instruments presented in chapters 4 through 8 are an excellent basic set; also very useful are instruments contained in Fox et al. (1973) and in Schmuck and Schmuck (1992). As the following five examples will show, the second capability consists of remembering that methods and instruments for formal data collection and feedback can and should be woven into each of the primary stages of a macrodesign.

1. *During startup, when data can be used to develop understanding and agreement about the project's objectives.* Doing OD with the staff and a large parent group in an elementary school, we first attended a meeting with a representative group composed of the principal, a few staff members, and representatives of the parent group. Before agreeing that we would help, we met separately with the whole staff and entire parent group to learn what they hoped to gain by working together and by having us work with them. At a second set of separate meetings, we reported a summary of the data collected during the first meetings, and each group discussed differences in how they perceived the purposes of the OD project. We then met again with the small group of representatives and proposed what the consultation could accomplish in light of those differences. The small group concurred with our proposal and agreed to serve as a steering committee to make decisions about the direction of the macrodesign over the next several months.

2. *During the first major OD event, when data previously collected might be fed back as part of the planned design, or might be collected on the spot and fed back immediately.* In an OD project with part of a community college faculty, Schmuck was invited to conduct a two-day event on the topics of improving meetings and clarifying decision making. Before the event, Schmuck interviewed all faculty members in the target system to find out how they defined meeting and decision-making problems. At the beginning of the event, he fed back a summary of those data and asked the participants to decide which specific problems were most important to deal with now. At the end of their meeting, when they had selected four problems for work, Schmuck gave them feedback about how the meeting had gone and how they had decided which problems to attack first. That on-the-spot feedback confirmed the participants' view that the major problems with their meetings and decision making included infrequent use of listening roles in meetings, sloppy procedures for meetings, and a lack of understanding about who was to decide what.

3. *After the first major OD event but before the follow up.* With a junior high school faculty we followed a two-day OD event in August with small-group interviews in September. The interview questions enabled us to find the faculty subsystems with the highest degree of mutual interdependence. Determining from the data that the pupil personnel subsystem (composed of counselors and the school psychologist) and the administrative subsystem (composed of the principal, vice principal, and two grade-level coordinators) were more recognizable than various departmental teams and more in need of coordinating their efforts than either was of coordinating its efforts with any other group, we proposed to continue the OD project by focusing on their interaction and to abandon immediate efforts to work directly with the total faculty. To enable other interested individuals to continue working with us, we proposed establishing a new subsystem that would be trained to serve as process consultants to any other faculty group requesting help. Those proposals were accepted at a brief meeting of the total faculty in October.

4. *In doing process coaching with a target system during one of its regular work sessions.* This is by far the most common setting in which we have used data-feedback designs—so common, in fact, that we have provided many examples of such designs later in this chapter. At this point suffice it to say that we have frequently distributed abbreviated questionnaires

during meetings, quickly tabulated the results, and reported the findings to the total group as a means of focusing debriefing. Our questions have included the following: To what degree have members' ideas been listened to at this meeting? How satisfied are you with your participation so far? Describe one thing that someone has done during the meeting that has been helpful to you. On a scale of one to ten, ranging from very unproductive to very productive, how would you describe the group's work during this meeting? See chapter 5 for more ideas.

5. *After the facilitator has completed work with the organiza-tion.* Most of our longer macrodesigns have concluded with a report that typically recounts the major events of the macro-design, summarizes major findings from data collection during and after the facilitation, and makes recommendations either to the participants or to other OD facilitators who would undertake similar work. When such a report is prepared for an audience other than the participants, we not only shield the identity of the individual participants but sometimes prepare two versions of the report—one for the target group and another for outsiders. Returning to the college or school to answer questions about either or both versions, we have often had to explain how data are displayed and the meaning of any research or statistical jargon used.

Training Designs

Chapter 1 introduced the view that to become self-renewing, an educational organization needs to improve interpersonal skill and subsystem effectiveness. Chapter 3 described a macrosequence to do that: improving communication skills, changing group norms through problem solving, and modifying organizational structure to support the new skills and norms. Chapters 4 through 8 described many skills, exercises, and procedures that could be incorporated into a training design. For example, training designs might make use of paraphrasing, the Five-Square Puzzle, the Planners and Operators, to name a few. Training designs consist of step-by-step plans to produce cognitive, behavioral, and normative change. They are used primarily when the facilitator and steering committee aim to refurbish interpersonal, group, or organizational functioning, and they assume that individuals and groups alike can learn to use new behavior, norms, and structures.

Another assumption in training designs is that individuals can alter their habitual behavior when encouraged to act in new ways by colleagues and when they internalize concepts to symbolize the new behavior. Yet another assumption is that the educational organization, too, can make change long-lasting when new norms and structures match and support the new behavior on the part of individuals. Cognitive change can be stimulated by means of information presented in the form of lecturettes or written handouts. Behavioral and structural change arises from experiential learning.

When presenting information and experiences about what ought to occur in an effective target system, the facilitator should maintain a directive stance, helping group members infer discrepancies between the ideal way of working together and their present way of working together. The facilitator should also design training events in a way that permits the educational organization as a whole to try out new norms and practice new ways of functioning successfully in real organizational life.

Experiential Learning

Since Kurt Lewin's research during the 1930s and early 1940s showed the importance of active group participation in helping people to learn new skills and attitudes, much social-psychological research has strongly supported behavioral tryouts or experiential learning, which is basic to OD training. Experiential learning places the responsibility for learning directly on the participant. Only by actually trying out new role behavior and by reflecting on the generalizations and conclusions that it produces can individuals make cognitive or behavioral changes in their interpersonal competencies. Only by means of active practice and conscientious self-reflection or debriefing do groups develop norms in support of, for example, surveying or creating the roles of convener and recorder. Likewise, new organizational structures, such as steering committees, link-pin arrangements for communicating information, or the regular use of buzz groups and Fishbowls in goal-setting conferences, do not emerge unless the educators involved can experience their utility.

The facilitators's job is to organize the OD training so that learners can experiment with their behavior, try out new skills and ideas, and make their own generalizations. By providing appropriate input, the OD facilitator helps participants summarize and build frameworks that organize what they have learned. In other words, learning occurs as a result of both the experiences themselves and the participants' own conceptualization of the meaning of their experiences. But OD work assumes further that cognitive and behavioral change on the part of individuals is insufficient without normative and system change as well. That is, subsystem and organizational change will not occur unless experiential learning opportunities teach new procedures, give practice in operating with new norms and roles, and allow reflection on organizational structures.

Experiential learning requires above all a deep commitment to the participant's self-determination. Because democratic values and procedures pervade the experiential learning strategy, OD facilitators must clearly communicate their own intentions so that participants are forewarned about the direction of the OD project. OD facilitators can do so by means of the demonstration techniques described in chapter 3. Because the commitment to the participant's self-determination further requires that the facilitator respect the participant's choice of whether to become involved at all, we also encourage clarity and specificity during contract building. We urge, too, that all participants be surveyed to determine whether enough of them will be engaged to justify an OD project at all.

In addition, OD facilitators should not label the participant's interpretation of what has been learned as either inaccurate or wrong. Everybody's interpretation is valid, no matter how bizarre it may seem to others. If, for example, participants perform an exercise for one purpose but offer debriefing comments on other matters, facilitators should show how these apparently disparate matters relate. Denying participants' interpretations not only violates the facilitator's commitment to the participant's self-determination, but also makes it unlikely that important or lasting learning will result.

Finally, it takes more than just skill to facilitate experiential learning successfully. Knowing how to give directions for an activity or exercise, knowing how to ask questions that stimulate thorough debriefing, knowing how to structure a session so that participants get practice in new organizational forms—all these are important, but other qualities and conditions are required as well.

1. OD facilitators should have become familiar with several theories of organizational functioning and with a good deal of the research on them. A theoretical understanding of how colleges and schools work serves to make OD projects more orderly and more easily described to others. Further, it yields sophistication about the methods of facilitation and about probable outcomes of various kinds of interventions.

2. Of the several kinds of support that OD trainers need, one is the participants' readiness to benefit from the training. For

participants to take responsibility for their own learning, they must want to do so, know how, and understand why, at least to some degree. The ready target system exhibits norms in support of collaboration and the acceptance of individual differences. If it does not exhibit those norms, preliminary work to raise readiness may be vital to enable even the most brilliant and skillful trainer to attract the organizational support necessary to an effective OD project.

3. Membership in an OD team or a cohesive steering committee can bring forth a third quality that trainers need: one that might be called will, courage, guts, self-initiating action, or "hanging in." Unfortunately, trainers "burn out" all too often in OD work. Without clearly differentiated and integrated roles, without norms for lending a hand and giving feedback, facilitators will sometimes find it impossible to accomplish their tasks or to maintain a cohesive team with their colleagues. We return to this point when we describe cadres of organizational specialists in the next chapter.

Guidelines for Training

Chapters 4 through 8 offer numerous exercises and games that can be part of a microdesign for OD training. Each exercise is in some way different from the others. For example, the exercise in chapter 5 for increasing participation is intended for use in groups, while Imaging, described in chapter 8, is used when two or more individuals or groups are brought together. At the same time, however, all exercises have some basic similarities. All provide some lesson to be learned by practicing with content chosen by the trainer, and all require particular behavior on the part of the trainer. We set forth below some concepts that OD trainers should keep in mind and some behavior they should exhibit.

Beginning the Activity. Carefully introducing an exercise or activity helps participants to know what is expected of them and how they might interpret the experience. Imaging, for example, might be introduced by explaining that its purpose is to show the character of relationships between two individuals or two groups and the problems that are contributing to conflict. Because paraphrasing and behavior description are important in this exercise, facilitators might review them briefly or encourage a 10-minute practice session in each group. Next the facilitators might present a brief overview of all phases of the exercise, giving greatest attention to the first phase and explaining that detailed instructions for each subsequent phase will be given as they begin. Approximate times for beginning each phase might be posted in some visible place, such as on newsprint or on a blackboard.

If the exercise requires participants to assume different roles, the behaviors expected of each role player and the differences between them should be clarified at the outset. When performing the One-Way, Two-Way Communication Exercise described in chapter 4, for instance, it is important to clarify what senders and receivers can expect of each other and what both can expect of observers. It is often helpful to encourage group members to paraphrase instructions. All questions about the facilitator's expectations should be answered, but those whose answers would reveal the solution to the simulated problem or puzzle should be fielded with the explanation that the purpose of the activity is for participants to discover that for themselves. Inaccurate paraphrasing or repeated questioning need not be annoying if the trainer regards it as evidence that the directions were ambiguous in the first place for those who need most to understand them.

Modeling the expected product of the exercise often helps participants understand what they are supposed to do. In explaining Hand Mirroring, for example, we have sometimes selected partners from among participants to demonstrate what we mean. To introduce the Blind Walk, we have used pairs of facilitators or steering committee members to demonstrate their individual styles for the purpose of stressing that many variations are possible in this exercise. If we expect participants to make lists on newsprint during the activity, we exhibit a possible format or a sample created by another group in a previous workshop.

During the Activity. Many relatively uncomplicated exercises allow participants to complete their work without interruption. For more complicated exercises, such as Imaging or the Planners and Operators Exercise, facilitators may have to remind participants of the rules or explain next steps throughout the event. In such cases, you should do only what you said you would do at the beginning, as interruptions to give an overlooked instruction or unsolicited comment can be annoying and disrupting to the participants' experience. This is not to say that attention to every detail before and during an exercise will prevent a flop, but only to reiterate that careful planning is very important. At the same time, however, overplanned designs that leave no wiggle room for surprises, freak accidents, or unanticipated side trips can produce a highly "tasky" atmosphere that leaves no room for ownership of learning, inventiveness, or "soul."

On one occasion, for example, we planned for the staff of a student services office in a college a half-day of training in giving and receiving personal feedback, using the first half of the morning for a third-party helping exercise. We planned to ask participants after a break to brainstorm the organizational forces that prevented them from using interpersonal feedback on their own. As we watched the exercise unfold, however, it became clear to us that many people resisted either hearing themselves described as "tough battlers" (a term used in the exercise) or telling others that they were regarded as tough battlers. In addition, many participants seemed to want much greater influence than they currently had over decisions about staffing and working with college students. During the break, several participants told us that there was a "vague something" about our design that did not quite meet their needs. After a brief huddle, we initiated the second half of the event by occupying the center of a Fishbowl and replanning the design. We ended by proposing, with the participants' agreement, that the discussion change to the issue of interpersonal influence in the group.

The rest of the half-day included an activity in which staff members rank-ordered themselves (i.e., lined up) according to the amount of influence they believed they had, following which the total group discussed where it believed various individuals should have placed themselves. As in the earlier exercise, we encouraged giving and receiving feedback. It developed that our willingness to redesign the second exercise on the basis of data collected informally during the first part of the morning spared us the necessity of conducting a training event from which group members would have learned little of importance to them.

Following the Activity. At the end of an activity in experiential learning, facilitators should provide concepts that enable participants to connect their generalizations and conclusions with OD theory. This phase begins with debriefing, in which participants share their observations, state their interpretations, or raise issues that the experience brought forth. The facilitator may sit in on debriefing merely to observe or to paraphrase what is being said or, more important, may provide reluctant or unskilled debriefers with leading questions, behavior descriptions, or impression checks to help them get started. Debriefing should not, of course, focus indefinitely on descriptions of feelings or behaviors. Questions like, What patterns did you notice? or What generalizations can be drawn? raise the discussion to a higher level of analysis. Almost always, final debriefing questions should encourage members of a target system to focus on how their performance in the exercise, or their satisfaction with it, are like or unlike what typically occurs at formal meetings in the college or school.

Once participants have discussed their experiences, OD trainers may wish to call attention once again to the main purposes of the exercise, relating it to organizational theory. A lecturette to this end may require no more than restating or summarizing what has already been said during debriefing, or this phase may take the form of a prepared presentation with only occasional reference to participants' comments. Examples of lecturettes we have often used include the Johari Awareness Model from chapter 4, task and maintenance leadership functions from chapter 5, and types of decision making (minority rule, voting, consensus, etc.) from chapter 7.

The nature of the facilitator's comments during the wrap-up will naturally depend upon the target group's success in performing the exercise or activity. To a group that completed the Five-Square Puzzle rapidly, and in which members greatly appreciated one another's helpfulness, the trainer may wish to note only helpful behavior. Providing a wrap-up for a less effective target group, however, may require very different tactics.

For example, we once asked the faculty of an elementary staff to divide into small groups for the purpose of building Tinkertoy models of "who talks to whom on this staff." Only one of three ad hoc groups was able to build a model; another group's model collapsed as members attempted to describe what it meant to them; after five minutes the third group abandoned the effort altogether and returned their Tinkertoys to the container. The debriefing of the total faculty revealed great discouragement and frustration with a task they had thought would be fun. Blaming one another was commonplace during the debriefing.

The lecturette we delivered after those events highlighted the need for sufficient, adequate channels of communication and reassured participants that many groups had far too few such links. We asked them to discuss who talked to whom in the school and who ought to be talking more. The thrust of the lecturette and the shift away from the frustrating Tinkertoy experience freed faculty members to discuss issues especially relevant to their group.

Designing for the Transfer of Learning

Because OD training aims to equip persons and groups with skills that will enable them to function successfully in real life, it is important to design microevents that include simulations or games for transfer of learning. Doing so, however, is complicated by the "cultural island" and "make believe" character of many OD exercises. It is true that a simulation helps to "unfreeze" daily mindsets, patterns, and expectations, and enables participants to stand off and take a fresh look at themselves. That can happen when a department of a college is asked to make decisions about surviving through Lost at Sea or when an administrative team is asked to assemble the Five-Square puzzle. But the very distance from ordinary work that such exercises bring about requires the facilitator to take special pains to ensure the transfer of learning.

When designing for transfer of learning, several guidelines are helpful. First, do not assume that transfer is automatic, but plan for it and discuss it with participants. Second, immediately after debriefing an exercise, allow participants plenty of time to consider its implications for their home setting. Third, include several of what classical learning theorists call "identical elements." For example, a large staff at a retreat might be grouped into its natural teams for an exercise.

For another example, in teaching some faculty members to design questionnaires for assessing the organizational climate in their college, Schmuck divided the group into two teams, each of which was to play both "facilitator" and "participant" to the other. Each team was given diagnostic information about the "client" team, including a description of the group's own history and problems. By designing questionnaires about and for themselves, the participants learned how to select and combine items to assess dimensions of the college climate. After trying out their first efforts and getting feedback from their "participants," the total group worked together to design an instrument actually to be used with others in the college.

Fourth, make sure the participants can learn the cognitive, affective, and motoric aspects of what they are expected to transfer. In helping members of a student council in a high school become better representatives of their homeroom constituencies, for example, we attended to the cognitive aspects of representation by giving a lecturette on what a good representative would and would not do. We encouraged thought about the affective aspects of being a representative in small-group discussions of hopes, fears, and concerns. Motoric aspects were taken into account as each member made to the rest of the group a practice presentation about the meeting that had just occurred; other council members were told to simulate a homeroom, with one student portraying the teacher.

Fifth, after the behavioral tryout, provide opportunities for debriefing in the real situation. The next workday meeting of the target system should begin with a discussion of "how we have worked as a group since our last meeting" and could go on to establish a next set of learning goals.

Themes and Designs for Training

If it is to succeed in teaching something of importance without eliciting cries of "information overload," an OD training design, regardless of its length, should be organized around some core theme. In the interests of clarification, we have often found it helpful during training events to post an agenda listing times, the name of the exercise, and the kinds of concepts the exercise is intended to teach. Note that we do not tell participants *what* they will learn (e.g., "You will learn that transactional communication is superior to one-way communication"); instead, we reveal the topic and purpose of the exercise (for example, "To explore the relative advantages of one-way and transactional communication and to relate the exercises to communication in your educational organization").

One theme could be simply activity or practice. Role-playing certain behavior before it is to be tried in the real setting is one way of using participants' natural urge to be active. A middle-school faculty that is talking about someday holding parent conferences, for example, may be helped to take initiative in doing so by pairing up and demonstrating such a conference to other pairs. Another design might call for enthusiastically praising the first group member who volunteers to try out the role of convener or those who take initiative in giving feedback to the facilitator on how the training session is going.

Achievement themes might include an activity like "strength bombardment," in which each person describes the special strengths that he or she perceives in every other person. Praising or otherwise acknowledging individual achievements that do not directly concern group work—for example, praising faculty members who complete home-improvement projects or who stay on their diets—can satisfy achievement motives by establishing the expectation that work well done will be rewarded. We have also encouraged groups to display activity charts on which to check off each task as it is completed, or to take time during the training event to exhibit their visible products—if only newsprint lists—to demonstrate to even the most product-oriented people that something is in fact being accomplished.

The best way of satisfying the achievement motive, of course, is to help members of a target system find real solutions to real problems. In one of our projects, for example (see Schmuck et al.,

1975), first- and second-grade teachers in a multiunit school had agreed to find a way for each teacher to teach reading to only half a class at a time while the other students engaged in interesting activities as part of a large group. But a lack of space and of additional personnel to run the large groups impeded achievement of this goal; in addition, schedules would have to be changed for the music teacher's visits to first and second graders and for use of the gym by third and fourth graders.

One problem was solved by brainstorming all possible space arrangements and by choosing those requiring the fewest people to move each day (an important criterion for the group). Sufficient personnel were found through soliciting parent-volunteers. Finally, other staff members were contacted so that the necessary schedule rearrangements and tradeoffs could be negotiated. As a result of finding these solutions, the teachers in the first- and second-grade unit were very proud, not only of their new reading program, but of their success in overcoming real problems that had stood in their way.

Opportunities to laugh together while working collaboratively on low-risk tasks can help groups build cohesion that satisfies members' needs for experiencing friendships. Affiliation themes are particularly important in brand-new groups or at the start of temporary systems such as workshops; thus we often include warm-up activities that encourage people to become better acquainted or to get ready to try out new behavior.

The Billy Goat Exercise described in chapter 5 allows people to try out unusual or unreal role behavior before the serious work begins of experimenting with real day-to-day role behavior. We have divided faculties into temporary teams to plan games that all could play together. One team devised a relay for building the tallest sandpile on a nearby beach in four minutes; another made materials so that everyone could play a popular TV game show; still another wanted each group to write a song parody about organizational life in their college. We have also asked groups to make chalk murals on large sheets of butcher paper and have suggested to others physical exercises, such as jumping jack or leapfrog. In short, affiliation themes can and should be fun to design and carry out.

Power motives can sometimes be satisfied by pointing out a group's range of goals and encouraging participants to think about how influential they are or wish to be, either within or beyond that range. On one occasion, for example, we worked with a parent-staff problem-solving group in a middle-school that was distressed about the unattractiveness of their school building and grounds. Complaining specifically about the drabness of the walls and the blacktop on the playground, their first ideas included placing flowers on the secretary's desk and posting colorful exhibits in the display case.

When the facilitators pointed out that they were not talking about painting walls or tearing up blacktop to plant a few trees, group members replied with *yeahbuts*: "*Yeahbut* the district has a policy about who should do the painting," or "*Yeahbut* the steering committee coffers are too empty to pay for landscaping labor or materials." By continually prodding the group to check whether its suggestions matched its complaints, the facilitators encouraged the members to get district policy changed so that they could do the painting if they used regulation-quality paint, to sponsor a workday on which parents and teachers were invited to bring tools and seedlings for playground refurbishment, and in general to expand their area of influence.

Many of the goal-setting activities described in chapter 6 can help members of target systems think about the areas of their environments that they wish to influence. Hand Mirroring and the Influence Line Exercises described in chapter 7 can be used when issues of interpersonal influence are salient. Imaging (chapter 8) and the Planners and Operators Exercise (chapter 7) are particularly useful for colleges and large schools in uncovering issues related to intergroup influence.

Confrontation Designs

Confrontation becomes necessary when a conflict between individuals or groups has become public, at least to the extent that the conflicting parties can both agree with the OD facilitator that conflict is present and that both parties know it is present. Note that both data-feedback and training designs often bring out conflict. Indeed, those designs are more appropriate than confrontation when conflict is hidden in an educational organization. Confrontation should occur after the conflict has become public.

Because confrontation designs are most often used in cases of difference or conflict, they usually focus on building a description of the conflict's dimensions, an analysis of the source of the differences, and a consideration of the consequences of the conflict for both parties. Confrontation designs enable facilitators to help either or both parties express their perceptions of the other's actions, focus on their differences, and engage in problem solving to resolve their differences. The elements of such designs usually include creating a setting for confrontation, uncovering and clarifying differences, and encouraging problem solving that leads to agreements for managing conflict.*

* Confrontation designs are explained in great detail by Walton (1969).

Arranging the Setting

The elements of a confrontation design that can be influenced by OD facilitators include the place in which the confrontation occurs, the amount of time allotted, and the amount of privacy provided. The place, for example, can be selected to give an advantage to one or to neither party. Neither party would feel more comfortable if Imaging were performed by academic department heads in the provost's office or by elementary and secondary school principals in the district's central office. On the other hand, staging an Imaging exercise in the school cafeteria might make outnumbered teachers more receptive to a large and angry parent group, and an instructor-department head confrontation might be appropriately set in the instructor's office to offset the department head's power advantage.

A highly formal setting is particularly useful when two groups greatly different in size are brought together in a confrontation. On one occasion in doing OD with one group of 12 and one of 60, we arranged two sets of chairs facing each other—one set in two rows of six chairs each, the other in 10 rows of six chairs each. By requiring persons in each front row to move to the back and all others to move forward a row every 10 minutes, we equalized participation with each group and minimized the effects of differences in total group size. Participants in the smaller group said that it was less threatening to be "six against six than twelve against sixty."

The amount of time allotted for a confrontation should be sufficient, specified in advance, and as free of interruption as possible, especially if the facilitator is to help the parties understand their differences, consider how much can realistically be accomplished in the time available, or determine the amount of time they wish to set aside to accomplish their goals. In other words, it is important to begin with either a clear time limit or a clear goal, but one or the other should be known in advance.

The facilitator should consider in advance whether adding extra people will help or hinder a confrontation and should be ready to change if the initial choice is not effective. Although extra persons can add relevant insights and be a source of support for either or both of the confronting parties, a private event avoids the risk that another person or third major group might inhibit the confrontation or complicate the procedure with other needs and goals.

Three-way confrontations effect a compromise between maintaining privacy and including others. We once divided the eighty participants in a school district demonstration event into three groups—central office personnel, building administrators, and teachers—to do a modified Imaging exercise in which each described its images of the other groups and examined their images of itself in return. We then asked each to describe problems between the other two, finally combining the three lists to find common problems. In addition to accomplishing the purposes of Imaging, this design gave a considerable number of people some initial experience in acting as third-party facilitators to groups in conflict.

Functions of the Third Party

As third parties to a confrontation, OD facilitators can perform a number of vital functions. First, they can equalize the energy that the parties bring to the confrontation by, for example, giving the more impatient party something constructive to do while working with the more passive or frightened party. In one case we planned a practice session in paraphrasing for one college group with the clear agenda while helping the less prepared college group make up its list of demands.

Second, facilitators can equalize the situational power of the two parties. If one party is more verbal than the other, facilitators can suggest a nonverbal activity or require both parties to put their ideas on paper first. Many of the suggestions for arranging the setting are intended to equalize situational power. When we conducted a role-clarification and negotiation session between some department heads and administrators of a community college, for example, we were aware that the administrators wrote annual performance reviews for the department heads. Therefore, we held the session in a room in which department heads sometimes met together and at a time on a Friday when the department heads had completed their responsibilities with faculty members for the week.

As it turned out, however, our attempt to make the department heads feel more secure about confronting the administrative team had the effect of shifting the power advantage too much the other way. Although the familiar setting gave the department heads confidence, repeated unexpected interruptions by instructors and even students looking for a department head caused the meeting to adjourn after two hours with very little accomplished. An evening meeting, or even a weekend meeting during which students and instructors were otherwise occupied, might have enabled both groups to focus more intently on their work.

Third, the facilitator as third party can help participants achieve similar definitions of issues before suggestions are made for resolving the conflict. The *S-T-P* procedure is useful; posting three sheets of newsprint labeled "Situation," "Targets," and

"Proposals" and asking each group to complete the first two before working on the third can frequently prevent premature decision making about solutions. By encouraging paraphrasing and impression checking, the facilitator can also reduce possible misunderstandings between parties, so that the expression of an unpleasant feeling by one party can be correctly interpreted either as an attempt to perpetuate the conflict or as a gesture of trust.

Fourth, the facilitator can maintain an optimal level of tension so that a sense of urgency produces an exchange without either rigidity or distortion. Encouraging the parties to persevere while the information is fresh or suggesting a break may both be appropriate in the same OD event. During a two-day event in which three groups used the Imaging exercise to uncover and find solutions to common organizational problems, we ended the first day by brainstorming a list of specific problems. Leaving the newsprint on the wall overnight, we encouraged participants to think about major categories that would guide the brainstorming of cross-role groups as they created proposals and action plans to recommend to the larger group.

Fifth, the third party can employ procedures and language that ensure clear communication. Use of the interpersonal communication skills described in chapter 4 is essential. The third party may have to be particularly active with paraphrasing and impression checking to encourage the participants to use those skills; it may also be necessary to ask questions that require each party to describe feelings or to describe the other's behavior.

The sixth function of the third party is often implicitly to convey a positive message. Simply by being present during the course of a confrontation, the OD facilitator can provide emotional support. This implicit way of saying that it is all right to express disagreements and that it is very productive to try do something about them can be extremely important in educational organizations whose norms do not support such behavior.

Encouraging Follow-through

One way of stimulating follow-through on agreements or on further dialogue after the initial confrontation meeting is to make explicit the techniques and principles that are being used as the meeting proceeds. By attempting to teach the means of effective confrontation, the facilitator should help enable the participants to continue or to repeat the confrontation on their own. Such empowerment must be well planned and well carried out, since parties to a conflict will not themselves normally think about how to avoid unproductive interchanges in the future.

Another means of encouraging follow-through is to change the larger organizational context in which the conflicting parties must survive. In order for them to continue their dialogue or carry out their conciliatory plans, it may be necessary to plan ways of informing others in the educational organization about the outcomes of the dialogue or to confront others about their lack of support. If participants have strong feelings about keeping their confrontation confidential, however, the facilitator should respect their wishes. In any case, the follow-up behavior of facilitator and participants alike should be clear before a confrontation meeting is regarded as complete.

A third means of ensuring that a dialogue will continue or action-plan be implemented is simply to "stick around." Just being available may give the parties confidence or remind them of agreements they have made. If the facilitator cannot be present continually, it may be wise to build another third party into the process at the beginning. If participants and the extra third party are willing, all may attend the initial encounter to become more familiar with the procedures of third-party facilitation. Of course, the most obvious way of facilitating follow-through is to ensure that the parties make an appointment to get together again, clarifying both the time and the purpose of the future meeting.

Process Observation and Feedback Designs

Much has been written about process observation and feedback (or more simply, process consultation), because many OD facilitators consider them the heart of any macrodesign. Designs for process consultation focus strongly on the immediate functioning of the target group and reflect the view that effective functioning is inseparable from the group's ability to see its problems while actually working on them. Otherwise uninvolved in the group's task, OD facilitators monitor group processes and individual behaviors and offer behavior descriptions, questions, hypotheses, and speculations about why the group works as it does. Facilitators encourage participants to report their own observations and attempt at the same time to focus attention on both task and social-emotional processes.

In contrast to training designs, process observation and feedback designs emphasize the inductive style of learning. By reflecting on many actions in one meeting or on many phenomena over several meetings, participants increasingly understand how to improve their methods of working together. In contrast to the OD trainer, the process observer maintains a low profile, is generally nondirective, reacts to what is happening rather than to what should be happening, and intervenes to help solve a particular process problem rather than to help beef up group functioning in general.

Foci

The contents of chapters 4 through 8 offer foci for process observation and feedback. As the theme of a particular event, the facilitator may also choose the target group's interpersonal relationships. Calling a group's attention to its cliques and coalitions, for example, leads to a different kind of discussion than do comments about dispersion of influence, struggle between group goals and individual satisfactions, clarity of communication, or phases of problem solving. Interpersonal or group process may also be enriched by focusing on the structure of the educational organization itself, including its integration and differentiation of roles, allocation and limitations of material resources, time-task relationships, intergroup linkages, and the like.

Opportunities

The OD strategy of process observation and feedback makes the target group aware of its own dynamics, usually getting a discussion of process on its agenda. During the initial OD events it may be suggested that 15 minutes be allocated for a process debriefing at the end of a meeting; during the later stages, facilitators can offer their own comments when any group member makes an observation about the group processes. It may take repeated efforts before group members will agree to an agenda item for discussing how they worked together on other agenda items, but getting them to do so is the process observer's goal.

Because of the immediacy of observational feedback, the process observer seldom has the luxury of building a design with as much care as the OD trainer, of analyzing data with as much leisure as the feeder back of data, or of structuring a meeting to the extent that a third-party facilitation must. At the same time, however, any occurrence in a target system provides the process observer an opportunity for feedback, and this quality of "winging it" often gives process consultation an advantage in flexibility. By this means participants come to use their own learnings, to invent creative solutions to their own problems, and to find the zeal and confidence to continue. In addition, process observation and feedback can easily include time for participants to analyze and criticize both the behaviors of the facilitators and the overall nature of the OD project itself.

Timing

Knowing when to comment on a group event and when to let it pass is a crucial skill for a process observer, and its effective exercise depends upon several factors. Consider, for example, the observer who, having the target group's permission to interrupt whenever something "significant" occurs, notices that one member has interrupted another member for the third time in a half-hour.

First, the observer must judge how ready group members are to consider their interpersonal relationships at this point. If a slow meeting has only just begun to accelerate, the time may be wrong for process examination and feedback. If the interrupted member has complained about interruptions in the past, however, the time may be right. In any event, a target group will ignore a facilitator's comments until its members are ready for them, and nothing is gained by premature feedback that is ignored or resisted. If the observed event is genuinely significant, it is likely to recur repeatedly.

If the facilitator offers an observation and is ignored, it is usually not a good idea to repeat and insist. When a target group ignores what the facilitator says, it almost always means that the group is busy with other matters and not ready to consider the facilitator's statement. The facilitator can go with the group's flow and repeat the observation at a more opportune time.

Second, facilitators must take their own feelings into account, recognizing that body language may reveal their feelings to participants and thereby make them the property of the target group. Whether to be transparent or opaque about one's feelings is a matter of personal preference. Some facilitators prefer to initiate a process discussion by saying, "I feel uncomfortable because Joe has interrupted Maria three times so far"; others will prefer to ask Maria how she feels about being interrupted or may ask the total group to discuss who has spoken, who has been interrupted, and who has remained quiet. Although the choice between relative opacity or transparency is largely one of style, facilitators should be aware that the choice is theirs, and they should pay attention to the consequences for the group of speaking out or remaining silent about their own internal feeling states.

Third, process observers may decide either to offer or to withhold feedback in the interests of dependency. The ultimate aim of OD facilitators is to work themselves out of a job by building into the educational organization a capability for monitoring its own processes and eliciting its own feedback. Thus, on one occasion, observers may withhold feedback to allow a group member with skill and understanding to do so instead; on other occasions they may encourage a target group to examine a particular phenomenon in order to sensitize members to that kind of issue, to reinforce something previously taught, or to model appropriate ways of giving feedback. In both cases the rationale centers ultimately on reducing dependency.

In addition to group readiness, the facilitator's preference for personal transparency or opacity, and the need to reduce participants' dependency, a fourth factor in timing is the culture of the target system. Groups that regard the singling out of individuals as taboo, for example, are not likely to appreciate attempts at behavior description or impression checking. Some groups of educators are more apt to discuss their processes when regularly interrupted to do so, while others seem to profit more from widely spaced interventions. Faculty groups that maintain a slow steady pace and whose norms scorn contributions that lack citations of literary, historical, sociological, or biological data will prefer feedback that is rich in abstract concepts and observable behavior, while a quickly paced faculty group may profit more from feedback given in small bits about immediate, tangible events.

Although we have implied throughout this chapter that OD facilitators alone make decisions about microdesigning, we recognize that they prefer a collaboration with participants in the real world of education. For that reason, we end this chapter with a brief section on ways of working with participants as an OD project is designed, implemented, and evaluated.

An Illustrative Case
Bringing a School Faculty and Parents into Effective Interaction

The following case, written by Jane and Richard Arends for an earlier edition of this book, shows how the four classical designs (data feedback, training, confrontation, and process observation and feedback) can be combined. In most actual designs for real schools and colleges the facilitator will indeed combine features of several of the classical designs. In this instance the OD team included members of a research and development team at the University of Oregon and representatives of a school-district cadre of OD specialists like those described in chapter 10. The case nicely illustrates some of the detailed planning that is required for microdesigns of OD projects. It is generic enough to be relevant for both schools and colleges. It also illustrates how microdesigns are fitted into macrodesigns.

The Context of the Microdesign

Thomas Elementary School, one of 32 elementary and 12 secondary schools in its district, had a student population of 250 drawn from a middle- and upper-middle-class neighborhood. Students had traditionally scored well above national norms for achievement, and both the parents and staff had expressed pleasure with the school's academic rigor for a number of years.

In the early seventies, some parents began to echo the concerns of popular educational critics who argued for parent involvement and humanized education. About 90 of these parents at Thomas School attended informal neighborhood meetings in the fall to discuss concerns they had with the school. The outgrowth of these meetings was the formation of a group that called itself the Parents' Advisory Committee. (Now, more than 20 years later, in the middle of the nineties, once again parents are striving to become influential within the elementary school. This time their involvement comes under the label of site-based management.)

That Parents' Advisory Committee of 20-some years ago sent a letter to the Thomas's principal in November that described "widespread concerns with school-to-parent communication, curriculum—especially in the arts— and the quality of the staff and its training." The principal passed the letter on to the 12 teachers in the school, who greeted it with disbelief, resentment, and disappointment. The principal then called upon the coordinator of the district's cadre of OD specialists, asking for "assistance in dealing with the parents' complaints."

The coordinator of the cadre called together a team of OD facilitators from outside the school district to outline a macrodesign that would guide the OD project. The team came up with a macrodesign that had as its overall theme a confrontation between parents and teachers. Within the basic theme were elements of training, data feedback, and process observation and feedback. The macrodesign included the following six stages:

Stage 1: Form and meet with a steering committee comprised of some teachers and a few parents to explain the macrodesign and get approval to proceed.

Stage 2: Provide demonstrations of OD to the faculty and to all interested parents so they understand the goals and procedures of an OD project.

Stage 3: Train parents and faculty members separately in the skills of interpersonal communication and group problem solving and help each group identify top-priority concerns. Collect data on impressions of intergroup climate and influence.

Stage 4: Bring the two groups together and feed back data on climate, concerns, and influence. Help the groups clarify intergroup communication and agree upon top-priority mutual concerns.

Stage 5: Form heterogeneous problem-solving groups of parents and teachers to design proposals to solve important mutual problems. Serve as process facilitators to these groups.

Stage 6: Bring all problem-solving groups together to share their proposals and to make decisions and plans for implementation.

According to the macrodesign, Stage 1 was to begin in November and Stage 6 was to be completed by June of the same academic year.

Features of the Microdesign

The six stages of the macrodesign did get carried out as scheduled. The following sections describe the microdesign elements that made that possible. This section concludes with a description of the project's outcomes and some ideas of things to consider when tailoring OD designs like this one for other educational organizations.

Meeting with the Steering Committee

On December 14, the facilitators met with the newly formed Steering Committee, a group composed of three teachers, the principal, and seven parents. The principal had identified these people as representative of the school and community and as both influential and energetic in their respective groups. Giving special attention to the parents' impressions of the needs of the school and the OD facilitators' definition of their role, the two-hour meeting began with a presentation and discussion of the macrodesign. Steering Committee members were surveyed and agreed that the facilitators should proceed with the demonstration events. Parents on the committee agreed to extend invitations to other parents, and the principal agreed to have the facilitators attend the next faculty meeting. All Steering Committee members agreed to meet about once a month throughout the school year to discuss progress in the OD effort and to give feedback to the facilitators.

Demonstration Events for the Faculty and Interested Parents

Two members of the OD team met with the whole faculty the following week. After informing the faculty of decisions made by the Steering Committee, the principal introduced the facilitators. The demonstration meeting had two main purposes: to explain OD and the facilitators' roles and to elicit the faculty's commitment to proceed. A slide-tape presentation on OD, a lecturette on OD facilitators as multipartisan helping agents,* and a question-and-answer session served the first purpose. A total-group discussion that concluded with a survey of individuals served the second.

The survey revealed that faculty members were generally hesitant and unwilling to become involved because they were concerned about the time it would take for OD training, whether the parents already involved were "truly representative of all parents," and whether they "as professionals" should listen and respond to parents. In addition, the facilitators became aware of the fact that teachers did not trust each other to take a united stand should parents' demands be difficult to implement. The facilitators paraphrased these concerns and did not attempt to influence the faculty, but the principal did not take the same stance; he pressed the faculty to approve of the project, saying, "We really have no other choice." A second survey showed that all teachers were willing to proceed but were skeptical about possible outcomes.

The first OD demonstration event for parents occurred at an evening meeting attended by 51 parents. The PTA president and the principal opened the meeting with a short business session and introduced the facilitators. After the facilitators gave a brief history of the OD project to date, described the interests and roles of the facilitators, presented a slide-tape show explaining OD, and outlined the macrodesign, parents formed small groups with members of the OD team for question-and-answer sessions. A summary of each group's discussion was reported to the total group after about half an hour.

The summaries revealed skepticism on the part of parents as to the faculty's commitment and ways to involve other parents. Recognizing a need to keep other parents informed and at the same time to avoid spending a lot of time continually bringing newcomers on board, the parents agreed that all parents should be informed of a second demonstration and that attendance at this or the next meeting be considered a prerequisite for being on the mailing list for future participation in the project. Parents on the Steering Committee ended the meeting by agreeing to send out invitations to all parents for the next meeting.

The second demonstration for about 50 parents began with a review of what had happened at the first meeting to bring the fifteen newcomers up to date. A lecturette on *S-T-P* problem solving was followed by work in pairs to describe frustrating situations and valued targets. After 20 minutes with two different partners, parents formed eight groups to list common situations and targets on newsprint. The facilitators urged paraphrasing and describing situations and targets in behavioral terms. The evening concluded as some parents volunteered to host OD training seminars for parents in their homes and all were given a questionnaire intended to elicit their impressions of who had influence in the school as well as handouts

---

* Multipartisan helping agents was a term coined by the OD facilitators for this project to emphasize that (1) they would not side with parents to attack the faculty any more than they would side with the faculty to ignore parents' demands, and (2) they were group process and organizational facilitators who would not tell teachers how they ought to teach or parents what to do in the school.

on *S-T-P* problem solving, communication skills, and an article on defensive communication (Gibb, 1961).

Training for Faculty and Parents

OD training for the faculty occurred at a two-day workshop in January when teachers had released time to prepare semester reports. The session began as communication skills were introduced through an exercise that required three groups of teachers to build Tinkertoy models depicting how staff members typically communicated with each other. After the staff assembled the models without speaking, they used communication skills to describe what the models represented. During the second half of the first day, staff members completed the Group Expectation Survey and were interviewed individually by the facilitators. The second day began with feedback of data collected and a lecturette on *S-T-P* problem solving. The faculty formed small groups to define more precisely problems related to faculty and parent relationships. The facilitators urged the faculty to postpone brainstorming solutions until the gap between situation and targets was clear. The day concluded with practice in small-group problem solving using the Five-Square puzzle exercise and with faculty members listing their individual resources on large sheets of newsprint.

In early February, 11 OD seminars for groups of four to six parents each were hosted in the homes of volunteer parents. Warm-up exercises and introductions were followed by reviews of communication skills. Parents then described experiences they had had at the school so all could practice the skills. After the *S-T-P* problem-solving model was reviewed, parents summarized their experiences as a definition of the situation and listed their individual goals. By paraphrasing and surveying, the interest others had in their individual goals was ascertained.

There was more OD training for faculty members as they met later in the month for two hours after school in three small groups. These meetings included time for additional practice in communication skills and *S-T-P* problem solving as well as time to administer the questionnaire on impressions of influence that had been given to parents.

Pinpointing Mutual Problems

In March a seven-hour meeting was held at the school in the afternoon and evening for parents and the faculty.* The session began with feedback of data collected through the questionnaire on influence. The facilitators emphasized that both groups saw the other as more influential than either saw itself and explained that this protocol is usually indicative of a history of poor communication. One OD trainer was assigned to meet latecomers at the door to catch them up; approximately 45 parents and 13 faculty members were present when the session began and only five or six parents came late.

---

* Students were sent home at noon so teachers and parents could be ready at 3:00. Parents had arranged for their own babysitters at home and the Steering Committee had called everyone to bring something for a potluck supper.

The Imaging exercise (compare the section "Imaging" in chapter 8) proceeded through the following six steps:

Step 1: Parents and faculty went to separate rooms to verify lists of helpful and unhelpful behaviors they thought the other group exhibited. These lists had been prepared in advance by the facilitators as their summaries of the comments repeatedly voiced by parents and teachers in earlier sessions. Each group modified its list until they found it acceptable.

Step 2: The two groups came back to the large multipurpose room and sat in chairs that had been arranged so that six parents at the front of the parent group would face six faculty members at the front of their group. The groups took turns presenting items from their lists and a member of the receiving group was asked to paraphrase as each item was read. The facilitators did not allow debate, explanation, or justification of any item. Twice during the session, participants played "musical chairs" so new people got the front-row seats where they were allowed to talk. This seating arrangement was designed to equalize participation between two groups that were very unequal in size.

Step 3: The two groups again went to separate rooms for an hour to discuss examples of their own behavior that might have contributed to the other group's image of them. The facilitators urged them to avoid defensiveness and to concentrate on why they had been viewed as unhelpful rather than to insist that they hadn't wanted to be.

Step 4: The parent group and the faculty each picked six people to represent them in reporting the discussions that had occurred in step 3. The 12 representatives sat in a Fishbowl for this discussion. Parents and faculty members took turns reporting items from their lists and a paraphrase was allowed and encouraged after each item.

Step 5: The facilitators reported five target areas they had summarized from all earlier faculty and parent comments. Participants then divided into four groups in the four corners of the room: parents and teachers of first and second graders, parents and teachers of third and fourth graders, parents and teachers of fifth and sixth graders, and the principal and auxiliary staff with the parents from the Steering Committee. Each group listed five to 10 major issues they wished to see become topics for collaborative problem solving. Each problem was stated in the form, "There is a lack of," and was written on newsprint.

Step 6: Members of the OD consultant team, in a Fishbowl, summarized the issues raised in the four groups. One consultant acted as convener until the 40 specific problem statements were combined into a list of seven. The seven were listed on separate sheets of newsprint and parents and faculty members signed up to work on the one that interested them most. The Steering Committee members spread themselves among the seven groups and agreed to serve as links across the groups over the next two months.

Joint Problem-solving Groups

During March and April, the seven problem-solving groups, composed of five to eight parents and one or two faculty members, met five times in homes of parents. Each group chose its own convener and recorder and had the same facilitator each time. During the course of the two months, each group made and worked with its own procedural agreements, carefully defined its problem, considered facilitating and restraining forces operating on the problem and its ability to find solutions, and located resources that might be brought to bear to solve the problem. One group prepared a questionnaire that its members administered to other parents and students, while other groups contacted people in other schools and the district's central office whom they had selected as appropriate technical consultants. Each group brainstormed possible solutions to its problem and planned what would be required in terms of financial, physical, and human resources if its proposal gained acceptance from others.

Total Community Sharing

At the last regularly scheduled PTA meeting of the year—in May— each group presented its proposal. The meeting was planned and convened by members of the Steering Committee so that proposals could be considered in some logical sequence. The proposal to restructure the PTA and to write a new constitution was quickly adopted and followed by election of PTA officers. Proposals to establish a parent volunteer program, make improvements to the building and grounds, and to start an after-school program for students, an artist-in-residence program, a handbook for students and parents, a regular newsletter, and a party for welcoming new and foreign families were then presented and adopted. Parents and staff members then signed up for committees that would oversee implementation of the proposals. The evening ended as the new PTA president convened a Fishbowl meeting of PTA officers to review summer activities.

Outcomes of the OD Project

Three kinds of outcomes of the OD project were documented by the OD team with methods that included follow-up interviews with 40 participants. The first set of outcomes had to do with implementation of proposals designed by the parent-staff problem-solving groups. Within a year, there existed in the school (1) a new parent organization that included parents in the process of making decisions about curriculum and staffing, (2) new forms of written communication from school to home, (3) improvements to the building and grounds, (4) parties for welcoming new and foreign families to the community and school, (5) many parent volunteers in classrooms and the library, and (6) an artist-in-residence program. Parents and teachers evaluated these innovations favorably.

A second set of outcomes had to do with improvements in the climate of interaction between staff and parents and in the climate of interactions among staff members. After the OD project, parents reported that they had better impressions of the school, could now get the information they wanted, and thought their input was welcomed by the teachers. When asked about changes they saw in the school, more than two-thirds of the parents noted that the emotional atmosphere was very different.

Faculty members reported being much more comfortable about having parents in the school, inquiring about the school's activities, and being effective in the PTA. Teachers did not totally endorse parental participation in other than subordinate roles as volunteer aides, but they did appreciate the efforts of some parents to make the library more accessible to students. In addition, two-thirds of the faculty reported a year later that working conditions and relationships within the school had improved. They were proud of their first steps at team planning and thought that their individual resources had been put to better use since they had started communicating openly with each other.

The third set of outcomes concerned changes in perceptions of own and others' influence. Parents perceived an increase in their own influence after the OD activities and did so without attributing less influence to the faculty. Faculty members, by contrast, didn't think they had gained or lost influence, but attributed more influence to parents. To both parents and the faculty, the PTA in its new structure was the vehicle through which the total amount of influence available to be shared had been increased.

Considerations for Tailoring

What happened at Thomas School cannot be expected to occur without alteration in other educational settings. In this case, the engaged parents were motivated and competent to confront and collaborate with the faculty even though they had been frustrated in their prior efforts to do so. In addition, the faculty came to realize—quite early in the OD effort—that confrontation and collaboration were inevitable and not as painful as they had expected them to be. Important questions remain, however.

1. What might happen with—let us say—a college faculty that, compared with that at Thomas School, has even stronger norms in support of autonomy, lower experience in interpersonal and problem-solving skills, a greater inability to recognize the implications of its posture, and more unwillingness to regard non-academic groups, such as lay boards, as legitimate?

2. What happens when groups similar to parents or adult college students

are not motivated or competent to make their wishes known, to suggest proposals to remedy important problems, or to pitch in and help implement new programs?

3. What happens when it is impossible to form an OD team of university personnel who have credibility and legitimacy with the college faculty?

4. Or even at other elementary schools, similar to Thomas, what happens logistically when a higher percentage of parents than at Thomas are employed in nine-to-five jobs, are spread over a much larger community, don't have phones, or don't volunteer their homes as meeting places?

5. What happens if the target school, instead of being one of the "best" in the district, is known to be one of the "worst," so that parents and faculty members feel discouraged at the outset and have to deal with basic needs before being creative about new, add-on programs?

6. What happens when there is more diversity within the community, so that finding a representative group of parents, such as at a senior high school, is a difficult chore rather than a fairly easy task?

Some of the facilitators who carried out this OD project began almost immediately to seek answers to these questions. And some of the OD team members found answers after conducting another project during the succeeding academic year. In this later project—another pilot effort in the sense that it was the OD team's first in an inner-city school serving seventh- and eighth-grade students—the outcomes sought were not achieved. Efforts to establish a Steering Committee to oversee the project were abandoned midway through the year, and efforts to train a group of teachers as group facilitators were to no avail in the sense that the group disbanded as soon as the OD team left. Nonetheless, the OD team learned several lessons in this second project which answered questions left over from the Thomas School project. These lessons were derived from comparisons of the project with the "ideal" described in theory and research on OD in schools. Seven major lessons were these:

1. Involve the total faculty in decisions to conduct a demonstration event about the OD process. Don't take the word of a few—even if they are administrators—that the faculty is ready to be helped.

2. Retain initiative for contacting parents until the faculty or other parents volunteer to take over this function. Don't leave to chance the notification of parents about meetings.

3. Provide training to volunteer subsystems or to ad hoc groups of individual volunteers. To be helpful to some people about some things, you need not wait until the whole faculty is ready.

4. Establish new subsystems only when a "critical mass" of the faculty agrees and funding to continue OD training is assured. Don't start to build a new group until others are ready to adjust to its presence and you are ready to stick around and help it become a more permanent structure.

5. Be extremely clear about OD project goals by portraying the ideally

functioning educational organization in a variety of ways. Find out which portrayal best matches the priorities and sequences of priorities that faculty members have in mind.

6. Include a variety of people on the intervention team—e.g., local people as well as outsiders, curriculum specialists as well as process consultants. Keep the differentiation among roles clear and include enough variety to make differentiation visible to participants.

7. Provide OD training that allows faculty members to "distance" themselves from traumas of the on-the-job world before encouraging application of learning. Teachers, in particular, invest so much energy in "keeping school" that they find it hard to think of change when they are in the midst of things, as they seemingly always have been.

To be sure, not all of the questions left over after the Thomas School project were answered by this second project in the junior high. The facilitators from Thomas School still look forward to the day when they and other OD facilitators will have a swifter and surer technology to bring about parent (or student) involvement in schools. In the meantime, they keep the questions in mind, keep reading new research, and are careful never to assume that what worked at Thomas School or any place else will work in the same way or with the same outcomes in yet another school.

An Exercise on Conflict:
Managing Conflict at Midurban Senior High School

We offer the following case as an exercise useful in giving training to neophyte OD facilitators. While particular aspects of the case are fictitious, the high school's organizational problems are based on fact. The sequence of this activity enables the trainee to (1) become acquainted with the fictitious school through the description that follows; (2) draw up an OD memorandum or arrangement for the project; (3) think up questions or observations for additional data collection; (4) simulate answers to the questions and observations; and (5) create the macrodesign (which could include alternative streams of activities at different points during the year), and (6) create examples of the microaspects of the macrodesign.

Background Information

Midurban Senior High School is a large urban high school of approximately 2,500 students located in a city of 300,000. The school has a professional staff of 56 full-time teachers, 18 teacher's aides, five counselors, a half-time school psychologist, a school nurse, and, during most semesters, at least 10 student teachers.

The student population of the school is well integrated and comes from a variety of ethnic and socioeconomic groups. Though it has no problems of desegregation or other racial sorts of tension, the school does have problems and tension. It is not highly regarded in the community. The absentee rate is the highest in the city, the achievement scores (reading and math) are the lowest, and occasionally there are acts of vandalism.

Staff morale was so low at the start of the year that the teachers from Midurban organized the other high school teachers in the school district for a strike. Most neutral observers of the strike seemed to think that the strike had no real issues and was only a statement of frustration. The aftermath of the strike left Midurban High polarized; some staff had supported the strike, but others had not.

There are now only three months left in a long and frustrating year. The principal of Midurban does not want to go through another year like this one, and decides that something must be done to improve the school's internal environment and its image in the community.

The principal decides that since teachers cannot be required to do anything differently (the fear is that they may strike again), perhaps a reorganization of the counseling services will help. After all, if better counseling were available, students would not skip school, and if they would stay in the classroom their achievement scores would increase.

The principal sends word to the counselors that he wants them to "shape up" and do something about the student problems. According to the principal, they have failed to address the needs of the Midurban student population. Also, the principal says teachers become very frustrated because they interact with about 200 kids a day and counselors sit in their nice offices and see about 15 to 20 a day individually. If counselors dealt more with the problems of the school, then maybe the teachers would be happier.

The counselors feel irritation at the principal's focus on them. In an effort to respond to the principal's demands, the five counselors decide to request feedback about their work from the teachers at a faculty meeting. At the meeting, not much is said when the counselors ask for feedback. Only two faculty members speak, and both of them say they think the counselors are doing all right. The principal is chagrined; he wonders why the teachers don't complain when they have the chance. Later that week, the principal creates a committee of two counselors and four teachers to discuss ways of improving the working relationships between the counselors and the teachers. The committee decides to collect data from the faculty. The committee collects data from the five counselors and from about three-fourths of the staff. The collected data are as follows.

The Data

Question 1. Imagine that you were working in your ideal school—the school you might sometimes dream about. What would the working relationships between counselors and teachers be like? (Please be specific.) The answers were as follows:

COUNSELORS' REPORT

1. Everyone would work together, not apart.
2. Counselors would consult with teachers about their needs.
3. Teachers would come to counselors when they have problems.
4. Counselors would help in the classroom sometimes.
5. Counselors and teachers would work together with problem students.

TEACHERS' REPORT

1. Counselors would know what teachers are teaching.
2. Counselors would work on emotional problems of the students.
3. Counselors would not make many mistakes in placing the students in classes.
4. Counselors would not let problem students off easy.
5. Everyone would work together instead of apart.

Question 2. What do counselors do now at Midurban High that is helpful for teachers?

COUNSELORS' REPORT

1. Try to relieve the stresses between students and teachers.
2. Tell students that they must do what teachers expect of them, not because teachers are always right, but because they have to do it to survive. That's how the system works.
3. Encourage teachers to send students to the counselors right away if they have any problems.
4. Contact parents for them, though I'd much rather the teacher did it.
5. Prepare students for the SAT.
6. Stay out of their way. Most teachers I've had dealings with seem okay, but I don't deal with that many. I don't want to be where I'm not wanted.

TEACHERS' REPORT

1. Work closely with me in programming kids.
2. Sometimes help me program a student.
3. Place kids in the right class.
4. Change class assignments to suit students' needs.
5. Send students for placement tests.
6. Refer gifted kids to me.
7. Come to confer with me when in doubt.
8. Reduce troubles students bring with them from home.
9. Talk with parents.
10. Reinforce standards—being uniform in their expectations.
11. I get information from some counselors sometimes, and that's helpful. On the whole, though, we don't work that closely.
12. Just knowing that I have their support is help enough.

13. Basically, I've had good vibes with the counselors; I get back good reports from the students.

14. Counselors are flexible; deal with teachers quite well. I have no negative feelings about counselors. They have never gotten in my way; they almost always do as I wish.

15. They are not usually obstructive; they help when they possibly can.

16. I don't think any of them get in my way; they are very helpful.

17. I don't think we ever get in each other's way.

Question 3. What do counselors do that gets in the way of the teachers?

COUNSELORS' REPORT

1. Insist on assigning students to their classes.

2. Pay little attention when I disagree about handling a student.

3. They feel sometimes we are responsible for over-crowding their classes.

4. They don't feel we work as hard as they do and sometimes that gets in the way when asking a favor of them.

TEACHERS' REPORT

1. Not knowing the required sequences of courses.

2. They do not know about prerequisites.

3. They don't make sure students have satisfied the prerequisites for a course.

4. Students get programmed into the wrong class. Sometimes counselors stereotype kids.

5. Misprogram students.

6. They overload my classes.

7. Change students' class assign-ments too late in the grading period.

8. Don't confer enough with me when programming.

9. They don't have enough career information.

10. They don't know how my classes are run.

11. They don't take care of the really bad kids.

12. They don't have uniform standards among themselves or with the faculty.

13. They have different procedures among themselves; they need a program that all teachers and students understand. Students should know when their counselors will be available.

Question 4. What do teachers do that is helpful for counselors?

COUNSELORS' REPORT

1. Generally, I've found teachers very cooperative; they don't seem to be on any power trip.

2. Some teachers are helpful.

3. Most teachers are cooperative.

TEACHERS' REPORT

1. Counseling students myself about course sequences.

2. Help with programming in my spare time.

3. Keep our own file on students' progress.

4. Work with students.

5. Take care of different needs of students.

6. Help students define their goals.

7. Help counselors with the testing program.

8. Give placement tests on short notice.

9. Join conferences with parents.

10. Visit families.

11. Handle an overcrowded classroom without complaining.

12. Not hassling them because they did not participate in the strike.

13. Stay alert to problems and let counselors know about them.

14. Invite them to sit in on my classes.

15. Are amenable to changes.

Question 5. What do teachers do that gets in the way of the counselors?

COUNSELORS' REPORT

1. Play games with me and with students. I send a student to join a class, and he comes back and tells me the class is full. Now what am I supposed to do?

2. Teachers are not helpful at all. Teachers will tell me it's too late for a student to get into a class. Sometimes I think they say so only to keep their roll books clean.

3. Shift rooms of classes too soon in the semester.

4. I wouldn't mind visiting a few classrooms; the problem would be with the teachers. They say they want us to help, but they really don't.

5. All any of these teachers seem to "know" about my job is that I'm sitting here with this fat job doing nothing. We get a lot of lip from people about all the stuff we should be doing.

6. When some teachers are not as competent as they ought to be, I hear that from students.

7. Some students tell me that they are not learning anything in a class. If teachers would teach well, there would probably be no problem about attendance.

8. Some teachers, especially the ones behind the strike, don't seem to care about teaching. I hate to put kids in their classes.

9. When we try to add a student to a class.

TEACHERS' REPORT

1. Insist that a class of mine is closed.

2. Changing students' classes late in the year and forgetting to tell the counselor.

3. Not getting grades in on time, leaving blanks in the forms, etc. But I think we have a pretty good record.

4. Not conferring with counselors often enough.

5. Usually what upsets them is not so much talking about one counselor, but talking about something that's wrong with the whole department; that gets in their way.

6. The school gets in their way because they are not directly in charge of registration, so they don't have the chance to meet all the students or even place them. They need to be more a part of the school.

10. Turn away students I send
    to join their classes.

Where the OD Facilitator Comes In

The committee is pleased with the openness and honesty of the counselors and teachers but is confused about what to do with the data. The committee wants help. The principal discovers that money for OD facilitators is available at the district office and is able to procure enough to hire one for 12 days during the next calendar year. The facilitator confers with the principal and the committee in April. Now the facilitator has the above data, the possibility of collecting additional data, and the requirement that he or she come up with a macrodesign by the middle of May. The OD project can last from this May to the next, and the staff can be available as a total group for OD (if desired) for three days in August, one day in October, and one day in March.

You, as OD facilitator, should take it from here. Create a strategy and design for proceeding. (1) Draw up a memorandum of agreement, (2) think up methods for additional data collection, (3) simulate answers, (4) create the macrodesign, and (5) create the microaspects of your macrodesign.

Features of Successful Microdesigns

OD facilitators should keep at least four principles in mind as they create their microdesigns: they should (1) get some participants to join in the microdesigning, (2) seek ways to increase all participants' motivation, (3) remain aware of the feelings of all participants and of how the ebbs and flows of change fit in their world, and (4) shift back and forth between the macrodesign and the microaspects to raise participants' consciousness about the nature of the planned OD.

Involving Some Participants in Microdesigning

To the extent that diagnostic data are collected and used, participants can be said to influence the designing process before an OD project event actually begins. But there are several more direct ways in which the facilitator can allow participants to influence the event in its early stages. Prior interviews that assess the target system's organizational, group-process, and one-to-one problems can also provide information about what the facilitator should or should not do during the OD project. During interviews, for example, we have asked participants whether they prefer to work all together or in small groups most of the time. In questionnaires we have asked for advice about when and where workshops and retreats should be held. We have also begun a few OD training sessions by proposing several different designs and asking participants which would best suit their needs.

Participants can also greatly influence microdesigning in the course of an OD project. For example, they might refuse to record all their ideas on newsprint but choose instead to record only each person's best idea. They may choose to interrupt the facilitator during a feedback presentation instead of waiting until the end or, as in one of our more devastating experiences, reject the facilitators' proposals in favor of using the time in their own way. OD facilitators who pay attention to the participants' behavior during an OD event can collect a great deal of diagnostic data for later use; indeed, all the factors related to the timing of process observation and feedback have application in this regard.

The importance of bringing participants into the designing process in the interests of increasing a faculty's capacity for self-renewal has been abundantly demonstrated by our own experience in both colleges and schools and by much research as well. In a study supported by the Rand Corporation, Berman and McLaughlin (1975) coined the phrase *mutual adaptation* to describe the modification of a project to fit a local academic situation while the local educational organization is changing in the direction of the goals of the originators of the project. They found, in addition, that this mutual adaptation is associated with a number of other conditions.

First, projects that participants view from the beginning as responsive to their needs and as a means of solving their problems have much more staying power than those that begin merely because money or other resources are available. Second, it is important that the project be supported from the beginning by target system members whom others regard as having a thorough knowledge of particular local conditions; in other words, most participants believe that the suitability of a project depends primarily upon local conditions, and they are right. Third, and most important regarding OD designing, mutual adaptation is accompanied by planning that establishes channels of communication between the OD facilitators and participants, sets forth initial goals and objectives with the assistance of representatives of the participant group, and is maintained continually throughout the project.

Fourth, it is important that practical, how-to-do-it, here-and-now topics have precedence over theoretical or inspirational content during the project. Both design and facilitator are likely to be judged unfavorably if they do not meet the participants' immediate needs. Fifth, projects are most often successful when they include what

Berman and McLaughlin call "local development of materials." That is, the quality of the finished product, whether it is to be an understanding of what is going on in the educational organization or a document outlining group agreements, is much less important than is the chance to participate in developing the product. Sixth, mutually adaptive planning and mutually adaptive interventions are likely to occur only when a critical mass of individual faculty members are participants.

Finally, we believe that by asking participants to collaborate in the designing process and to criticize the design before it is executed, while it is in progress, and after it is completed, OD facilitators can get important information that will enable them to do a better job next time. We believe that participants will take the risks involved in criticizing and evaluating if time is allowed for the purpose and if the facilitators are receptive to their feedback. One can begin collaborative planning by asking participants what they think can be done to meet a list of OD goals and by referring to those goals during debriefing. The facilitator can also ask to what degree each OD goal has, in fact, been met. Another method of ensuring that participants give feedback is for facilitators to engage participants in designing a postmeeting reaction questionnaire before an OD event begins and to use the questionnaire when the session is ended.

Motivating All Participants

OD designs cannot be sustained without the active involvement of the participants. The facilitator must keep in mind the motives discussed in chapter 1: achievement, affiliation, and power. Microdesigns should be created to raise the participants' feelings of competence and mastery, friendship and social support, and influence and power. OD facilitators can arrange to enhance those motives by selecting the appropriate exercise or procedure and then, after performing the activity, by leading the debriefing in the direction of the three motives.

In selecting an OD activity or in leading a debriefing after the activity, the OD facilitator should strive to increase participants' engagement and involvement while reducing their reticence and defensiveness. When executing survey-data-feedback, for example, the facilitator can ask participants for examples of particular issues that the data pointed up. By asking for examples, the facilitator acknowledges the participants' closeness to their own system and the fact that they are involved in it and understand it better than the facilitator. At the same time, the facilitator strives to communicate that issues like those under discussion arise in educational organizations of all kinds, and that participants need not feel embarrassed, since the problems are common. The facilitator tries to walk a fine line between the poignancy of a concrete problem and the wisdom of viewing organizational problems in schools and colleges as universal.

Going with the Flow

To communicate effectively, to obtain a basis for building sound strategy, and to express empathy, the facilitator must understand how participants view themselves and how they view the culture of their college or school. This means "starting where the educational system is"; it requires that the facilitator be adept in fitting into the flow of the change.

An important skill for the OD facilitator is the ability to show understanding for the here and now while communicating respect for the past and excitement for the future. Timing is of the essence. At one moment a summary of current events is appropriate, at another a reminder of past events. And at still another time, painting pictures of the future is necessary to inspire the participants. There are patterns and rhythms to OD projects; the competent consultant learns to discern them.

Shifting Between the Macrodesign and Microaspects

The OD facilitator should keep in mind the place of each microaspect within the larger macrodesign, and should articulate such information to the participants as the design unfolds. In this way, the particular OD design takes on a past, present, and future for the participants and serves as a metaphor for more general self-renewal in the college or school. At each stage of the OD sequence, the facilitator can raise activity to a higher level of significance by relating it to the macrodesign as a whole. The facilitator can talk about the contract, for example, in relation to the past and possible future of the school or college. He or she can relate the past to the future through diagnosis by asking what in the present might be changed in the future. Skills, exercises, and procedures serve as transition steps from an older style of problem solving to a new, more systematic type of problem solving. Though each part of an OD sequence is performed for its own sake, no part can be isolated from the whole. The facilitator's expertise and credibility are rooted in large measure in an ability to reveal to the participants the interdependencies between macro- and microdesigns.

Chapter Ten

Institutionalizing OD in Colleges and Schools

On Thursday evening, the budget committee of the school board met. The total funds requested by various parts of the school district had exceeded the expected revenue. A few budget items had to be cut. The committee came to a line in the budget that read, "Organizational support services." That didn't sound important. Besides, what did it mean? The committee crossed it out.

That line was in the budget to support the school district's cadre of OD specialists—an arrangement for providing continuous OD facilitation to the schools and to subsystems within them.

The budget committee met again on Saturday morning to make final recommendations. The room was crowded with visitors who wanted to be heard. Many were members, clients, and friends of the district's cadre of OD specialists. Principals told the committee how the OD cadre had helped save time in meetings, speed curricular changes, reduce conflicts, and improve relations with parental groups. Teachers told how the cadre helped them to work more effectively in teams. Several students who were members of the student government in a high school explained that they had learned from the cadre facilitator how to work with faculty in ways that improved friendliness, trust, and accuracy of communication between students and teachers. They also reported that their attitudes toward the school as a whole had changed for the better. A researcher from the nearby university described how the OD cadre functioned and presented data on its effectiveness. In the end, the district budget committee put back into the budget sufficient money to support the cadre.

That episode, an actual one, illustrates how easily support for OD in a school district or in a college can be lost. It also shows how support for OD can be marshalled. The clients of OD often give it its firmest support.

This cadre of OD specialists had been active in the school district for five years, but the budget committee had not heard about its work and could not estimate its value—or even interpret a reference to it in the budget. The voices of approval for the cadre's work did not reach them until the last moment. But the voices did reach them. Some members of the OD cadre had been present Thursday evening. They spent the rest of that night and most of Friday telephoning other members, clients, and friends. As a result, the breadth and intensity of the testimonials at Saturday's meeting impressed the members of the budget committee. The testimonials altered the committee's thinking about the cadre's usefulness to education in the district.

Those present on Saturday morning were people the budget committee cared about. They were people whose approval or disapproval was capable of making the committee members feel good or bad about their actions. From principals to students, the speakers were those the budget makers saw themselves as serving. The committee members would feel rewarded if they took an action that would bring praise and joy from those people.

To put it differently, some *norms* were at work. The committee and the audience agreed about many kinds of work in schools that they thought *ought* to be done—work they approved and saw as important. Also, the visitors showed strong and common approval of some further kinds of actions in the schools designed to help the actions the committee already knew about and approved. In particular, the visitors showed strong support for OD and wanted the committee to show similar support.

When an action brings clear and agreed-on approval or disapproval from many people, and when the person acting cares about that approval or disapproval, then a norm is operating. When people show approval and disapproval to a person acting in an organizational capacity, they are sending messages about what they consider to be proper behavior on the part of that person. They are sending specifications, so to speak, for the person's behavior in his or her organizational role. To put it in a phrase, they are *role senders*. The visitors at the meeting on Saturday morning were role senders to the budget committee.

Organizational behavior is held in place by norms, and the norms are transmitted by role senders. OD is institutionalized in a school district or in a college or university when role senders make it an approved and expected part of the organization's activities. Several methods have been used in schools and colleges to make OD projects approved, expected, and customary. We will describe those ways and then return to the use of role senders in maintaining OD as an expected activity in educational organizations, but before that let us look at an OD cadre in higher education.

Here is another story.

The meeting of the board of trustees of the community college was unusually packed with faculty members and students. The board had asked the vice-president for academic affairs to talk to it about the work of the OD cadre, a group of 15 department heads and faculty members who had been trained to act as OD facilitators.

After the vice-president described how, at first, the 15 participants had been trained to apply OD concepts and techniques to their own departments and classrooms, and later had offered OD facilitation to faculty committees and the student government, she went on to introduce two cadre members: the head of the faculty curriculum committee, and the president of the student government. As occurred at the school district meeting described above, those three talked about how with OD their meetings had improved, how conflicts had been brought into the open and solved, and how the general emotional climate of the college had improved.

A few board members who had experience with OD in business asked about the similarities and differences between industrial OD and educational OD. Another wondered how OD was different from strategic planning. Another asked about how Total Quality Management related to OD and to the sort of training that the cadre carried out. That board, indeed, was well-informed about contemporary innovations in human resource development. The members were so impressed by the report on the work of the OD cadre at the college that they asked the cadre to help them improve their communication and problem solving. The board members had become role senders to the vice-president and to the OD cadre; they were saying that they approved the cadre and expected it to be a part of the organization's activities.

Methods of Maintaining OD Projects within an Educational Organization

A lot of help giving goes on in schools and colleges. In fact, some jobs consist mostly of help giving: those of librarians, computer specialists, assistant principals and deans, and custodians. And of course instructors and counselors are always helping students.

OD facilitation is one kind of help giving. It is a sort of peer consultation. The term *consultation* means giving information, giving advice, showing how, and guiding practice. Colleges and schools maintain the availability of consultation of one kind or another by various means. We will distinguish three kinds of educational consultation: content, process, and OD. Within each of those, we will distinguish inside from outside consultation.

Content Consultation

Most consultation in colleges and schools is *content* consultation. An example is the in-service course or workshop in which an expert trains educators in such subject matters as computing, academic curriculum, sexual harassment, and retirement planning. Other examples include psychologists who teach educators about issues of mental health, mathematicians who help educators with new instructional or research strategies, student services personnel who help instructors with students who have emotional or learning problems, and specialists in instructional strategies who help instructors use various teaching techniques.

Inside Consultation. Colleges and schools maintain some consultants full time—computer specialists, for example. Frequently, school districts maintain central-office departments of curriculum, and colleges maintain a center for instructional improvement. For other kinds of consultation, colleges and schools call upon personnel who spend most of their time performing duties other than consultation but who are experts in needed topics. An instructor who is expert in cooperative learning, for example, may be called upon occasionally. Or, a professor who is expert in statistics may be called upon to help analyze data.

The advantages of inside consultation are that (1) the inside consultant is more easily available than the outsider; (2) the insider knows useful information about the setting, can get to the task faster than an outsider, and can avoid political mistakes an outsider might make; and (3) the insider shares a "common fate" with the participants and can inspire their immediate trust. Participants know that the insider will continue to be within easy reach and will have a continuing personal stake in achieving a favorable outcome and in avoiding discomfort to individuals.

The disadvantages of inside consultation are that (1) inside people usually have work loads calibrated to average demand and are therefore unable to undertake exceptionally large projects without putting aside other regular duties; (2) simply because they are locals, they may not be seen by the participants as experts; (3) their knowledge of the organization may be biased; and (4) the very fact of their "common fate" with the participants may dissuade them from taking risks that a change project requires.

Outside Consultation. The advantages of outside consultants are that (1) they can more easily take on large projects beyond the ready capacity of the target system; (2) they have expert power; (3) they can collect information for an unbiased diagnosis uninfluenced by having been members of the target system; (4) to the extent that they are trusted—and some people usually trust an outside expert immediately—some staff members will confide in them things they would be fearful of telling an insider; and (5) they are freer to take the risks of change.

The disadvantages are that (1) it takes time and effort to find the right consultant; (2) outside consultants require more time for getting to know a school or college regardless of how open some participants may be; (3) although some participants will trust them immediately, others may take longer to trust outsiders, worrying that outside consultants will be more likely than insiders to embark upon risky journeys; and (4) they require a cash outlay. We might also mention the risk of picking the wrong consultant, but that applies equally to insiders and outsiders.

Content consultation in education is important, of course. For making organizational changes in support of the content, however, the expertise does not lie in the content. The expertise rarely lies with the curriculum committee, the payroll department, or the bus schedule. It lies in the norms and skills of organizational development—in particular, in the four metaskills described in chapter 1.

Process Consultation

Process consultation within an educational organization aims to improve the interpersonal *procedures* used by educators to reach their educational objectives. It focuses on the *how* of interpersonal interactions rather than the *what* of their content. Process consultants deal with such matters as the patterns of communication, leadership attempts, underlying group tensions, problem solving, and decision making. Examples of inside consultation include counselors meeting with an academic department or team of instructors to offer constructive feedback on the group's procedures, an administrator acting as a third-party mediator between an angry student or parent and an uneasy instructor or department head, and a specialist in cooperative learning giving feedback to the class and teacher about their interaction patterns. The emphasis is on procedures; process consultants do not deal directly with the subject matter of interactions.

Inside Consultation. Like content consultation, process consultation can be provided from inside either by full-time or part-time people. Some colleges and schools have positions for "human relations." Counselors, psychologists, mental health specialists, administrators, and others sometimes give process help.

Content consultants almost always deal with individuals (even when they work with groups), and unless they move into process consultation, they can have little effect on the norms that hold organizational procedures and structures in place. Since they deal frequently with interpersonal processes, process consultants can begin to affect organizational norms.

The advantages and disadvantages of process consultation from inside are much like those of content consultation. Since process consultants more often run afoul of organizational norms, however, they are likely to be weakened more by being embedded in the organization.

Much process consultation focuses on interpersonal norms. To the extent that it does so, it can be carried on with a subsystem in temporary isolation from the rest of the organization. An inside process consultant can train an academic committee in meeting skills, for example, while doing little about those skills in other groups in the college or school. But the procedures in the academic committee cannot be kept secret. Indeed, to the extent that the committee members find the new skills useful, they will want to use them elsewhere. They will probably talk about them in other faculty groups. And to the extent that the new skills differ from the old, people who have not shared the committee's gradual transformation and the rewards its members found in the new skills will be leery, even frightened, of what they hear. These others may come to think of the freshly trained committee members as people they want to avoid, and they may come to think of the consultant as an irritant, or even a danger, rather than a helper. In brief, it is easy for inside consultants, especially when they are dramatically successful with one part of the college or school, to find people in other parts fending them off.

To the extent that a process consultation deals with many parts of an educational organization, the consultant will become known personally and gradually to people in those parts. Participants will come to know the consultant through direct experience rather than rumors. The consultant can move forward with each faculty group at its own pace but at the same time maintain communication among groups, so that no group is suddenly surprised by what is happening in other groups. But it is difficult for an inside consultant to break the time loose to work with an entire college or school of any size, not to mention an entire university or school district. And at the other extreme, if the consultant is a member of a very small academic department, college, or school, the other disadvantages of being embedded in the tiny organization are exacerbated.

Outside Consultation. The advantages and disadvantages of process consultation from the outside, too, are much like those of content consultation. Again, however, because process consultation deals with interpersonal and organizational norms, there are some differences. The proverbial hat of the expert on process will be less persuasive to many educators than that of the content expert, because they will be unable to visualize what will come from under the process hat. They will know, or think they know, what a content consultant will do, but they will have little idea about what a process consultant will do. And the difficulties of gaining trust are magnified for the outside process consultant when the participants discover that the consultant seems bent on unhinging the existing norms.

OD Facilitation

OD facilitation is a kind of process consultation. To institutionalize it, we want to magnify the advantages of both inside and outside consultation, with due regard to the special delicacies of process consultation with intact systems. We want to put OD facilitation into the hands of those who are close to influential members of the college or school. We want to reach administrators, of course, but we also want to reach instructors and others who are influential in informal ways. Those with informal influence are almost always important role senders to the administrators.

Inside Consultation. Many colleges and schools have no member skilled in OD. Some have one or two but lack a formal structure to support the local application of OD. Only a handful of educational organizations worldwide have some internal capacity for OD, and many of those have an administrative department for OD.

An administrative department for OD has advantages:

1. It is close to the heart of organizational power. Its members can communicate easily in one direction with the superintendent or president or with assistant superintendents or the provost's staff, and in the other to the principals or deans. If the OD department carries out consultation that pleases the central administrators, its direct links to them give OD the strength of their support.

2. The connection of the administrative department with authority brings its members immediate attention when they approach a school or an academic department.

3. When the staff of the OD department is full-time, it has the advantage of being able to put large blocks of undistracted time into a project.

4. Because of their position near the top of the organizational hierarchy, the OD staff gains an additional aura of expertness.

5. Potential participants (or users) can find the department easily.

6. Like all insiders, the OD staff accumulates first-hand knowledge of its own educational organization.

An administrative department also has disadvantages:

1. Its close connection with authority causes some people to treat OD with caution and initial distrust.

2. Because the top administrators (the superintendent or the president) see OD as part of the central administration, they are likely to believe that it should carry out their purposes. The fact that the OD office is in their suite reminds them that OD might be useful to them. They sometimes might press the OD staff to carry out projects in parts of the educational organization against the will of the people there. The price of refusal can be loss of support.

3. When the OD department does carry out a successful OD project, other people in the organization may attribute the success only to the pressure of authority, not to the validity of OD.

4. As with the other insiders, the knowledge of the OD staff about its own educational organization may be biased and spotty. The

information the OD staff gets from educators within will usually be thinned by the careful editing they will give their communications to the top.

5. Frequently a superintendent or a president and their respective staffs will not themselves use OD skills or adhere to its norms. Like other members of the educational organization who have not had direct experience of OD, they may be fearful of norm changes and may press the OD staff to limit itself to innocuous and picayune projects.

All those constraints infect every OD department in one degree or another, because they stem from the characteristics of hierarchy. No amount of competence or skill on the part of the members of the OD department will erase them.

Outside Consultation. To the advantages and disadvantages of outside consultation mentioned earlier, we have two disadvantages to add in the case of OD. First, it is costly to hire an external consultant for every OD project and a team of external consultants for large projects. Second, OD consultants with experience in colleges and schools are hard to find. OD consultants with experience in other kinds of organizations can often be helpful, but it always takes them a while to learn about the special qualities of educational organizations.

Fullan, Miles, and Taylor (1978) located 308 consultants who had been doing extensive OD with schools in the United States and Canada during the previous five years. That is a heartening number, but it is not enough to touch many of the 16,000 school districts in the United States, not to speak of Canada. No study exists on the number of OD consultants in higher education; we believe that the number is very small, however, and that only a handful of colleges and universities have OD consultants inside.

When OD consultants with educational experience are not located nearby, they cannot respond quickly to sudden needs. Responding quickly can sometimes be crucial to the progress of a project. And if the distant consultant is to be on site frequently, travel costs mount.

Role Sending and Institutionalization

Conducting OD in a college or school requires that some people take on the role of OD facilitator and others that of participant. To institutionalize OD, these roles must become expected and stabilized. A role is stabilized by norms about the proper behavior of the person acting in it. When people say, "That's the way we do things around here," or "That's *not* the way we do things around here"—that is, when they express approval or disapproval of an action—you know that norms are at work. OD becomes institutionalized when the norms support it—when the practice of OD itself causes no eyebrows to rise, when special skill in it draws compliments, and when deviations from its norms draw frowns.

The people who express approval or disapproval, who convey standards of behavior, are the role senders to the person in the role. Here, we will use the term *role sending* to abbreviate long phrases such as "expressing approval or disapproval of selected behavior on the part of a person acting in a particular organizational role." The best arrangement for maintaining OD in a college or school is one that puts knowledgeable and supportive role senders in communication both with the central office and with potential participants in the educational organizations.

But superintendents and presidents come and go, citizens' groups suddenly get riled, and the state department board of higher education issues new regulations. What then? What can protect the norms of OD within a school or college from onslaughts by role senders who hold to contrary norms of organizational behavior? What we need, obviously, are role senders who can strongly support OD when others send disapproval. Furthermore, the role senders should be placed where they can be most effective.

A method of institutionalizing OD should make use of supportive role senders in educational organizations who can voice approval for actions and opinions that go in the direction of OD and disapproval of contrary actions and opinions. Outside consultants cannot be those voices, since they are usually not in the organization between consultative visits. Nor can OD departments usually provide them, since department members rarely spend time in the faculty lounge, the hallways or pathways on campus, or at faculty meetings where they can affect role behavior. And even when they do, they may not be the people whose approval and disapproval the teachers care most about. The most effective role senders in support of OD in an educational organization are educators who have had experience with OD either as participants or as facilitators and who are present to speak when the topic comes up.

Further, a method of institutionalizing OD should put supportive role senders not only in the educational organizations that are making use of OD, but also in those that have not yet done so. Obviously, outside consultants do not spend time in organizations where they are not consulting. Members of OD departments, too, spend most of their time in those subsystems that ask them for help.

A method of institutionalizing OD should include supportive role senders to central administrators. An OD department can usually do that very well. Outside consultants are weak in this respect owing to their on-again-off-again visits.

Finally, a method of institutionalizing OD should entail role senders who can support OD in education when they interact with the community. Such role senders are most effective when they can actually help, for instance, conduct meetings, coordinate among groups, and solve problems with PTAs, college boards, youth groups, social service agencies, and so on. People who are active in community affairs are often those who attend and speak at school or college board meetings and who communicate directly with— that is, who are themselves role senders to—school teachers, college instructors, principals, deans, superintendents, presidents, and the like.

We turn next to a method of institutionalizing OD that puts knowledgeable role senders into closer contact with participants in educational organizations and the community than either an OD department or outside consultants can do.

Peer Cadres

In J. D. Salinger's novel, *The Catcher in the Rye*, Holden Caulfield tells of his recurring dream of patrolling the edge of a high field of rye to keep the children playing there from falling over the cliff. Through that poetic image, Holden poignantly portrays for his little sister, Phoebe, the sort of job he would like to have as an adult. He would be the catcher in the rye, he says.

Metaphorically, OD facilitators catch educational administrators, instructors, and students before they fall off organizational cliffs. They are catchers in education. And like Holden Caulfield, OD facilitators don't want to tell educators what games to play, where to stand, and where to run. They don't want to be breathing down their necks all the time. Rather, facilitators want their participants to look around for help every now and then. If educators look for help, it will be easier for the catcher to catch them when they get too close to the edge.

Even if a catcher were available for every college or school, however, the strategy of stationing one at the cliff's edge would contain an irreparable flaw. We and others have learned from experience that participants in OD can become too dependent on their facilitators. The facilitators' charisma and expertise, though advantageous in the short run, can become drawbacks in the long run. After all, the OD facilitator has helped design the diagnoses, the retreats and workshops; brought all faculty members through the stages of problem solving; initiated the evaluation and feedback; and led the follow-up support to put new structures and procedures into place. It was the facilitator who knew about the exercises and procedures, and it was the facilitator who took leadership when events turned confusing or highly emotional. Under those circumstances, it is not surprising that participants come to depend on the facilitator. Still, ideally, we think that the OD facilitator should act more like a guide on the side than a sage on the stage.

We have been concerned in our designing, therefore, with creating ways of gracefully disengaging from our OD facilitating roles with the participants. We have sought to remove ourselves from dependency relationships, for example, by asking participants to take leadership in convening sessions for their own faculty. But even after successful year-long projects from which we gradually extricated ourselves from our powerful roles, we were sometimes not fully satisfied that the college or school in which we had been working had achieved a capacity for self-renewal.

In one of our first experimental efforts with OD in schools, we were well into a research project with an entire school district we will call Keele. It became obvious that we would be unable to provide continuing OD facilitation to the district, or even to one school, after we completed our research project. Other suitable OD resources in the region were scarce. And even had there been more consultants available, they would have suffered the disadvantages of outside consultants. It was then that Schmuck conceived the idea of a peer cadre to provide continuing OD help to an educational organization (for his conception, see Schmuck, 1982; for other writings on peer cadres, see Schmuck, 1977, and Schmuck and Schmuck, 1992).

In our project with the Keele district, we (and 11 assistants) carried out OD during one academic year in two elementary schools, one junior high school, and two high schools. Then, in the spring of that year, we informed Keele personnel that training would be offered in June after classes were over for those wishing to become "communication consultants" for the district. A printed circular stated that the trainees would become knowledgeable and skilled in communication, simulations, diagnosis, feedback giving, problem solving, and OD designing. We solicited applications from all levels of the school district; the 23 people eventually selected represented a wide cross-section of the district, including teachers, counselors, elementary and secondary principals, curriculum and student personnel specialists, and assistant superintendents who were members of the superintendent's cabinet.

We gave the Keele peer cadre its initial training in OD facilitation during two weeks that June. Then, from September to March of the next school year, we assisted them by working side by side with them and helping them with their planning and OD projects. We gave them constructive feedback during and after each of their OD projects.

Ten rules for an OD cadre in schools and colleges grew out of our work at Keele:

1. Draw members from all ranks and from throughout the larger educational organization. Since the initial peer-cadre project at Keele, cadres have been drawn from the following, in order from larger to smaller numbers: instructors, counselors, department heads, principals and assistant deans, central administrators like assistant superintendents and assistants to the provost, secretaries, and students or parents.

2. Assign members part time to the cadre—perhaps for 10 or 15 percent of their time.

3. Do not impose cadre services; let the cadre respond to requests. The cadre should, however, advertise its services and give demonstrations.

4. Do not assign cadre members to OD projects with units (academic departments, central-administration departments, etc.) in which they are regularly employed.

5. Appoint a cadre coordinator to work at least half time.

6. See that the cadre has at least 10 active members. A couple of dozen is better in educational organizations of any size.

7. Train cadre members to provide OD services through temporary *teams* drawn from their membership. A cadre member should do an OD project alone only in exceptional circumstances.

8. Plan three weeks (15 full days) of initial training for cadre members and at-the-elbow help to teams of cadre members during their first OD projects.

9. Give the cadre its own budget.

10. Provide time for the cadre's own self-renewal: recruiting and training new members, distributing information about the educational organization among members, acquiring new skills, renewing the cadre's cohesiveness, planning for the future.

Rules 1 through 7 serve to maximize the advantages of both inside and outside consultants and to minimize their weaknesses. Because cadre members are employees of the educational organization (Rule 1), they are perceived as insiders. They have a common fate with their fellow participants. They cannot pull out and vanish; they must live with the outcomes of their OD projects. That brings them trust more quickly than outsiders can give it. Because they continue to work most of the time in their regular jobs (Rule 2), they have a great deal of intimate information about what is going on in the educational organization and about its history. That saves them from many mistakes, especially political mistakes, that outsiders might make, no matter how thorough their diagnosis might be. Because they work in all ranks in the larger educational organization, their information is not screened as information is to a central-administration department. They get the information that goes to instructors and secretaries as well as that going to central-administration department heads. Their knowledge still has some of the bias to which insiders are prone, but the wide spread of its sources minimizes the bias. Rules 7 and 10 (working in teams and setting aside time for self-renewal) help the cadre to distribute information among its members.

Because the cadre has members throughout the educational organization who can give accurate information, because it advertises its services and gives demonstrations of its work (Rule 3), and because it engages colleagues in all parts of the organization in OD, it is less likely than a smaller group of consultants or a central-administration department to suffer from the growth of antagonistic rumors—that is, to get walled off.

Because cadre members do not do OD in their own units, but are always assigned to facilitate elsewhere in the educational organization (Rule 4), they are outsiders to their participants. They collect systematic diagnostic data to learn what they need to know. They get the trust that some participants give to outsiders. They are willing to take some risks they would not take if they were members of the participants' unit, the target system. And they can come in with at least a little of the aura of the outside expert.

Because the cadre contains a fair number of members (Rule 6), it has flexibility in meeting demands. If the available time of some members is committed, others can be assigned. Because cadre members work only part time in that role (Rule 2), some can negotiate more released time when a project of large scope looms. The coordinator (Rule 5) facilitates those allocations. The flexibility of any cadre has its limits, of course. The available time of cadre members and the willingness of administrators to release more of their time can become overstretched. On the whole, however, because cadre members are continuing members of the organization (Rule 1), because the coordinator is in the organization's phone book, and because of the other reasons we gave, the cadre can respond to most requests with alacrity.

The cadre's direct link to the central administration through its coordinator has advantages and disadvantages. It makes the cadre easy to find, and it gives cadre members a formal place in the organization. And as long as the cadre does work of value to the central administrators, the coordinator can draw support for the cadre that is important to its morale and stability. On the other hand, the cadre can find itself pressed by administrators to go out and solve problems that are administrators' problems, not educators' problems, and it can further find itself pressed to limit itself to work that does not rock the boat. The coordinator can act as a buffer against that pressure, and the cadre can counterpoise its participants' demands against those of the administrators. The latter defense is usually the better, especially if some administrators have participated in OD themselves. Nevertheless, pressures for conformity to administrators' demands will crop up intermittently, and the cadre must withstand them.

Finally, the cost of a cadre is moderate. Figures from some of the cadres we will describe below are representative. Start-up costs in Keele and Eisner were about $37,000 in 1982 dollars. The Bold Community College cadre invested perhaps $9,000 during the first year, and the Carpenter College cadre perhaps $6,000. In today's dollars the Carpenter College cadre spends about $24,000 per year. One reason for the lower costs of the latter two, at least for start-up, is that those college cadres spread initial training over a longer period than did the two school district cadres of Keele and Eisner.

Maintaining a cadre costs less than starting one up. Fullan, Miles, and Taylor (1978, vol. V, p. 12) say that the cost of a typical OD program is "perhaps one-half of one percent of total budget, and is comparable to amounts usually spent on in-service education." Some educational organizations do use part of their staff-development funds for supporting their cadres. Annual maintenance costs in Eisner have varied between $25,000 and $40,000. Writing about the cadre in a large city district, Milstein and Lafornara (1980) said,

> The actual cost of the direct maintenance of [the cadre] has been about $25,000 annually. Buffalo's 1979–80 budget was approximately $126,000,000. [The cadre's] cost, therefore, represents less than [two hundredths of one percent] of that budget. Another way of looking at the situation is to note that it would cost substantially more to support even one full-time change agent in a school district than it does to support a skilled internal change team of twenty teachers and administrators.

All those advantages of the cadre's structure help it to do good work. When it does good work, it gets approval from its participants, and it can influence persons who have power to keep it going or destroy it. In brief, the OD cadre can institutionalize itself. In their nationwide study of school-based OD, Fullan, Miles, and Taylor (1978, vol. V, p. 7), report that " 'classical' OD, plus two other system-oriented, comprehensive approaches . . . were most likely to show clear impact, positive attitudes and institutionalization." The term "classical OD" characterizes cadres.

The way a cadre is organized puts role senders in important places. Members in all parts of the educational organization (Rules 1 and 2) can voice their support of OD both with the faculty ranks and in central-administration departments. Because they have experience *outside* their own units (Rule 4), they are often seen to have a wider knowledge of the facts than their colleagues within the unit. Because they respond to requests from all over the larger organization (Rule 3), they are not known as the captive agent of any one team, committee, department, school, or faction. Since many of the cadre's members are connected to the bottom of the organization through their own jobs and to the top through their coordinator, they have an open channel for conveying role expectations from bottom to top and back again. Since they have various jobs in the organization, they can convey the expectations of various groups.

Because the coordinator reports to someone in the central administration (Rule 5), he or she can act as role sender from the cadre's members and participants to the central administration. The coordinator can keep the central administration informed of the demands for its services and of the satisfaction of its participants. It almost always happens, too, that the cadre is called upon by groups in the community. When that happens, the cadre stimulates role sending from community to the college or school.

The many links and opportunities for communication and role sending by an OD cadre promote its stability. In the example of a school-based cadre we gave at the opening of this chapter, the cadre almost lost its funding because it had not set out to influence the budget committee. But the cadre members were not out of touch. They knew the budget committee was meeting, they knew the meetings were critical, they knew when the proceedings would allow them to be heard, and they attended. When the need arose, they were able to round up participants—principals, teachers, students—overnight. Their presence at the meetings, their quick communications, and the support of their clients saved the day.

One test of stability is longevity. Our first cadre in Keele started operation in the fall. That November, an auditor discovered a shortage of $1.85 million in Keele's operating budget of $12 million. Programs were cut, jobs were eliminated, and administrators were moved back to classrooms. But the cadre survived. The superintendent wrote to us later to say that the OD delivered by us and the cadre there had been a major asset in helping the district to weather the crisis. Then, two years later, a new superintendent arrived. When he encountered a conservative and vocal segment of the community who believed the cadre was doing "sensitivity training," he became first ambivalent about the cadre and then unsympathetic. The cadre's budget was cut and then abolished. Nevertheless, the cadre continued to receive requests from schools for OD, and it continued work (the varieties of its work are described in Runkel, Wyant, Bell, and Runkel, 1980). In the end, however, the difficulties of getting released time for cadre work without central-administration support, the pressures of overtime work, and other matters became too much; the Keele cadre disbanded six years after it was started. The fact that the Keele cadre was perceived as a help rather than a luxury during the terrible budget crisis, and the fact that it went on working for several years after it lost its budget, testify to its durability.

The cadre in Eisner began its work 23 years ago. It has survived five changes of superintendent, 10 changes of coordinators, two teacher strikes and budget cuts in recent years. It continues strong. The literature is full of accounts of educational innovations, particularly curricular changes, that fade away a year or two after the departure of the outside resources. In view of that record, the staying power of the Eisner cadre is remarkable. We will tell about other cadres in the next section.

Rules 7 through 10 help the cadre to maintain its own internal strength. Rule 7 specifies delivering OD facilitation by teams, not individuals. Especially when cadre members are new at their work, they find it comforting to have a colleague alongside. Doing OD is stressful enough without having to be alone on the firing line. Even when cadre members are highly experienced, it is still useful to exchange informal diagnoses with partners, to discuss possible alterations in the plan for the next hour, and to give and get feedback about performance. Partners can divide the work, too. While one is leading a session, for example, another can be observing and noting participants' reactions to parts of the session. Finally, when making informal judgments about outcomes, the presence of two or more judges increases reliability.

Rule 8 specifies that cadre members be adequately trained before they are released to work on their own—still in teams, but without the original trainer at the elbow. The training is necessary to build in the members an adequate repertoire of skills, but it is also necessary to develop confidence among cadre members in one another's skill and trust in their support. When they go to work in teams, each must feel that the other members will be a help, not a hindrance. The initial training includes many exercises requiring interdependence for success.

Rule 9 specifies a budget for the cadre. According to the information we have from several cadres, the biggest expense is usually for retreat time for participants and cadre members. In some cases, money for retreat time is part of the cadre's budget and is used to release both participants and cadre members. In other cases, participants request expenses directly from the central administration. Some cadres get along on very little money. Beyond expenses for retreat time, cadres need money for the coordinator's salary, secretarial time, supplies and materials, rental of space when the cadre mounts a session away from its own property, and the occasional outside OD expert when the cadre engages one to help it with its own self-renewal. Sometimes there are transportation costs as well. A cadre can hardly plan well without its own budget; we know of no cadre that has none. Besides the practical considerations, a cadre's budget serves as a symbol that the unit is a legitimate and honored part of the college or school.

Rule 10 provides time for the cadre to recruit and train new members, bring in outside experts to teach old and new members new skills, exchange information about what is going on in their own organization, and plan for the future. This rule is also vital for renewing trust and solidarity among members—by resolving conflicts and coping with feelings of affront and injury. The work of a cadre never becomes routine, for the unit must continually make adaptations to changing circumstances. Every change in the administration calls for a conference among cadre members. Every OD project carried out by the cadre changes the climate of acceptance in the organization—a little or a lot—and the impact of the change must also be assessed. Adaptability requires communication among cadre members that is frequent, accurate, quick, and honest, and it requires cadre members to trust that help and support, when they are needed, will be strong and quick. Time for self-renewal and professional development is vital in maintaining such communication and support.

Two other rules not only help the cadre to do good work and to become institutionalized, but also help it to maintain its internal strength and cohesiveness. Rule 1, drawing members from all ranks, enables the cadre to get support from all ranks. If a cadre discovers that it cannot recruit new members from some sectors, it should worry that it is losing support from those sectors. Drawing members from all ranks also brings the cadre direct information about its own status in the organization.

Rule 5, having a coordinator, provides for a central person

through whom arrangements can be made. Participants call the coordinator. The coordinator finds members to make up an OD team—members who have the skills needed for the particular OD project, who will work well together, and who are personally acceptable to the participants in the target system. Having a paid coordinator also adds legitimacy to the cadre.

Examples of Peer Cadres

In this section we describe the organizational features and OD activities of a number of cadres in schools and colleges in the United States and elsewhere. In most cases we use pseudonyms to protect the schools and colleges from being in the spotlight. Our information comes from published and unpublished documents and from our own experience. We also draw upon the work of Kelsh (1983) and Leatt and Schmuck (1988).

Keele Schools

At the beginning of one school year, the Keele district had just hired several new assistant superintendents to cope with the problems of a ballooning student population and an increased number of schools. The superintendent wanted us to clarify roles and improve the communication among departments, committees, and schools. We struck a bargain: we would do that if we could conduct research on OD as we went along. The full story of the Keele project, including displays of data on outcomes, is told by Runkel, Wyant, Bell, and Runkel (1980).

Entry and preparation of questionnaires for summative evaluation took place from August to January. In January we collected data from Keele and from two neighboring districts for comparison; we did so again in May, again one year later, and again two years after that. We also collected diagnostic and formative data by means of interviews, observations, documents such as newspapers and district memos, and occasional brief questionnaires.

Our macrodesign included OD help in the form of teambuilding for the superintendent's cabinet and three central-office departments, and OD projects for two high schools, one junior high, and two elementary schools during one academic year. In the spring of that year, we recruited volunteers for the cadre of organizational specialists—the name they chose for themselves was "Communication Consultants." We sought people who, after training, would spend 10 percent of their time acting as OD facilitators within the district. From the volunteers, we selected 23 for training.

The initial workshop for the cadre lasted two weeks. The first week was devoted to exercises to develop the cadre's skills in group work and to help it become cohesive. The neophyte specialists were also given experiences as cotrainers in exercises on particular OD skills and then conducted them for their colleagues. During the second week, new temporary OD teams formed, members of each team shared resources and experiences. Then the cadre as a whole generated a list of potential clients for their OD projects. Each team selected an actual target system, carried out start-up, gathered diagnostic data, and returned to the cadre's training site to review its data and design its OD activities.

The following fall, cadre members found two schools in the district willing to become the cadre's first target systems. Members of our own university-based team collaborated in those OD projects. During the following spring, we gradually withdrew our presence; we ceased active collaboration at the end of that school year. In the meantime, seven elementary schools had requested the cadre's services, and the cadre delivered OD to all of them during the following August. Later, the cadre provided OD facilitation to other elementary and secondary schools and to administrative groups. Cadre members taught several in-service courses in communication skills, which later turned out to be one of the best sources of future members for the cadre. In one way or another, the cadre also aided two schools in other neighboring districts, teachers' and principals' groups, PTAs, a League of Woman Voters local, and social agencies.

The first coordinator of the Keele cadre was a curriculum coordinator who worked in the central administration. He and all later coordinators were drawn from the cadre membership. The cadre also organized a "decision-making group" of four or five members to aid the coordinator. That group decided things that came up between meetings of the whole cadre. Members of the decision-making group were highly trusted, but were also held to account at the meetings of the whole.

Eisner Schools

One spring we were completing an OD project with six elementary schools in Eisner and Worthington, two school districts in Oregon (the project is reported in Schmuck, Murray, Smith, Schwartz, and Runkel, 1975). The Eisner cadre grew out of the interest in OD that arose in the Eisner district during that project.

Throughout that same spring, two teacher leaders in Eisner and the two of us recruited members for the Eisner cadre. We put a printed notice in the district's annual catalogue of summer workshops. We attended several meetings of the central-administration, of principals, and of the teachers' association to inform people about the project. A great deal of information, we discovered, was spread informally at parties, in faculty rooms, in supermarkets, and so on. In all, 72 people responded. We invited the respondents to a two-hour meeting to hear about OD and how it works. After that meeting, we asked interested persons to fill out an application; 51 people handed one in. The four of us, along with the assistant superintendent of personnel, acted as a panel of judges. We selected 27 respondents for initial membership: three assistant superintendents, six central-administration coordinators, three secondary administrators, two elementary administrators, one secondary counselor, two elementary counselors, four secondary teachers, and six elementary teachers. We selected the 27 on the basis of their educational experience in group dynamics, the nature of their interest in the cadre, and the diversity of role, sex, and race. The 27 candidates represented 14 of Eisner's 44 schools and several different sections of the central administration.

The formal training of the 27 consisted of two two-hour introductions to OD in May, 10 workshop days in June, five workshop days in August, and cofacilitations with us throughout the following academic year.

Our intention in the 10-day workshop was not to produce sophisticated OD facilitators quickly, but to give the trainees a thorough introduction to communication skills, setting goals, working with conflicts, improving meetings, solving problems and making decisions in groups. We included lecturettes and some practice in start-up, organizational diagnosis, designing, and evaluation. We made use of mimeographed sections from the manuscript of the first *Handbook* (Schmuck, Runkel, Saturen, Martell, and Derr, 1972).

Day 1. After introduction, cadre members formed triads to discuss "What I hope the cadre can do for me." We gave a lecture on paraphrasing and asked cadre members to overuse paraphrasing during the workshop. They then formed new triads to discuss "What I hope the cadre can do for the district." Next came a lecturette on the clients, issues, and strategies with which OD is concerned. Then, after we spoke briefly on the skill of behavior description, participants formed cross-role groups to list goals for the cadre in behavioral terms. We then lectured on describing one's own feelings, after which we formed new small groups to build Tinkertoy models of "What this district is like." Participants discussed what the models revealed about the district and the group processes they noted while constructing their models. We then held a discussion on checking one's impressions of another's inner state. Finally, we asked cadre members to fill out the questionnaire entitled Team-Expectations Survey (chapter 4).

Day 2. We gave a lecture on the technique of survey-data-feedback, displayed data from the Team-Expectations Survey, and asked new small groups to design and administer brief questionnaires to the whole group. Together with the cadre members, we criticized the newly created questionnaires. Next, we asked the cadre members to list their personal goals and resources and then to exchange that information with one another. As homework, we assigned the mimeographed *Handbook* chapters on clarifying communication and establishing goals.

Day 3. After lecturing on constructive openness and the interpersonal gap, we asked cadre members to form new triads to review their personal goals. Next, after discussing the use of conflict to uncover problems, participants grouped with persons in jobs similar to theirs to practice the Imaging exercise. By the end of the day, they had completed Stage 1 (generating images of the other groups) and Stages 2 and 3 (clarifying the images with the other groups). We assigned for reading the chapter of the *Handbook* on improving meetings, which was similar to chapter 5 in this book.

Day 4. After going on with the Imaging exercise through Stage 4 (listing own behavior from which others might have formed their images) and Stage 5 (clarifying the listed behavior), cadre members completed the exercise by forming cross-job groups to discuss problems in the school district that were brought out by the exercise. The entire group discussed the strengths and limitations of the exercise. We then conducted the Planners and Operators exercise. We assigned for reading the *Handbook* chapter on making decisions.

Day 5. After we lectured on task and social-emotional processes in groups, cadre members discussed ways in which those processes are related to decision making. They formed small groups to list skills they would need as cadre members and then formed pairs of groups to exchange lists. Next, we lectured on techniques of process observation and feedback, after which each pair of groups formed a Fishbowl. The inner groups discussed restraints the cadre would encounter in using its skills in the district, while the outer groups acted as process observers. Then the roles and physical positions of the inner and outer groups were reversed to give everyone a chance to play both the content and the process functions. We asked participants to read the *Handbook* chapter on theory and technology, similar to chapter 1 in this book.

Days 6 to 10. The second week contained a similar mix of lectures, procedures, exercises, simulations, and anticipations of future work. We gave lectures on entry and start-up, diagnosis, designing, types of OD designs, and problem solving. For exercises and simulations, we used the Five-Square puzzle, Lost on the Moon, One-Way, Two-Way Communication, and again Planners and Operators. We used a lot of time in demonstrating *S-T-P* problem solving with the cadre's own anticipated problems. At the end of the week, the superintendent attended and expressed his support for the cadre.

Days 11 to 15. During the five days in August, we helped cadre members get ready to cofacilitate with us during the following school year. We wanted to move from the rehearsal of specific exercises and procedures toward the wider application of skills associated with start-up, writing memos of understanding, diagnosing participants' needs, macrodesigning and microdesigning, and evaluating members' facilitative efforts.

We encouraged cadre members to discuss the norms that were being established within their group. We encouraged them to ask, Are we being open with one another? What does it mean to learn from others? How can we put resources within the group to best use? What commitments to one another have we made or are willing to make? In addition, we encouraged cadre members to become more self-analytic about the emerging structural arrangements for their cadre. We encouraged them to discuss these questions: What will the coordinator's role be? What sort of governance structure will direct the cadre's actions? How can the cadre work to be accepted by others in the district while at the same time maintaining its autonomy and neutrality?

On the first day, we divided the participants into the six teams that would do the OD projects. Each team was made up of four or five members, and each team member typically held a job in the district different from those of his or her teammates. We asked the teams to discuss how their group composition would limit or enhance their ability to work effectively, and then to brainstorm ways of overcoming the group's potential limitations. In two teams, group memberships were changed. Then we devoted 10 minutes to each of the following topics: problem solving, communication, OD phases, organizational issues, OD procedures, OD exercises, and survey-data-feedback. We asked participants to spend the last two hours of the day making agreements in their teams about their preferred norms for working together, using the Group Agreement Exercise.

As the week continued, the cadre made agreements about the role of the coordinator, the role and composition of the steering committee, the decision-making procedures, matters of ethics, and the manner of functioning of the separate teams. Members also made plans for advertising the cadre's services. They selected one person from each team to serve on the steering committee. On the last day, the steering committee selected some future self-renewal events, and the cadre as a whole discussed and revised them. Schmuck (1982) gives more detail on these 15 days.

After Day 15. During the entire next academic year, we joined cadre members in carrying out some initial OD projects with an assortment of target systems. Three teams provided follow-up facilitation to schools with which we ourselves had already worked, and one team helped a high school staff develop the skills and structure for participatory decision making. Another team did teambuilding for the superintendent's cabinet to help it improve vertical and lateral communication in the district. A sixth team designed and started an in-service course on communication and problem solving for anyone in the district who might like to attend. Though this last group was not "doing OD," its work was deemed important both to inform a wider audience in the district about cadre skills and to motivate key teachers, counselors, and principals to request an OD project in their schools. One of us or one of our advanced graduate students aided each of the OD teams. At the end of that school year, our active involvement and leadership with the cadre ended.

As others have done, the Eisner cadre has focused its OD projects on intact work groups such as school staffs, teaching teams, and administrative cabinets, helping them overcome interpersonal and organizational constraints to productive collaboration. The following are some examples of the kinds of tasks they have undertaken:

- Diagnosing communication skills
- Diagnosing general organizational functioning
- Convening (facilitating) meetings at schools and the central administration
- Training in communication skills
- Training in meeting skills

- Facilitating communication by direct observation and immediate oral feedback (i.e., "process consultation")
- Training in methods of group decision making
- Training in methods of systematic group problem solving
- Training in team building and team leadership skills
- Building cohesiveness and coordination in the faculty of a new school
- Facilitating conflict negotiations
- Helping choose near-term goals
- Intervening in units facing crisis and applying diagnosis, conflict management, and negotiation (crises have included interpersonal hostilities, financial shortages, communication lags between superintendent and staff, and the like)
- Providing instruction and guided practice in management and leadership styles
- Conferring with administrators or others to design a strategy for change
- Conferring on classroom management and implementation of programs
- Training in time management and scheduling
- Evaluating effectiveness of projects
- Teaching self-development classes in interpersonal communication, group processes, and meeting skills
- Helping school faculties put site-based decision making into place
- Helping elementary teacher teams with non-graded classrooms

The overall sequence of most OD projects by cadre members includes an initial period of start-up and the memo of understanding followed by diagnosis and design. Then a series of sequential OD sessions follows, interspersed with data collections for formative evaluation. A typical OD project will last from a few months to an academic year. Evaluative data serve as the springboard for redesign and more OD sessions, until cadre and participants agree that the necessary structures and procedures for self-renewal have been built. Finally, data are often collected for purposes of summative evaluation and are offered to policy makers, such as members of the governing board or of funding agencies.

After the Eisner cadre had acquired some experience, and after new participants requested their services, the teams originally formed the first summer no longer served. Since then, members have repeatedly sorted themselves into teams to suit new tasks as they have arisen. Members now typically choose the team to which they want to belong, using criteria such as willingness to work with others on the team, making a balance among the regular jobs of the members, and showing significant interest in the task to be done. It is fairly typical for individual specialists to focus their energies on such functions as designing interviews, training large groups, service as process facilitators, or coaching individual participants such as principals or team leaders. All team members provide one another with helpful feedback and carry out continual evaluation as the OD projects move along.

Fifteen years after the Eisner cadre was established it contained one supervisor-consultant for training, one specialist in assessment and planning, three central-administrator coordinators, one computer specialist, one principal, three assistant principals, two counselors, fifteen teachers, four secretaries, and one receptionist.

Cash outlay for the Eisner cadre at that time was about $4,000, not counting salaries, ordinary materials, telephone, rental space, and the like. The $4,000 paid for the cadre's continuing training, expenses of courses they taught in communication skills, and released time for conducting OD projects during the school day. There had been an exceptionally low need for released time that year. In contrast, the cadre recently estimated that a cash outlay of about $10,200 is needed currently. In addition to those funds, the district still designates quarter time for the coordinator even though, like other school districts in Oregon, Eisner is under severe pressure to cut its budget.

Cadre members in Eisner volunteered time outside their regular work day during a recent year to conduct 18 OD projects and to attend cadre meetings and training sessions. At regular pay rates, the donated time was worth $54,000.

Large City District

Some years ago, the Buffalo (New York) Public School District was presented with a court order to desegregate its schools. Having already encountered difficulties in desegregating its schools, and being aware of the difficulties encountered in Louisville, Boston, and other cities, the leaders of the Buffalo district knew that a "supportive institutional environment" would be necessary. They determined to provide to individual schools skill, encouragement, and social support for dealing with the myriad problems that they knew were inevitable. Michael Milstein, of the State University of New York at Buffalo, was asked to assist.

As a result, the Buffalo district established the School

Improvement Resource Team (SIRT). It was modeled on the kind of cadre of organizational specialists described above, but it took on a shape of its own suitable to its locality and its mission. In particular, under the pressure of the desegregation order, SIRT could not observe the rule of waiting for invitations from schools. Milstein and Lafornara (1980) explained:

> In urban school environments, . . . invitations are not readily forthcoming . . . Schools needing help are usually identified by central office administrators. . . . Efforts are [then] made to (1) explain how SIRT functions, (2) clarify . . . the issues at the school, and (3) obtain faculty-wide commitment. . . . SIRT's experience is that the involvement of entire school facilities is not practical, since interventions usually take place after school or at week-end sessions. SIRT's response . . . has been to rely on volunteers who are vitally interested in the issues involved. As a result, SIRT sessions typically draw from a minimum of four or five teachers up to a maximum of about 25 percent of a faculty.

In spring of SIRT's first year, 16 of 65 applicants for membership in SIRT were accepted. The group received three weeks of initial training that summer. The stressful conditions are indicated by the facts that five of the original members dropped out during the first week of training and that the central administration pressed the team to take on tasks even before it was fully prepared. In August, nevertheless, SIRT conducted one-day workshops in three high schools and did a week of teambuilding with "liaison teams," which would in turn conduct in-service activities in eight other schools.

Beginning in the fall of the following year, SIRT met monthly for further training, to renew its internal dynamics, and to deal with business affairs. The following spring, 10 of 45 new applicants were added to SIRT, and the entire group received another two weeks of training that summer. SIRT conducted numerous facilitations during the next two academic years.

The operation of SIRT, its embedding in the school district structure, the stresses it experienced in bringing itself to active and competent performance, and other matters have been reported by Milstein (1978), Milstein (1979), and Milstein and Lafornara (1980). The following descriptions of some of SIRT's 1980 projects are condensed from Milstein and Lafornara (1980).

The Student Relations Committee (SRC). SRC contained about 50 students from three academic high schools undergoing the greatest extent of desegregation. The students, their teacher-advisers, and a SIRT subteam met monthly for all-day sessions to develop skill and to deal with such issues as discipline, student morale, teacher-student relations, school spirit, and class cutting. After the SRC began, it replenished its ranks several times. In each of the three SRC schools, members maintained events calendars to keep students informed about school activities. Each SRC group met regularly with school administrators to discuss strategies for school improvement. Action committees dealt with issues and concerns unique to each school. For example, one SRC group formed an action committee to curb "hall walking" and false fire alarms.

High Schools. After the first workshops with high schools, the SIRT discovered it would have to rely on volunteers at a time when the teachers' union was urging its members not to volunteer for any projects. Nevertheless, as many as 25 percent of a school's teachers volunteered to attend after-school meetings. At one school confronted with severe disciplinary problems, teachers at first focused their efforts on "hall sweeps," in which groups of staff members walked the halls to get students back into class and to remove those who were from other schools or who were dropouts "just visiting." The result was an immediate improvement in discipline and a more favorable perception of SIRT activities by other staff members. The school's administrators became actively involved, volunteers doubled in number, and the group expanded its work to nondisciplinary matters.

A second high school also initially focused on discipline, but developed another strategy. Volunteers at this school developed a schedule card to be carried by all students. This "Omega Card" served as a long-term solution to problems of student identification, hall walking, and class cutting. Other high school principals were contemplating similar methods.

This second high school was the city's newest. Under court order, it was slated to be closed as a secondary school and reopened as an elementary school. Before the court order was handed down, SIRT had been helping the school's faculty develop activities to strengthen school traditions and clarify special resource needs for grants-in-aid proposals. After the court order, SIRT turned its efforts to helping the school faculty to buoy up its sagging morale and minimize the impact of the pending closing on the educational programs. As a result of those efforts and the subsequent intercession of a board member, the school underwent a gradual phase-out instead of the abrupt one-year closing originally prescribed.

Elementary Schools. SIRT's work with elementary schools began in response to requests from schools that had one or more faculty members in SIRT. In one school, the staff asked for process help in refining their individualized mathematics program. The staff, meeting weekly for a semester, developed a schoolwide resource file for math materials, an individualized diagnostic test, and a procedure for assessing student progress in mathematics. A second school was faced with absorbing a junior high school staff. Teachers and ancillary staff met for a semester to develop new policies, disciplinary procedures, and report card procedures. The group was also successful in obtaining a small grant to develop a basic skills task force in the school.

SIRT also was called upon to help three elementary schools slated for closing. SIRT trained school-based liaison teams to help the schools close in orderly fashion.

Nonschool Interventions. SIRT helped a citywide citizens' advisory council establish goals and assess needs related to desegregation. Two projects were conducted with groups established by the board of education to monitor and recommend policy for schools in their areas. SIRT conducted several sessions with them to pinpoint and resolve problems.

SIRT had not one coordinator, but two. Together, they oversaw SIRT's budget and kept tabs on the OD projects. Other leadership activities were distributed among the members. At monthly meetings, the roles of convener, group-process helpers, and observers were rotated. Every OD project had its own leader. SIRT-wide functions such as overall evaluation and public relations were delegated to members.

At first, SIRT was assigned for administrative purposes to a central administrator in charge of school integration. He did not find much time for SIRT, and several important items of information failed to reach the right place in the hierarchy. Later, another central administrator was assigned who had been a participant in one of SIRT's early OD projects; he had attended SIRT's meetings, observed interventions, and participated in budgetary decisions. That person served as an effective role sender to the central administration.

After desegregation had been satisfactorily achieved, federal funds were withdrawn, and the district ceased to provide funds for released time or for training new members. The cadre no longer met as a formal organization. Milstein told us, however, that the associate superintendent for instruction still called on ex-members of the cadre for help with organizational problems. Milstein's own work with the district changed to giving aid with stress reduction, and ex-members of SIRT often helped him with that effort. Milstein continues his work on stress reduction and on the preparation of neophyte school administrators at the University of New Mexico.

Australian Schools

During the late 70s, the Director of Services of a very large state department of education in Australia circulated a paper to his staff. It proposed that the Division of Services establish OD teams for school improvement. William Cameron, an officer of the division, proposed to train a team of school heads to act as OD facilitators and change agents to a number of schools. Cameron met with the director of the Macquarie North Region (a fictitious name), and they agreed to mount a project with the following characteristics (this list is abridged from Cameron, 1982):

1. Cameron would train a team of OD facilitators. The team would assist faculties of schools to attain goals they would choose.
2. The OD facilitators would be school heads.
3. The facilitators would be released from their regular jobs for one-half day per week to carry out OD projects in other schools.
4. The facilitators would work in pairs, each pair to be assigned to one target school during the project.
5. The decision to participate in the OD project would be made by the school faculties.
6. The schools in the project would not receive any additional resources.
7. The project would run for about two years.

Cameron also obtained the support of the local teachers' federation for the project.

Cameron and the Director of Macquarie North selected three "experimental" schools in which pairs from the larger OD team would intervene: Raworth Primary, with 30 faculty members; Blue Gum Primary, with 32; and Redleaf High with 75. They selected four comparison schools: Mountview Primary, with 30 faculty members; Highfield Primary, with 25; Ridgeway Primary, with 17; and the Parklands High with 70. Cameron visited the schools and explained OD to the faculties. He promised every school a survey-data-feedback diagnosis. He promised the experimental schools a weekend retreat and facilitator support afterward for about two hours per week for two years. All school faculties voted by large margins to join the project.

The start-up phase of the project ran for seven months. It included survey-data-feedback, the selection of OD facilitators, and the weekend retreats.

The Director of Macquarie North submitted to Cameron the names of 25 school heads who had been nominated by inspectors of schools. Cameron visited the nominees. From the 11 who were interested, he selected seven who had moderate needs for control, achievement, and affiliation, and who could act in a "reflective and supportive" role with the faculties in the schools. The seven-member OD team then received two days of training during the winter and three days the next spring. Between the two sessions, members of the OD team carried out the survey-data-feedback on current school operations.

Next the faculty of each experimental school participated in a weekend retreat for training in problem solving. After that the active problem-solving phase of the project ran for 10 months. Temporary problem-solving groups were formed in each of the experimental schools. They were intended to place emphasis on task (rather than process), to use peer pressure to keep themselves on task, to represent interest groups in the school, and to be a link with the rest of the school. During the active problem-solving phase, the OD facilitators demonstrated their competence as helpers and showed that they could be trusted by the faculties.

Each school formed three problem-solving groups, each group to undertake a particular task, as shown in Table 10-1. The problem-solving groups at the schools carried out a variety of activities that engaged all staff members, but particularly the problem-solving group members, in gathering information, making decisions, and taking action. Activities included surveys, inventories, displays,

Table 10-1. Problem-solving Tasks Undertaken by Three Schools in the Australian OD Project

School	Team Number	Number of Members	Task
Raworth	1	9	Resource organization
	2	unknown	Curriculum development in culture activities
	3	7	Teaching methods
Blue Gum	1	7	Relationships within and among major work groups
	2	7	Student evaluations, including reports to parents
	3	7	Resource organization
Redleaf	1	8	Expectations for faculty
	2	9	Student behavior
	3	10	Student evaluation

resource purchasing, curriculum developing, role playing, mounting in-service courses, developing teaching aids, role negotiating, and outcome evaluating. Overall, a great deal of energy was expended by school staffs in planning and development in addition to their normal teaching duties.

As the time for withdrawal of the OD facilitators approached, Cameron intended for the facilitators and their target schools to find teachers or others who would serve as internal facilitators, gradually taking over the helping role from the outsiders. Little of that happened. A year later Cameron visited Redleaf and discovered that "nothing more had happened at the school with regard to collaborative problem solving." Principals at Raworth and Blue Gum, however, did continue to call the Division of Services for materials to aid staff development. Both reported that collaborative activities were continuing; Raworth's principal held another weekend retreat, and Blue Gum's principal asked Cameron for an after-school refresher course in problem solving. One year later the two principals reported serving each other as OD facilitators. Two years later six of the original seven OD facilitators were actively leading a variety of OD projects in their own schools.

Bold Community College

The cadre in Bold Community College grew out of the college's effort in 1986 at strategic planning. Discussions with Schmuck actually began two years before a project steering committee was formed. The steering committee, made up of two administrators and four faculty members, recruited 20 instructors, counselors, administrators, and students to become a cadre of part-time OD facilitators. With the help of Schmuck, the steering committee began training the cadre one spring and the cadre began its field work the following spring. The cadre carried out 17 OD projects during its first two years of field work. All OD efforts were linked to the college's commitment to engaging as many stakeholders as feasible in strategic planning.

When a department or administrative unit requested help from the cadre, a team from the cadre and a committee from the target unit merged to become a planning team to conduct a diagnosis and design the OD and strategic planning. Some examples of the cadre's work were (1) improving working relations among members of a Nursing Department, (2) surveying community attitudes toward the business program, (3) helping an English faculty state its goals and helping the department head find ways to aid the faculty in reaching them, (4) training students as discussion leaders and data gatherers, and (5) facilitating a workshop on strategic planning for the governing board of trustees, a faculty committee, and a few administrative personnel. Generally, the cadre gave aid in diagnosis, communication skill training, goal setting, planning, decision making and team building. In a few instances, the cadre helped academic departments apply the *S-T-P* problem-solving procedure to their efforts at strategic planning. Teams from the cadre ranged in size from two to six members.

Two years after the cadre was launched, it began training new members. Sixteen trainees were selected from 35 applicants. The new members came from 10 different academic departments and from the central administration. The new members completed their training in one year. The college then unfortunately suffered drastic budget cuts and over the next few years the cadre was entirely disbanded. In a visit to the college recently, however, Schmuck found that at least half of the department heads originally trained in OD facilitation still were using OD procedures in their faculty meetings and committee work.

Jackson College

While the Bold cadre was still alive, a few of its key members helped establish a new cadre at Jackson College, a rather small college in a neighboring state.

Jackson is divided into four academic divisions (Math and Science, Arts and Letters, Humanities, and Social Studies). The cadre is divided into four corresponding teams with five cadre members on each team. Each OD team focuses its effort on one of the academic divisions. No cadre member is allowed to act as an OD facilitator to his or her own academic division.

The cadre's work is paid in part through budgets of each of the divisions. The college allocates annually $250 per faculty member to each division for staff development. The division can use that money to pay the cadre's expenses, including expenses for retreat time.

Two years after the cadre was started, 14 members were working in three divisions to improve their meetings' skills. Another team of three cadre members was helping staff members in the health center and counseling center think through how to reduce drug and alcohol abuse on campus.

Apparently, the cadre lasted for four years in all after which it was eliminated when a new president took over.

Sousa County Education Department

The cadre in Sousa County, Florida, came into being in the late 70s. It contained 14 people, including the then superintendent. The cadre was expanded and reorganized in the 80s. The 24 members of the 80s cadre received two weeks of training one summer. The OD training used the program called "Preparing Educational Training Consultants" published by the Northwest Regional Educational Laboratory. Another training cycle began in the middle 80s; it offered 27 hours of training over a nine-week period. In addition to the 24 persons already then in the cadre, eight potential recruits were also invited to attend.

The Sousa cadre follows the rules of doing OD in teams and of refraining from leading the OD project in members' own units. Cadre members volunteer to join OD teams when the coordinator notifies members of requests. The cadre as a whole meets irregularly, chiefly to receive further training in OD concepts and techniques.

The Sousa cadre assists schools in assessment, goal setting, and other phases of school improvement. It also offers in-service workshops. Ten years ago the district suffered financial restrictions, and money for training time was not available. Nevertheless, the district office still supported the cadre in other ways, and the coordinator reported "every possibility for success." We do not know how the Sousa cadre is doing today.

South Murphy County

Also in the late 70s, George Richmond was on the staff of the South Murphy County Office of Education, an office serving 23 districts in suburban California. Richmond proposed a cadre to two small districts: Millwood and Bunche. He attended meetings of principals, teachers, and classified staff in those two districts and recruited 22 potential members.

Training for the cadre ran for 30 hours in six evening sessions one fall using the *Second Handbook of Organization Development in Schools*. In addition, each person completed at least 10 hours of internship. At the end, 16 people chose to continue with the cadre. When, however, Richmond left education three years later to work in private industry, the cadre languished.

A few years after that Richmond returned to the South Murphy County Office as a private consultant. He discovered that 14 of the original 16 members wanted to revive the cadre. They brought in other potential members. The new cadre received training from him, emphasizing the memo of understanding, diagnosis, and macrodesign. A month later, with members from the Bunche, Millwood, and San Luis school districts, the new cadre was formally established. Five years later, the cadre had 18 members and, Richmond said, was "strong and healthy."

Carpenter College

Five years ago, at the instigation of President Helen Adams, Carpenter College, a two-year junior college for women, established the position of Coordinator of OD and hired Sharon Yocum for the job. Yocum built the Carpenter cadre.

She got nominations for potential cadre members from administrators and department heads. These recruits received two five-day blocks of OD training by Richard and Patricia Schmuck; the third edition of the *Handbook of Organization Development in Schools* was used. Of the 17 persons attending the training, 12 became the members of the cadre. Administrators, instructors, classified staff, and counselors composed the group. Some further OD training was given during the cadre's monthly meetings. The cadre began field work four years ago.

Burt Allen was coordinator during 1990–91. The cadre advertised for new members in October and November 1990 and took in three. Cadre members received little new training during that year, though monthly meetings continued.

Joan Marshall was coordinator during 1991–92. Cadre members received little new training during this year, either. Monthly meetings continued, and in March, 1992 the cadre held a retreat for business and group maintenance. During that same month, the cadre took in another two members; one was a department head and one was from the president's staff. By August 1992, the cadre had 17 members, of whom 14 were active.

The Carpenter College cadre had work waiting for it at the start. Student enrollments had been declining, and some faculty members were facing dismissal or reassignment. During 1990–91, the original 12 cadre members worked with faculty and students to analyze why enrollments were dwindling. They also helped an organization of alumni with its meetings. In addition, they taught courses in human relations, recommending that entire academic departments attend. And they recommended that departments send groups composed of the department head and at least two instructors to the course on effective meetings. Part of the problem of dwindling enrollments was connected to low faculty morale and high student dissatisfaction with some faculty members.

During 1991–92, the cadre sought to deal with conflict resolution in teaching teams, conflict resolution between faculty and administrators, and meetings of the college's management team. It also set up a series of meetings with students to engage the students in problem solving about how to improve the emotional climate at the college.

During 1991–1992, the cadre focused its efforts on faculty-student discussions about how to improve the climate of the college. The president required the department heads of departments with poor reputations among the students to use the cadre's services at least once. Two of the four used the cadre's services extensively. In addition, in one department, faculty members carried out a six-month project in "becoming more supportive of students as individuals."

At various times during its existence, the cadre also helped change the teaching techniques of three instructors, aided conflict resolution with faculty committees, and gave further help to the alumni organization.

The Carpenter College cadre has observed the rules of working in teams and refraining from doing OD in members' own units. In addition, the custom has developed of asking that requests from faculty members for help in their classes be routed through the department head so that he or she is sure to be aware of why the cadre members are visiting the faculty member's classroom.

The cadre has had the continuing support of the president of the college who is now in her tenth year in that job. Also, the college's board of trustees has continued to give strong support to college-wide OD. The college has paid for all retreat time needed. In 1992–93, as an example, the amount needed came to about $24,000. The money has been well spent since the emotional atmosphere of the college has improved significantly and student enrollments have started to rise.

For other examples of OD in higher education see Hopkins, Wideen, and Fullan (1984).

Bowman Schools

The School Climate Cadre in Bowman, Idaho, began as a joint project of the Teacher Resource Center, the Bowman Education Association, and the school district. The purpose of the cadre was "to maintain and enhance the working atmosphere of our schools ... primarily through the initiation of support groups within schools."

One August, the nine-member cadre received its first OD training, partly from two members of the Eisner cadre. Training covered personal effectiveness, stress management, decision making, and problem solving. During the next school year, the cadre gave workshops on those topics to seven hundred members of the Bowman school district.

The following August, the cadre, then numbering 12, received more training in OD. Three months later, the cadre contained 14 members: one assistant superintendent, two facilitators for the gifted and talented, two psychologists, one principal, two assistant principals, three counselors, two teachers, and a half-time coordinator.

In the fall of the next academic year, and again in the spring of that academic year, the Bowman cadre offered, among other courses, one entitled "Management Techniques for a Positive Climate." Several cadre members participated in the instruction. The text used was the *Second Handbook of Organization Development in Schools*. In a subsequent session, one principal attended with six of his school's teachers.

In a flyer distributed a year later, the cadre offered workshops in communication skills, effective meetings, team building, reaching consensus, problem solving, conflict resolution, increasing job satisfaction, nutrition, exercise, relaxation, stress and time management, dealing with difficult people, and developing assertive skills.

Though the Bowman cadre started by offering workshops, it also began early to prepare itself to conduct OD projects. After the cadre had existed for two years, the staff of an elementary school wanted to learn how to run its own meetings, and the principal approved. The cadre provided OD training to the staff in meeting effectiveness. By the end of that school year, the principal was telling the benefits to other principals.

The cadre's budget, in early 80s dollars, not counting salaries, was $2,000 in the first year, $4,000 in the second year, and $8,000 in the third year. One cadre member said after the third year that although the cadre was no doubt in its honeymoon period, everything seemed to be going well so far.

Like most others, the Bowman cadre holds meetings monthly.

In the examples above, you can see variations on the prototype we described in the first part of this chapter. Also apparent are differing origins or precipitating conditions and similarities in the cadres' work style.

We have also heard of cadres or cadrelike groups in schools and colleges in other parts of North America and in northern Europe, but we have only vague information about them. For some details about cadres of OD facilitators in education see Leatt and Schmuck (1988).

The Organization's Readiness for a Peer Cadre

Before launching a cadre, whoever is thinking of doing so should examine the college or school's readiness in four areas: (1) the top administrators, (2) the cadre's potential trainers, (3) the cadre's potential membership, and (4) the potential coordinator.

Administrative Readiness

First, as with other innovative educational programs or projects, establishing a cadre requires the institutional legitimacy that only top-level decision makers can provide. Although a cadre need not be initiated by top administrators (in Eisner and Bold, for example, much of the early work to establish those cadres was done by regular faculty members), the superintendent or president and other key personnel in influential positions should acknowledge the usefulness of OD and clearly state their commitment to support it.

Second, top administrators must be clear about where the cadre fits into the overall organizational structure. They must know to whom the cadre will go when it needs to explain its work or to request cooperation, and they must recognize, if the cadre is not to be viewed as simply an extension of top administration, that the cadre services should be equally available to all the organization's subsystems.

Third, the top administrators and their staffs should be very clear with the nascent cadre about the amount of money they will commit and then be determined to carry out the commitment.

Fourth, though it is not necessary for the top administrators to have had extensive experience with OD, they should be aware of both its costs and benefits. A new cadre will get off to a good start if a sizeable number of educators in the target system are ready to ask for OD help as it is offered.

Fifth, top administrators should feel a need for change and have confidence that crises can be averted through long-range efforts. Administrators of colleges or schools undergoing profound or pervasive crisis may believe they cannot afford the long view. If they believe they cannot, they should delay starting a cadre until emergencies seem less pressing.

Finally, the target organization must evidence the skills and norms necessary to build and maintain a new subsystem. Are people present who can plan where the new subsystem will fit in relation to other departments, projects, and programs? Are they willing to allocate resources to an OD effort? Are they receptive to the idea of part-time work by cadre members, responsive to the interdependent needs of the new subsystems, and confident that their own resources are necessary?

The Readiness of Trainers

The skills needed in a cadre are best learned in real OD projects under the tutelage of one or more experienced OD experts who are also good educators. Trainers should be ready to make a commitment of several months' duration.

Private OD consultants who often are based in universities or regional labs can serve during the first year of establishing a cadre. They are sometimes hard to find, especially in some locations, but with persistence it is possible to do so. You may not find an OD expert nearby who has had experience in education, but the experience of those who have worked in other human service organizations is often transferable to schools. Still, we strongly recommend that you search for OD experts with experiences with OD in colleges and schools.

As you search for outside OD consultants, you might call us to ask for the names of appropriate OD experts.

Center for Organization Development in Education
Division of Learning and Instructional Leadership
College of Education
University of Oregon
Eugene, OR 97403

Or you might call the psychology department, sociology department, or college of education at a nearby university.

The professional organizations named below maintain lists of OD consultants, some of whom have the necessary skills. You can use these lists to find consultants in your region. Even if you reach people who have had no experience in colleges or schools or who show no interest in your project, they might be a good source of referrals.

Director of Program Management
NTL Institute
1501 Wilson Boulevard
P.O. Box 9155, Rosslyn Station
Arlington, VA 22209

The Organization Development Institute
6501 Wilson Mills Road, Suite K
Cleveland, OH 44143

Potential trainers of cadres need information to determine whether the project has clear objectives and goals, the support of key personnel, and other resources required to initiate and sustain a training effort. In exchange, the district's leaders will want to assess the motivation, competencies, and resources of outside experts before contracting for training. At best, the contract should be a written document detailing the goals of the collaboration between expert and district, the obligations of each, and a clear statement of the resources (money, prestige, logistical support) being exchanged.

The Readiness of Potential Cadre Members

Two categories of people should exist in an educational organization before a cadre can be launched: individuals who want OD training and a few groups ready to use the services of an OD cadre once it is formed. When volunteers for the project are being recruited, it is important to inform the greatest number of people possible, giving potential members a chance to ask questions and to ascertain their commitment. Two-way communication is essential at this point, because many educators will be unclear about organization development, and especially about the purposes of cadres and their manner of working. Those who view the OD training as an opportunity for personal growth may lack the commitment to serve as OD cadre members after training. Others may view the project as only another administrative push toward improving a specific curriculum or implementing another technical innovation.

As potential OD cadre members are selected for training, at least five considerations are important. First, because they will take on cadre duties in addition to their regular full-time jobs as educators, applicants should demonstrate special motivation and understand the extent of the commitment required of them. Second, potential cadre members should either have some facilitation competencies already or have the ability to learn them. While many OD skills can be taught in workshops, the scope of the training task and the amount of time required to prepare the cadre will depend on the trainees' prior level of skill and understanding. Third, applicants should feel optimistic about their ability to influence others and change situations around them. Fourth, people who have previously exhibited leadership ability, who have participated in other innovative projects, who have high visibility in the college or school, and who have good rapport and a favorable reputation with persons in the administrative and faculty ranks should find it easier to help others.

Finally, the individual criteria for selection should be sufficiently relaxed to enable the creation of a 15- to 25-member group representing all important role groups in the college or school district. Role balance is important if cadre members are to help one another understand the target system's organizational forces and problems, provide ready-made links to various groups within the system, and reduce the likelihood that they will be perceived as pursuing the interests of any particular group over others. For the same reasons, target organizations might also pay attention to factors of sex, race, age, years of experience in the local organization, membership in professional organizations, and academic assignment. Some cadres include noncertified staff secretaries—for example—among their membership. At least one has a student or parent. Expanding cadre membership to include parents and students would add to the task of coordination, but we believe the benefits to be gained would make the experiment worth the effort.

The Coordinator

Once the decision has been made to develop a cadre and firm agreements have been reached between the educational organization and the outside consultants, the target organization must find someone to build support for the cadre and to recruit potential specialists and clients. This same person should later coordinate the cadre and link the specialists with the outside consultants, with others in the target organization, and with one another.

In Keele, Eisner, Bold, and Carpenter, we found that this person had to understand organization development, have experience as a facilitator, be familiar with the working arrangements of educational organizations and cadres, and have the skills necessary to coordinate the efforts of diverse individuals and groups. In addition, we sought a coordinator who had leadership and administrative talents, had earned a high degree of trust and respect from colleagues, and had demonstrated ability in working successfully with others at difficult tasks. Skill as a trainer or facilitator is important but not paramount. The critical factor is the person's ability to link the cadre with other groups of educators and to coordinate its efforts.

People with all these qualities are probably rare in educational organizations, although many of the skills are similar to those needed in convening adult task groups. Colleges and schools may look to their own personnel for someone who either has these qualifications or who could be trained to fill the position. A qualified coordinator from outside will need help in becoming settled and familiar with the educational organization.

Training the Cadre

In training the Keele, Eisner, Bold, and Carpenter cadres, we had the following four objectives—shared, we believe, by the trainers of the other cadres described above:

1. The cadre was to develop into a cohesive subsystem with clear goals, roles, norms, and procedures both for internal functioning and for delivering OD help within its larger organization.
2. The specialist trainees were to feel enthusiastic about their tasks and their own potential influence as OD facilitators.
3. They were to learn about OD theory, intervention designs, and techniques.
4. They were to develop skills in data collection, communication, problem solving, convening meetings, and managing conflicts, and to convert those skills into strategies and designs for helping others.

During the initial training, cadre members learned about OD by experiencing process analyses during their own team building. They received lecturettes and reading assignments designed to increase cognitive understanding, and the practice and experiential learning were used to teach skills. Most workshop activities were designed to be self-analytic, self-reflexive, and self-directed. Structured activities such as games, simulations, and role playing were used in the early days of training, but were gradually replaced by realistic procedures and skills that would often be more useful for accomplishing actual tasks. Cadre members worked in several different groupings during the initial training, enabling them to become well enough acquainted with one another to build functional interdependence and cohesiveness. It is important for cadre members to work and play together sufficiently, and to talk about their working and playing together sufficiently, so that they develop strong trust in one another.

Doing OD in educational organizations has its stressful episodes, which are not usually felt as poignantly by outside consultants.

Strong trust among cadre members (or clarity about a lack of trust where it occurs) is needed to help facilitators weather the storms of stressful episodes. As an example, a principal of an elementary school once called one of our cadres to say that he had arrived that morning to find resignations on his desk from 12 of his teachers. In response, a cadre team interviewed the entire faculty. In a faculty meeting with the principal present, the team members reported the concerns they had discovered. They then helped to resolve the conflicts, and several days later all but two of the 12 teachers withdrew their resignations.

Another example of very high stress occurred in a school district when the teachers went on strike. A few teachers and most administrators crossed picket lines to go to work. Some of the members of the cadre in that district found themselves having to look other cadre members in the eye as they crossed the lines. The strike put severe stress on the fabric of the cadre, but their cohesiveness was strong enough to enable them to understand that their conflicts during the strike were due to the system they were all caught in and to the role conflicts it forced upon them. The cadre had to use several of its meetings for members to air their emotions, but it survived the episode as strong as ever.

Colleges also present their share of challenges to cadre members. In addition to difficult facilitating tasks and events in a college beyond a cadre's control, the way the cadre is embedded in the college will also bring episodes of stress. For example, department heads will sometimes show reluctance to have certain cadre members do OD in their departments, because the department heads feel competitive with the cadre members' home departments. Cadre members will sometimes find their work as facilitators in conflict with that of their regular jobs. And sometimes one member will suddenly get sick and someone else will have to step into an OD project in which he or she does not feel competent.

Because of those inevitable and recurring stresses, it is important that the initial training enable cadre members to come to know one another much more deeply than colleagues at work usually do. They must feel fully confident that they know each other's hopes and fears, strengths and weaknesses. They must know on whom they can count and for what. They must know that all the cadre's active members feel devoted to the welfare of the group and to that of its members as friends and admired colleagues. And they must know that when a sudden need arises, any active member will stretch an extra muscle and give up an hour of sleep to get the job done.

Cadre members cannot have those requisite attitudes and that confidence unless it actually becomes true that members will respond to one another's needs with solidarity. The initial training and the cadre's regular self-renewal sessions must enable solidarity to develop and continue. We have, therefore, always taken time in the initial training for participants to debrief thoroughly after the exercises—that is, to tell the feelings they had about one another during the exercise and the feelings they anticipate having about one another in an actual OD project. When a lack of trust or a lack of competence has surfaced, we have arranged further sessions to build new trust or competence. In doing so, we have been explicit about our reasons for making the rearrangements, thus modeling the honesty and openness necessary for maintaining a high level of competence among all members.

In brief, the strong emotions of solidarity become the armor against the strong emotions of threat and conflict the cadre will meet in its work.

Maintenance and Renewal

When a cadre is well trained at the outset, half the battle is won. But the other half—maintaining the strength and resilience of the cadre while replenishing its membership from year to year—goes on forever. We review here the most important matters requiring continued attention.

Structure

The organizational structure of a cadre radiates from the coordinator, who (1) participates as a team member in some of the cadre's OD projects; (2) arranges demonstrations for potential participants; (3) assists in the start-up and contract-building stages of OD projects; (4) coordinates the various OD teams; (5) explains the goals, methods, and work of the cadre to people in the college or school district; (6) arranges for outside experts when they are required; (7) links the cadre with the central administration; and (8) links the cadre to groups outside the organization, such as other cadres, research universities, county or state departments of education, and research and development centers.

Every cadre forms committees to help with some of the coordinator's duties and with such tasks as organizing self-renewal sessions and recruiting new members. A cadre of some size, however—say more than 10 members—also needs a decision-making body. In Eisner, membership in this body rotates among people currently active in OD consultation teams. In contrast, the

Carpenter cadre used a four-person group elected at large. This central body, whatever it is called, copes with matters that must be decided between plenary meetings of the cadre. Also, it typically helps in preparing budgets, allocating resources, planning self-renewal events, deciding on responses to requests from participants, and recruiting new members.

When enough money is available, the question usually arises whether it might be advantageous to pay some members to work in their cadre roles half or full time. It might also be advantageous in a cadre of some size to rotate a few half-time assignments. That goes contrary to the egalitarian norm that is often strong in cadres, but it can work if cadre members watch for signs of resentment and cope with them promptly. It is desirable in any case to pay overtime for work beyond the call of duty.

Every cadre finds that its members differ a great deal in the amount of time they can give to cadre work. Some find some kinds of work not to their liking. Others find that they had originally overestimated the amount of time people in their regular work units would suffer them to be gone. The Eisner cadre established three formal categories of membership: (1) "active members," those currently working in OD teams and attending most meetings of the cadre; (2) "supporting members," those who attend meetings only occasionally but speak and act in support of the cadre in their own units and elsewhere; and (3) "inactive members," those who have suspended all their activities with the cadre for a limited time. Persons who stop all activity without any estimate of a return date are dropped from the rolls.

Using teams, not individuals, to provide OD help is an important part of the cadre's structure. Working in teams enables cadre members to pool their skills, give one another emotional support, and demonstrate to clients by their own behavior that collaboration among people in different jobs is not only possible but actually enjoyable.

The OD teams are not permanent. A new one is formed for each OD project. Each member of the cadre works with a variety of colleagues as the months go by. That rotation is one more structural feature that maintains the cohesiveness of the cadre. Using temporary teams also allows new members to join teams as apprentices to get practical experience gradually with helpful colleagues at their elbows.

Support from the Top

Lively support in the central administration is vital to the cadre. Such support can help cadre members get released time from their regular assignments. Central administrative support can also make a continuing budget more likely and give potential participants more confidence in asking for the cadre's help.

The coordinator is in large part responsible for the vital link between the central administration and the cadre. But the coordinator cannot do it alone, and therefore the cadre maintains membership from all ranks in the larger organization. In their regular jobs, cadre members are the grassroots to which most administrators are responsive; they are role senders. Beyond that, the central administrators who are also members of the cadre can influence other central administrators directly.

It often happens that central administrators who join a cadre find later that they cannot devote as much time to it as they originally hoped. In both Keele and Eisner, we noted some decrease, after the cadres were first established, in the percentage of central administrators active in the cadre's work. Most of the administrators, however, continued to attend meetings often enough to remain well informed about the cadre's doings, and they provided very important support for the cadre among their administrative colleagues. A cadre should cherish and nurture those connections.

Relationships with Participants

Doing good work is essential, of course, though a cadre can overcome the disappointments of some failures, especially if participants enter the OD project with a high awareness of the risks. Beyond good work, however, some other considerations are important.

Awareness. Although the cadre should not press its services on participants, it should advertise itself and give demonstrations of its kind of work. A cadre can use handouts, circulars, announcements in newsletters, posters, and even slide-tape presentations.

A very effective way for the cadre to build informed awareness is to offer free courses to individuals in communication and group-process skills. The Eisner cadre has offered three courses of increasing complexity, each made up of 10 three-hour sessions. Participants get actual experience with some of the kinds of work the cadre does. They can tell others about that work and about the competence with which the cadre members do it. If the unit in which they work considers asking for the services of a cadre team, participants are likely to show optimism about the cadre's helpfulness. The courses have those outcomes among almost all enrollees, because they acquire practical skills they can put to use quickly.

The Eisner cadre did a good job of building awareness. In a study of that cadre, Burr and Bell (1976) say,

> During the first five years of the cadre's tenure, the 35 or 40 people who have been members (approximately two percent of district employees) have exerted a surprising amount of influence on this district of 2,000 staff. The results of the study show that a sizable amount of knowledge exists about the cadre, and 67 percent of their knowledge is accurate. Attitudes toward the cadre are substantially more favorable than unfavorable, particularly in schools where cadre interventions have taken place.

Now, 20 years later, there continues to be evidence that the Eisner cadre is successful.

Collaboration. Doing OD only when invited to do so lays the necessary foundation for good collaboration between the cadre and its participants. Never acting as a formal facilitator to one's own unit also models collaboration, since the participants see that members of their own group who are also members of the cadre do not therefore set themselves apart, but collaborate with the cadre team just as the participant group does.

A cadre maintains collaboration with participants throughout an OD project. Cadre members demonstrate that they value democratic and humanistic relationships by showing in their own behavior with participants the kinds of behavior they hope their participants will emulate: interdependence, collaboration, openness, and the use of rational inquiry for organizing and getting work accomplished. During each step of an OD project, they strive to remain open to feedback concerning their own performance and their helpfulness or unhelpfulness.

Long-term Work. Because organizational problems are a continuing part of college and school life, they are seldom resolved in a brief workshop; they almost always require an extended OD design. Short-term efforts may lead to undesirable consequences. We have learned, for example, that fewer than about 24 hours of OD training with a school staff in communication skills can do more harm than good. Even when a short-term project seems highly successful, short-term gains usually fade quickly. Through demonstration and discussion, OD specialists reveal to potential participants the futility of quick interventions, and they refuse participants who desire one-shot events except as a means of demonstrating longer term OD designs.

Telling participants that a short OD project will not get them what they want is discouraging to some participants, but it also impresses them with the cadre's sense of responsibility and integrity. Usually, a request for a short OD effort with unrealistic goals can be converted into a short demonstration of the kind of work the cadre does, purposely giving the participants direct experience upon which to base the choice of whether to undertake a longer project. If the participants are still tentative, the OD project can be made tentative also, with the understanding that a new memorandum of agreement will be made after each part of a longer play is carried out. But if participants insist on an unrealistic agreement, the cadre is better off to refuse it.

When the cadre takes the long-term view, participants know that the cadre cares about their own long-term welfare—that it is not just dipping in for some gain of its own. This stance also conveys to central administrators that the cadre cares about the long-term welfare of the college or school—that it is not just playing around.

Self-renewal

To remain effective, cadres must renew and upgrade their skills. They must be on the lookout for new ideas and methods, and they must solve problems that arise about their own internal coordination and that arise between themselves and parts of their larger organization. Because they work in teams, each tightly interdependent but rotating in membership, they must do those things as a group. Cadres use monthly meetings on evenings or weekends, occasional seminars, summer workshops, and annual retreats for this sort of renewal.

Cadres periodically hire outside experts to explain theory and methods of diagnosis or evaluation, show new OD techniques, and serve as facilitators at the cadre's longer convocations. As noted earlier, OD experts who have worked with colleges or schools are not easy to find, but it is much easier to find consultants nearby whose skills or experience can be *adapted* to use by the cadre. Cadres have shown themselves very capable of doing that.

The renewal meetings of a cadre differ, of course, from most staff-development activities. The distinguishing features are these:

1. A cadre initiates its own self-improvement. It determines its own needs, recruits its own outside experts and usually helps design its own training. That fact heightens commitment, readiness to learn, and the readiness of cadre members to apply their learning.

2. The new learning is directed to group functioning, not to individual functioning. Training sessions for a cadre are usually devoted to skills to be exercised in teams, not by individuals.
3. Training sessions are not lectures, but practice. Lecturing and reading are used to illustrate practice, but it is practical skill that is emphasized. Any outside expert always has to answer the demand, "All right, that sounds good. Now can you show us how to do it?"
4. A cadre deals constantly with interpersonal relations among members. The strong emphasis on collaborative teamwork demands high levels of trust and confidence. If someone fails to do his or her part, others cannot take refuge in the claim that they have done their duty, leaving the weaker member to be cast out by some superior. The solution of the problem always requires airing feelings about how both the stronger and weaker team members act.

Maintaining a skilled, lively, and cohesive cadre takes time. We have some figures from a report made to the district in January 1993 by the coordinator of the Eisner cadre. Between July 1992 and January 1993, the Eisner cadre distributed its person-hours as follows:

Conducting OD projects	65	
Planning for OD projects	48	
Giving other kinds of help	40	
Total for all consultations		153
Upgrading members' own skills	83	
Attending to cadre business	131	
Total for maintenance		214

During those months, the Eisner cadre spent many more person-hours on maintenance compared with carrying out OD in the schools. A similar tally 10 years earlier had revealed similar proportions.

Recruiting

Cadres periodically send circulars around the organization advertising openings in their ranks. They try to recruit more members than immediate prospects of OD will require, because (1) having more members than are immediately necessary reduces the shock of sudden overloads, (2) some new members inevitably drop out for various reasons, (3) some become relatively inactive—that is, they become what the Eisner and Bold cadres call supporting members—and (4) it is always useful to have members throughout the college or school as role senders.

Circulars always include a brief description of the cadre and of OD's goals and techniques. Many people in the educational organization will not be knowledgeable about the cadre's methods, and many will not even have heard of the cadre. The circulars include the coordinator's telephone number or e-mail address for those who want more information. They may also include an application blank, though that stage can be left for later.

The circular does not ask people to commit themselves to joining the cadre. Rather, it invites them to attend a meeting where they can learn more about the cadre's work and ask questions. Many persons will lose interest after that first meeting. The remainder can be invited to a second meeting to go into more detail, or they can be interviewed individually. After that, a few more will drop away. Some of those who still want to join the cadre will be selected, and others will be advised to prepare themselves by enrolling in the free courses conducted by the cadre or by some other means.

Several cadres offer free courses both to spread skill in communication and group dynamics (or knowledge about them, at least) around the college or school district and to generate a pool of likely recruits. Most "graduates" of these courses become useful role senders on behalf of the cadre.

Outside Threats

Compared with many organizational innovations, cadres seem exceptionally sturdy. Nevertheless, not all cadres have survived the slings and arrows of outrageous fortune. Is it possible to design a cadre or some other arrangement that would be impervious to any possible outside threat? We think not.

Nor do we consider it a good idea to try. No human system is an island. Any human system is shaped not only by itself but also by the other human systems around it. If a college or school district changes, the cadre must change. If social problems change, educational organizations and cadres must change. As college curriculum changes, the cadre's OD focus will change. As budgets change, a cadre's mode of operation must change. And so on. Our hope in our design of the cadre is not that our 10 rules will suffice forever. Rather, we hope that sufficient adaptability grows out of those rules to enable most cadres to bend and evolve, without shattering, as they meet challenges to their capabilities. We do not hope that every cadre will look 20 years from now as it did 20 years ago, nor that it will be following the same 10 rules. Instead, we hope that colleges and school districts will have institutionalized a way to help members deal cooperatively with their own organizational problems. If that kind of mutual help continues and grows, we may still see something recognizable as cadres in school educational systems 20 years from now, but we may not.

Our society exhibits two strong and opposite trends. One is the growing trend toward local self-sufficiency and participative democracy. That is certainly true of our colleges and schools and that is the trend of which cadres partake. The other is the trend toward centralization and far-flung hierarchy. That is the trend of big government, litigation, and accountability enforced from the top. And that is the trend when pressure groups try to get colleges and schools to change in a particular way. When governmental regulations make life more difficult in a college or school, they make the work of a cadre more difficult also. When a group of citizens demands that its own idea of education be enforced upon all students, the participative democracy (the nourishing pluralism) of our educational system is threatened, and the cadre finds it harder to foster mutual self-help. When the courts issue rulings about what all educational organizations must do, that much local self-sufficiency is nibbled away. We are not here taking sides about any one law, regulation, or court decision. We are pointing out that these two trends oppose each other and that the cadre, along with the typical educational organization, is pulled both ways. We think that this two-way tugging is the source of most of the severe conflicts to which educators of all types and cadres must nowadays adapt.

We are often asked how a cadre or any other organizational arrangement can be made invulnerable to the turbulent societal environment of today. Beyond urging colleges and schools to build in as much adaptability as possible, we do not know the answer to that question. Indeed, we think there is a point of diminishing returns beyond which the effort to make an educational organization impervious to threat is effort wasted. It is better to turn the effort to sensing environmental trends and searching for ways of coping with new conditions. That may mean letting the old ways "fail" and vanish. The continuity comes in using the lessons learned to build anew. Individuals die, but the species continues. Old ideas become quaint, but the culture remains strong. Adaptability, we think, is not a suit of armor, but a phoenix.

The Ultimate Target

Near the beginning of this chapter, we wrote about the catcher in the rye. A disturbing aspect of that metaphor is that the catcher stands apart. The catcher is not a member of the group, but assumes the special role of savior, who saves the others from their own inadequacies. The role is paternalistic and even arrogant. When an OD facilitator takes that stance and when the participants accept it, the latter become dependent upon the facilitator, and the likelihood dwindles that the participants will ever learn to manage their own affairs. We would like to see educators managing their own affairs, even their own organizational self-renewal. We think the cadre is a large step in that direction.

Nevertheless, the danger remains that cadre members will fall into the same savior role as an outside facilitator might. We think cadres can democratize the management of colleges and schools best if they encourage their participants to become facilitators to themselves in the same way that cadre members become facilitators to themselves within the cadre—through open communication, using personal resources as the tasks demand, helping one another apply strengths and strengthen weaknesses, giving the supports of energy and loyalty when stresses mount, and rotating the process roles in helping. Conditions being right, the cadre can teach participants how to do without the cadre. We don't mean to be categorical about this, of course. Cadres do call upon outsiders occasionally to help them in their work, and people in colleges and schools should call upon the cadre occasionally even when they are themselves skillful in their own OD. But we want to encourage people all the way down the hierarchy—even students—who would otherwise depend on a catcher, to practice self-help. And we also summon the individual college professor or the individual classroom teacher to apply OD concepts and practices to his or her own classroom instruction.

At its best, OD offers concepts and procedures to carry democracy into the work place, where people seek achievement and productivity, control over their own work domain, and friendship and affection. To do that in colleges and schools, OD should come to include not only administrators and teachers, but also students, parents, classified personnel, and perhaps other citizens with a stake in the community's educational infrastructure.

What steps might a cadre encourage?

First, the cadre might help heads of educational units learn how to initiate and support the norms, structures, and procedures needed for organizational problem solving. Although heads cannot easily remove themselves from the flow of organizational life, they can start the conditions necessary for communicating, goal setting, problem solving, and decision making. Indeed, heads can act as OD facilitators in their work with colleagues without even using the words *organization development*.

It is not impossible, in fact, for the head of an educational unit to step out of the authority position, at least temporarily, to act as a guide on the side. In one case we know of, the principal of a senior high school did just that: for an entire academic year while on sabbatical leave and studying for a doctorate, he served as an organizational facilitator to his own staff and student body (for an account, see Flynn, 1976). Data from questionnaires answered by all faculty members indicated that the principal was able to step out of his role and be effective as a facilitator with the majority of his staff. Thirty-four of 58 faculty members perceived him to be in the role of OD facilitator throughout the experimental year; 14 saw him in a halfway position; and only 10 still saw him in the role of principal as authority throughout the year. The 34 who saw him in the facilitating role thought he was more competent, more facilitating, more open, and more willing to let the faculty members find things out for themselves than the last 10 did. The latter had difficulty in viewing him as helpful. The evaluation also showed that the faculty members' communication improved, their participation in group meetings and their initiation of influence attempts became more widespread, and by the end of the academic year they were clarifying and developing a new, more participative decision-making structure.

Second, instructors, counselors, and department heads might act as OD facilitators within their own colleges, at least in matters in which they do not have too strong a personal stake. They might act as observers and coaches in Fishbowl arrangements or as conveners or recorders in meetings, and they might regularly model communication skills and helping roles in groups. They might also form helping pairs to facilitate one another's professional growth, both as instructors in the classroom and as staff members, observing each other, giving each other feedback, and generally supporting one another through personal change. Indeed, Schmuck has recently worked with a group of college instructors who in striving to use OD practices in their classrooms have paired off to offer encouragement and feedback to each other.

In relation to OD for the entire organization, instructors and others might serve as members of a collegewide or schoolwide renewal committee to collect data on the systematic effectiveness of their organization and to arrange to feed data back to the faculty to stimulate collaborative problem solving. A few of the members of the renewal committee might also act as trainers in S-T-P problem solving. Goodlad (1984, p. 278) has recommended a similar body.

Third, it is not unreasonable to consider giving interested parents OD functions in elementary school. As an arm of a schoolwide renewal committee, for example, they could collect questionnaire and interview data from other parents and citizens in the community, analyze those data and put them into tables and figures, and present the data to the staff with the collaboration of the principal and teachers. Moreover, parents could participate in staff and team problem solving, adding their thoughts to the general reservoir of ideas obtained during brainstorming. And there could be instances in which parents would be helpful facilitators to helping pairs—for example, when a pair is wrestling with ways of increasing the engagement of particular parents in their children's education.

Finally, students remain an untapped resource as OD facilitators to their own secondary schools and colleges. At first, that concept sounds crazy, but it seems crazy only when students are viewed as the clients or as the "products" of education. Consider students as organizational participants in some aspects of educational diagnosis and planning, educational problem solving, and faculty decision making. Indeed, a failure to consider students as organizational participants could partly explain low student motivation and high student alienation. A case in point was Carpenter College before the OD effort there. Instructors and administrators can become so preoccupied with their own management efforts that they lose touch with the students. For their part, students can feel "put down," even oppressed, by imposed rules and become alienated when their ideas and energies have not been used.

Perhaps the most straightforward procedure for helping students participate in the educational organization is to use the social studies curriculum. A course for high schools, for example, has been developed by Arends et al. (1981) and Schmuck and Schmuck (1992) to help students understand the dynamics of the school as a formal social organization, to delineate their roles as potential organizational participants, and to teach the students the skills required to design and participate in a schoolwide improvement program. Through experiential activities, reading, and group discussions, students learn how the motives of affiliation, power, and achievement can be satisfied or frustrated through organizational participation. They practice communication skills to facilitate their discussions about interpersonal relations in the school. They explore the roles of individuals, groups, and the organization as a whole in carrying out the school's mission and in satisfying the needs of both students and adults. In one activity, students prepare "maps" of the informal structure of the school, designating the groups in which they spend their time out of school. They compare the maps with rosters of students in classrooms and discuss the congruence of friendship groups with work groups. In another activity, students collect questionnaires about the climate of the school from teachers, administrators, and other students. They analyze the data and present a summary in a colloquium for members of their class and interested adults in the school. That kind of activity can easily be adapted in colleges. It offers an entry point for students to act not only as organizational participants, but also as OD facilitators to their own high school or college.

We believe that educational participants, including students, can successfully act as OD facilitators to themselves and that they can bring into being a self-renewing organization without the need for large amounts of outside expert help. Perhaps the concept of participants as OD facilitators serving themselves is no more radical or outrageous than that of consciously watching the effect of one's own behavior or of being aware collectively of how a social system is operating. After all, what the OD facilitator offers is an organizational mirror. And once the participants can look at themselves in the mirror, they can manage changes in their own system. Self-renewal, one might say, is simply self-reflection accompanied by concerted, collaborative action to right the wrongs that are discovered. Can participants as OD facilitators to themselves learn to hold up the organizational mirror together? We know they can.

References

Alderfer, Clayton P. *Existence, relatedness, and growth*. New York: Free Press, 1972.

Allport, Gordon W., and Leo F. Postman. The basic psychology of rumor. *Transactions of the New York Academy of Sciences* (Series 2), 1945, *8*, 61–81.

Arends, Richard I., R. A. Schmuck, M. Milleman, J. Arends, and J. Wiseman. *School life and organizational psychology*. New York: Teachers College Press, 1981.

Bachman, J., C. Smith, and J. Slesinger. Control performance and satisfaction: An analysis of structural and individual effects. *Journal of Personality and Social Psychology*, 1966, *42*, 127–136.

Bales, Robert F. *Interaction process analysis: A method for the study of small groups*. Reading, MA: Addison-Wesley, 1950.

Bass, Bernard. *A program of exercises for management and organizational psychology*. Pittsburgh: Management Development Associates, 1966.

Bassin, Marc, Thomas Gross, and Patricia Jordan. Developing renewal processes in urban high schools. *Theory into Practice*, 1979, *18*(2), 73–81. Published by the Ohio State University.

Bavelas, Alex. Communication patterns in task-oriented groups. *Journal of the Acoustical Society of America*, 1950, *22*, 725–730.

Berlew, David E. Leadership and organizational excitement. In D. A. Kolb, I. M. Rubin, and J. M. McIntyre (Eds.), *Organizational psychology: A book of readings* (2nd ed.). Englewood Cliffs, NJ: Prentice-Hall, 1974, pp. 265–277. Also in *California Management Review*, 1974.

Berman, Paul, and Milbrey McLaughlin. *Federal programs supporting education change*. (Vol. 6) *The findings in review* . Santa Monica, CA: Rand, 1975.

Birnbaum, Robert, James P. Begin, and Bert R. Brown. *Cooperation in academic negotiations: A guide to mutual gains bargaining*. New Brunswick, NJ: Institute of Management and Labor Relations, Rutgers University, 1985.

Boulding, Kenneth. *Ecodynamics*. Beverly Hills, CA: Sage, 1978.

Bowers, David G. OD techniques and theory in 23 organizations: The Michigan ICL study. *Journal of Applied Behavioral Science*, 1973, *19*(1), 21–43.

463

Buckley, Walter. *Sociology and modern systems theory.* Englewood Cliffs, NJ: Prentice-Hall, 1967.

Burr, Ann M., and Warren E. Bell. The Eugene cadre: An internal group of OD specialists—their impact on a school district. Eugene, OR: Center for Educational Policy and Management, 1976. (Mimeo)

Cameron, William G. The in-service school development project: A case study in consultancy for planned change. Doctoral dissertation, University of New England (Australia), 1982.

Coch, L., and John R. P. French. Overcoming resistance to change. *Human Relations,* 1948, *1,* 512–532.

Cohen, Michael D., James G. March, and Johan P. Olsen. A garbage can model of organizational choice. *Administrative Science Quarterly,* 1972, *17,* 1–25.

DeCharms, Richard. *Personal causation.* New York: Academic Press, 1968(a).

DeCharms, Richard. Personal causation training in the schools. *Journal of Applied Social Psychology,* 1968(b), *2*(2), 95–113.

DeCharms, Richard. *Enhancing motivation: Change in the classroom.* New York: Irvington (distributed by Halstead Press), 1976.

Derr, C. Brooklyn. Organizational development in one large urban school system. *Education and Urban Society,* 1970, *2,* 403–419.

Derr, C. Brooklyn. An organizational analysis of the Boston School Department. Doctoral dissertation, School of Education, Harvard University, 1971.

Dowling, William F. Conversation: An interview with Fletcher Byrom. *Organizational Dynamics,* 1978, *7*(1), 37–60.

Flynn, C. Wayne. Collaborative decision making in a secondary school: An experiment. *Education and Urban Society,* 1976, *8*(2), 172–182.

Foa, Uriel G., and Edna B. Foa. *Societal structures of the mind.* Springfield, IL: Charles C Thomas, 1974.

Fosmire, Fred, and Carolin Keutzer. Task-directed learning: A systems approach to marital therapy. Paper presented at the meeting of the Oregon Psychological Association and the Western States Psychological Association, May 1968.

Fox, Robert, R. A. Schmuck, E. Van Egmond, M. Ritvo, and C. Jung. *Diagnosing professional climate of schools.* Fairfax, VA: NTL Learning Resource Corp., 1973.

Francisco, Richard. The Documentation and Technical Assistance Project in urban schools. *Theory Into Practice,* 1979, *18*(4), 89–96.

French, John R. P., and Bertram H. Raven. The bases of social power. In D. Cartwright (Ed.), *Studies in social power.* Ann Arbor: University of Michigan Press, 1959, pp. 150–167.

Fullan, Michael, Matthew B. Miles, and Gib Taylor. *OD in schools: The state of the art* (5 vols.; final report to the National Institute of Education under contract Nos. 400-77-0051 and 400-77-0052). Toronto: Ontario Institute for Studies in Education, 1978. Three extractions from the original report appear elsewhere: (1) M. Fullan and M. B. Miles. OD in schools: The state of the art. In W. W. Burke (Ed.), *The cutting edge: Current theory and practice in organization development.* San Diego:

University Associates, 1978. pp. 149–174. (2) M. Fullan, M. B. Miles, and G. Taylor. Organization development in schools: The state of the art. *Review of Educational Research*, 1980, *50*(1), 121–183. (3) M. B. Miles and M. Fullan. The nature and impact of organization development in schools. In M. M. Milstein (Ed.), *Schools, conflict, and change*. New York: Teachers College Press, 1980, pp. 72–95.

Gardner, John. *Self-renewal: The individual and the innovative society.* New York: Harper & Row, 1963.

Gibb, Jack R. Defensive communication. *Journal of Communication*, 1961, *11*, 141–148.

Goldman, Paul, Diane Dunlap, and David Conley. Facilitative power and nonstandardized solutions to school site restructuring. *Educational Administration Quarterly*, 1993, *29*(1), 69–92.

Goodlad, John. *A place called school*. New York: McGraw-Hill, 1984.

Hale, James R., and R. Allen Spanjer. *Systematic and objective analysis of instruction training manual.* Portland: Northwest Regional Educational Laboratory, 1972.

Hall, Jay. *Systems maintenance: Gatekeeping and the involvement process.* Monroe, TX: Teleometrics International, 1969.

Harrison, Roger. Role negotiation: A tough-minded approach to team development. In W. W. Burke and H. A. Hornstein (Eds.), *The social technology of organization development*. Fairfax, VA: NTL Learning Resources Corporation, 1972, pp. 84–96. Another version appears in R. T. Golembiewski and W. B. Eddy (Eds.), *Organization development in public administration, Part 2*. New York: Marcel Dekker, 1978.

Harrison, Roger. How to design and conduct self-directed learning experiences. *Group and Organization Studies*, 1978, *3*(2), 149–167.

Harrison, Roger, and Jim Kouzes. The power potential of organization development. *Training and Development Journal*, 1980 (April), 44–47.

Hedberg, Bo L. T., Paul C. Nystrom, and William H. Starbuck. Camping on seesaws: Prescriptions for a self-designing organization. *Administrative Science Quarterly*, 1976, *21*, 41–64.

Hersey, Paul. *The situational leader*. Escondido, CA: Center for Leadership Studies, 1984.

Hirschman, Albert O. *Exit, voice, and loyalty*. Cambridge: Harvard University Press, 1970.

Hopkins, David, Marvin Wideen, and Michael Fullan. Organizational development in faculties of education. *Group and Organizational Studies*, 1984, *9*(3), 373–398.

Hornstein, H., D. Callahan, E. Fisch, and B. Benedict. Influence and satisfaction in organizations: A replication. *Sociology of Education*, 1968, *412*, 380–389.

Jackson, Philip W. *Life in classrooms*. New York: Holt, Rinehart, & Winston, 1968.

Johnson, David W., and Frank P. Johnson. *Joining together: Group theory and group skills* (1st and 2nd eds.). Englewood Cliffs, NJ: Prentice-Hall, 1975 and 1982.

Johnson, David W., and Roger T. Johnson. *Learning together and alone:*

Cooperation, competition, and individualization. Englewood Cliffs, NJ: Prentice-Hall, 1975.

Katz, Daniel, and Robert L. Kahn. *The social psychology of organizations* (2nd ed.). New York: Wiley, 1978.

Katz, Elihu. The two-step flow of communication: An up-to-date report on an hypothesis. *Public Opinion Quarterly*, 1957, *21*, 68–78.

Kelsh, Bruce. Effects of a teachers' strike on an organization development cadre. Doctoral dissertation, University of Oregon, 1983.

Knutson, Andie L. Quiet and vocal groups. *Sociometry*, 1960, *23*, 36–49.

Kouzes, James M., and Paul R. Mico. Domain theory: An introduction to organizational behavior in human service organizations. *Journal of Applied Behavioral Science*, 1979, *15*(4), 449–469.

Lawrence, P. R., and J. W. Lorsch. *Organizations and environment: Managing differentiation and integration.* Boston: Harvard Business School, Division of Research, 1967.

Leatt, Desmond, and Richard Schmuck. *Cadres of organization development consultants in schools: A progress report.* Eugene, OR: UCEA Center on Organizational Development in Schools, 1988.

Leavitt, Harold J. Some effects of certain communication patterns on group performance. *Journal of Abnormal and Social Psychology*, 1951, *46*, 38–50.

Leavitt, Harold J., and Ronald Mueller. Some effects of feedback on communication. *Human Relations*, 1951, *4*, 401–410.

Lewin, K. *Field theory in the social sciences.* New York: Harper & Row, 1951.

Lewin, Kurt, Ronald Lippitt, and Ralph K. White. Patterns of aggressive behavior in experimentally created "social climates." *Journal of Social Psychology*, 1939, *10*, 271–299.

Likert, Rensis. *New patterns of management.* New York: McGraw-Hill, 1961.

Likert, Rensis. *The human organization: Its management and value.* New York: McGraw-Hill, 1967.

Likert, Rensis, and Jane Gibson Likert. A method for coping with conflict in problem-solving groups. *Group and Organization Studies*, 1978, *3*(4), 427–434.

Longabaugh, Richard. A category system for coding interpersonal behavior as social exchange. *Sociometry*, 1963, *26*, 319–344.

Lortie, Dan C. *School-teacher: A sociological study.* Chicago: University of Chicago Press, 1975.

Luft, Joseph. *Group processes: An introduction to group dynamics* (3rd ed). Palo Alto, CA: Mayfield, 1984.

McClelland, David C. Methods of measuring human motivation. In J. W. Atkinson (Ed.), *Motives in fantasy, action, and society.* New York: Van Nostrand, 1958, pp. 7–42.

McGregor, Douglas. *The professional manager.* New York: McGraw-Hill, 1967.

Maier, Norman, R. F., *Problem solving and creativity.* Belmont, CA: Brooks-Cole, 1970.

March, James, and H. Simon. *Organizations.* New York: Wiley, 1958.

Maslow, A. J. *Motivation and personality.* New York: Harper & Row, 1954.

Meyer, John W., and Brian Rowan. Institutionalized organizations: Formal structure as myth and ceremony. *American Journal of Sociology,* 1977, *83*(2), 440–463.

Miles, Matthew B. Organizational development in schools: The effects of alternate strategies of change. New York: Horace Mann-Lincoln Institute of School Experimentation, Teachers College, Columbia University, 1963. (Mimeographed research proposal.)

Milstein, Michael M. Evolution of an internal change team: Expectations, design, and reality. Paper read at meeting of the American Educational Research Association, Toronto, Ontario, Canada, 1978.

Milstein, Michael M. Developing a renewal team in an urban school district. *Theory into Practice,* 1979, *18*(4), 106–113. Published by the Ohio State University.

Milstein, Michael M., and Paul A. Lafornara. The institutionalization of an internal change agent team: The Buffalo experience. Paper presented to the annual meeting of the American Educational Research Association, 1980.

Pfeiffer, J. William, and John E. Jones (Eds.). *Handbook of structured experiences for human relations training.* San Diego: University Associates, 1969–present.

Pfeiffer, J. William, and John E. Jones (Eds.). *Annual handbook for group facilitators.* San Diego: University Associates, 1972–present.

Pilon, Daniel H., and William H. Bergquist. *Consultation in higher education: A handbook for practitioners and clients.* Washington, DC: Council for the Advancement of Small Colleges, 1979.

Porterfield, Robert W., and Illah J. Porterfield. School-based renewal coordinators. *Theory into Practice,* 1979, *18*(4), 82–88. Published by the Ohio State University.

Raven, Bertram, and William Kruglanski. Conflict and power. In P. G. Swingle (Ed.), *The structure of conflict.* New York: Academic Press, 177–219, 1975.

Runkel, Philip J., Spencer H. Wyant, Warren E. Bell, and Margaret Runkel. *Organizational renewal in a school district: Self-help through a cadre of organizational specialists.* Eugene, OR: Center for Educational Policy and Management, 1980.

Salinger, J. D. *The catcher in the rye.* Boston: Little, Brown, 1951.

Schein, Edgar H. *Process consultation: Its role in organization development.* Reading, MA: Addison-Wesley, 1969.

Scheinfeld, Daniel. A design for renewing urban elementary schools. *Theory into Practice,* 1979, *18*(2), 114–125. Published by the Ohio State University.

Schindler-Rainman, Eva, Ronald Lippitt, and J. Cole. *Taking your meetings out of the doldrums.* Columbus, OH: Association of Professional Directors, 1975.

Schmidt, W., and Robert Tannenbaum. How to choose a leadership pattern. *Harvard Business Review,* 1958, *36*, 95–101.

Schmuck, Richard A. Peer consultation for school improvement. In C. L. Cooper and C. P. Alderfer (Eds.), *Advances in experiential social processes*. Sussex, England: Wiley, 1977, pp. 137–159.

Schmuck, Richard A. District cadres of OD consultants. In J. Alpert (Ed.), *Psychological consultation to schools: Case studies*. San Francisco: Jossey-Bass, 1982, pp. 247–274.

Schmuck, Richard A. Organization development in the schools. In Cecil R. Reynolds and Terry B. Gutkin (Eds.), *The handbook of school psychology* (2nd ed.). New York: John Wiley, 1990.

Schmuck, Richard A. The heart of participatory management. In Allan Hoffman and Daniel Julius (Eds.), *Managing community and junior colleges: Perspectives for the next century*. Washington, DC: College and University Personnel Association, 1994.

Schmuck, Richard A., Donald Murray, Mary Ann Smith, Mitchell Schwartz, and Margaret Runkel. *Consultation for innovative schools: OD for multiunit structure*. Eugene, OR: Center for Educational Policy and Management, 1975.

Schmuck, Richard A., and Philip J. Runkel. *Organizational training for a school faculty*. Eugene, OR: Center for Educational Policy and Management, 1970.

Schmuck, Richard A., and Philip J. Runkel. *The handbook of organization development in schools* (3rd ed.). Prospect Heights, IL: Waveland Press, 1985.

Schmuck, Richard A., Philip J. Runkel, Jane H. Arends, and Richard I. Arends. *Second handbook of organization development in schools*. Palo Alto, CA: Mayfield, 1977.

Schmuck, Richard A., Philip J. Runkel, Steven L. Saturen, Ronald T. Martell, and C. Brooklyn Derr. *Handbook of organizational development in schools*. Palo Alto, CA: National Press Books (now Mayfield), 1972.

Schmuck, Richard A., and Patricia A. Schmuck. *A humanistic psychology of education: Making the school everybody's house*. Palo Alto, CA: Mayfield, 1974.

Schmuck, Richard A., and Patricia A. Schmuck. *Group processes in the classroom* (6th ed.). Dubuque, IA: Wm. C. Brown, 1992.

Tannenbaum, Arnold S. *Control in organizations*. New York: McGraw-Hill, 1968.

Wallen, John L. Emotions as problems. In Charles Jung, Rosalie Howard, Ruth Emory, and Rene Pino (Eds.), *Trainer's manual: Interpersonal communications*. Portland: Northwest Regional Educational Laboratory, 1972.

Walton, Richard E. *Interpersonal peacemaking: Confrontation and third-party consultation*. Reading, MA: Addison-Wesley, 1969.

Weick, Karl E. Educational organizations as loosely coupled systems. *Administrative Science Quarterly*, 1976, *21*(1), 1–19.

Weisbord, Marvin R. *Productive workplaces*. San Francisco: Jossey-Bass, 1987.

Williamson, John N. The inquiring school: Toward a model of organizational self-renewal. *Educational Forum*, 1974, *38*, 355–371, 393–410.

Wyant, Spencer H. The effects of organization development training on intrastaff communication in elementary schools. Doctoral dissertation, University of Oregon, 1974.

Name Index

Subject Index

475

YORK COLLEGE OF PENNSYLVANIA 17403

0 2003 0150956 4

SCHMIDT SHELVES
LB 2805 .S3825 1994
Schmuck, Richard A.
The handbook of
organization development

DISCARDED

YORK COLLEGE
PENNSYLVANIA

LIBRARY

GAYLORD FG